Peoples versus States

Peoples versus States

Minorities at Risk in the New Century

Ted Robert Gurr

UNITED STATES
INSTITUTE OF PEACE PRESS
Washington, D.C.

UNITED STATES INSTITUTE OF PEACE
1200 17th Street NW, Suite 200
Washington, DC 20036-3011

First published 2000. Second printing 2002.

Printed in the United States of America

The paper used in this publication meets the minimum requirements of American National Standards for Information Sciences—Permanence of Paper for Printed Library Materials, ANSI Z39.48-1984.

Library of Congress Cataloging-in-Publication Data
Gurr, Ted Robert, 1936–
    Peoples versus states : minorities at risk in the new century / Ted Robert Gurr.
        p. cm.
    Includes bibliographical references and index.
    ISBN 1-929223-03-X (cloth) — ISBN 1-929223-02-1 (pbk.)
    1. World politics—1989– 2. Ethnic relations—Political aspects. 3. Minorities.
I. Title.

D860 .G872 2000
323.1'1'09049—dc21   00-027280

Contents

The sketches of representative groups from the Minorities at Risk study describe the preconditions and nature of ethnopolitical conflicts. Although each sketch is self-contained, all are designed to illustrate general issues discussed in various chapters.

Foreword

WHEN OUR Grant Program awarded Ted Robert Gurr a grant to work on a sequel to his highly acclaimed *Minorities at Risk,* we looked forward to seeing another volume of conspicuous excellence: compendious, rigorous, insightful, instructive, invaluable. Thus, when Professor Gurr delivered his final draft of *Peoples versus States,* we were impressed but not surprised by the manuscript's breadth, depth, and wealth of data and analysis. What we had not expected, however, was that *Peoples versus States* would be a book with such an encouraging assessment of such a discouraging subject.

Like *Minorities at Risk,* which the United States Institute of Peace published in 1993 to numerous critical plaudits, laudatory reviews, and a substantial readership, *Peoples versus States* surveys the world for signs of conflict between governments and "identity" groups. The nature of those governments varies (from autocracies to democracies and everything in between), as does the core of the groups' identities (ethnic, national, religious, and so forth) and the level of conflict (from party politics and street demonstrations all the way to full-scale, armed rebellion). The focus, however, is always conflict and its consequences.

Conflict, of course, is intrinsic to human society and is often an agent of reform, adaptation, and development. But conflict can also engender destructive violence, and a depressing number of the conflicts featured in *Minorities at Risk* had spawned dreadful violence. Indeed, as that book chronicled with such precision, the late 1980s witnessed a dramatic increase in the incidence and severity of violent confrontations between security forces and minority groups bent on secession or at least on securing a much greater say in the government of their lives. Wherever one looked—from Kashmir to Kurdistan, Nagorno-Karabakh to Zaire—it seemed that roiling disaffection kept erupting into bloody civil conflict.

So, when we first began to read *Peoples versus States*, we anticipated a similar story of intolerance and discrimination, of repression and rebellion. And, to be sure, the world had not been transformed in the half-dozen years since the publication of *Minorities at Risk*. As the reader will discover in the pages of this book, the twentieth century has bequeathed to the twenty-first literally hundreds of conflicts between contending identity groups or between identity groups and governments. These disputes tend to have deep social and historical roots; fueled by enduring grievances as well as ongoing inequalities, they stubbornly resist resolution. Many have escalated far beyond the level of nonviolent protest and diplomatic negotiation. One need only scan a newspaper for, say, January 1, 2000, to find evidence of this global scourge: Chechnya, East Timor, Sierra Leone, Burundi, Kosovo.

But while *Peoples versus States* confirmed our anticipation of widespread and ongoing intrastate strife, it also offered altogether more encouraging news. Despite the persistence of considerable discrimination, repression, and unrest, reports Professor Gurr, the overall trend is toward a decline in violence: "Comparative evidence shows that the intensity of ethnonational political conflict subsided in most world regions from the mid- through the late 1990s and that relatively few new contenders have emerged since the early 1990s."

Gurr, it should be noted, is not the first to draw attention to this decline. Other scholars have also suggested that the tide of civil wars reached its highwater mark in the last years of the century and is now ebbing, and these observations have been reported even in the press and on television. Gurr's more considered conclusions, however, carry unusual weight, especially because they are based on unusually strong evidence. With his colleagues at the Center for International Development and Conflict Management at the University of Maryland, Professor Gurr has developed a database of impressive scope, containing coded information on 275 politically active ethnic and other communal groups. He has also mastered the complex and delicate art of interpreting this data. His conclusions about overall trends are hard to challenge, his explanations for those trends are persuasive, and his predictions as to future sources of conflict demand the attention of policymakers as well as scholars.

Equally heartening are the three reasons Gurr gives in *Peoples versus States* for the reversal in the tide of ethnic war: First: "The shocks of state reformation in the Soviet sphere and Eastern Europe have largely passed," closing the windows of opportunity for ethnopolitical activism in that region. Second: "Civil capacities for responding to ethnopolitical challenges have increased, especially in democratic societies. Democratic elites are less likely to rely on strategies of assimilation and repression, more likely to follow policies of recognition, pluralism, and group autonomy." And third: "States and international organizations, prompted by intense media attention and the activism of nongovernmental organizations, as well as their own security concerns, have been more willing to initiate preventive and remedial action."

If Gurr's analysis is correct, we have grounds to be guardedly optimistic about the future. After all, reasons number two and three suggest that the world is slowly learning what to do, and what not to do, in addressing the concerns and ambitions of discontented ethnic, religious, and national groups. A violent, heavy-handed response by governments to ethnonational challenges rarely brings lasting peace (as Russia may have learned in Chechnya). Instead, the keys to channeling identity conflicts into nonviolent forms of expression, and to building enduring stability, are to recognize and accommodate differences at home—something that democracies are constituted to do.

Peoples versus States is, then, an encouraging volume for those who have promoted, applauded, or otherwise supported efforts to resolve intrastate conflicts through dialogue between the protagonists and the active engagement of the international community. Yet, as *Peoples versus States* also makes clear, much remains to be done. The intensity of ethnopolitical conflict may indeed have declined on a global scale, but many individual conflicts are still being contested with ferocity and (as detailed in chapter 7) many more have the potential to escalate or re-escalate into bloody strife. Furthermore, the "emerging global regime governing relations between communal groups and the state in heterogeneous societies" is *not* perfect, has *not* been embraced by many nondemocratic states, and is *not* uniformly effective.

Readers interested in finding out more about specific ethnonational conflicts and the means by which they might be peacefully resolved are encouraged to review some of the other books recently published by the United States Institute of Peace. In the past year, the Institute has published Ahmedou Ould-Abdallah's firsthand account of Burundi's intercommunal strife, *Burundi on the Brink, 1993-95: A UN Special Envoy Reflects on Preventive Diplomacy;* John Wallach's *The Enemy Has a Face: The Seeds of Peace Experience,* a book about the divide between Israelis and Arabs and Wallach's own innovative youth program that tries to bridge that chasm; and *Watching the Wind* by Susan Collin Marks, which recounts grassroots efforts to prevent racial violence from derailing South Africa's journey from apartheid to democracy in the early 1990s. Other recent volumes have addressed a wide array of practical approaches to settling intrastate—and interstate—conflict. These include three edited volumes, each featuring a dozen or more preeminent practitioners and analysts: *Herding Cats: Multiparty Mediation in a Complex World* and *Managing Global Chaos: Sources of and Responses to International Conflict*, both edited by Chester Crocker, Fen Osler Hampson, and Pamela Aall; and *Peacemaking in International Conflict: Methods and Techniques*, edited by I. William Zartman and J. Lewis Rasmussen.

All of these publications share with *Peoples versus States* the goal of providing policymakers, practitioners, academics, and indeed all interested citizens with timely information and analyses relevant to the promotion of nonviolent solutions to conflicts throughout the world. It is a goal that Ted Robert Gurr has achieved in this impressive, richly detailed, powerfully argued, and ultimately encouraging book.

Richard H. Solomon, President
United States Institute of Peace

Preface

THE TSUNAMI of ethnic and nationalist conflict that swept across large parts of Eurasia and Africa in the early 1990s raised grave doubts about the future of the international system of states and the security of their citizens. The pessimistic tone of scholarly and policy analysis at the time is reflected in book titles with phrases such as "conflicts unending," "pandemonium," and "clash of civilizations."[1] By the mid-1990s armed conflict within states had abated: there was a pronounced decline in the onset of new ethnic wars and a shift in many ongoing wars from fighting to negotiation. Some of my colleagues have referred to this pause as the "short peace."[2]

One objective of this book is to document the "short peace" and to analyze the conditions responsible for it. Comparative evidence shows that the intensity of ethnopolitical conflict subsided in most world regions from the mid- through late 1990s and that relatively few new contenders have emerged since the early 1990s. The exceptions to this generalization are found mainly in Central and West Africa and in South and Southeast Asia. Most protagonists in the ethnic wars that continue at the beginning of the new century are veterans of past episodes of protracted communal conflict, not new contenders. This is true of Hutus and Tutsis in the Great Lakes region, and equally true of the Kosovar Albanians. Their conflicts took dramatic and deadly turns in the mid- to late 1990s, but in no sense are they new.

Three reasons can be suggested for the general decline in ethnic wars. First, the shocks of state reformation in the former

Soviet sphere and Eastern Europe have largely passed. The breakup of old states and the formation of new states and regimes in these regions opened up opportunities for ethnopolitical activism; now windows of opportunity in the postcommunist states have closed. Second, civil capacities for responding to ethnopolitical challenges have increased, especially in democratic societies. Democratic elites are less likely to rely on strategies of assimilation and repression, more likely to follow policies of recognition, pluralism, and group autonomy. Third, international efforts at publicizing and preventing violations of group rights increased markedly after the Cold War. States and international organizations, prompted by intense media attention and the activism of nongovernmental organizations, as well as their own security concerns, have been more willing to initiate preventive and remedial action. Public and private pressures also have helped persuade governments in some countries with mixed human rights records to improve their treatment of minorities in ways that vary from cosmetic to substantive.

Events of 1997–99 in Kosovo, the middle belt of Africa, and Indonesia suggest that the "short peace" may indeed be transitory, perhaps only a lull before the onset of new waves of ethnic and other kinds of war within states. The second general objective of this book is to analyze the general preconditions of past and future ethnopolitical conflict. These arguments are documented and elaborated in later chapters.

- The political assertion of ethnic and other communal identities that spawned new episodes of ethnic warfare during the 1980s and early 1990s will continue, for two reasons. The politics of identity are based most fundamentally on persistent grievances about inequalities and past wrongs, conditions that are part of the heritage of most minorities in most countries. Moreover, movements based on identity have succeeded often enough in recent years to justify emulation and repetition.

- The ethnic conflict management strategies favored by Western states and international organizations are not uniformly effective. Democratic institutions and elections in weak, heterogeneous states often provide incentives and opportunities that increase the chances of ethnopolitical conflict rather than channeling it into conventional politics. Internationally brokered settlements and the atmospherics of cease-fires, amnesties, and signing ceremonies that accompany them are sometimes a facade behind which protagonists jockey for political advantage and resources that fuel the next round of fighting.

- The states and international and regional organizations that promote democratic and negotiated management of ethnic tensions often walk away after multiparty elections and settlements. Failure of outside parties to provide sustained political and material resources in postconflict situations all but guarantees the eventual renewal of conflict.

The outlook suggested by this study is conditionally positive. Deadly rounds of ethnopolitical conflict are likely to occur or reoccur in new, impoverished states with ineffective governments and sharp communal polarities. When they erupt they will pose severe humanitarian problems. However, most such conflicts are foreseeable, they are likely to be concentrated in a few regions— the middle belt of Africa and parts of Asia and the Middle East—and in principle they can be contained and transformed through constructive and sustained regional and international action. The grave risk is that powerful global and regional actors will become so weary of remedial action, and so preoccupied with other issues, that they will give only marginal attention and resources to the management of local conflicts in peripheral regions.

The first specific task of this study is to document the rise and decline of political action by ethnic and other communal groups from 1986 to 1999— the years in which ethnopolitical challenges rose sharply and then fell. The evidence comes from the Minorities at Risk project's coded information on the status and conflicts of 275 politically active ethnic and other communal groups in the 1990s.[3] The virtue of relying on this broad base of information is that it enables us to identify and interpret global patterns and trends and to delineate differences among world regions. It also enables us to test suppositions about the causes and outcomes of ethnopolitical conflict using information on all relevant cases rather than a handful of case studies. The liability is that some details and qualifications revealed by more narrowly focused case and regional studies are glossed over.

The second task is to sketch a theory of the conditions associated with the political assertion of ethnic and communal identities. Two major arguments are developed. The conditions in which communal identities become salient enough to provide the basis for joint political action are specified in chapter 3. Four characteristics of groups and their immediate political environments explain when and why they are likely to mobilize: *the salience of communal identity* and *groups' incentives, capacities,* and *opportunities* for ethnopolitical action. All these factors tended to increase in the 1980s, some because of long-term processes of state building and economic development, others through global and regional transitions—especially the collapse of hegemonic states and the promotion of democratic institutions in states with traditions of authoritarian governance.

Discrimination and repression against national and minority peoples are a pervasive source of poverty and resentment and provide strong incentives for ethnopolitical mobilization, protest, and rebellion. Chapter 4 examines global and regional patterns of political, economic, and cultural discrimination in the 1990s. It also surveys new evidence on strategies of state repression in the 1980s and 1990s, evidence that suggests that severe repression is substantially more likely to intensify than contain conflicts over contested identities.

Perhaps the most striking finding of this study is evidence of a pervasive shift in public policies toward ethnic contenders in the middle years of the decade. This is the study's second major argument. The shift from assimilation and control to pluralism and accommodation is strongest in democratic societies, old and new, but also evident in some autocratic societies as well. Several kinds of evidence are examined. Chapter 5 shows that the introduction of democratic governance in the 1980s and 1990s usually was followed by a shift in strategies of ethnopolitical action from rebellion to protest. Political and cultural restrictions on national and minority peoples also declined during the 1990s, a shift that was strikingly evident in new democracies. The process of democratization can also prompt extreme nationalism and trigger new rebellions, but these outcomes have occurred mainly when democratization was attempted in newly independent states, not in established states. In chapter 6 we survey the outcomes of more than fifty ethnonational wars fought during the last forty years and find strong evidence of crisscrossing trends during the 1990s: new ethnic wars declined, and there was a striking increase in negotiated settlements, which usually provided for significant substate autonomy.

The third general task of this book is to assess the risks of future ethnopolitical conflicts. Despite the short-term decline in conflict and the ascendance of efforts at reform and accommodation, many of the conditions of future ethnopolitical conflict persist. Chapter 7 builds on the results of comparative analysis to identify some ninety groups that are at medium to high risk of conflict and repression at the beginning of the twenty-first century.

The concluding chapter reviews the evidence for an emerging global regime governing relations between communal groups and the state in heterogeneous societies. This regime consists of a set of principles about intergroup relations in heterogeneous states, a repertoire of strategies for institutionalizing the principles, and agreement on civil and international policies for responding to ethnopolitical crises and conflicts. But this new regime of managed ethnic heterogeneity is imperfect. Its proponents are the established democratic states, mainly those in the global north, and its effectiveness is severely tested by past, ongoing, and future communal conflicts and humanitarian crises in central Africa, Asia, and parts of the Middle East.

This study's broad comparative analysis is complemented by fourteen vignettes of ethnopolitical groups—their grievances, mobilization and political actions, and the prospects for peaceful accommodation of their interests. The sketches are designed to give substance and examples, especially for nonspecialists, to generalizations based on comparative data. They are chosen to represent the diversity of the 275 groups included in the study and to suggest the richness of the case study materials used in preparing the Minorities at Risk data set.

Acknowledgments

The Minorities at Risk project monitors and analyzes the status of politically active communal groups throughout the world. It has been based at the Center for International Development and Conflict Management, University of Maryland, since 1988 and has been supported by grants from the United States Institute of Peace, the National Science Foundation, the Hewlett Foundation, the Korea Foundation, and International Alert (London) plus substantial institutional support from the University of Maryland at College Park.

The Minorities project is a long-term, labor-intensive study that has depended on the knowledge, skills, and commitment of many graduate assistants. The project coordinators who have played a key role in sustaining the project since the mid-1980s include Monty G. Marshall, Scott McDonald, Shinwha Lee, Michael L. Haxton, and Anne Pitsch. James Scarritt, my colleague at the University of Colorado in the 1980s, directed a research team that did the first round of coding for Africa. Statistical analyses and graphs for this book were prepared by Minorities project coordinators Michael L. Haxton (1994–96) and Anne Pitsch (1996–present); by Göran Lindgren of the Department of Peace and Conflict Research at Uppsala University; and by Monty G. Marshall, who is now a faculty associate of the Minorities project. Graduate and postdoctoral researchers who prepared the case studies and coded the data used for this book include Pamela L. Burke, Ken Cousins, Michael Dravis, Jonathan Fox, Mizan Khan, Deepa Khosla, Shin-wha Lee, Marion Recktenwald, and Anne Pitsch, and also undergraduates Alex Tanoyue and Ari Wilkenfeld. Ongoing work is directed by Anne Pitsch with Victor Assal, Michelle Boomgaard, Deepa Khosla, and Lyubov Mincheva.

Chronologies and assessments for most groups cover the full decade of the 1990s and are available from the project's site on the World Wide Web, address www.bsos.umd.edu/cidcm/mar. A code book, *Minorities at Risk Dataset Users Manual.899,* and a data set consisting of 975 variables for each group are provided on the Web site.

A special note of thanks is due Professor Peter Wallensteen and his colleagues of the Department of Peace and Conflict Research at Uppsala University, who provided a supportive setting in which the first draft of this book was completed. Stephen Saideman and Jack Snyder read the draft in its entirety and provided a number of comments that helped guide the revision. Monica Duffy Toft provided useful comments on chapter 7. I also express my appreciation to participants in 1996–97 seminars at the Universities of Uppsala, Lund, and Stockholm and the Stockholm Peace Research Institute (SIPRI) and to students in my 1998–99 graduate seminars at the University of Maryland, especially Victor Assal and Robert Tomes, who provided thought-provoking critiques of drafts of some of the chapters. Other useful comments have come from participants in seminars at the World Bank, the National Security Agency, and the Center for International Development and Conflict Management.

Finally, my enduring gratitude to Barbara Harff of the U.S. Naval Academy, who has been a source of inspiration, criticism, and encouragement throughout the life of the Minorities project.

Peoples versus States

1

The Ethnic Basis of Political Action in the 1980s and 1990s

THE ASSERTION of peoples' cultural identities within and across the boundaries of existing states has reshaped the political landscape in all world regions during the last half of the twentieth century. Proponents of cultural identity groups have sought collective recognition, rights, and autonomy from governments that often have reacted to these demands as threats to civic identity and state security. The title of this study, *Peoples versus States*, symbolizes the tension between governments and challengers who represent cultural, ethnic, religious, or national identity groups. The study offers a broad but systematic account of the trends and outcomes of these identity-based conflicts. They have had major consequences for the status of identity groups, for the ways in which heterogeneous societies are governed, and for the norms and structures of the international system of states. This chapter discusses the nature of communal identities and groups and summarizes some global data on politically active identity groups. The next chapter reports on the long-term rise in identity-based conflicts from the 1950s to the early 1990s and the subsequent decline.

Assumptions about Ethnicity

Most people have multiple identities. They see themselves as members of a clan or a national minority, as citizens of a state, and sometimes as part of a larger entity such as the European Community or the *umma arabiyya*, the community of Arab peoples. *Ethnic group*, as the term is used here, refers

3

to people who share a distinctive and enduring collective identity based on common descent, shared experiences, and cultural traits. They may define themselves, and be defined by others, in terms of any or all of a bundle of traits: customary behavior and dress, religious beliefs, language, physical appearance ("race"), region of residence, traditional occupations, and a history of conquest and repression by culturally different peoples. They are also referred to in this study as *communal* and *identity* groups. The bases of communal or ethnic identity vary greatly and provide the basis for a typology of groups, specified at the end of this chapter.

There are serious debates among scholars about the intrinsic nature of ethnic identities and their plasticity. The essence of the "primordial" view is that ethnic identities are more essential and transcendent than others and that groups defined by ethnicity are more enduring than other collectivities, states included. The "instrumental" view is that ethnicity is one of many alternative bases of identity. It gains social significance mainly when ethnic symbols are invoked and manipulated by political entrepreneurs in response to threats or opportunities. The "constructivist" view, which underlies the Minorities at Risk project, is that ethnic identities are enduring social constructions. As Virginia Q. Tilley observes, they are "adaptive and contingent" but are "not entirely malleable. . . . they are attached to myriad social experiences, collective memories and norms, that carry their own logics and inertia." The content and significance of group identity can and do change but usually in response to changes in the group's social and political environment. The criteria by which people are judged to be group members also can change but usually around the margins.[1]

The question of how ethnic identities are constructed is not central to this study. For most purposes we take ethnic identities as given and focus attention on their contemporary political consequences. Nonetheless, we recognize that identities can be created as well as re-created and that how this happens shapes identity politics. Identity creation is sometimes the work of myth-makers who build on a preexisting sense of groupness. More often it is a consequence of policies and acts by powerful agents—states and dominant groups—who define groups by assigning them labels and treating them differentially over generations. J. M. Coetzee observes that in South Africa during apartheid "the status of 'Coloured' was, across almost the entire range of people who it implicated, accepted, so to speak under protest, as an identity forced upon them. Insofar as there is or was a 'Coloured' community, it was a community created by the common fate of being forced to behave, in the face of authority, as 'Coloured.'"[2] Indigenous identities in the Americas were formed, or if not formed then aggregated, in similar way, by collective labeling and subordination of people from many different cultures. Identities formed or re-formed by force and differential treatment not only are likely to persist but also often provide the basis for mobilization and action aimed at redressing the shared grievances that are the common result of collective mistreatment.

In short, we assume that ethnic identities are enduring social constructions that matter to the people who share them. *How much* they matter depends on people's social and political circumstances, as discussed in chapter 3. Ethnic identities are not "primordial" but nonetheless based on common values, beliefs, and experiences. They are not "instrumental" but usually capable of being invoked by leaders and used to sustain social movements that are likely to be more resilient and persistent than movements based solely on material or political interests.

From Ethnic Identity to Ethnopolitical Conflict

The social fact that many people value shared cultural traits is not intrinsically a source of conflict with other identity groups or the state. It probably is universally true, as Martin O. Heisler has observed about Europe, that ethnic identity "tends to be a partial, part-time aspect of people's self-concepts." His larger argument is that ethnicity varies in salience, being less salient and fundamental to social relations in Western societies than elsewhere.[3] The generalization probably is accurate, but it raises the causal question of why salience should differ, not just across regions, but among groups, and within groups over time. What shapes the *salience* of ethnic identity is therefore a central issue in Heisler's essay and in the analytic framework proposed in chapter 3.

TERMINOLOGY SUMMARIZED

Ethnic groups are people who share a distinctive and enduring collective identity based on a belief in common descent and on shared experiences and cultural traits. They are also referred to here as communal and identity groups.

Ethnopolitical groups are identity groups whose ethnicity has political consequences, resulting either in differential treatment of group members or in political action on behalf of group interests.

The first question for the study of ethnopolitical conflict is, When does ethnic identity lead to political action? The essence of the answer proposed here is, When ethnicity has collective consequences for a group in its relations with other groups and with states. More exactly, to the extent that ethnicity is a major determinant of a people's security, status, material well-being, or access to political power, it is likely to be a highly salient part of their identity. In *Minorities at Risk,* the book to which this is the successor, I summarized the argument this way: "treat a group differently, by denial or privilege, and its members become more self-conscious about their common bonds and interests. Minimize differences, and communal identification becomes less significant as a unifying principle."[4]

When ethnic identity is highly salient, it is likely to be the basis for mobilization and political action. The term *ethnopolitical group* is used in this study to denote groups whose ethnic identity is the basis for either differential treatment or collective political action, or both. Most ethnopolitical movements of the past half century have emerged in response to changes in identity groups' political environment that have prompted some of their members and leaders to find more effective ways to promote or defend interests that they define in collective terms. In short, mobilization is ethnopolitical when it draws support from and appeals to the interests of African Americans or Albanians or Amazonian peoples rather than the working class or the disenfranchised or the victims of environmental degradation. The concept of "ethnopolitical group" is consistent with the constructivist approach because it focuses attention on the changing circumstances in which ethnic identity becomes the basis for collective political mobilization and action.

Ethnonationalists are the most visible of ethnopolitical groups in the late twentieth century. Nationalism is a distinctively modern doctrine that links ethnic identity to a hegemonic political program. The proponents of nationalism—Basque, Russian, Greek, Kurdish—claim that national identity trumps other identities, including parochial identities of clan and locality and transcending identities such as those of faith. They also claim that a national people has the right to govern a sovereign state in which the interests and identities of other peoples are subordinated or assimilated to the dominant nationality. Nationalist doctrines and the movements they have inspired have had a transforming impact on the international system of states: they have contributed to the breakup of empires and segmentary states throughout the twentieth century and provided the rationale and energy for building new nation-states in the aftermath of World War I and again after World War II. Ernest Gellner attributes the rise of nationalist doctrines and movements to intellectuals who are responding to the examples of successful national states elsewhere. They are, in Gellner's conception, constructions of aspiring elites with instrumental objectives. Anthony D. Smith gives more weight to the enduring ethnic identities that provide the basis for nationalist movements.[5]

If national identities are intellectual constructions derived from preexisting group identities, under what circumstances are they most likely to be articulated in ways that capture the imaginations of peoples and mobilize their political energies? Political upheaval, collective insecurity, and conflict with other groups are implicated in the origins of most modern nationalist movements —as they are in the origins of most other ethnopolitical movements. The American sense of nationhood was forged in the colonists' adversarial relationship with the British crown and the ensuing war of independence. Modern Zionism developed in the late nineteenth century in reaction to the persecution of Jewish communities in East Central Europe. Eritrean nationalism is almost entirely the product of a thirty-year conflict that eventually united tribal and urban people, Muslims and Christians in a successful war of independence from Ethiopian rule. Rashid Khalidi, in his account of the origins of Palestinian nationalism, shows that Palestinian self-consciousness crystallized following the collapse of Ottoman rule in the Middle East. Local resistance to expanding Zionist settlement and the eventual establishment of the state of Israel gave specific content to the sense of collective victimization that is a central element in modern Palestinian nationalism.[6]

Identifying Ethnopolitical Groups

The units of observation in the Minorities at Risk project are *ethnopolitical groups,* as defined in the preceding section. The study includes groups that meet one or both of two general criteria:

- The group collectively suffers, or benefits from, systematic differential treatment vis-à-vis other groups in a society. We also include groups that are persistently disadvantaged, either economically or politically, relative to dominant or mainstream groups. The assumption is that persistent disadvantages either originated with or are reproduced by social practices and public policies of advantaged groups.

- The group is the basis for political mobilization and action in defense or promotion of its self-defined interests. In practice we look for evidence of associations—movements, parties, committees, militias—that claim to act on behalf of the group. Ethnic groups that nominally control a regional government are not automatically included by this criterion; inclusion requires evidence of associational activities by a group outside of governmental structures.

Ethnopolitical groups are not necessarily "ethnic" in the narrow sense. Many shared attributes can contribute to the sentiments and interests that lead to joint action. As observed earlier in the chapter, the salient bases of collective identity include a common language, religion, or national or racial origin, shared cultural practices, and attachment to a particular territory. Most ethnopolitical groups also have a common history or myths of shared experience, often of conquest and victimization by others. Vamik Volkan refers to the latter as the group's "chosen trauma," a belief that helps define the group and focus its hostility on the "other." For example, Khalidi observes that everywhere in the Palestinian diaspora people are still likely to identify themselves according to where their families lived in 1948, before they fled the first Arab-Israeli war.[7] The counterpart to "chosen trauma" is the belief nurtured by advantaged groups that they are inherently superior to others. The sense of group pride is also an important element in collective identity.

No one trait is essential to group identity. What counts, most fundamentally, is the belief—by people who share some such traits and beliefs, and by those with whom they interact—that the traits set them apart from others in ways that justify their separate treatment and status. Ethnic identities may be "constructed" in the sense that they are malleable in scope and content, but that does not detract from their social reality or their persistence.

The salience and political consequences of group identity change over time in response to large events such as the breakup of multinational states and

GROUPS IN THE MINORITIES AT RISK STUDY

The 275 ethnic or communal groups in the Minorities at Risk study are included because they are disadvantaged by comparison with other groups in their society, usually because of discriminatory practices, or because they have organized politically to promote or defend their collective interests. Most are numerical minorities; a few are majorities such as the Shi'is in Iraq. Also included are advantaged minorities such as the Chinese in Indonesia. Small groups are excluded, and so are groups in countries with a population of less than half a million.

local events such as changes in government policies toward minorities. These processes are analyzed in chapter 3. As a consequence, the numbers of groups that meet the two general criteria also change. In the 1980s the Minorities at Risk project identified 233 ethnopolitical groups that made up 17.3 percent of the world's population in 1990. The comparable figures for 1998 are 275 groups and 17.4 percent. These numbers are to some degree arbitrary and reflect the application of six operational rules:

- Include groups only in countries with a 1995 population greater than five hundred thousand. This rule excludes politically significant communal contenders in smaller countries and dependencies such as Surinam and New Caledonia.

- Include groups only if in 1995 they numbered at least one hundred thousand or, if fewer, exceeded 1 percent of the population of at least one country in which they resided. This rule, like the previous one, excludes a few small groups whose human rights status and political activities are of significant local concern, for example, the Ainu and Okinawan minorities in Japan.

- Include groups separately in each country in which they meet the general criteria. For example, the Lezgins are counted and analyzed separately in Russia and Azerbaijan. From their own perspective the Lezgins are a single people, but the focus of this study is on relations between peoples and states. The Lezgins, like the Kurds and other, better-known, transstate peoples, have been carved into segments, each of which has a distinctive set of relations with state authorities.

- Include advantaged minorities like the Sunni Arabs of Iraq and the overseas Chinese of Southeast Asia, but do not include advantaged majorities— "minorities" being defined as groups with less than 50 percent of country population. Advantaged minorities are included on grounds that their privileges usually make them vulnerable to challenges from disadvantaged communal groups and retaliatory treatment, for example, the episodic attacks on the economically advantaged Chinese minority in Indonesia. Fearon and Laitin observe that this rule excludes politically self-conscious *majorities* such as Hindus in India, people of German birth in Germany, and Serbs in present-day Yugoslavia who are in many respects comparable to advantaged minorities elsewhere.[8]

- Count and code groups at the highest within-country level of aggregation that is politically meaningful. All Hispanics in the United States are treated as a single group because they usually are regarded and treated by

Anglo-Americans as one collectivity. Most native peoples in the Americas are similarly treated, except that in Mexico, Ecuador, Peru, and Bolivia we make analytic distinctions on political and cultural grounds, for example between native highland and lowland peoples in the Andean countries. This rule means that some group segments with distinctive identities and political agendas—examples are the three subclans that make up the Isaaq clan that dominates Somaliland, and indigenous peoples like the Navajos in the United States and the Quechua in Ecuador—are not separately profiled. As a practical matter we cannot profile most such subgroups because study resources are limited. As a conceptual matter, coding segments within groups detracts from the study's objective of analyzing the general relations between identity groups and states.[9]

■ Estimate membership in a group using the widest demographic definition, even though not all people who are nominal members of a group necessarily identity with it. The accuracy of these estimates is confounded by lack of census data in most countries and contending estimates of group size by protagonists for whom numbers are symbolic weapons. Where possible we rely on standard sources; in other instances we have made case-by-case judgments about the reliability of alternative estimates. All estimates are expressed as percentages of country population in the estimate's year of reference and those percentages are applied to estimates of country population for 1995 and 1998. The sources and procedures are summarized in appendix E.

The numbers of groups meeting these criteria and their distribution among world regions are shown in table 1.1 along with estimates of their aggregate population. They range from a low of 11.7 percent of the population of Western democracies and Japan to a high of 35.7 percent in Africa south of the Sahara. Comparisons in table 1.2 show the macro-changes in numbers and percentages between the late Cold War era and the late 1990s. The groups and their 1998 population estimates are listed in appendix D.

Despite the apparent precision of the numbers in tables 1.1 and 1.2, the coverage of the study is open to criticism on two grounds. First, the project's roster of groups is not "complete" for various reasons. For example, it is difficult to specify precisely and in cross-culturally comparable ways the thresholds of "discriminatory treatment" and "political mobilization." Moreover, the information needed to judge reliably whether a group is above or below these thresholds is sometimes inadequate. Therefore, the 1990s phase of the study includes some groups that are in the zone of indeterminacy, such as the

Table 1.1. Minorities at Risk in the 1990s, by World Region

World Region (number of countries)	Number of Countries with Minorities at Risk	Number of Minorities at Risk	Population of Minorities at Risk (1998 estimates)	
			Total (in 000s)	Percentage of Regional Population
Western democracies and Japan (35)	15	30	99,453	11.7
Eastern Europe and the newly independent states (28)	23	59	57,058	13.9
East, Southeast, and South Asia (44)	20	59	428,976	13.4
North Africa and the Middle East (24)	13	28	101,538	26.0
Africa south of the Sahara (51)	27	67	221,079	35.7
Latin America and the Caribbean (45)	18	32	124,028	25.8
Total countries (227)	116	275	1,032,132	17.5

Note: Politically significant national and minority peoples greater than one hundred thousand or 1 percent of country population in countries with 1998 populations greater than five hundred thousand. The list is based on current research by the Minorities at Risk Project, Center for International Development and Conflict Management, University of Maryland. Changing political circumstances and new information lead to periodic updates in the inclusion and exclusion of groups under observation. Numbers of countries above the five hundred thousand threshold in 1998 are shown in parentheses in the World Region column. The population estimates for national and minority peoples usually are approximations and are listed in appendix D. Population percentages are calculated from 1998 estimates for all countries in each region.

The Western democracies region includes Canada, the United States, Australia, New Zealand, and Japan in addition to Western Europe. The Middle East includes North Africa, the Arab states, Turkey, Cyprus, Iran, and Israel. Asia includes Afghanistan, the Indian subcontinent, Southeast Asia, and Pacific Asia. Africa includes South Africa but excludes North Africa. Latin America includes Central America and the Caribbean.

Table 1.2. Changes in Minorities at Risk, 1980s to 1998

World Region (number 1980s/1998)	Number of Minorities at Risk		Minority Percentage of Regional Population	
	1980s	1998	1980s	1998
Western democracies and Japan (21/21)	24	30	10.8	11.7
Eastern Europe and the USSR/NIS (9/27)	32	59	35.0	13.9
East, Southeast, and South Asia (21/24)	43	59	10.2	13.4
North Africa and the Middle East (19/20)	31	28	28.8	26.0
Africa south of the Sahara (36/45)	74	67	42.3	35.7
Latin America and the Caribbean (21/24)	29	32	11.0	25.8
Total (127/161)	233	275	17.3	17.5

Note: See note to table 1.1. The World Region column shows in parentheses the numbers of countries above the 1 million population threshold in the late 1980s and above the five hundred thousand threshold in 1998.

Basters of Namibia and the Hui of China, and omits others that may have a stronger claim to inclusion. New groups are added from time to time, based on suggestions by users and information from our Web searches. Under consideration for future inclusion are the Flemish and Walloons of Belgium, the Tamils of south India, and a substantial number of African groups such as the Krahn in Liberia and the Ijaw in Nigeria, Christians in Pakistan, and Mongols in China.[10] Appendix C provides an initial list of groups planned for inclusion in the next phase of the Minorities project.

The second specific criticism is that groups engaged in collective action are more likely to come to the attention of observers (and coders) and thus are

GLOBAL DISTRIBUTION OF MINORITIES AT RISK

Disadvantaged and politically active minorities are present in 116 of the world's 161 larger countries. They include about one-sixth of the global population. Minority populations are proportionally largest in Africa and the Middle East and smallest in the Western democracies. The postcommunist states and Asia have a relatively large number of minorities, but they make up a small proportion of the regional populations.

more likely to be included than politically quiescent groups. As a result, generalizations and comparisons about the conditions of ethnic conflict may be biased.[11] This criticism is misplaced because the Minority project's principal objective is to identify and analyze only the groups that meet its criteria for political significance, that is, differential treatment and political action. The main research question is why some differentially treated ethnic groups act politically and others do not. The term *ethnopolitical group* is used to emphasize this narrower demarcation of the universe of analysis. If the focus of research is "why ethnic groups rebel," however, the criticism is appropriate. A sample of politically quiescent minorities will be added to the project in the next phase.

Changes in Ethnopolitics from the 1980s to the 1990s: A Regional Overview

This section reviews changes in the number and traits of ethnopolitical groups between the last decade of the Cold War and the first post–Cold War decade.

In *Western democracies* the 1990s saw no major change in the extent or strategies of ethnopolitical action. Mobilization around issues of group rights and regional autonomy in Western democracies dates mainly from the 1960s.[12] By the 1990s almost all cultural groups with potential claims of this sort were already politically active. The only significant exceptions were immigrant workers in some European states—Switzerland, for example—whose foreign workers are subject to systematic discrimination—and therefore included in the survey—but have not organized politically. The increase in numbers of ethnopolitical groups from the 1980s to 1998 is due, first, to inclusion of a handful of new groups such as the Scots (they should have been included in Phase I as well) and, second, to the separate analysis of Roma (Gypsies) in the four Western European states in which they meet the one hundred thousand population criterion. The Bretons of France, included in the 1980s survey, have been omitted because they no longer meet either general criterion.

The most substantial changes have occurred in *Eastern Europe and the newly independent states* (NIS, i.e., the successor states to the USSR), where the creation of new states and the politicization of ethnic cleavages within them has increased sharply the number of politically active minorities from thirty-two to fifty-nine. The increase in number of groups is offset by a decline in their aggregate proportion of the regional population by a ratio of almost 3:1. The decline in the aggregate minority population is mainly due to the independence of the non-Russian republics of the USSR, most of whose titular nationalities were "at risk" in the 1980s, and also due to the secession of Croatia and Slovenia from Yugoslavia and of Slovakia from the Czech Republic.[13]

The increase in numbers of ethnopolitical groups in the region reflects, first, the assertion or reassertion of identities that were dormant under state socialist rule, for example, among the Serbs in Croatia and Bosnia; and among regional peoples such as the Sandzak Muslims, Abkhaz, Ossetians, Tuvinians, and Yakut, all of whose political status and objectives changed due to the dissolution of Yugoslavia and the USSR. A second set of additions are Russians in the newly independent states, collectivities whose status changed abruptly from representatives of the dominant group in the USSR to potentially threatened minorities in the NIS. All of them meet the "differential treatment" criterion for inclusion, but few have mobilized politically, except in the Baltic states and Crimea. Emigration to Russia has been their main response to threats to their status and security. A third factor that affects comparisons between the 1980s and 1990s is technical: the Roma, who were counted in the 1980s as a single aggregate group for the region as a whole, are now analyzed separately in the eleven Eastern and Central European countries where they are estimated to number more than one hundred thousand.[14]

In *Asia* both the numbers and proportional size of groups increased from the 1980s to the 1990s. Most important, new communal contenders have emerged in India's northeastern states (in Assam in particular) and have resurfaced in Afghanistan. In the latter country the Islamic bonds that held together the mujahedin opposition to the communist regime in Kabul have dissolved and been replaced by communally based rivalries among Tajiks, Uzbeks, Pashtuns, and Hazaris contending for either regional control or a share in central power. The Taliban, which had secured control of most of the country by mid-1998, is based mainly on the Pashtuns, numerically the largest and historically the country's dominant group. The others remain in open or latent opposition. The 1980s to1990s comparison also is affected by a technical decision to categorize Pakistan and its six ethnopolitical groups as part of Asia rather than the Middle East.[15]

In the *Middle East and North Africa* the intensity of communal conflict has varied but not the contenders. The politically significant minorities and national peoples in the region are much the same in the 1990s as they were in the 1960s, with three additions: Turks in Cyprus, Shi'i in Bahrain, and Christians in Iran.[16] The Palestinians and other immigrant workers in the Gulf States are outside the scope of this study. The guideline used in the Minorities study is that immigrants are "minorities" only when informed observers conclude that many of them have become permanent residents. The Turks in Germany and the Muslim North Africans in France qualify as minorities by this criterion. Foreign workers in the Gulf States and the hundreds of thousands of migrant workers in western and southern African states do not. The same general principle applies to refugees: Only those whose settlement is tacitly accepted as permanent by the host society qualify for inclusion in the Minorities study. The Palestinians in Lebanon are one such Middle Eastern group.

Africa south of the Sahara is the only region with a significant decrease in both numbers and proportions of ethnopolitical minorities from the 1980s to the 1990s. This observation may appear counterintuitive, in light of the intensification of ethnopolitical conflict in Africa in the early 1990s. In part our data reflect a real shift toward depoliticization of some communal identities that were significant immediately after independence. This trend is particularly evident in francophone West Africa. The decline also reflects more stringent application of the general criteria for "at risk" status to African groups and the availability of better information. The lines of communal cleavage and contention in most of Africa are fluid, however, and a number of additional African groups will be included in the next phase.

Perhaps the most important point to be made about communal conflict in Africa is that the "new" ethnic wars across the middle belt of Africa from Somalia and Kenya through Rwanda and Burundi to the Congo basin are most of them recent manifestations of long-standing conflicts. The Banyarwandans of the former Zaire are an example. The Banyarwandans are Hutus and Tutsis (Banyamulenge), some of whom have lived in what is now northeastern Democratic Republic of Congo (formerly Zaire) for a number of generations, others of whom were refugees from genocidal conflicts in Rwanda and Burundi from the 1960s to the 1990s. Most were citizens of Zaire, at least until the Zairian government sought to deprive them of citizenship in the early 1990s. In reaction to Zairian repression, the Banyamulenge began the rebellion led by Laurent Kabila that culminated in Mobutu's overthrow in May 1997. They also participated in the Rwanda-sponsored rebellion against Kabila's government in mid-1998 and were targets of retaliatory killings in Kinshasa when the rebellion was suppressed in the western Congo. In short, the Banyamulenge are a segment of the Tutsi, a people who have been victims and protagonists in communal conflict in central Africa throughout the postcolonial period.[17]

In *Latin America and the Caribbean* the Minorities at Risk survey includes all indigenous peoples and all peoples of African descent. Almost everywhere both groups are disadvantaged and subject to discrimination as a matter of social practice, though not usually of government policy. Indigenous peoples in all the Americas have been politically active throughout the 1980s and 1990s, Afro–Latin Americans much less so.[18] The only change from the 1980s to the 1990s is the inclusion of all Afro-Brazilians in the population at risk, rather than only Brazilians of pure African descent. This change is due to evidence of political activism in the 1990s that potentially mobilizes all Afro-Brazilians (see the sketch on pp. 100–104). They are one of the three largest minorities in the world, numbering an estimated 82 million in 1998. Including them doubles the regional population at risk in Latin America by comparison with the estimate for the 1980s.

Types of Ethnopolitical Groups

The 275 ethnopolitical groups vary greatly in their defining traits, goals, and relations to the state. We use a typology to distinguish more homogeneous sets of groups, sets that can be used for both descriptive and analytic purposes. The most basic distinction is between national peoples and minority peoples. *National peoples* are regionally concentrated groups that have lost their autonomy to states dominated by other groups but still preserve some of their cultural and linguistic distinctiveness. Their political movements usually seek to protect or reestablish some degree of politically separate existence. *Minority peoples* have a defined socioeconomic or political status within a larger society —based on some combination of their race, ethnicity, immigrant origins, economic roles, and religion—and are concerned mainly about protecting or improving that status. To make the distinction most sharply, national peoples ordinarily seek separation from or greater autonomy within the states that govern them, whereas minority peoples seek greater rights, access, or control. The distinction can change depending on political circumstances: a group's leaders may seek access at one time, exit at another. And sometimes groups are represented by contending factions that pursue both objectives.[19]

There are distinctive types of ethnopolitical groups within each of the two broad divisions, most of them illustrated in the group sketches that accompany the text. The national peoples include *ethnonationalists* (see the discussion of nationalism on pp. 6–7), *national minorities,* and *indigenous peoples.* The types of minority peoples are *ethnoclasses, religious sects,* and three subtypes of *communal contenders:* disadvantaged, advantaged, and dominant. Following are the definitions.

NATIONAL PEOPLES

Ethnonationalists. Regionally concentrated peoples with a history of organized political autonomy with their own state, traditional ruler, or regional government who have supported political movements for autonomy at some time since 1945. See sketches of Tibetans in China (pp. 212–217) and Gagauz in Moldova (pp. 218–222).

National minorities. Segments of a transstate people with a history of organized political autonomy whose kindred control an adjacent state but who now constitute a minority in the state in which they reside. Examples are Hungarians in Slovakia (pp. 183–187) and Russians in Ukraine (pp. 57–63).

Indigenous peoples. Conquered descendants of earlier inhabitants of a region who live mainly in conformity with traditional social, economic, and cultural customs that are sharply distinct from those of dominant groups. Examples are indigenous peoples of Ecuador (pp. 96–99) and Bolivia (pp. 178–182). Indigenous peoples who had durable states of their own prior to conquest, such as Tibetans, or who have given sustained support to modern movements aimed at establishing their own state, such as the Kurds, are classified as ethnonationalists, not indigenous peoples.

MINORITY PEOPLES

Ethnoclasses. Ethnically or culturally distinct peoples, usually descended from slaves or immigrants, most of whom occupy a distinct social and economic stratum or niche. Examples are Turks in Germany (pp. 21–26) and Afro-Brazilians (pp. 100–104). If an ethnoclass is a politically organized contender for a share in state power, such as the Chinese in Malaysia, it is classed as a communal contender.

Communal contenders. Culturally distinct peoples, tribes, or clans in heterogeneous societies who hold or seek a share in state power.

1. *Disadvantaged.* Communal contenders who are subject to some degree of political, economic, or cultural discrimination but lack offsetting advantages. See the sketches of Burundi (pp. 188–194) and Kenya (pp. 261–265): the Hutus in Burundi and the Kikuyu, Luo, and kindred groups in Kenya are examples. Also see the sketch of Chinese in Malaysia (pp. 133–137), whose economic advantages are offset by state-imposed political and cultural restrictions.

2. *Advantaged.* Communal contenders with political advantages over other groups in their society. See the sketch of Kenya (pp. 261–265): the Kalenjin

and Maasai are now politically advantaged. Communal contenders can quickly gain or lose advantage, as happened in Rwanda in 1994.

3. *Dominant.* Communal contenders with a preponderance of both political and economic power. See the sketch of Burundi (pp. 188–194): the Tutsis are a dominant minority; so are Sunni Arabs in Iraq—with the qualification that their advantages accrue mainly to the Arabs of Takriti, the hometown of Saddam Hussein.

Religious sects. Communal groups that differ from others principally in their religious beliefs and related cultural practices and whose political status and activities are centered on the defense of their beliefs. Examples are Copts in Egypt (pp. 138–142) and Muslims in India (pp. 266–274). Islamist movements in contemporary Egypt, Algeria, and other Arab states are not included as communal groups in this study. They are new religiopolitical movements that may, in the long run, evolve into durable identity groups distinct from more secular segments of their societies.

Numbers of each of the eight types of ethnopolitical groups are shown in table 1.3, categorized by world region. National peoples (151) are somewhat more numerous than minority peoples (124). Ethnonationalists and ethnoclasses are situated in almost all world regions. Indigenous peoples also are widely dispersed, though more numerous in Asia and Latin America than elsewhere. The other types of groups tend to cluster in particular regions. Communal groups defined principally by religious belief are located in and on the borders of the Islamic world: some are non-Muslim minorities in Islamic states; others are Muslim minorities in societies dominated by other religious traditions.

Most national minorities live in East Central Europe, where they are the legacy of historical processes of the expansion and contraction of national states. Russia, Serbia, Poland, and Hungary all have substantial numbers of kindred in neighboring states who at one time were part of, and governed by, the metropole. They are sometimes called diasporas, a misleading term for peoples many of whom have lived for generations in what they regard as part of their national homeland. The term seems more appropriate for Chinese minorities on the periphery of the People's Republic, most of whose ancestors migrated to their countries of residence within the past century or so.[20]

Communal contenders are found mainly in Africa south of the Sahara. They are the unintended legacies of colonial policies that carved out territorial entities that consisted of multiple "tribes" and kingdoms, some of whom became antagonistic rivals because of colonial policies that favored some peoples at the

Table 1.3. Types of Ethnopolitical Groups by Region in 1998

World Region (number of countries)	Number of Groups	National Peoples (151)			Minority Peoples (124)		
		Ethno-nationalists	National Minorities	Indigenous Peoples	Ethno-classes	Communal Contenders	Religious Sects
Western democracies and Japan (21)	30	8	3	6	12	0	1
Eastern Europe and the newly independent states (27)	59	9	32	8	9	0	1
East, Southeast, and South Asia (24)	59	10	6	20	4	14	5
North Africa and the Middle East (20)	28	8	3	4	1	6	6
Africa south of the Sahara (45)	67	6	0	8	7	46	0
Latin America and the Caribbean (24)	32	0	0	20	10	2	0
Totals (161)	275	41	44	66	43	68	13

Note: See text for definitions of group types.

expense of others. The most politically successful of postindependence leaders have governed through relatively stable coalitions that incorporate most or
all contenders. The least successful have used patronage policies to maintain
the hegemonic advantages of their own group at the expense of others. By doing
so they have reproduced the conditions of protracted communal conflict and
ethnic war.[21]

The next chapter evaluates trends in ethnopolitical conflict based on information that was collected using the definitions and distinctions sketched in
this chapter. Its conclusions are valid within those limits.

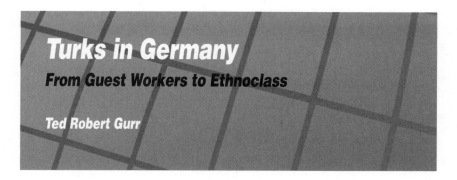

Turks in Germany
From Guest Workers to Ethnoclass

Ted Robert Gurr

Labor migrants of one era may become the ethnoclass minorities of the next, depending on whether the host society emphasizes incorporation or exclusion. The Turks in Germany also illustrate the politics of conservative reaction to immigrants in many Western societies and the ways in which immigrants resonate to the political conflicts of their countries of origin.

THE TWO MILLION Turkish residents of Germany are one of the new "visible minorities" in Western industrial democracies, people who have immigrated from countries in the global south mainly for economic reasons. The Turks, like the Maghrebins in France and recent Hispanic immigrants to the United States, have made some economic gains but often encounter social and cultural discrimination. The Turks in Germany, even those who are born there, also have faced serious barriers in gaining citizenship. They thus lack some of the political rights and influence that would facilitate their incorporation into German society. This pattern of political exclusion and informal social discrimination is as serious a problem as the widely publicized xenophobic attacks of the early and mid-1990s that targeted Turks as well as asylum seekers. The attacks have been checked, but discriminatory treatment continues. And because many Turks live on the margins of German society, they are more readily mobilized by Islamist and Kurdish national organizations seeking support for challenges to the Turkish government.

BACKGROUND

The presence of Turks in Germany is a consequence of policies of the former German and Turkish governments. West Germany's rapid economic growth in the 1950s and 1960s created a demand for labor that was met in part by a 1961 bilateral agreement between the two governments under whose terms

21

650,000 Turks migrated to the Federal Republic. Virtually all were Muslims, and 20–25 percent were members of Turkey's Kurdish minority.[1] Both governments expected that the *Gastarbeiter* (guest workers) would be temporary and would return to Turkey. The Federal Republic experienced an economic slump in the early 1970s and, beginning with the *Anwerbestopp* of 1973, initiated policies to stem the flow of new workers and encourage their repatriation. Relatively few Turks and other foreign workers left Germany; most sought instead to bring in their families and establish permanent residence. Polls taken during the 1980s showed that more than 80 percent wanted to remain in Germany, including virtually all who were born in the country. Most live in old inner-city neighborhoods, including 150,000 in Berlin's Kreuzberg district. In the industrial city of Duisburg the population of 550,000 includes 60,000 Turks. Many Turks, like other immigrants to Germany, still work at menial, entry-level jobs, but some have been modestly successful: in the early 1990s there were thirty-three thousand Turkish-owned businesses.

POLITICAL RESTRICTIONS

All immigrant workers in Germany face legal liabilities. The *Auslaendergesetz* of 1965 gave the state the right to restrict their freedom of assembly, association, movement, and choice of occupation. Unless they acquire citizenship, they cannot vote in national or most local elections, although they can and do participate in unions and civic organizations. The elected head of one of Germany's largest trade unions in 1999 is of Turkish origin. Ironically, despite the economic power he wields, as a noncitizen he cannot vote. Employed workers from countries of the European Community (since 1993 the European Union) have long had automatically renewable residence permits, whereas, until recently, Turks could qualify as permanent resident aliens only after eight consecutive years of work and residence.

Restrictions on citizenship are a major source of grievance for long-time Turkish residents and their children. Under German law citizenship is generally limited to those of German descent, and the law excludes from citizenship children born and raised in Germany by foreign nationals. The law in effect in 1998 allowed foreigners who had lived in Germany for fifteen years—or for eight years if they were under the age of twenty-three—to apply for citizenship. Doing so meant giving up foreign citizenship, which many migrants have been reluctant to do because it precludes a future return to Turkey or inheritance of property in Turkey. Further, substantial fees were required, and many applicants reportedly were rejected by police investigators on technicalities. As a consequence only 13,000 Turks were able to gain citizenship between 1977 and 1990. In the 1990s the process was eased so that in 1996 citizenship was granted to 46,300 Turks. But only 160,000 Turks were eligible to vote in the 1998 federal elections, and only 1 of 672 members of parliament, a representative of the Green party, was of Turkish origin.

In late 1998 the new government in Bonn, a coalition of Social Democrats and Greens, proposed legislation to reduce the residency requirement for all foreigners to eight years and to allow dual citizenship. The proposal was fiercely opposed by the Christian Democratic opposition, not least because virtually all Turkish-German citizens voted for the Social Democrats in 1998. Public resistance to the proposal also contributed to the Social Democrats' electoral defeat in subsequent elections in the state of Hesse, a long-time party stronghold. Revised legislation, passed in 1999, provides that children with foreign-national parents who have lived eight years or more in Germany have dual citizenship until the age of twenty-three, when they must choose between German citizenship and that of their parents.

The state does provide Turks and other foreign residents with the full range of social services and most of the benefits to which citizens are entitled. Criticisms of discrimination against Turkish youths in schools have declined in recent years. They are enrolled at all levels of the school system, including the gymnasiums, the academic secondary schools that are the gateways to higher education. The fact remains that most German-born Turks are now more German than Turkish in their language and culture but are not German citizens. As one authority remarked, German-born Turks are "not foreigners with German residence permits, but Germans with foreign passports."[2]

SOCIAL DISCRIMINATION

A special liability faced by Turks is widespread prejudice and social discrimination, based on the pervasive perception that Turks are a culturally alien group who cannot be assimilated into European society. Opinion polls in the 1980s showed widespread resentment against Turks; two-thirds of Germans thought *Gastarbeiter* should return to their homelands, regardless of their own wishes. The sources of resentment include the belief that Turks compete with Germans for jobs, that they take undue advantage of social programs, that they are potential supporters of militant Islam or extreme Kurdish nationalism, and that they are dirty and disorderly. Antidiscrimination laws are on the books, but enforcement efforts appear limited. These attitudes and practices translate into day-to-day acts of discrimination and hostility that limit Turks' personal security, cultural expression, and access to housing and private facilities. Two examples from 1997 serve to illustrate. In Duisburg leaders of two mosques applied to the city to broadcast their muezzins' call to prayer once a week, as in other cities in the region. The application, though approved, prompted hundreds of protest letters and newspaper advertisements decrying "Islamic sovereign territory Duisburg." On New Year's Eve, in a village near Berlin, ten skinheads attacked the Turkish proprietor of a fast-food stand. He defended himself with a meat cleaver. When police arrived, they let the skinheads go but arrested the proprietor and held him for two days.[3]

The most serious manifestations of antiforeigner discrimination have taken the form of deadly arson attacks on Turkish homes and assaults, some of them fatal, on Turks in public places. These attacks were perpetrated mainly by skinheads and neo-Nazis in the early to mid-1990s. They occurred in the context of widespread insecurity in Germany due to the economic impact of reunification and an unprecedented influx of asylum seekers and of Germans from the East. The attacks were directed more or less indiscriminately against all visible minorities, not just Turks, and were gradually brought under control by state authorities. Right-wing attacks against all targets declined from 1992 to 1994 by nearly two-thirds, from 2,277 to 860. In 1997 the German agency that monitors such attacks reported 669 episodes, more than half aimed at foreigners. The attacks and lesser acts of harassment are especially common in the towns and villages of former East Germany, where foreigners make up a much smaller proportion of the population than in the former West, but where unemployed youths are numerous and neo-Nazi sentiments are widely held.

GROUP IDENTITY AND POLITICAL ACTION

Despite political and social discrimination, Turks have rarely joined in collective action against German authorities, though they have joined German citizens in demonstrations and vigils to protest antiforeign arson and murder. But many have organized and acted in behalf of Islamic and Kurdish causes, prompting public and official concern. The German domestic intelligence service reported in 1997 that some twenty-eight thousand Turks belonged to militant Islamic organizations such as the Islamic Community Milli Goerues, which wants to replace the Turkish secular state with an Islamic republic.[4] Kurds in Germany have repeatedly protested policies of the Turkish government.

Examples from 1998 include an April demonstration of fifty thousand Kurds in Dortmund in support of a peaceful solution to the Kurdish conflict in Turkey and November demonstrations by twenty thousand Kurds in cities throughout Germany to support the extradition of PKK leader Ocalan to stand trial in Turkey.

Political action by Turks (and Kurds) in Germany thus poses a puzzle. Their lack of protest against discrimination suggests a degree of complacency about a status that German and other observers think is insecure and inequitable, especially given the proactive efforts to incorporate immigrants by some of Germany's neighbors.[5] On the other hand, Turks are quick to engage in political action in behalf of contentious issues in Turkey, which suggests continued identification with groups and issues in that country. The answer to the puzzle is this: as many studies have shown, Turks in Germany are not a cohesive group, except perhaps in the perceptions of many Germans. Second- and third-generation Turkish Germans probably have enough of a stake and enough security in Germany that they identify more with German than Turkish society. More recent immigrants, though, are still outsiders—a status reinforced by government policy and social discrimination—and therefore are more likely to value their old communal ties. Many came as political refugees in the 1980s and are responsive to the appeals of political entrepreneurs to take sides in homeland politics.[6]

IN SUMMARY

The Turks can in principle be incorporated into German society in much the same way that immigrant minorities have been and are being incorporated in other Western societies. The legal means to this end include ensuring equal access to educational and economic opportunities, active enforcement of anti-discrimination laws, and reducing the barriers to citizenship. In 1999 Germany adopted a policy followed in virtually all other Western countries, that children born to foreign residents gain citizenship at birth or on reaching adulthood. By doing so the government has broken with the old principle that Germany is not a "society of immigration." Widespread social prejudice against immigrant minorities remains. Change in citizenship policy is an essential precursor to the long-term erosion of discriminatory social practice and the prejudices from which it derives. It also may help channel the political energies of Turkish-origin Germans away from homeland issues and into domestic German politics.

NOTES

1. News accounts in the mid- to late 1990s estimated the number of Kurds in Germany at about four hundred thousand.

2. Klaus J. Bade, ed., *Population, Labor, and Migration in Nineteenth- and Twentieth-Century Germany* (New York: St. Martin's Press, 1987), 149.

3. "Muezzin's Call to Prayer Reveals Religious Differences in Duisburg," Deutsch Presse-Agentur, July 15, 1997; "Right-Wing Violence on Rise in Eastern Germany," *Washington Post,* March 5, 1998.

4. "Islamic Extremists Alarm Germany," Deutsche Presse-Agentur, September 11, 1997.

5. Citizenship is readily obtained by immigrants in the Netherlands, Belgium, and the Scandinavian countries, for example. The German rejoinder is that German society has much larger numbers and proportions of immigrants than other European countries.

6. A detailed study that supports this interpretation is Nedim Ögelman, "Organizations, Integration, and the 'Homeland Hangover': The Case of Germany's Turkish-Origin Community" (paper presented to the Annual Meeting of the American Political Science Association, Atlanta, September 1999).

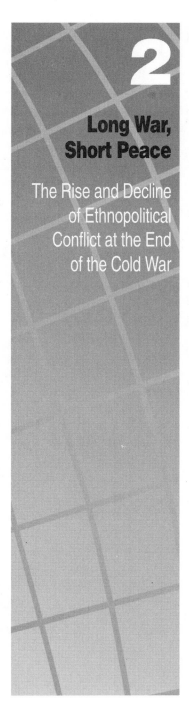

Long War, Short Peace

The Rise and Decline of Ethnopolitical Conflict at the End of the Cold War

THE MOST COMMON MODE of political action among ethnopolitical groups in the 1990s is not rebellion; it is symbolic and organizational politics. Here is another factual challenge to conventional wisdom about the pervasiveness of deadly ethnic conflict: in 1995 as many of the groups in the Minorities at Risk survey were politically quiescent (seventy-one groups, or 26 percent) as were engaged in rebellions (seventy-one groups).[1] The types of political action observed among groups in each region are summarized in table 2.1. This information, coded annually for all groups since 1985, also provides the basis for the following analysis of global and regional trends in ethnopolitical conflict. The nature of the coded data is summarized briefly in the first section, followed by discussion of the reversing trend in intensity of ethnopolitical conflict between 1985 and 1998. The last part of the chapter focuses on the groups that initiated violent challenges to the state in this period and on the antecedents of their rebellions.

Dimensions of Ethnopolitical Conflict

Politically organized communal groups often pursue their interests through electoral politics, lobbying, or control of local or regional governments. These are the strategies of conventional politics. The focus of this chapter is the extent to which communal groups pursue their interests outside the institutional frameworks established by the state, using means that scholars

Table 2.1. Highest Level of Political Action among Minorities in 1995, by World Region

World Region (number of groups)	Inactive in 1995	Mobilization	Demonstrations and/or Rioting	Small-Scale Rebellion	Large-Scale Rebellion
Western democracies and Japan (30)	5 (17%)	11 (37%)	8 (27%)	6 (20%)	0 (0%)
Eastern Europe and the newly independent states (59)	12 (20%)	27 (46%)	9 (15%)	6 (10%)	5 (8%)
East, Southeast, and South Asia (57)	19 (32%)	8 (14%)	5 (9%)	13 (22%)	12 (21%)
North Africa and the Middle East (26)	5 (19%)	10 (38%)	4 (15%)	6 (23%)	1 (4%)
Africa south of the Sahara (66)	23 (35%)	14 (21%)	10 (15%)	16 (24%)	3 (5%)
Latin America and the Caribbean (30)	7 (23%)	16 (53%)	4 (13%)	2 (7%)	1 (3%)
Totals (268)	71 (26%)	86 (32%)	40 (15%)	49 (18%)	22 (8%)

Note: Groups are categorized according to the highest level of conflict recorded in the Minorities at Risk profiles for 1995. See table 2.2 for coding categories.

Inactive = Protest and rebellion both coded 0.

Mobilization = Verbal opposition, symbolic resistance, or organizing activity.

Demonstrations and/or rioting = Demonstrations or riots; any level of participation.

Small-scale rebellion = Political banditry, terrorism, local rebellions, or small-scale guerrilla activity.

Large-scale rebellion = Intermediate or large-scale guerrilla activity, protracted civil war.

characterize as political action or "unconventional politics." This analysis distinguishes two general strategies of political action: protest and rebellion. The essential strategy of protest is to mobilize a show of support that prompts officials to take action favorable to the group. The Chinese minority in Malaysia (pp. 133–137) acts almost entirely through political parties and communal associations, through activities characterized here as "conventional politics." The indigenous peoples of Ecuador, by contrast (pp. 96–99), have relied heavily on political action—marches, demonstrations, and blockades—to press their demands on the government.

The essential strategy of rebellion is to mobilize enough coercive power, or cause sufficient disruption, that governments are compelled either to fight or to negotiate change. The leaders of the Gagauz in Moldova (pp. 218–222) organized a local rebellion with scattered clashes that stopped short of warfare; the dispute between the leaders of the Chechens and the Russian government escalated into a protracted civil war. Demonstrators also may use violence but ordinarily do so in episodic and unplanned ways, typically in reaction to coercive acts by the police and military. The use of violence by rebels, however, is usually proactive and part of a larger strategy.

The distinction between protest and rebellion is not absolute, because ethnopolitical leaders, or different factions within a group, may use both strategies either in sequence or simultaneously. In the United States between 1960 and the mid-1970s, different elements of the African-American community participated in civil rights marches (nonviolent protest, mainly in the early to mid-1960s), urban riots (violent protest, mainly from 1965 to 1969), and armed attacks on police (small-scale rebellion, from 1969 to 1975).[2]

We profiled the history of political action of each group in the Minorities survey using scales of the severity and extent of protest and rebellion. The scales in table 2.2 take into account the number of people involved and the intensity of their actions. Each group was coded for the most widespread and intense action of each type recorded during a period. From 1945 to 1984 the groups were coded for successive five-year periods; after 1985 they were coded annually.

Communal groups often are caught up in open conflict with rival groups as well as the state or are attacked by rival groups acting at the instigation of officials. Intercommunal conflict can take the form of harassment and violent attacks on group members of the kinds directed by neo-Nazis and other xenophobes against Turks in Germany (pp. 21–26) and by the government-aligned Kalenjin against the Kikuyu in Kenya (pp. 261–265). It also can take the form of communal attacks initiated by a group, exemplified by episodic

Hutu attacks on Tutsis in the postcolonial histories of Rwanda and Burundi (pp. 188–194). Some of this violence has been officially encouraged; some has been initiated by local communal activists. The scale of intercommunal conflict in table 2.2 is used to record the most severe kind of action recorded during a period. From 1945 to 1989 each group was coded by decade; after 1990 groups were coded annually.

Global and Regional Trends in Ethnopolitical Conflict

A half century of global trends in magnitudes of ethnopolitical protest and rebellion are depicted in figures 2.1 and 2.2.[3] Upward movement in ethnopolitical conflict began shortly after the end of World War II and continued to accelerate through the 1980s. The numbers of groups using protest and rebellion show a similar upward trend until the early 1990s. The intensity and volume of both kinds of political action also increased over the same span. After 1994, though, the indicators suggest that ethnopolitical conflict leveled off: the number of active groups steadied, and the intensity of both protest and rebellion began to decline. The asterisks for 1995–98 in figures 2.1 and 2.2 are a warning that because this period includes data for only four years, the numbers of active groups may be slightly understated by comparison with previous five-year periods.

The global data suggest two important qualifications about the conventional wisdom that ethnopolitical conflict exploded at the end of the Cold War. First, the upward trends were evident as early as the 1950s and accelerated sharply in the 1970s. Second, the trends reach their height in the early 1990s, but thereafter they turn downward. Is conventional wisdom wrong, or are the data wrong? The next section examines the details and alternative interpretations.

It is necessary to consider two alternative explanations for the long-term upward trends. Are they due to better reporting about group conflict rather than a real increase? Or can they be attributed to our neglect of groups that were politically active in the 1950s and 1960s but not since then? More thorough and accurate reporting probably has increased the project's capacity to document recent ethnic protest and minor episodes of intercommunal conflict, especially in the global south, but not rebellion or intercommunal warfare: armed conflict is always "news" that sooner or later reaches outside observers and journalists, even from states with tight media controls. "Neglect" led to omission of a few historically active communal groups like the Walloons of Belgium, the Tamils and the Telagu-speakers of India, and no doubt some

Table 2.2. Scales for Coding the Highest Level of Collective Action by Communal Groups

---

Antigovernment protest

0 = None reported.

1 = Verbal opposition (public letters, petitions, posters, publications, agitation, etc.). Requests by a minority-controlled regional government for independence are coded 1.

2 = Political organizing activity on a substantial scale, symbolic resistance or destruction of property. Mobilization by a minority-controlled regional government for autonomy or secession is coded 2.

3 = One or more demonstrations, rallies, strikes, and/or riots; total participation less than 10,000.

4 = Demonstrations, rallies, strikes, and/or riots; estimated total participation between 10,000 and 100,000.

5 = Demonstrations, rallies, strikes, and/or riots; total participation over 100,000.

Antigovernment rebellion

0 = None reported.

1 = Political banditry (often the last stage of guerrilla wars), sporadic terrorism.

2 = Campaigns of terrorism.

3 = Local rebellions: armed attempts to seize power in a locale. Declarations of independence by a minority-controlled regional government are coded 3.

4 = Small-scale guerrilla activity.[a]

5 = Intermediate-scale guerrilla activity.[b]

6 = Large-scale guerrilla activity.[c]

7 = Protracted civil war, fought by rebel military units with base areas.

Intercommunal conflict (targeted at or initiated by a communal group)

0 = None reported.

1 = Individual acts of harassment against property and persons, no fatalities.

2 = Political agitation, campaigns urging authorities to impose restrictions on a group, etc.

3 = Sporadic violent attacks by gangs or other small groups, some of them fatal.

4 = Anti-group demonstrations, rallies, marches.

5 = Intercommunal rioting, armed attacks.

6 = Intercommunal warfare (protracted, large-scale intergroup violence).

---

[a] *Small-scale guerrilla activity* has these three traits:
- fewer than 1,000 armed fighters;
- sporadic armed attacks (fewer than six reported per year); and
- attacks in a small part of the area occupied by the group or in one or two other areas.

[b] *Intermediate-scale guerrilla activity* has a mix of small- and large-scale traits.

[c] *Large-scale guerrilla activity* has these three traits:
- more than 1,000 armed fighters;
- frequent armed attacks (more than six reported per year); and
- attacks affecting a large part of the area occupied by the group.

Figure 2.1. Long-Run Global Trends in Ethnopolitical Protest

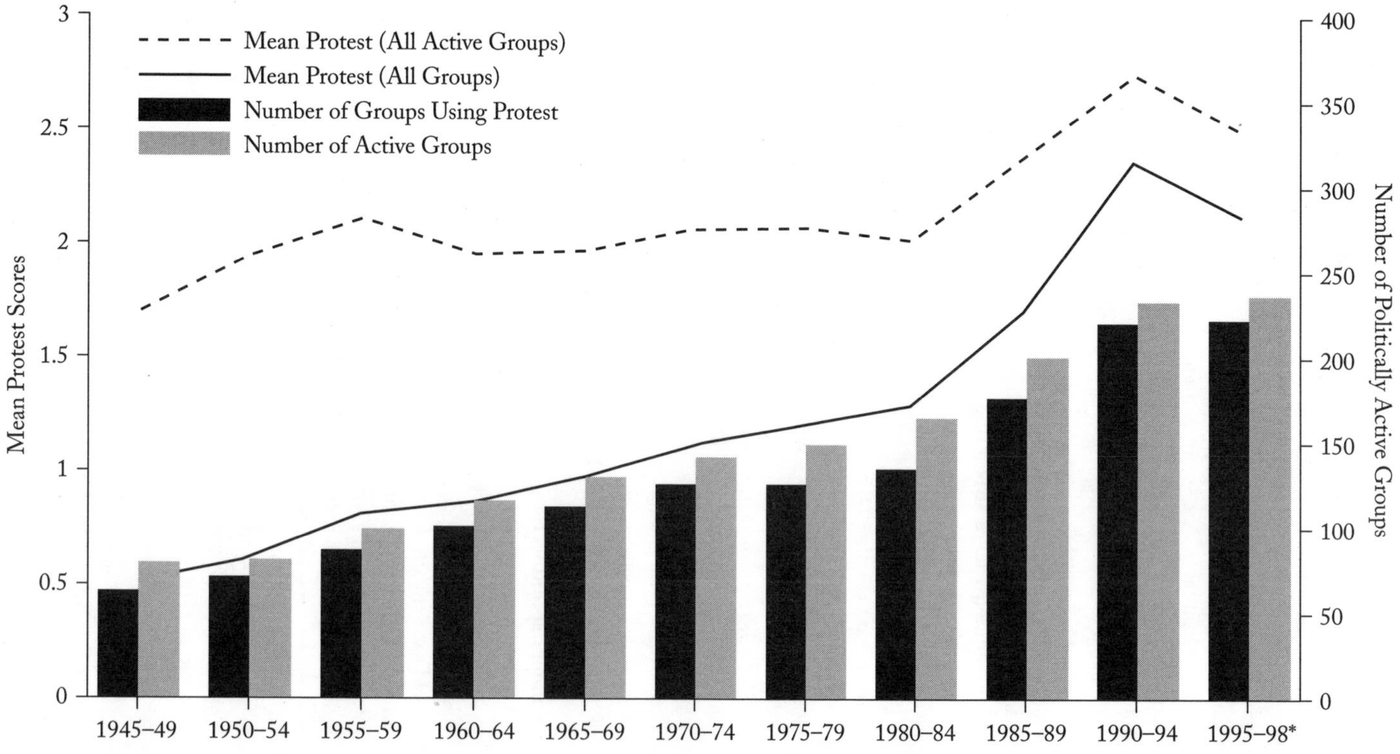

Figure 2.2. Long-Run Global Trends in Ethnopolitical Rebellion

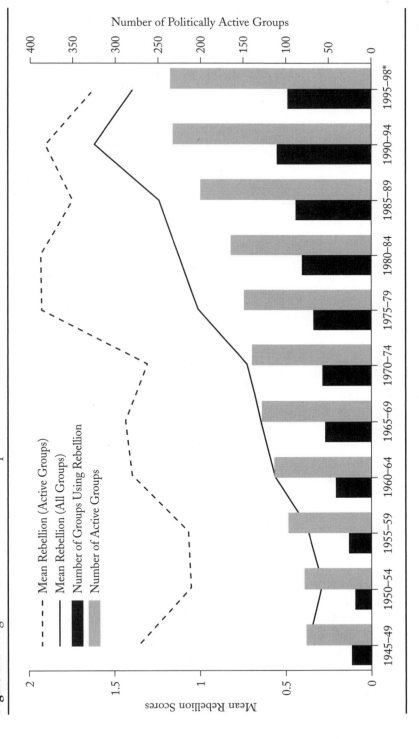

others, but groups in open rebellion against the state almost surely have not escaped our searches through historical sources. Neither factor, therefore, is a plausible explanation for the long-run increase in ethnic war, which is the form of conflict of greatest contemporary concern.

The annual data for 1985–98 suggest a retelling of the story.[4] Figure 2.3 shows that the intensity of ethnopolitical protest by all active groups reached a global peak in 1990–91, followed by a gradual decline. The number of groups in rebellion also peaked in the early 1990s but the average intensity of rebellion has been declining since the late 1980s. The inference is that the spate of new rebellions that began at the end of the Cold War were less intense, on average, than rebellions already under way. The more general point is that a sea change in ethnic conflict has been under way for much of the 1990s, a reversal in a forty-year trend that cannot be explained away as an artifact of changes in reporting or global attention. To the contrary, the global spotlight has focused throughout the 1990s on issues of minority status, ethnic mobilization, and communal warfare.

Other sources provide confirming evidence about the decline in serious ethnic conflict. Annual surveys of armed conflict prepared by Peter Wallensteen and his associates show that these conflicts—the great majority of which are ethnic wars—have followed the same trajectory as the Minorities project's indicators of trends in protest and rebellion. Wallensteen and Sollenberg identify forty-seven armed conflicts in 1989, fifty-five in the peak year of 1995, but only thirty-six in 1998. The decline was especially pronounced for the most serious conflicts, defined as those with more than one thousand battle-related deaths in a given year: their number peaked at twenty in 1991 and 1992 but declined to only six in 1996 before increasing to thirteen in 1998—an increase due mainly to the onset of non-ethnic conflicts.[5] PIOOM, a Dutch non-governmental organization (NGO) that monitors human rights violations, reports an apparent increase in total number of armed conflicts in the 1990s, from 106 in 1993 to 200 in mid-1998, but its researchers acknowledge that the increase is due to the inclusion of larger numbers of low-intensity conflicts and the disaggregation of complex conflicts into multiple, separately counted elements. The number of high-intensity conflicts, defined by PIOOM as those with more than one thousand fatalities annually, fell from twenty-two in 1993 to sixteen in mid-1998.[6] A third confirming study, by Byman and Van Evera, evaluates the factors that contributed to the decline in serious conflict in the mid-1990s.[7]

Numbers of refugees from internal conflicts also have risen and then declined during the last decade. In 1989 there were an estimated 15.1 million

Figure 2.3. Global Trends in Ethnopolitical Conflict, 1985–98

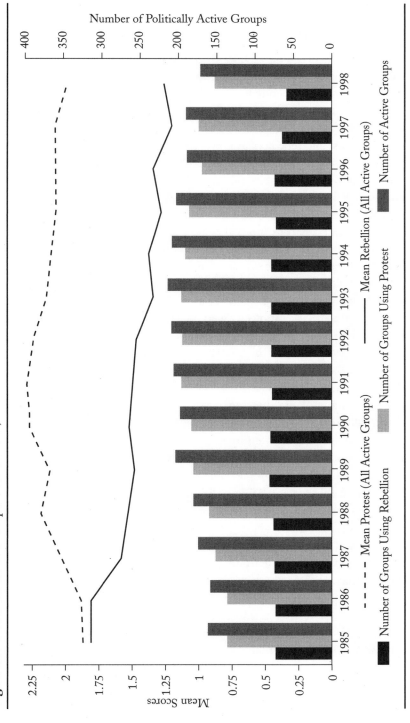

- ■ Number of Groups Using Rebellion
- ▨ Number of Groups Using Protest
- ■ Number of Active Groups
- --- Mean Protest (All Active Groups)
- — Mean Rebellion (All Active Groups)

refugees in need of assistance outside their countries of origin, rising to a peak of 17.6 million in 1992. By 1997 the number of people being repatriated to their homelands had substantially exceeded the outflow of new refugees and the global total had been reduced to 13.6 million.[8]

The global trends are open to various interpretations. The dissolution of the USSR and Yugoslavia contributed substantially to the 1989–92 maximum in ethnic protest and rebellion, as is evident in figure 2.4. However, the general pattern of rise and decline is also evident elsewhere. It can be seen from figures 2.5 through 2.9 that ethnopolitical conflict increased during the 1980s and early 1990s in most world regions. In Asia and Africa protest and rebellion both intensified, while in Latin America and the Western democracies protest increased. Most regions also show evidence of declining ethnopolitical conflict in the mid- to late 1990s. Rebellion declined sharply in the Middle East from the mid-1980s onward and held steady in Asia during the 1990s. Numbers of active groups and the intensity of ethnopolitical action also declined somewhat in the Western democracies, the postcommunist states, and Africa. Latin America showed diverging trends in the 1990s: the number of groups using rebellion fell, whereas protest intensified.[9]

The disengagement of the USSR and the United States from local rivalries may help to explain the rise in ethnopolitical conflict in parts of Asia and Africa, as some observers have suggested.[10] When a hegemonial power withdraws from a weak and heterogeneous state, the result often is what Barry Posen calls a security dilemma. Constraints on ethnic rivals are reduced, mutual uncertainty about intentions increases, and the rivals are prompted to mobilize and take preemptive action against one another. The argument fits Afghanistan well, for example. But the end of Cold War rivalry cannot be held responsible for escalating political action by ethnoclasses and ethnonationalists in the advanced industrial democracies or among indigenous peoples in Latin America.

Second, the increase in the late 1980s in the intensity of ethnopolitical protest, seen in figures 2.1 and 2.3, is associated with the "third wave of democratization." As the level of democracy increases in a heterogeneous state, the opportunities for and potential payoffs of ethnic mobilization and protest increase relative to more violent forms of political action. In Latin America it is clear that democratic transitions provided incentives and opportunities for mobilization of indigenous peoples, as is illustrated by the sketches of Bolivia and Ecuador on pages 178–182 and 96–99. The Roma of postcommunist Europe are far more politically active under democratic regimes than they were under state socialism.

Figure 2.4. Trends in Ethnopolitical Conflict: Postcommunist States, 1945–98

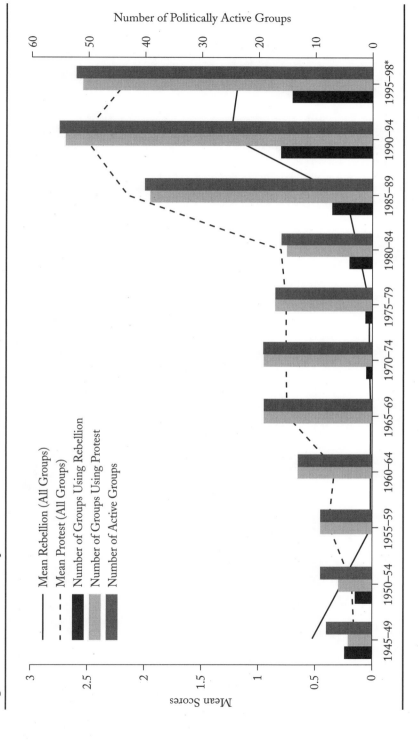

Figure 2.5. Trends in Ethnopolitical Conflict: Western Democracies and Japan, 1945–98

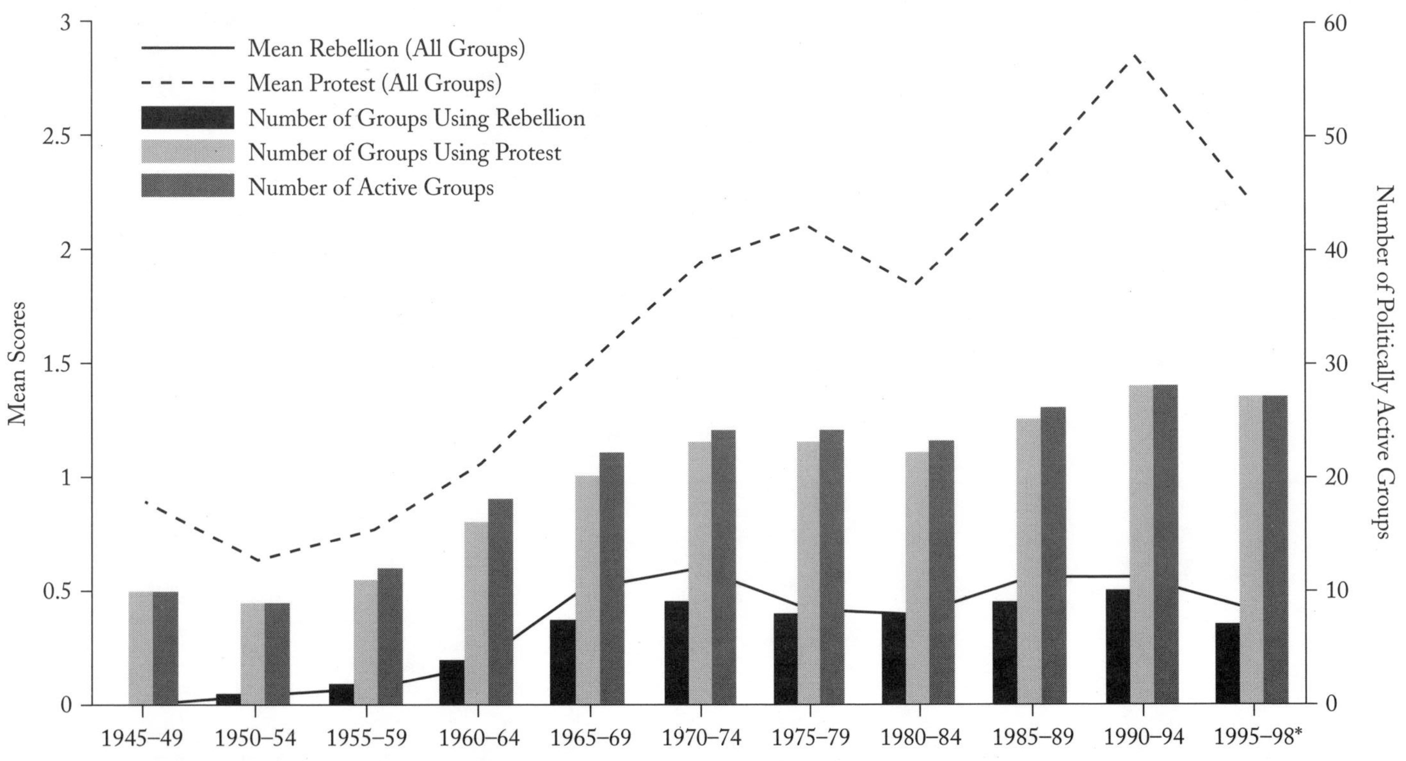

Figure 2.6. Trends in Ethnopolitical Conflict: Asia, 1945–98

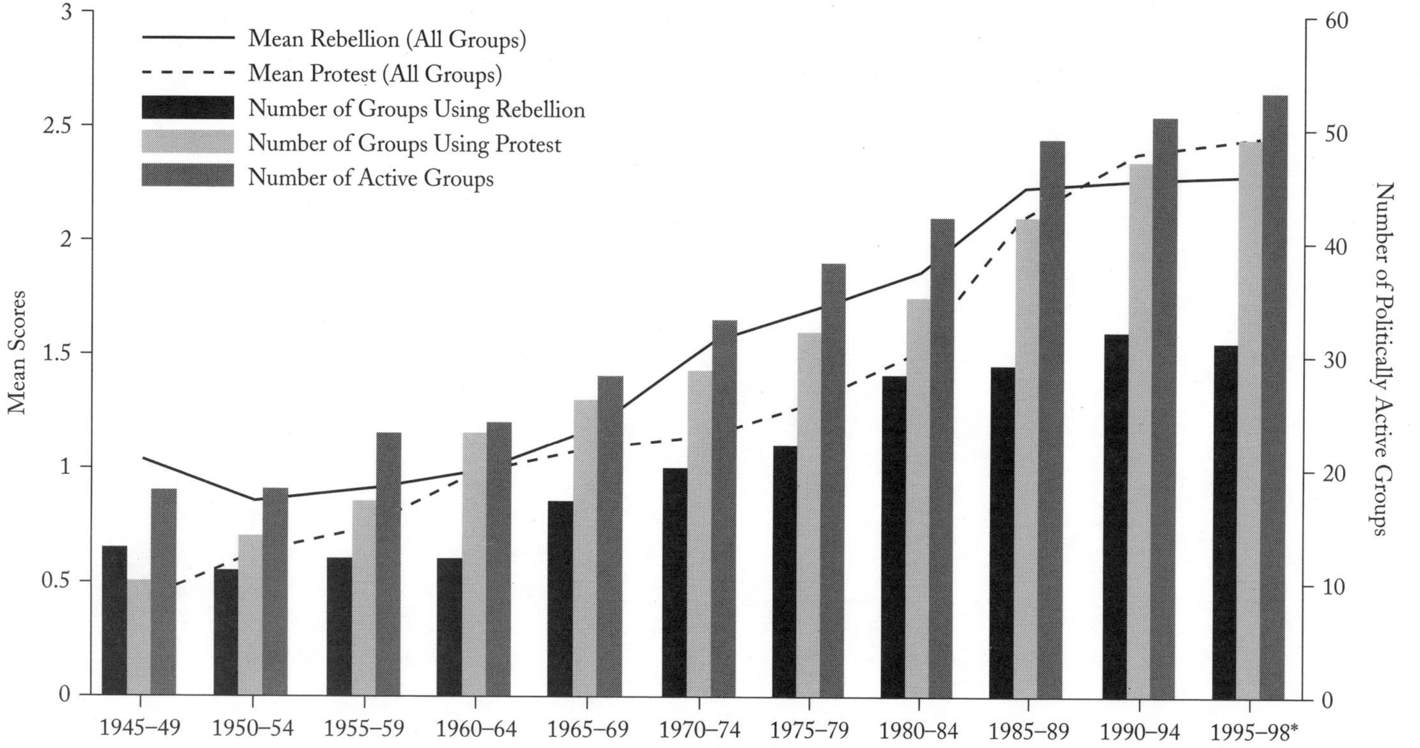

Number of Politically Active Groups

Mean Scores

— Mean Rebellion (All Groups)
- - - Mean Protest (All Groups)
■ Number of Groups Using Rebellion
▨ Number of Groups Using Protest
▨ Number of Active Groups

1945–49 1950–54 1955–59 1960–64 1965–69 1970–74 1975–79 1980–84 1985–89 1990–94 1995–98*

60 50 40 30 20 10 0

3 2.5 2 1.5 1 0.5 0

Figure 2.7. Trends in Ethnopolitical Conflict: North Africa and the Middle East, 1945–98

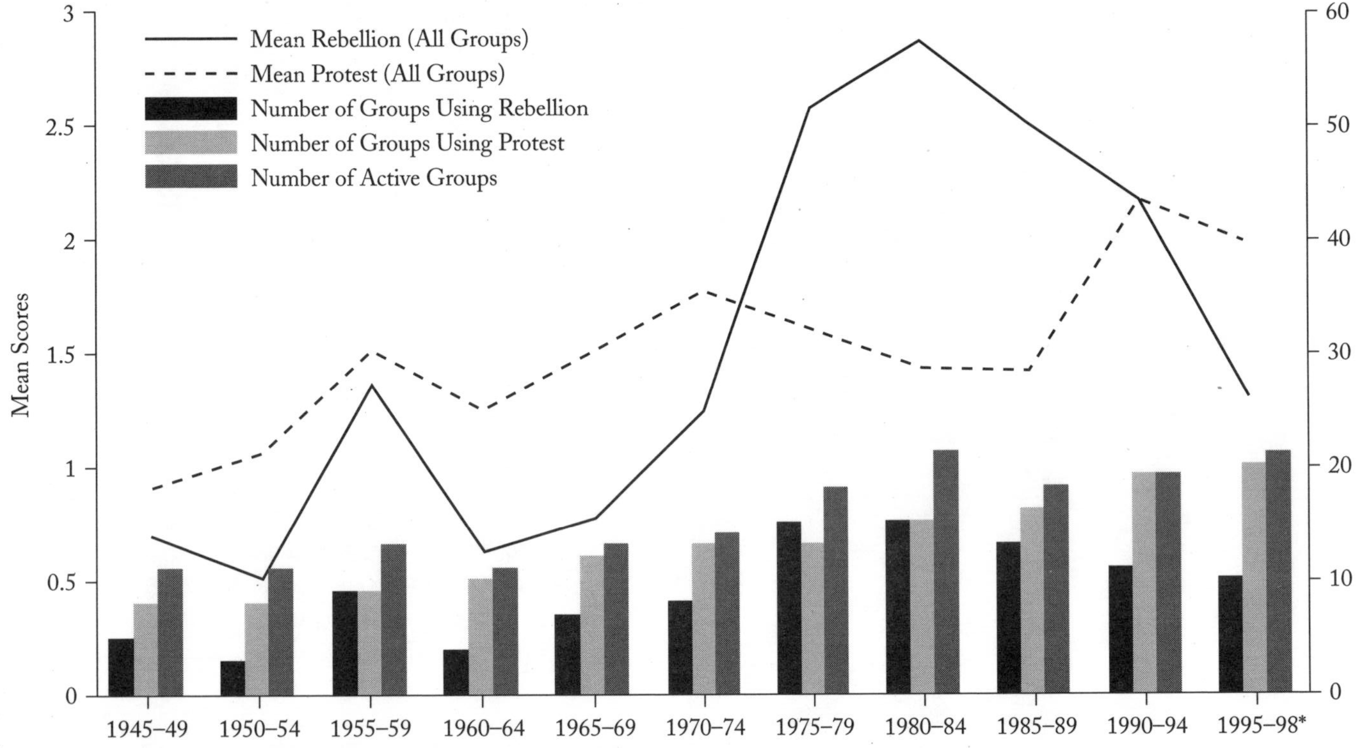

Figure 2.8. Trends in Ethnopolitical Conflict: Africa South of the Sahara, 1945–98

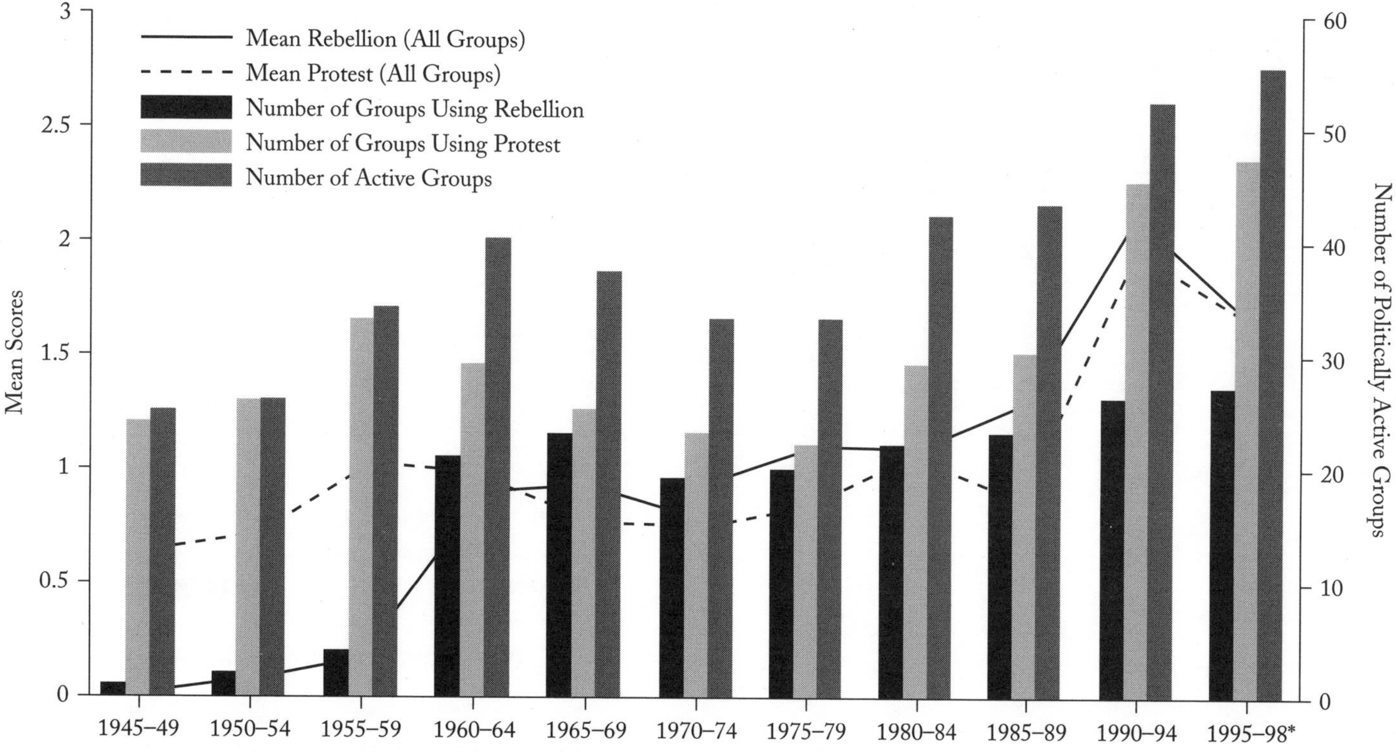
Mean Rebellion (All Groups)
Mean Protest (All Groups)
Number of Groups Using Rebellion
Number of Groups Using Protest
Number of Active Groups
Mean Scores
3
2.5
2
1.5
1
0.5
0
Number of Politically Active Groups
60
50
40
30
20
10
0
1945–49
1950–54
1955–59
1960–64
1965–69
1970–74
1975–79
1980–84
1985–89
1990–94
1995–98*

Figure 2.9. Trends in Ethnopolitical Conflict: Latin America and the Caribbean, 1945–98

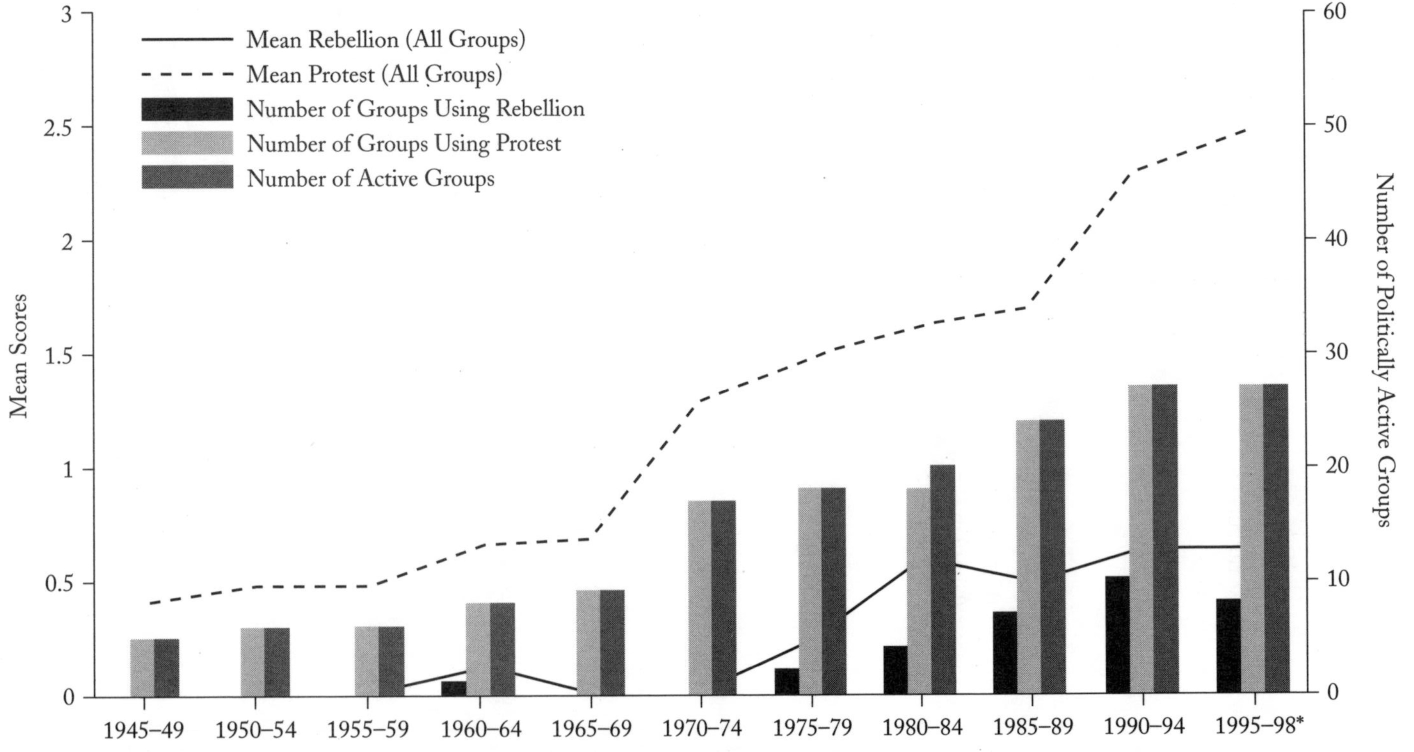

Under some circumstances democratization may also precipitate rebellion. In southeast Europe political entrepreneurs—some of them postcommunist, others recycled communists—took the democratic opportunity to make appeals for electoral support based on national identities and interests. The subsequent process of "outbidding" polarized interethnic relations and, in Croatia, Bosnia, and Kosovo, led to ethnic war. But these are exceptional, not typical, consequences of democratization. Moderate democrats prevailed early in the democratic transitions in Czechoslovakia, Bulgaria, and Macedonia, and eventually in Romania (1996 elections) and Slovakia (1998 elections). Except in Macedonia, moderate democrats opened up their governments to more effective participation by national minorities. In Macedonia, however, the 30 percent Albanian minority were marginalized until the November 1998 elections, when they along with other opposition parties ousted the ruling Social Democrats and formed a coalition government.[11] Chapter 5 provides a general assessment of the consequences of democratization on minority rights and political actions in all world regions.

The New Contenders, 1986 to 1998

Another perspective on trends in ethnopolitical conflict is to ask how many groups are or have been engaged in serious conflict at different times. Table 2.3 shows the results of such an analysis of all the groups included in either phase of the Minorities project. The global trend is by now a familiar one. A substantial increase in the number of rebellious identity groups in the 1970s and 1980s was followed by a veritable explosion in the early 1990s. The regional trends are more varied; virtually all the increase in the early 1990s is specific to Europe and Africa. In the Middle East the number of groups in serious ethnopolitical conflicts has varied relatively little over the past half century. Latin America is remarkable for the scarcity of serious ethnopolitical conflicts.

The tabulations for the late 1990s show further evidence of the retreat from serious conflict in most regions. The decline from 115 to 95 groups in serious conflicts from the early to the late 1990s is modest, not dramatic. More telling is the balance between escalation and de-escalation. We examined the annual rebellion codes from 1995 to 1998 for fifty-nine groups that were above the "local rebellion" threshold in table 2.2. De-escalating rebellions outnumbered escalating ones by twenty-three to seven, with the remaining twenty-nine conflicts showing no short-term trend.

Table 2.3. Numbers of Ethnopolitical Groups Involved in
Serious Conflicts between 1945 and 1998, by Region

Period	Europe	Middle East	Asia	Africa	Latin America	Total
1945–49	7	6	12	1	0	26
1950–59	2	15	14	8	0	39
1960–69	3	4	15	20	0	42
1970–79	1	16	20	22	2	61
1980–89	10	13	28	19	6	76
1990–94	21	14	35	40	5	115
1995–98	16	10	31	31	7	95

Note: Groups are tallied for each period in which they participated in mass protest (more
than 100,000 participants in demonstrations or riots in at least one year), local rebellions,
guerrilla activity, civil war, or deadly intercommunal conflict, based on codings in Phases I
and III of the Minorities at Risk project. Protagonists and victims in intercommunal conflict
are both counted. Groups participating in more than one such type of conflict in a period
are counted only once. The analysis does not include seven groups in small countries (populations 500,000 to 1 million) added to the project in 1998.

Next we take a closer look at the timing and circumstances of new episodes
of ethnoprotest and rebellion between 1986 and 1998. The "new" episodes
are those initiated in these years by politically active ethnic groups that had
no post-1945 history of collective action *plus* episodes initiated by groups that
resumed action after a decade or more of inactivity.[12] Examples from group
sketches in this book are new episodes of protest by the indigenous people of
Ecuador in 1992 and Turks in Germany in the same year. New rebellions began
among the Hutus in Burundi in 1988 and the Gagauz of Moldova in 1990.

The timing of the onset of new episodes is shown in tables 2.4 and 2.5, with
striking results: more than half the ninety-one new protest campaigns during
the thirteen years began between 1988 and 1991. New ethnorebellions were
even more tightly clustered, with more than half beginning between 1990
and 1992. The decline in new episodes after 1992 is especially pronounced.
An average of eight new ethnorebellions began each year between 1989 and
1992; after 1992 the average was two per year. The regional breakdowns provide a more precise diagnosis.

THE WESTERN DEMOCRACIES AND LATIN AMERICA

New episodes of ethnopolitical conflict in the Western democracies and Latin
America between 1986 and 1998 were relatively few in number (nineteen

Table 2.4. New Campaigns of Ethnopolitical Protest, by Region and Year of Onset, 1986–98

Year	Western Industrial Democracies and Latin America	Postcommunist States	Middle East, Asia, and Africa	Totals
1986	0	0	0	0
1987	1	2	1	4
1988	3	3	2	8
1989	2	7	4	13
1990	3	6	11	20
1991	1	6	4	11
1992	3	3	2	8
1993	3	5	3	11
1994	0	0	1	1
1995	1	2	1	4
1996	0	1	0	1
1997	0	0	3	3
1998	2	1	4	7
Totals	19	36	36	91

Note: Based on annual codings of protest on the five-category scale in table 2.2. "New" protest movements are those that shifted, in a given year, from a decade or more of political quiescence or low-level opposition activity (coding category 0, 1, or 2) to strategies of demonstrations, strikes, rallies, or riots (coding categories 3 to 5). The tabulation does not differentiate between groups whose use of collective action was short-lived and groups who employed it for a longer time.

episodes of protest, eight of rebellion) and were more or less evenly distributed across time. Indigenous peoples began most of these new episodes of collective action, including Native Americans in Ecuador, Hawaii, Honduras, Mexico, Panama, and Venezuela, and Aborigines in Australia. Other new episodes were initiated by ethnoclasses: African Americans in Brazil and Colombia, Muslims in France and Greece, Roma in Italy. Virtually all these peoples had long-standing grievances about differential treatment and restrictive policies, but, in most instances, their situations did not worsen in the 1980s. With some exceptions noted below, their political action was proactive: they had new leadership, new organizations, and new opportunities, especially openings provided by democratization and examples of effective action by similar groups elsewhere.

Four indigenous rebellions are counted in table 2.5. In the Brazilian Amazon in 1992–94 a series of violent clashes (which we coded as a local rebellion)

Table 2.5. New Ethnopolitical Rebellions, by Region and
Year of Onset, 1986–98

Year	Western Industrial Democracies and Latin America	Postcommunist States	Middle East, Asia, and Africa	Totals
1986	1	0	0	1
1987	1	0	0	1
1988	0	1	3	4
1989	0	0	4	4
1990	1	5	7	13
1991	0	3	6	9
1992	0	3	3	6
1993	1	0	1	2
1994	1	0	2	3
1995	0	0	0	0
1996	2	0	3	5
1997	0	2	0	2
1998	1	0	1	2
Totals	8	14	30	52

Note: Based on annual codings of rebellion on the seven-category scale in table 2.2. "New" rebellions are counted for groups that shifted, in a given year, from long-term inactivity, protest, or banditry or sporadic terrorism (rebellion code = 1 or less) to strategies of terrorist campaigns, local rebellion, or guerrilla or civil war (rebellion = 2 or more). The tabulation does not differentiate between groups whose new rebellions were short-term and groups whose rebellions were of longer duration.

punctuated a protracted but usually nonviolent conflict in which indigenous hunting-and-gathering peoples have resisted, without much success, the incursions of miners and settlers. The widely publicized rebellion of the Maya of Chiapas, which began in 1994 and was still under way in 1999, was initiated by leaders external to the group who capitalized on the Maya's marginalized and deteriorating status. The Zapotecs of south central Mexico have a much longer history of political action organized and led by indigenous leaders. Their political movement, COCEI, has controlled the municipal government of the Oaxacan city of Juchitan for most of the last thirty years, and periodic fights have erupted with officials of the Revolutionary Institutional Party (PRI) who have tried to displace them. Zapotecs live in both Oaxaca and Chiapas and in 1996 became involved in a local rebellion linked to the ongoing conflict in Chiapas that also drew in neighboring indigenous communities. The Maya, Zapotecs, and other indigenous peoples thus account for three "new" rebellions that really reflect the convergence and escalation of indigenous activism that is widespread in southern Mexico.

Two new episodes of rebellious terrorism were initiated in Western Europe by small ethnonational groups with a long history of political activism. A scatter of bombings by South Tyroleans in Italy in 1986 and by Jurassians in Switzerland in 1987 attracted attention almost as transient as the actions themselves.

THE POSTCOMMUNIST STATES

New episodes of ethnopolitical conflict in the postcommunist states began well before the breakup of the USSR. The first, in 1988, was the rebellion of Armenians in Nagorno-Karabakh against the Azerbaijan republican government, prompted by anti-Armenian pogroms. New conflicts in the postcommunist world peaked in 1989–92.[13] In Georgia, for example, new protest movements began in 1989 among the Abkhaz, Adzars, and South Ossetians; rebellions soon followed among the Ossetians in 1991 and the Abkhaz (encouraged by their local Russian allies) in 1992. Most new ethnonational movements in the (former) Soviet republics were proactive efforts to capitalize on political opportunities for group autonomy that opened up in new and weak states. Most were facilitated by external support, for example, by Russia for the Abkhaz and by the Armenian Republic for rebels in Nagorno-Karabakh.

Ethnonational movements in the breakaway republics of Yugoslavia took place in two stages. Slovenian, Croat, and Bosnian nationalism of the late 1980s was a proactive response of local ethnic entrepreneurs to new political opportunities, analogous to what was happening in the non-Russian republics of the USSR. The second stage was a far more deadly and protracted reaction by minority nationalities in Croatia and Bosnia to threatened loss of political status—with ample political and material support from nationalists in Serbia. The Krajina Serbs first openly opposed the Croatian republican government in 1988; political violence began in 1990, more than a year before independent Croatia gained international recognition. Serbs in Bosnia began organized protest in 1990; a year later they shifted to open rebellion.

Albanian ethnonationalism is responsible for the two rebellions that began in 1997. The Kosovo Liberation Army (KLA) began a terrorist campaign in 1997 that escalated the following year into a full-blown separatist civil war. A cluster of bombings attributed to Albanians also occurred in neighboring Macedonia in 1997, but by mid-1999 there had been no evidence of further escalation. There is no equivalent of the KLA in Macedonia, most of whose Albanians pursue their claims for greater political rights by electoral and other conventional political strategies. The participation of a major Albanian party in a coalition government since late 1998 reinforces their reliance on nonviolent strategies.

Though many experts have warned of the potential for new ethnic rebellions in the postcommunist states, we have identified none—with the Albanian exceptions—that began after 1992. This finding cannot be explained away by claiming that there are no more potential ethnonationalists. For instance, of the nine significant ethnonational movements we have profiled in the Russian Federation, only two have used violent means (the Chechens and, episodically, their Ingush neighbors). The others have chosen peaceful and cooperative means of pursuing their objectives, choices that seem best explained by the lack of external threats and the high potential costs of confrontation strategies. Unlike with the Chechens, the Moscow authorities have accepted claims by Tatars, Tuvinians, and others to republican sovereignty (low threat). But opportunities for further gains by ethnonationalists are limited: there is not much more that might be conceded by the weakened government in Moscow and always the risk that greater demands or militant action will provoke a nationalist reaction. The Russians' devastating war against Chechen rebels in 1995–96 may have failed in its immediate objective, but it probably had a sobering effect on the aspirations and strategic calculations of ethnonationalists elsewhere on the Russian periphery.

Because ethnorebellion is usually preceded by protest activity, the most likely candidates for future rebellion in the postcommunist states are to be found among groups that initiated or escalated protest activities between 1993 and 1998. There were nine such groups, of whom six are singled out for comment here.[14] Three are Roma—in Hungary, the Czech Republic, and Slovakia. The Roma have never resorted to campaigns of political violence anywhere in Europe. They are a fragmented and dispersed people whose traditional response to persecution has been to move, not resist. The risk that their protest activities will escalate into rebellion is virtually nil. Two other new episodes of ethnoprotest are more threatening: their protagonists are the Russians in Crimea and elsewhere in Ukraine (mainly the Donbas region of eastern Ukraine).[15] The government in Kiev thus far has been very cautious about policies that might threaten Russian or any other minorities. The risk of future rebellions by Russian ethnonationalists in Ukraine depends on future policies of the Kiev government, especially on language issues, and on external support from nationalists in Russia. Thus far Russian nationalists have found other, less disruptive, means of pursuing their interests in Ukraine.[16]

Another new episode of protest originated with the Hungarian minority in Slovakia, a group that faced sharply restrictive policies by Slovakian nationalists

for much of the 1990s. The threat of escalation has been averted by a combination of factors: first, in 1996 the Slovakian government signed a bilateral
treaty with Hungary that offered guarantees for the Hungarians in Slovakia;
second, the nationalist government led by Vladimír Mečiar was ousted in
1998 elections. The changing status of the Slovakian Hungarians is examined
in more detail in the sketch on pages 183–187.

THE THIRD WORLD

In the Third World new episodes of ethnoconflict also spiked in 1988–92.
More than half occurred in Africa, including so many new ethnorebellions,
more than at any time since the early 1960s, that they might be labeled "new
wars of African independence." Almost all were manifestations of enduring
postcolonial rivalries among communal contenders. Most were by protagonists who sought to protect or improve their share in regional or national
political power. Some ethnorebellions took place in the context of attempts to
introduce democratic reforms in authoritarian systems, for example, among
Hutus in Burundi, Ewe and Kabre in Togo, and Bemba and Lozi in Zambia.
Opening up the political process, however slightly, threatened the status of
some groups and provided political opportunities for others.

However, most new episodes in Africa had little or nothing to do with
democratization. They included new or renewed rebellions by the Tuareg in
Niger (1988) and Mali (1990); Cabindans in Angola and Merina in Mada-
gascar (1990); the Temne in Sierra Leone and Afars in Djibouti (1991);
and southerners in Chad, westerners in Cameroon, and the Casamançais in
Senegal (1992). The co-occurrence of so many rebellions correlates with the
fact that most African economies were in free fall during the 1980s. Economic decline provokes intensified competition for access to resources, and
in most of Africa the state is the main source of money and position as well as
power. Easterly and Levine show that the stagnation of African economies by
comparison with growth in most Asian countries is due in substantial part to
the ethnic fragmentation and polarization of African politics. If, as is suggested
here, economic stagnation has become a major source of communal conflict
in Africa, then many African states have been trapped in a degenerative cycle
in which the ethnicization of politics and economic stagnation reinforce
each other.[17]

A smaller number of new episodes of ethnoconflict began in Asia: seven
protest movements and nine new ethnorebellions. Political context does not
help explain where they occurred. New regional rebellions began in established
democracies (three in India, one in Papua New Guinea), in a quasi-democratic

state (Pakistan), and in authoritarian states of all stripes (Bhutan, Burma, China, Indonesia). The Middle East had by far the fewest new episodes of ethnoconflict. Four groups initiated or escalated collective protest, including the Shi'i of Saudi Arabia (1987) and the Arabs in Israel proper (1990). Both seem to have been prompted mainly by external circumstances—Iranian support for the Shi'i, emulation of the intifada by Arabs in Israel—rather than by increased domestic threats or opportunities. The Shi'i of Iraq initiated the only new rebellion in the region in 1991, a new and violent phase in a conflict that had persisted in other forms since the early 1950s. Iraq's defeat in the Gulf War provided the opportunity; Iranian support facilitated it.

The Antecedents of Ethnorebellion

The outbreak of ethnorebellion often follows a period of conventional political activity and organized protest, as is suggested by some of the cases cited earlier in this chapter. This is consistent with a pattern observed in Western democracies from the 1940s to the 1980s, where an average of thirteen years elapsed between the onset of political activism by minorities and their first resort to violent protest or terrorism.[18] If such time lags are a universal phenomenon, two important implications follow. One is that communally based protest movements are leading indicators of potential future rebellion; the other is that responses by states and other actors during the protest phase may change the dynamics of conflict in ways that enhance or minimize the risks of escalation. The fifty-two new ethnorebellions of 1986–98 provide a baseline for analyzing time lags between the onset of political activism and the outbreak of new rebellion. For fifty of the fifty-two groups we have examined the track record since 1945 of political activism, protest, and rebellion.[19] Some of the results are summarized in table 2.6 and discussed in greater detail below.

Significant political action preceded virtually all the new ethnorebellions of 1986–98 in the Western democracies, Latin America, and the postcommunist states. The one exception, out of twenty-three new episodes tabulated in the first two data columns of table 2.6, was the rebellion of the Croat minority in Bosnia in 1992—an event for which there were ample antecedents, though not ones to which the Minorities coding scheme is sensitive. The differences are in the lead times: the duration of protest tended to be shortest—three years—in the postcommunist states, compared with twenty years in the Western democracies and Latin America. This difference is readily explained by two factors. First, the policies of state socialist regimes discouraged open

Table 2.6. Open Conflict Prior to the Onset of New Ethnopolitical Rebellions of 1986–98

Antecedents	Western Industrial Democracies and Latin America	Postcommunist States	Middle East, Asia, and Africa	Global Total
Number of new rebellions	8	14	30	52
Of which 8 were new episodes of protracted rebellion:	0	1	7	8
Of which 37 were preceded by mobilization and protest:				
20 years +	4	2	5	11
11–20 years	3	0	2	5
6–10 years	0	2	6	8
3–5 years	0	3	2	5
1–2 years	1	5	2	8
Of which 7 were not preceded by mobilization and protest:	0	1	6	7
Median years of open conflict before new rebellion begins:	20	3	10	10

Note: Prior group protest and rebellion are estimated from Minorities at Risk codings of reported collective actions by each group beginning in 1945. The lowest recorded levels of group mobilization and protest are verbal opposition, scattered acts of sabotage, and political organizing activity. If a group was politically inactive for a decade or more and then resumed protest, it is categorized here in the period it resumed action.

Protracted conflicts are episodes of rebellion and intercommunal warfare between long-time antagonists that resumed in 1986–98 after a decade or more during which there was little or no violent contention.

The median years of open conflict are calculated for all cases including those with 0 years of prior protest and protracted rebellions, which are dated from the first year of their initial episode.

manifestations of ethnonationalism until the late 1980s; and second, the threats and opportunities that prompted rebellion increased very quickly thereafter. Most ethnoprotest movements in the postcommunist states that subsequently escalated into rebellion began in 1988 or 1989. Three exceptions are the Kosovar Albanians, who have sought autonomy since the end of World War II; the Abkhaz in Georgia, who had asked to be joined to the Russian Republic from the 1950s onward; and the Armenians in Azerbaijan, who first registered demands for unification with the Republic of Armenia in the early 1960s (according to our coded data).

The time lags between ethnoprotest and rebellion in the Middle East, Asia, and Africa—shown in the third data column of table 2.6—are much more varied. More than five years of protest or low-level violence preceded thirteen of the thirty new ethnorebellions in these regions. The two most protracted examples are the Kashmiris in India and the Turkomen of China's Xinjiang province. The predominantly Muslim people of the Indian state of Jammu and Kashmir have sought greater autonomy, usually by conventional political means, since the partition of the Indian subcontinent in 1947; insurgency did not begin until 1989. The Muslim peoples of China's northeastern province of Xinjiang—Uighers, Kazakhs, and others—had a period of brief, unrecognized independence in the 1940s and have opposed political control from Beijing since the communist regime took power. There was a brief episode of violent resistance to the initial imposition of communist rule in the early 1950s, then a long period of low-level political activism until 1990, when a campaign of terrorism began—possibly with support from exile groups based in the newly independent Central Asian states.

Seven new episodes of ethnorebellion in the Third World were flareups of what we call protracted rebellions, defined by recurrent violence over a period of several decades. Each resumed between 1986 and 1998 after being dormant for a decade or more. Six of the seven are listed, with information on previous periods of political activism:

Aceh in Indonesia: new regional rebellion in 1989, prior rebellions in the 1950s and late 1970s, episodic protest from the early 1950s through the early 1980s.

Shi'i in Iraq: new rebellion in 1991, prior rebellion during the Iran-Iraq war (mainly by exiled Iraqi Shi'i based in Iran), sporadic protest and resistance at a lower level of intensity from the 1950s.

Cabindans in Angola: new rebellion in 1990, prior rebellion (during the Angolan war of independence and subsequent civil war) from the early 1960s to the late 1970s.

Hutus in Burundi: new rebellion by militants in 1988, prior rebellion in the early 1970s, episodic intercommunal conflict with and victimization by Tutsis since the 1940s.

Tutsis in Burundi: new rebellion in 1996 by extremists, including elements in the army, who opposed concessions to Hutus, another manifestation of long-standing intercommunal conflict.

Hutus in Rwanda: new rebellion in 1994 by militant supporters of former Hutu regime, mainly from exile, the latest phase in violent intercommunal conflict and repression that began when Hutu revolutionaries overthrew the Tutsi monarchy in 1963.

To recap, all but a handful of the episodes of ethnorebellion in the Third World that began between 1986 and 1998 were new manifestations of open conflicts of long duration. They were visible enough that informed outsiders could and often did monitor them, and interested international actors in principle could have encouraged and supported efforts at peaceful conflict management prior to the onset, or resumption, of armed conflict. Some of them did attract such attention, particularly in Central Africa, but not enough to forestall intensive violence.[20]

Finally, it is worth looking at some of the exceptions. These are instances of new ethnorebellions with no antecedent political actions that were evident in the open sources used in the Minorities at Risk project.

Bodos in India's Assam state: These tribal people began a rebellion in 1989 that was continuing as of 1999. They are the newest entrants on a rather long list of regional contenders in India's northeast who have fought rebellions for autonomy, usually with some success (Nagas, Tripuras, Mizos).

Bougainvillians in Papua New Guinea: At the time of Papua New Guinea's independence in 1975, political leaders on Bougainville asked, to no avail, that they be joined to the neighboring Solomon Islands. This latent separatism provided the background to Bougainvillians' mobilization in a 1988 protest against alienation of their lands by a large-scale mining enterprise. Protest escalated quickly into terrorism and then low-level insurgency that ended in a cease-fire and negotiations in 1998.

Tuareg in Mali: The Tuareg, who live on the margins of the Sahara, suffered badly from regionwide drought in the 1980s. They are situated on the political as well as geographic peripheries of the countries in which they live and began localized rebellions for autonomy in Niger in 1988 and in Mali in 1990. The Niger rebellion was preceded by mobilization and protest and thus is not enumerated here; the inspiration for rebellion by Tuareg in Mali, where we detected no prior mobilization, presumably came from their kindred. By 1994 both governments had concluded agreements with the Tuareg that ended the conflict in Mali and largely contained it in Niger.

Afars in Djibouti: The Afars are communal contenders who shared power in Djibouti with the more numerous Issa clan of the Somalis. A political rupture with the Issa precipitated a 1991 rebellion that was largely ended by a negotiated settlement in December 1995.

Amharas in Ethiopia: The Amharas' century-long domination of the Ethiopian state ended in early 1991 when the radical military regime, the Derg, was overthrown by Tigrean and Eritrean rebels. Later that year a political movement that represented mainly the Amhara supporters of the old regime mounted a short-lived counterrebellion.

Kabre in Togo: A brief 1991 rebellion by military representing the interests of the Kabre people was an outgrowth of regional and political rivalries.

Temne in Sierra Leone: The Temne were the main supporters of the Revolutionary United Front (RUF), which began a protracted rebellion in 1991. The conflict metastasized into a multisided civil war that prompted intervention by a regional force, led by Nigeria, and intense diplomatic engagement that achieved a fragile settlement in 1999. The rebellion was an outgrowth of long-standing communal rivalries over access to official positions and largess. One justification offered by the RUF leaders was to eliminate the "hegemony of the Mende" in Sierra Leone's government.

Two different patterns are evident in these seven rebellions. The first three —in Assam, Bougainville, and Mali—were movements for greater autonomy by regionally concentrated indigenous peoples[21] who were reacting to what they thought was neglect by or abuses of central authority. The other four rebellions, all in Africa, grew out of rivalries among communal contenders for power. In other words, all new rebellions that occurred without prior rebellions or protest movements were manifestations of long-term political processes of conquest, exploitation, and contention for power in multiethnic states.

New Contenders, Old Issues, Unanswered Questions

The evidence reviewed in this chapter can be summarized in the following general observations.

- The global incidence of new ethnopolitical conflicts, and the emergence of new contenders, peaked at the beginning of the 1990s and has since declined.

- The onset of new ethnopolitical conflicts in 1989–93 was pervasive but most pronounced in the postcommunist states and in Africa south of the Sahara. In Latin America a number of new contenders followed the lead of the global indigenous rights movement by using strategies of protest. The Middle East had the fewest new communal conflicts of any world region.

- The upsurge in ethnopolitical conflict in the postcommunist states is readily explained by the reassertion of old nationalist claims and by contention over power and autonomy among proponents of competing nationalisms. In Africa long-standing communal rivalries over access to state power were exacerbated by serious economic decline and attempts at democratization.

- In the postcommunist states and Africa there are instances of diffusion (ethnoconflict spilling across state boundaries) and suggestive evidence of contagion (ethnoconflicts prompted by examples set elsewhere). Contagion also helps explain the near-simultaneous emergence of new protest movements among indigenous peoples in the Americas and among the Roma in Europe. But it is not plausible, or necessary, to postulate a global contagion process for ethnic warfare. Stephen Saideman argues persuasively that secessionist movements are contagious mainly within states, not among them.[22] The cresting wave of ethnoconflict at the beginning of the 1990s had more immediate, concrete, and probably sufficient explanations.

- Most of the fifty-two new ethnorebellions that began between 1986 and 1998 were outgrowths of longer-term conflicts that were known to outside observers. In the typical (median) case, a decade elapsed between the emergence of protest movements, or the last violent phase, and the outbreak of new rebellions. Such long time lags have alternative interpretations. Optimists may see them as ample lead time for conflict management efforts by civil and international authorities that have the will and means to forestall serious violence. Pessimists could conclude that the underlying issues are intractable and that escalation is inevitable. Our impression from case studies of conflicts that escalate from protest to rebellion is that the intervening years are mostly characterized by inconsistent and expedient state policies, often a mix of limited and partly implemented reforms with repression.

- Relatively few new ethnopolitical protest movements have emerged among the 275 groups in the Minorities survey since the peak years of 1989–91. This finding suggests that there are few potential ethnic wars just over the time horizon: the decline in new ethnopolitical movements since 1992 may be a trend rather than a lull. Before jumping to comforting conclusions, though, it is necessary to survey the conditions that signal future conflicts in these 275 groups—and in other communal groups not included in the survey. Those issues are dealt with in chapter 7.

The cresting wave of ethnopolitical conflict at the beginning of the 1990s does not have a simple explanation. The rise of protest and rebellion by identity groups resulted from regionally specific conjunctions of local and international conditions, including the collapse of hegemonic control in the postcommunist world, successful democratic transitions in Latin America, and systemic political and economic failure in Africa.

The global recession of serious ethnopolitical conflict after 1992 also lacks a simple explanation. Security dilemmas and militant nationalism can be expected to engender persisting conflicts, not transitory ones. The contention, documented in chapters 5 and 6, is that the post-1992 decline in the number and intensity of ethnic wars is due mainly to an increase in civil and international capacities for managing ethnopolitical conflict. Democratic and nondemocratic regimes alike have learned to employ a wider range of techniques to accommodate, deter, and co-opt communal challengers. International attention to the collective rights of nonstate peoples, and international and regional efforts to check violent ethnic conflicts through preventive diplomacy and peacekeeping, have reinforced the disposition to manage ethnopolitical conflict short of armed conflict. But many of the preconditions persist and others can be reinvented. A framework for understanding these conditions and how they are interconnected is developed in the next chapter.

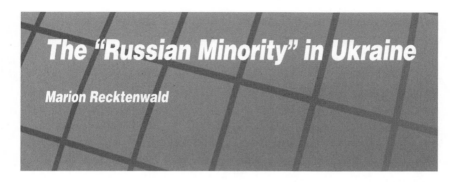

The "Russian Minority" in Ukraine

Marion Recktenwald

The "Russian minority" in Ukraine is a complex ethnopolitical group whose shifting boundaries and multifaceted identities are shaped by both historical and current influences from the homeland. The group's reliance on institutional politics to pursue collective interests has contributed to relative peace and stability while also shaping Ukraine's domestic and foreign policies in ways favored by certain patrons in the Russian Federation.

THE "RUSSIAN MINORITY" in Ukraine is in many respects atypical of national peoples elsewhere. This "minority," usually referred to by Ukrainians as Russian-speakers,[1] includes ethnic Russians living in Ukraine and those non-Russians influenced by Russian and Soviet social engineering efforts. Many are descendants of the ethnically mixed Russian-speaking settler communities who migrated as guardians of Moscow's interests and whose privileges, and socioeconomic and political values, were heavily intertwined with the Russian and Soviet empires. Most reject being labeled as a minority, because of their size and influence, long-standing residence on Ukrainian territory, and centuries of indoctrination that ingrained in them the belief that Ukraine is an integral part of a greater Russian or Soviet entity. Many regard Ukraine not as an alien new host country, but instead as their legitimate homeland. Ethnocultural grievances are of limited significance. Instead, socioeconomic and political factors determine the salience of group identity and political actions.

The key to ethnopolitics in Ukraine is the willingness of Ukrainian and Russian communists to pursue the diaspora's interests and aspirations through institutional politics. This willingness has helped to modulate extremism and avert open ethnic violence between the supporters of this sizable, relatively resource-rich, and influential group and their Ukrainian counterparts. However, it has also slowed formation of a distinct Ukrainian state identity, impeded socioeconomic reform, and limited Kiev's ability to distance itself from Russia and to integrate with Western institutions.

THE SHIFTING BASES OF GROUP IDENTITY

The collapse of the Soviet Union in 1991 left Ukraine with about eleven million ethnic Russians (20.1 percent of its total population), just under half the entire contingent of ethnic Russians stranded in the "New Abroad." Their large numbers and declarations that Moscow would defend the diaspora in the New Abroad evoked concerns that Russia would provoke secession and ethnic war. This has not happened, because the "Russian minority" in Ukraine is not oppressed, disadvantaged, or subject to discrimination. Rather, the group's historical legacies and the ample opportunities provided by the Ukrainian state for institutional politics have enabled many of its members to place themselves in positions of economic and political influence rather than fomenting revolt or secession.

The "Russian minority" did not exist as a structured group at the time of Ukraine's independence, nor does it now. Instead, group boundaries have included people from throughout Ukrainian society whose values and aspirations predispose them for mobilization around issues defined as "Russian." National origin is not the sole criterion by which Ukrainians identify with the "Russian minority." The pro-Russian communist movement in Ukraine has included a large number of ethnic Ukrainians, whereas some ethnic Russians, such as the former Ukrainian minister of defense Morozov, have been loyal supporters of the new Ukrainian state.

"Russian-speaking" is another indicator of affiliation with the segment of Ukraine's society from which the "Russian minority" is drawn. Voting patterns show that preference for political candidates promoting Russian ethnocultural and political rights largely coincides with linguistic distribution. Although Russian-language use is an additional indicator of affiliation with things Russian, it is still not automatic or sufficient grounds for identification with the "Russian cause" and loyalty toward an external Russian homeland. When, for instance, one asks an ethnic Russian in Kiev (an area well known for centrist positions on issues of legitimacy of independent Ukraine) whether he feels like a Russian or a Ukrainian, it is not atypical to receive a differentiated answer, such as, "I am ethnic Russian, I prefer to speak Russian, but I am also supportive of independent Ukraine." Were one to ask an ethnic Ukrainian activist in the heavily Russified and Sovietized area of Donbas the same question, the typical answer would be, "I am ethnic Ukrainian, I know Ukrainian, but I prefer speaking Russian and am in favor of Ukraine joining some type of union with Russia."

The official 1994 Russian statement of "Moscow's policies and obligations toward its diaspora in the 'New Abroad'" plays on political affinities in defining the group. Rather than limiting Russia's "diaspora" to ethnic Russians or to their "compatriots . . . defending their ethnocultural rights," this official program says the "diaspora" includes "all those who wish to maintain their culture and ties with Russia," thus giving priority to the desire for maintaining a relationship with the external Russian homeland.[2]

Once we recognize that the identity of the "Russian minority" is based on a crosscutting combination of socioeconomic aspirations and political affinities, as well as culture and national origin, we can begin to understand why, on the one hand, some ethnic Russians have been loyal defenders of Ukrainian integrity and economic reform, whereas, on the other hand, the Ukrainian procommunist movement has spearheaded defense of Russian ethnocultural rights and promoted reintegration with the Soviet Union. The latter group includes a large number of ethnic Ukrainians from the Russian-speaking regions in southern and eastern Ukraine.

HISTORICAL LEGACIES

The policies of Tsarist and Soviet states shaped modern-day Ukrainian identities. Both Tsarist Russia and the USSR were multiethnic empires that sought to unify their diverse communities by constructing multilayered state and national identities. The Soviet leadership, in particular, downplayed Russian national identity, emphasizing instead the language and the socioeconomic and political characteristics of their system. Tsarist Russia and the Soviet Union also sought to reshape group identities to fit Moscow's foreign and domestic policy objectives. To maximize control over vast territories, both empires relied on ethnically mixed Russian-speaking communities. The settler communities' privileges depended on the existence of empire, and they, along with local populations, were subject to ongoing Russification and social engineering. In the Soviet era, leadership went to great lengths to socially engineer a new transcendent identity in the form of the "Homo Sovieticus." In Ukraine specifically, Stalin's deadly policies, combined with the demographic havoc wreaked by World War II, left an amorphous society, linguistically fragmented and characterized by political apathy and absence of a civic culture.

The degree to which the territories of modern-day Ukraine have been subjected to social engineering varies. Western Ukraine, due to its earlier incorporation in the Austro-Hungarian and Polish empires and repeated German occupation, was not subjected to intensive Russian and Soviet social engineering until after 1945. Consequently, the Ukrainian language is widely preserved and remains the preferred means of conversation. It is also here that the ethnocultural, socioeconomic, and political vectors of identity point consistently toward Ukrainian identity.

In southern and eastern Ukraine, the unrealized efforts to construct the "Homo Sovieticus" left their tenacious mark. For example, Moscow's societal and economic policies fostered substantial intermarriage[3] and created islands of mixed Russian-Ukrainian language and culture, especially in parts of central Ukraine. They cultivated a mixed Russian/Ukrainian and Soviet identity that, according to post-Soviet opinion polls, is centered in southern and eastern Ukraine and makes up a quarter to a third of Ukraine's total population.

THE MOBILIZATION OF A "RUSSIAN MINORITY"

The sudden and peaceful independence of Ukraine was largely accomplished because most of the Russian-speaking population in southern and eastern Ukraine voted for independence in the December 1991 referendum. Popular opinion shifted sharply from March 1991, when 70 percent of all Ukrainians voted for preservation of the Soviet Union, to December, when 90 percent supported independence. For many, this support was conditional, however, based on the hope that Ukrainian independence would lead to an improved living standard. Russian-speaking populations also expected that policies of ethnocultural assimilation by the new Ukrainian state would be marginal. The closeness of Russian and Ukrainian cultures, a legacy of ethnic and social peace, the regional concentration of Russians and Russian-speaking populations, and the reassuring words and deeds of the new national-communist leadership in Kiev, all encouraged Russian identifiers to think that they would be secure in a Ukrainian state.

This conditional support for Ukrainian statehood soon crumbled. Kiev's liberal ethnic laws, grants of considerable regional cultural autonomy, and the decision to enact only a limited "Ukrainization" of state and society could not fully offset the psychological difficulties that the previously privileged ethnic Russian and "Russian-speaking" populations experienced in adapting to the realities of living in a new state that embodied the symbols of the Ukrainian titular nation. This adaptation has been more difficult, given centuries of Russification in which Ukrainian language and culture were denigrated as inferior to Russian. Hence, pro-Russian elites in Ukraine—often supported by patrons in the Russian Federation, including the official Russian state TV station Ostankina—initiated a media disinformation campaign that exaggerated the nature and extent of Kiev's Ukrainization policies. Ethnocultural grievances were taken seriously and became the basis for political action largely because of the broken dream of a better life in independent Ukraine. Nostalgia for the Soviet past emerged.

The bankruptcy of the Ukrainian version of the Soviet economy and Ukraine's heavily asymmetric dependence on the Russian economy, particularly for energy supplies, were major economic weaknesses. They were exacerbated by a variety of economic pressures from Moscow and by the persistent media campaign by pro-Russian elites in Ukraine and Russia. By early 1993, hope was increasingly displaced by real and perceived economic hardship. Whereas economic difficulties did not undermine overwhelming support for Ukrainian independence in western Ukraine, in the south and east, with their Russian-oriented ethnocultural features and Soviet-derived socioeconomic values, economic grievances became the basis for political initiatives aimed at restoration of the USSR or its best approximation.

MODES OF POLITICAL ACTION AND THEIR IMPLICATIONS

The political manifestations of these grievances have ranged from spontaneous protests and strikes to sabotage, espionage, and talk of secession. Both local Ukrainian and external Russian players (the Russian Orthodox Church, segments of the Russian military and security establishment, the Russian Club and the Congress of Russian Communities, and a number of official and quasi-official Russian elites) have supported such actions. These groups have impeded independent state formation, derailed socioeconomic transformations, and helped intensify popular grievances. Though these actions carry substantial costs and risks, they have not led to violent political action nor have they had a decisive effect on the stability of the Ukrainian state. The essential reason is that most political energies of Ukrainians who identify as Russians have been directed into conventional political institutions.

Ukraine's emerging political and economic institutions provided new and effective opportunities for minority politics. With its comparative advantage in terms of organizational and political skills, resources, and potential electoral support from the "Russian minority," the communist movement channeled diaspora politics into the new institutional realm. More precisely, the Communist Party and its sympathizers in Ukraine and abroad[4] were able to mobilize this electorate by articulating a political agenda reflecting Soviet-style values in domestic and foreign policies and by exploiting ethnocultural, socioeconomic, and political grievances, particularly among Russian-speakers and the people of southern and eastern Ukraine. In the 1994 and 1998 elections this support approximated 40 percent.

As Ukraine's strongest and best-organized party, the Communist Party, and its sympathizers, has used its political leverage to preserve regional autonomy and impede implementation of Kiev's policies. The leftist movement also has used its influence to support presidential candidates thought to support its interests, first Kuchma and in mid-1999 three candidates: Leonid Symonenko, Natalia Vitrenko, and Olexander Moroz.[5] It supported initiatives to curtail presidential power and pursued legislative policies to influence Ukraine's domestic and foreign policy. In the domestic realm the communists did not achieve their goal of making Russian a second state language, but they did impede the extent and speed of Ukrainization efforts. Socioeconomic reform has been one of the most significant realms of political struggle. By thwarting reforms, the leftist movement in Ukraine has perpetuated economic stagnation and contributed to decreased Western assistance and investment. In foreign policy, leftist support of a Russian-Ukrainian friendship treaty has been part of a wider array of efforts to promote closer ties and some sort of union with Russia. Keeping the Russian-speaking population suspicious of Western institutions, and using the war in Kosovo to further devalue prospective NATO membership in the minds of their electorate, the communists have been a major impediment to Kiev's ability to move toward the West.

The procommunists have amplified economic grievances and secured, for the time being, a substantial electorate but have fallen short of more ambitious goals. They are internally divided[6] and have not achieved a majority vote. As the November 1999 presidential election results showed, pro-Russian and procommunist tendencies, particularly strong among Russian-speaking populations in south and eastern Ukraine, are not sufficiently strong to overcome the majority's aversion to old-style Russian and Soviet politics.[7] Moreover, whereas "ethnic" politics is significant during electoral campaigns, it loses impetus in the interim, when the day-to-day struggle for economic survival and interregional rivalries between various economic clans tend to dominate. More important, diaspora politics will outlive much of its attractiveness as the older generations give way to the younger. True economic reform and progress are likely to become the first priority for most segments of the Ukrainian elite and society. But because economic difficulties will not soon disappear, and given the possibility of a decline in Western interest in Ukraine, the Communist Party will continue to engage in "minority politics" and to mobilize Russian-speaking populations for power and influence.

NOTES

The author is an expert on regional and international security issues in East Central Europe who received her doctorate in 1998 from the University of Maryland's Department of Government and Politics. This essay is drawn from her dissertation, "The Russian 'Diaspora' in Ukraine: Russian Influences on Its Political Behavior."

1. *Russian-speakers* is in itself an ambiguous term. Depending on an individual's definition of the term, the group constitutes between 17 million (11.4 million Russians plus 4.6 million ethnic Ukrainians and 1 million other non-Russian ethnics declaring Russian their "mother tongue") and 26-28 million (11.4 million Russians plus 15–16 million ethnic Ukrainian and other non-Russian ethnics identifying Russian as their "language of convenience"). The latter figure is slightly over half Ukraine's total population. These figures are derived from the 1989 Soviet census. For a discussion see Valerii Khmel'ko, "Dva berehy—dva sposoby zhyttya," *Demoz,* no. 1 (1995): 17–20.

2. For details on the August 1994 official Russian program on the "strategic line of Russia's policy toward the compatriots," see, for instance, Igor Zevelev, "Russia and the Russian Diasporas," *Post-Soviet Affairs* 12, no. 3 (1996): 293.

3. By the 1970s intermarriages varied between 35 percent and 55 percent in eastern and southern Ukraine. See Kuzio Taras, "The National Factor in Ukraine's Quadruple" (paper prepared for the conference on Soviet and Post-Soviet Ukraine: A Century in Perspective, Yale University, April 23–24, 1999).

4. Note that the Communist Party of Ukraine, while forging alliances with pro-communists at home and abroad, also on occasion joined forces with pro-Russian nationalist organizations in Ukraine and Russia.

5. "Presidential Candidates Release Financial Statements," *Ukrainian Weekly* 57, no. 22 (May 30, 1999): 1, 6.

6. "Tkachenko's Announcement Leaves Leftists More Divided," *Ukrainian Weekly* 57, no. 24 (June 13, 1999): 2.

7. See, for instance, "Kuchma and Symonenko to Face Off on November 14," *Ukrainian Weekly* 57, no. 45 (November 7, 1999).

3

The Etiology of Ethnopolitical Conflict

THIS CHAPTER SKETCHES a theoretical framework for understanding the causes of ethnopolitical conflict.[1] More precisely, it provides general answers to two questions. In what circumstances do groups that define themselves using ethnic or national criteria, such as the Mayan-speaking peasants of Chiapas and the Bosnian Serbs, mobilize to defend and promote their collective interests in the political arena? And what factors determine the shape, intensity, and persistence of their actions?

The first step is to define ethnopolitical conflict. Stavenhagen suggests that a conflict is *ethnic* if the contending actors or parties identify themselves or one another using ethnic criteria.[2] Consistent with Stavenhagen and with the definitions in chapter 1, *ethnopolitical conflict* here refers to conflicts in which claims are made by a national or minority group against the state or against other political actors. The framework that accounts for ethnopolitical conflict may also explain intercommunal violence, such as attacks by indigenous Dayaks on Indonesian settlers in Borneo (winter 1996–97) and anti-Chinese and anti-Christian riots in Indonesia (1998–99), but that is tangential to its main objective.

The second step is to identify four general factors, or variables, that provide answers to the theoretical questions:

1. The salience of *ethnocultural identity* for members and leaders of the group.

2. The extent to which the group has collective *incentives* for political action.

3. The extent of the group's *capacities* for collective action.

4. The availability of *opportunities* in the group's political environment that increase its chances of attaining group objectives through political action.

Propositions about these four factors are derived from existing theories of collective action and are central to explaining political action by any kind of identity group.[3] The key to analyzing the origins of ethnopolitical conflict is to show how each factor is activated by the characteristics and circumstances of communal identity groups. The framework is used here to integrate many of the specific factors that observers have identified as causes of ethnic conflict. It also incorporates the effects of state actions on communal groups' identities, incentives, capacities, and opportunities. But it does not deal directly with the objectives and strategies of states in conflict with communal groups. As Virginia Q. Tilley points out, many contemporary states embody the interests and political agenda of a dominant ethnopolitical group. In these circumstances, the framework also provides a beginning point for analyzing state policies toward subordinate communal groups.[4]

The argument rests on assumptions about the nature of ethnic identities and the motivations for ethnopolitical action that are argued in the first chapter. The motivations at the heart of ethnopolitics are assumed to be a mix of grievance, sentiment, solidarity, ambition, and calculation. It is simplistic to argue that one kind of motivation is primary and the others subsidiary. Ethnopolitical protest and rebellion are consequences of complex interactions among collective experience, normative commitments, contention for power, and strategic assessments about how best to promote individual and collective interests.

The Salience of Ethnocultural Identity

The general proposition is that the greater the salience of ethnocultural identity for people with shared descent, cultural traits, and historical experience, the more likely they are to define their interests in ethnocultural terms and the easier it is for leaders to mobilize them for collective action. I assume that cultural identities—those based on common descent, experience, language, and belief—tend to be stronger and more enduring than most civic and associational identities. Nonetheless, the salience of cultural identity varies widely among and within groups and is subject to change over time. The description question is, How salient is ethnocultural identity at any point in time? The conceptual question is, What factors determine changes in its salience?

Scholars recognize that communal identities are multidimensional. There is no warrant for assuming that any one basis for ethnic identity, such as race, language, religion, or a common homeland, is intrinsically more important than another. Some traits, though, are associated with particularly strong and durable collective identities. In multiracial societies, shared physical attributes ("race") are almost always primary markers of group identity.[5] Religion also is a strong source of group cohesion, except in societies where its force has been eroded by secularism. The historic European schism between Catholics and Protestants is paralleled, in the late twentieth century, by communal cleavages in the Third World between Shi'i and Sunni Muslims and between Muslims and non-Muslims.[6] A group's language is another key marker of identity, a source of group cohesion, and a recurring issue of contention among groups in heterogeneous societies. But David Laitin argues convincingly that language disputes alone are not a common source of deadly rivalries, because language differences, unlike racial and religious ones, are subject to individual and collective compromises. Individuals in heterogeneous societies can and ordinarily do speak several languages, but they cannot be both black and white or both Hindu and Muslim.[7]

If cultural factors are variable, does salience originate in a people's material interests, as Marxists have argued? It is true enough that claims made by ethnopolitical groups include material and political demands as well as claims based on their ethnocultural interests. But I do not think it is reasonable to explain away the significance of cultural identity by arguing that what "really" motivates the leaders and members of such groups is the quest for material benefits or power. The decisive factor is that ethnopolitical groups organize around their shared identity and seek gains or redress of grievances for the collectivity. It is misleading to interpret the Zapatistas of Chiapas only as a peasants' revolutionary movement or the Bosnian Serbs as the equivalent of a political party. Their strengths derive from associations built on a prior sense of communal identity and shared interests that are defined in terms of that identity. It is a commonplace that manipulative leaders like Slobodan Milosevic and Franjo Tudjman used appeals to Serbian and Croatian nationalism as a means to advance their personal political agendas. It is equally important to recognize that most who followed them did so because they thought their collective interests were best served by militant nationalists.

The basic proposition is that the salience of ethnocultural identity depends on how much difference it makes in people's lives, as mentioned in chapter 1. Three specific propositions are suggested. First, the greater a people's dissimilarity from groups with which they interact regularly, the more salient their identity is likely to be. The self-awareness of indigenous peoples and *mestizos* in Latin American societies is illustrative. The cultures of indigenous peoples are sharply distinct from that of the dominant group, that is, people of European descent, whereas *mestizos,* as the word suggests, are genetically and culturally in between. Indigenous peoples in these societies in the late twentieth and early twenty-first centuries are likely to identify with and pursue the agenda of the global indigenous rights movement, whereas *mestizos* tend to identify with class-based parties and revolutionary movements.

Second, ethnocultural identity is important when it contributes to a group psychology of comparative advantage or disadvantage. Groups in heterogeneous states make comparisons of relative worth, as Horowitz demonstrates at length, based on their collective experiences and myths. Advantaged groups often feel superior because they share a belief that they are the original people of a place (the Malay claim to be "sons of the soil") or that they have exceptional skills (the European claim to a civilizing mission toward colonial peoples) or that they have overcome adversity and hostile challengers (the basis of Afrikaners' sense of superiority over black Africans).[8] The belief in comparative superiority helps to explain ethnic domination and the resistance of advantaged groups to communal challenges. It also motivates some separatist movements by relatively advantaged peoples, for example, the Catalans of Spain.

Comparative superiority is the other side of the coin of Volkan's "chosen traumas" (see chapter 1, note 7) and the grievances of disadvantaged peoples. For the latter, their ethnocultural identity is salient because it is the source of invidious distinctions—the inequalities in status, economic well-being, and access to political power that are maintained by advantaged groups. Insofar as a people's race, culture, or beliefs provide others with grounds for discriminating against them, the salience of their ethnocultural identity is likely to be high.

Third, open conflict with the state and rival groups sharpens the salience of group identity. Many of the appeals used by ethnopolitical leaders aim at increasing the salience of group identity by invoking historical memories and symbols of victimization. Serious episodes of conflict leave bitter residues in people's memories and for a long time afterward can be used by leaders to justify political action. Serbian nationalists, for example, made effective use of fifty-year-old memories about atrocities committed by the Croatian Ustashi to mobilize Serbian support for their 1991–92 war with the newly independent state of Croatia. Labeling helps: Serb leaders referred to Croats as Ustashi.

To summarize, the salience of a people's ethnocultural identity at any point in time is due mainly to three factors: (1) the extent to which they differ culturally from other communal groups with whom they interact, (2) the extent to which they are advantaged or disadvantaged relative to other groups, and (3) the intensity of their past and ongoing conflicts with rival groups and the state. This set of propositions and others developed in this chapter are shown in figure 3.1.

Incentives for Ethnopolitical Action

The second general proposition is that the greater the shared incentives among members of an ethnocultural identity group, the more likely they are to support and participate in ethnopolitical action. *Ethnopolitical action* refers to any organized activity in pursuit of the group's objectives, beginning with mobilization, the process by which people are recruited into movements. Once people are mobilized, participation can take diverse forms, depending on a group's political environment and the strategic and tactical decisions of its leaders. The range of actions includes conventional politics, collective action (strikes, demonstrations, nonviolent direct action), and rebellion.

The incentives that prompt political action by identity groups can be categorized into three major types: *resentment about losses suffered in the past, fear of future losses,* and *hopes for relative gains.* The relative importance of each of these factors depends on a group's changing position in relation to other groups and to the state. This proposition builds on familiar arguments about the causes of relative deprivation. People who have lost ground relative to what they had in the past are said to experience decremental deprivation and are motivated to seek redress for what was lost. Those who anticipate losses, especially reversal of an improving trend, are said to experience progressive deprivation that disposes them to support movements that defend and promote the group's present status and attainments. Groups in which nationalist or revolutionary expectations have taken hold are motivated to seek a fundamental change in their political status.

I do not assume that the incentives of communal groups are nonrational or that they inherently dispose people to ethnopolitical violence. Instead they constitute a potential for goal-directed political action. They are analogous to what Charles Tilly characterizes as the collective interests that form the basis for group mobilization.[9] But incentives for ethnopolitical groups are different from Tilly's calculated "collective interests" because they have an intrinsic affective component. Members of identity groups usually resent their disadvantages and seek redress not only, or even necessarily, with self-interest in mind, but with passion, self-righteousness, and solidarity with their kindred.[10]

Figure 3.1. The Etiology of Ethnopolitical Conflict

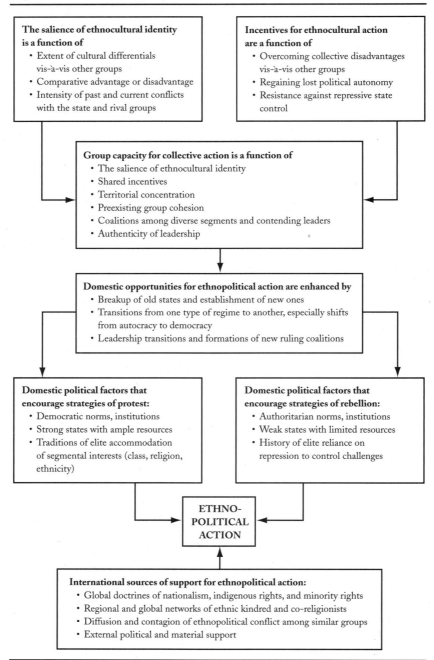

COLLECTIVE DISADVANTAGES

For theoretical and practical purposes we need ways to judge the nature and extent of group incentives that are independent of, and prior to, mobilization. Comparative and case studies point to four general conditions that strongly affect group incentives. First, the greater a group's collective disadvantages vis-à-vis other groups, the greater the incentives for action. *Disadvantage* means socially derived inequalities in material well-being, political access, or cultural status by comparison with other social groups. I proposed earlier in the chapter that a group's sense of comparative superiority or inferiority strengthens the salience of its identity. The argument here is specific to disadvantaged groups: inequalities provide incentives for remedial action. The combination of disadvantages and overtly discriminatory policies gives people powerful incentives for action because the combination focuses their resentment on the agents of discrimination. A recent empirical study by Dudley and Miller uses 1980s data on 203 groups from the Minorities at Risk data set to test alternative explanations of ethnic rebellion. They find that indicators of relative deprivation (country economic performance, group grievances) were more important predictors of the occurrence and magnitude of rebellion than indicators of diffusion or state capabilities.[11]

THE LOSS OF POLITICAL AUTONOMY

Regaining political autonomy is a second major incentive. Virtually all ethnonationalists, national minorities, and indigenous peoples either were once independent of external control or were part of political entities other than the states that now govern them. The American conspiracy that deposed the last ruling monarch of independent Hawaii in 1893, the fragmentation of the Hungarian nation into a half-dozen segments in 1919, and the conquest of Tibet in 1951 are historical facts that give rise to persistent grievances and hopes for restoration. They are potent symbols for political entrepreneurs whose projects are to restore indigenous rights or regain national autonomy. The greater the loss of autonomy, and the more recently it occurred, the greater the likely effect of such appeals.[12]

REPRESSION

Repressive control of a communal group is a third major source of incentives for collective action. The general principle is that the use of force against people who think it is unjust may inspire fear and caution in the short run but at the same time provokes resentment and enduring incentives to resist and retaliate.[13] White supremacy in the American South was maintained until the early 1960s by legal repression and extralegal violence. Long before the Russians' first invasion of secessionist Chechnya in December 1994, Russian governments had used force to establish and maintain control of the region. In both cases repression left enduring legacies of anger and resentment, which in the United States animated a decade of direct action and violent protest by African Americans and in Chechnya motivated widespread, intransigent resistance to Russian attacks in 1994–95 and 1999. Kenya's President Moi in the early 1990s encouraged his Kalenjin supporters and their Maasai allies to burn Kikuyu and Luo villages and thus force their inhabitants from rich agricultural land in the Rift Valley Province, as described in the sketch of Kenya on pages 261–266. Short-term objectives were gained at the long-term cost of a desire for retribution against the Kalenjins and Maasai that is likely to fuel future intercommunal and political conflict.[14]

FRAMES FOR ETHNOPOLITICAL ACTION

Empowering ideas about national self-determination and collective rights also give impetus to ethnopolitical movements because they provide frameworks that justify actions. Theorists of social movements describe these kinds of orienting ideas as "frames," or cognitive understandings. In Tarrow's summary, "Inscribing grievances in overall frames that identify an injustice, attribute the responsibility for it to others and propose solutions to it, is a central activity of social movements."[15] The most effective frames for identity groups are those that fit their cultural predispositions and immediate circumstances. Three doctrines that have been widely used as frames by contemporary ethnopolitical movements are national self-determination, indigenous rights, and minority rights.

Nationalism has a long Western pedigree. In the guise of the principle of national self-determination, it has inspired three major waves of empire breaking and nation building in this century—in East Central Europe and the Middle East after World War I, in colonial Africa and Asia during the 1940s and 1950s, and in the postcommunist world at the end of the Cold War. The doctrine continues to exert considerable force. As of 1998, the Minorities at Risk survey identified forty-one politically active ethnonationalist groups (table 1.3, above).[16] Some of the forty-four groups we categorize as national minorities, such as the Kosovar Albanians, also frame their demands in the language of self-determination and independent statehood.

The doctrine of indigenous rights, with antecedents in nineteenth-century petitions by conquered peoples like the Maori, had little impact until the late twentieth century. It was first given effective voice by regional and global coalitions of indigenous activists in the 1970s and 1980s and amplified by nongovernmental organizations concerned with indigenous rights and environmental protection. The doctrine's political impact follows from the success of many of these activists in achieving substantial gains for their own peoples. In normative terms its influence depends on the United Nations system's recognition of the validity of indigenous claims of group rights—protection of a group's land, resources, culture—as embodied in various declarations and draft conventions. In the 1970s and 1980s, according to evidence from the Minorities at Risk project, protest and rebellion by indigenous peoples escalated more rapidly than political action by any other type of minority. In 1998 the Minority project's global survey included sixty-six politically active indigenous peoples, most of whom used the language of indigenous rights doctrine to frame their political demands.[17]

International efforts to specify and guarantee the rights of religious and cultural minorities have a long historical pedigree. A number of recent international declarations specify minority rights that are binding on signatory states. The Council of Europe and the Organization for Security and Cooperation in Europe (OSCE) have issued detailed guidelines for the protection of ethnic, cultural, linguistic, and religious identities. The UN Commission on Human Rights has drafted a similar declaration (issued on February 21, 1992) that extends such protections to minorities everywhere. The documents reflect the views of many politically active minorities and, in turn, are used by their leaders to exert moral and political pressure on governments to grant them the rights stipulated.[18]

Is it plausible to think that frames derived from these empowering doctrines are an independent source of incentives for collective action by identity groups? Perhaps they are for intellectuals and aspiring leaders. For collectivities as a whole, though, the effect of these doctrines probably is contingent on other kinds of incentives and on the closeness of their ties to the group. People are more likely to frame their situation and actions in such terms if they already have a sense of injustice about disadvantages and repression. And group identifiers are more likely to accept these doctrines if they learn of them through networks of communication within the group and from credible leaders.

To summarize, the incentives of an ethnopolitical group for collective action are shaped by three features of their interactions, past and present, with other groups and with the state: (1) the extent of their material, political, and cultural disadvantages; (2) the historical loss of political autonomy; and (3) the extent to which force has been used to establish and maintain their subordinate status. The three conditions are analytically distinct but often converge in practice. In the presence of these conditions, the doctrines that frame ethnopolitical action have catalytic effects—they activate and amplify incentives that arise from a group's disadvantaged position vis-à-vis other groups and the state.

THE DYNAMICS OF PROTRACTED CONFLICT

The theoretical argument to this point incorporates some strong feedback effects. The salience of group identity is attributed in part to repression and disadvantages imposed on the group as a consequence of previous episodes of resistance. If salience and disadvantages in their turn provide incentives for present and future conflict, how is it possible to identify "root causes"? Steven Saideman characterizes this as the "chicken-and-egg" issue in explaining the origins of ethnopolitical conflict.[19] There is no single answer to the question: the answer is different for different groups. It is precisely this mutually reinforcing dynamic that generates protracted or recurrent ethnopolitical conflicts such as those between Catholics and Protestants in Northern Ireland, Hutus and Tutsis, Palestinians and Israelis, Tamils and Sinhalese. Historical analysis should pinpoint the particular conjunction and sequence of conditions that set off a given episode. Once these conflicts have gone through several cycles, however, they tend to become self-generating.

The general analytic solution to the chicken-and-egg problem is to examine the consequences of each episode of protracted conflict using the concepts employed here. If repression is used and disadvantages reinforced without any compensatory gains, then we should expect to observe a resentful reinforcement of group identity and a disposition (incentives) to wait and work for future opportunities to rebel.

The Capacity for Ethnopolitical Action

The third general proposition is that the greater the cohesion and mobilization of an ethnocultural identity group, the more frequent and sustained its participation in political action. And, one can add, the more likely it is to gain concessions and greater access to power. Cohesive groups are those held together by dense networks of communication and interaction. *Mobilization as process* refers to the ways in which members of ethnopolitical organizations are recruited and motivated. *Mobilization as variable* signifies the extent to which group members commit their energies and resources to collective action in pursuit of shared interests.[20]

A sense of collective identity and some awareness of common interests (salience of identity and collective incentives, analyzed earlier in the chapter) are necessary preconditions for cohesion and mobilization. A widely used strategy of ethnopolitical organizations is to build a sense of common interest by employing frames that incorporate symbols of shared identity and grievance.[21] But commitment to ethnopolitical organizations cannot be constructed or maintained from nothing. If people's cultural identity and incentives for joint action are weak, they seldom can be mobilized by any leaders in response to any new threat or opportunity. On the other hand, the conjunction of shared incentives and a strong sense of group identity—a conjunction found among black opponents of apartheid in South Africa and among Shi'is and Kurds in Iraq after the Gulf War—provides highly combustible material that fuels what may appear to be spontaneous action in response to new opportunities. Four general factors, in addition to shared identity and incentives, shape a group's capacity for sustained and effective political action: its geographic concentration, its prior organization, its formation of coalitions, and the authenticity of its leaders.

TERRITORIAL CONCENTRATION

Rebellion is feasible for groups that have a territorial base but very difficult to organize for dispersed and urban groups. Observers of the breakup of the USSR and Yugoslavia have suggested that particular kinds of settlement patterns contributed to ethnorebellion. One element of Posen's argument about the security dilemma in ethnic conflict (see chapter 1) is that a "first strike" against ethnic opponents is most advantageous when they live in concentrated pockets or exclaves. Van Evera suggests that the risks of ethnic warfare are greatest in situations of "local intermingling," such as that which characterized settlement patterns among Serbs, Croats, and Muslims in Bosnia-Herzegovina.[22]

Two recent empirical studies have used large-n comparisons in conjunction with case study materials to test these arguments. Erik Melander asks which kinds of territorial relationships among rival groups (including rivalries between minorities and states) were most likely to lead to violent conflict in the 1990–94 period. The answer is "ethnoterritorial dominance": when the smaller ethnic group in the conflict dyad made up more than 70 percent of the population of its home region, violent conflict was substantially more likely. In a similar study, Monica Duffy Toft examined seventy-two ethnic-based civil wars since 1945 and found that 88 percent involved groups that were regionally concentrated compared with only 6 percent that were dispersed. A reanalysis of the Minorities at Risk data set by Fearon and Laitin confirms Toft's results and observes that geographic concentration predicts to rebellion in all world regions. By contrast, the groups least likely to rebel are those concentrated in urban areas.[23]

PREEXISTING ORGANIZATION

The cohesion of an identity group is a function of high and sustained levels of interaction among its members. Speaking a common language and sharing home ground both promote interaction. So does preexisting social organization. Cohesion is high among people who practice a common religion (Shi'is in Iraq, Saudi Arabia, Bahrain), share an economic niche (Chinese entrepreneurs in Southeast Asia), or dominate a political establishment (Hausa-Fulani in the Nigerian officer corps, Mende in Sierra Leone's government ministries). The organizational basis for the U.S. civil rights movement came from black southern churches, colleges, and the NAACP, all of which expanded rapidly from 1930 to the mid-1950s.[24]

Moreover, established political institutions usually are more cohesive than new political movements and can mobilize members at lower cost. For example, the capacity for collective action is relatively high in groups whose traditional authorities still command respect, as they do among the Afars in Ethiopia and Hazaris in Afghanistan. The same is true of groups that control an autonomous regional government. The constituent republics of the USSR provided the institutional framework within which nationalists in the Baltic, the Caucasus, and Ukraine built independence movements in the late 1980s. Similarly, the non-Russian republics of the Tatars and a dozen other national peoples in the Russian Federation since 1991 have been the base for ethnonational movements that have sought and gained substantial autonomy from Moscow. I am not suggesting that all regional political entities, such as states in India or organized tribes in the United States, are intrinsically disposed to ethnorebellion. The point is that, given incentives and opportunities, it is easier to build ethnopolitical movements among people who have significant cohesion due to frequent and routine interaction as members of an existing institution. In the language of collective action theory, cohesion reduces the costs of organizing collective action. And it also is likely to increase the incentives, especially the normative incentives of meeting the expectations of others with whom one interacts on a regular basis.[25]

OVERCOMING FACTION, FORGING COALITIONS

The capacity for ethnopolitical action further depends on overcoming narrower loyalties to clans, classes, and communities. Theorists of collective action and revolution emphasize the importance of establishing cooperation across diverse groups. Lichbach writes, "Revolution results from an antiregime coalition that consists of multiple disgruntled collective actors. . . . Coalition formation is a critical link between collective dissent and revolution."[26] Identity groups are heterogeneous, and, as I observed in chapter 1, their boundaries are fluid. The effective boundaries of an ethnopolitical group may depend more on coalition formation than on the scope of group identity. Palestinians, for example, are dispersed throughout the Middle East, include adherents of two major religions, are stratified by class, and support competing political organizations. The effectiveness of the Palestinian national movement, now on the verge of statehood, is due to the incorporation of most of these elements into the Palestine Liberation Organization. Founded in 1964, the PLO was one of many organizations competing for Palestinian support until 1968–69, when it was joined by a number of guerrilla organizations, including Yasir Arafat's al-Fatah. During the 1970s and 1980s the PLO was able to extend acceptance of its leadership with the symbolic and material support of the Arab states, which in 1973 recognized the PLO as "the sole, legitimate representative of the Palestinian people." External support and recognition, combined with Arafat's adroit leadership, have made the PLO a viable and effective political force that has overcome most sources of faction in the Palestinian diaspora.

If the aspiring leaders of ethnopolitical groups fail to build inclusive coalitions, mobilization and joint action are impeded, resources are deflected into factional fighting, and it is easier for states to co-opt and deflect communal opponents. Prospects for accommodation with authorities also are handicapped by factionalism. Bardhan concludes a discussion of ethnic mobilization with the observation that "intraethnic animosities make interethnic compromises more difficult as the moderates are afraid of their conciliatory actions being decried as a 'sellout' by the extremists."[27]

Kurdish nationalism offers a counterpoint to the Palestinian example. From the 1920s to the 1990s, Kurds in Turkey, Iraq, and Iran have fought a series of ethnonational rebellions seeking autonomy or independence. But Kurdish leaders have rarely coordinated political action across state boundaries, and most of their rebellions have been crippled by rifts among the rebels themselves. Kurds in northern Iraq achieved and maintained de facto independence after their 1991 rebellion against the weakened regime of Saddam Hussein only because of Allied (U.S. and British) protection. The rivalry between their two principal factions, the Kurdish Democratic Party (KDP) and the Patriotic Union of Kurdistan (PUK), became so bitter that in August 1996 the KDP collaborated with the Baghdad government in a military campaign to suppress the PUK.[28] If the Kurds could have coalesced in a coherent and durable political movement, they might not now be the Middle East's largest nation—numbering 20 million to 30 million people—without a state.

AUTHENTICITY OF LEADERSHIP

As described in the preceding section, effective mobilization in divided groups depends heavily on the formation of coalitions among diverse segments and contending leaders. The role of leadership is central to the mobilization process, not just for overcoming divisions within groups. *Leadership* refers to a set of skills whose effectiveness in identity groups depends on context, not a manual of organizational behavior or a body of revolutionary doctrine. *Authenticity* of leadership may be the most critical factor. The concept is analogous to legitimacy in the arena of conventional politics. Ethnopolitical leaders are *authentic* if they are perceived as representing the most essential values and aspirations of the group and if their actions are thought to be in the common interest. Authenticity is a matter of degree and can be gained or lost. Established leaders usually have intrinsic authenticity; entrepreneurial leaders need to attain it.

Established leaders usually have authenticity by virtue of their position. They control resources, command preexisting loyalties, symbolize group identity, articulate group interests and demands, and manage coalitions. They thus have ample means for overcoming the collective action problem, that is, the reluctance of most individuals to commit to the risky enterprise of protest and rebellion. But they can lose authenticity by wrong words and deeds. Aspiring entrepreneurial leaders are quick to capitalize on errors by their established counterparts. Entrepreneurial leaders—those who aim to build new ethnopolitical movements—face greater obstacles than the leaders of established organizations. They control fewer resources and depend more on symbolic skills and personal example. Entrepreneurial leaders are more likely to articulate "frames" that give people a new sense of hope and power. Often they are risk takers who help convince and attract followers by dramatic personal acts of resistance. And they are especially likely to appeal to supporters who are dissatisfied with established leaders and organizations.

The Nagas of northeastern India provide an illustration of conditions for successful entrepreneurial leadership. The Naga National Council and its successors fought a seventeen-year civil war that was settled in 1963 when the government in New Delhi recognized Nagaland as a separate state of the Indian Union. With the passage of time, the leaders who dominated the new state government lost their authenticity as representatives of Naga interests because they were seen as serving the interests of their own supporters, the federal government in New Delhi, and the Congress Party. Entrepreneurial young Nagas, mainly university students, established new and more militant organizations. Factional competition escalated into renewed separatist violence in 1972 that pitted rebel groups such as the National Socialist Council of Nagaland against both state and federal governments. A negotiated settlement was reached in 1999 with a familiar outcome: the new generation of entrepreneurial leaders will be joining the ranks of Nagaland's political establishment.

■   ■   ■

To summarize the argument thus far, an ethnopolitical group's capacity for political action depends, first of all, on the salience of group identity and shared incentives. Capacity is enhanced if the group has preexisting organizational networks and authentic leaders who successfully bridge internal divisions, whether by coalition building or by other means. And it is easier to build ethnopolitical movements and sustain campaigns of political action if most of the group shares a common homeland. This general proposition, like the preceding ones, is shown schematically in the top portion of figure 3.1.

The argument sketched here also incorporates a response to writers who prefer the instrumental, or "bad leaders," interpretation of ethnopolitical movements. Skillful leaders can strengthen existing group ties and provide a greater awareness of shared interests, but they cannot create them. Given the existence of identity and interest, ethnic entrepreneurs can build effective political movements, but only within limits of group members' expectations about acceptable objectives and actions. If ethnic leaders fall out among themselves or pursue the interests of one segment at the expense of others, they can undermine the cohesion of the group as effectively as any outside agency.[29]

Opportunities and Choices

The ways in which identity, incentives, and capacity are translated into ethnopolitical action are complex. They depend on political and cultural context in ways that are difficult to summarize in general propositions. Some actions are spontaneous and reactive, such as racially motivated riots in Los Angeles in 1965 and 1992, each of which was provoked directly or indirectly when police used force against individuals resisting arrest. But most ethnopolitical action, including all sustained campaigns of protest and rebellion, is shaped by the strategic assessments and tactical decisions of the leaders and activists of politically mobilized communal groups.

The concept of *political opportunity structure* refers to factors external to a group that influence decisions about how to pursue ethnopolitical objectives. As discussed in the preceding three sections, the salience of group identity, incentives, and networks are the elements from which leaders build ethnopolitical movements. They determine a group's *capacity* for political action. *Opportunity structures* are external to the group. Two analytic distinctions are useful: first, between durable and transient opportunity factors; second, between domestic and international opportunity structures.

Durable opportunity factors include the political character of the state and its resources and whether an ethnopolitical group has long-term alliances with other groups in the domestic political arena. These durable factors are properly labeled opportunity *structures:* they shape the ways in which groups organize, and they affect their long-term choices about strategies. Changes in the structure of a group's political environment are *transient* opportunity factors. Examples include changes in political institutions, turnover of elites, shifts in government policy, and the emergence of new political allies. Transient factors can give a boost to mobilization and morale, enhance the credibility of some leaders and frames, and lead to shifts in group claims and strategies. They also help determine the targets and timing of political action.[30]

The impact of transnational structures and actions on ethnopolitics has become so pervasive since the 1980s that it is useful to extend the concept of political opportunities from the domestic to the international level. The role of external support for ethnopolitical groups has long been recognized, especially the political and material assistance that external patrons provide for separatist movements. Deepa Khosla has examined the range of political, material, and military support given by foreign states to ethnopolitical minorities in the Third World in the 1990s. Slightly more than half (95 of 179 minorities in her study) received foreign support. All but 2 of 23 ethnonationalist groups benefited from foreign support, and so did half (32 of 64) the communal contenders and nearly half (24 of 52) the indigenous peoples. Communal contenders and ethnonationalists both received more military than nonmilitary support.[31]

The concept of *international political opportunity structure* used here encompasses an ethnopolitical group's international allies and opponents, its kindred groups, and regional and international organizations. Recent studies of transnational networks show that they also have patterned effects on political mobilization and strategies of some kinds of ethnopolitical groups. For example, indigenous groups in Latin America have developed durable transnational links with one another, with global indigenous movements, and with some environmental NGOs. These transnational organizations and networks are sources of a wide variety of information and assistance to local indigenous organizations and represent their interests in a great many venues, for example, the U.S. Congress, the European Union, and the World Bank.[32] From a local perspective, therefore, the international domain is as much a part of the opportunity structure as the domestic political arena is. The next two sections specify some of the most important opportunity factors shaping choices and outcomes of ethnopolitical action at the beginning of the twenty-first century.

THE STATE CONTEXT OF ETHNOPOLITICAL ACTION: EFFECTS OF STATE POWER AND DEMOCRACY

The state's political institutions and capabilities structure ethnopolitical groups' choices about the objectives to pursue and the means used to do so. First, the resources and administrative capabilities of the state set limits on what groups might obtain. Second, the openness of the political system affects group leaders' choices about whether to participate, protest, or rebel. Evidence from the Minorities at Risk study points to the special significance of three factors: *the scope of state power,* the political values and practices of *institutionalized democracy,* and the transient effects of *democratization.* Detailed empirical evidence of the impact of democracy and democratization on ethnopolitical conflict and accommodation is reported in chapters 5 and 6. This section develops the general argument and provides a number of examples.

Uses of State Power

State power is a durable opportunity factor. Strong states are those that have ample resources and the administrative and political capacity to control or regulate most economic, social, and political activity. The strongest states in the late twentieth century have included most of the advanced industrial democracies, China, and, until the 1980s, some Soviet-bloc states. Postcolonial and postrevolutionary leaders throughout this century have sought to build strong states on the Western or Soviet model. Because almost all new states in the global south govern ethnically plural societies, state building usually has meant policies aimed at assimilating individual members of cultural groups, restraining their collective autonomy, and extracting their resources and labor for the state's use.

The expansion of state power is likely to have crosscutting effects on national and minority peoples. State strategies of subordination and assimilation almost invariably increase collective grievances: administrative restraints

are imposed, lifeways are altered, traditional cultures are denigrated or marginalized. At the same time the potential costs of collective action increase
because the agents of an expanding state are usually intrusive and vigilant. On
the other hand, groups whose leaders have countervailing resources, or low-cost
access to decision-making processes, may be able to maintain group autonomy
and secure payoffs for cooperating with dominant groups. All such statements are fraught with "maybes" because they depend on the dominant state's
ideology and on the abilities of group leaders to obstruct, to adapt, and to
acquire and deploy influential allies. In Lenin's USSR the Communist Party
recognized the principle of national self-determination for non-Russians, and
Stalin accepted the more limited principle of cultural-national autonomy. In
Ataturk's Turkey, however, no political or cultural alternatives to Turkish
identity were tolerated. The People's Republic of China follows the principle
of cultural autonomy for minority peoples but adamantly opposes "splittists,"
such as Tibetan and Taiwanese nationalists who seek or, in the latter instance,
want to maintain political autonomy.

The outcomes of minority peoples' resistance to state building are problematic. Strong, resource-rich states have the capacity either to accommodate or
to suppress national peoples and minorities at relatively low cost, depending
on the preferences of state elites. Gains are most likely to be won by identity-
based movements that maintain sustained, nonviolent campaigns for reforms
that do not threaten state security. Rulers of weaker states face more stark, zero-
sum choices when confronted by communal challenges. They can expand the
governing coalition at risk to their own positions, or they can devote scarce
resources to all-out warfare against communal rivals. The Tutsi-dominated
government of Burundi was under international pressure during the 1980s
and early 1990s to incorporate the Hutu majority and, to its credit, attempted
to do so by democratic means. The plan foundered in a coup and a welter of
killings by militant Tutsis who rejected sharing power with Hutu leaders who
won 1993 elections.[33] In Rwanda in the early 1990s, the Hutu elite faced pressures to accommodate Tutsis from a rebel army and international actors but
chose genocide rather than compromise.

A third alternative to incorporation or warfare is to negotiate independence
or autonomy with ethnonationalists. The nonviolent deconstruction of the
USSR, a powerful but declining state, provided a strong precedent. In 1993
Czechoslovakia fissioned peacefully into two independent republics. Among
the states that are candidates for political fragmentation at the onset of the
twenty-first century are Canada, Belgium, South Africa, Serbia-Montenegro,
Iraq, Sri Lanka, Russia, Pakistan, Ethiopia, Burma, Sudan, and the Democratic

Republic of Congo (former Zaire). A supplement to this list consists of countries in which breakaway regions have already established de facto independence: Somalia (Somaliland's independence is already gaining recognition from a few other states in the region), Georgia (de facto independence for Abkhazia), and Moldova (the Trans-Dniester Republic). The states are listed roughly in order of declining state strength. The first three, Canada, Belgium, and South Africa, are relatively strong states that command substantial resources. The next seven have serious weaknesses and face serious challenges from regional contenders. The last five—Sudan, Congo (former Zaire), Somalia, Georgia, and Moldova—are failed states: they have lost control over substantial tracts of territory that are now controlled by secessionist peoples.

The examples cited here suggest that the connection between state strength and opportunities for successful ethnonational rebellion at the end of the twentieth century is a curvilinear one. Secession or autonomy is most likely to be gained either in relatively strong or very weak states: in strong states such as Canada and Belgium because democratic elites may be persuaded that peaceful divorce is less costly than civil war, and in weak states such as Moldova and Georgia because they lack the means to reclaim secessionist regions by force or inducements. Between these extremes are states with enough will and resources to wage war with ethnonational rebels but not the means to bury them or buy them out. These are the states most at risk of protracted communal wars.

What does this argument imply for political opportunity structures? From the perspective of ethnonational and other communal contenders, state strength and elite commitments are both critically important. A rebellion against a semi-strong state is a reasonable strategic choice only under certain conditions: (a) if the challengers have high incentives and capacity, and (b) if the state shows signs of loss of either strength or will. Alternatively, (c) communal strategists may be convinced that rebellion itself will eventually erode the state's capacity and will to fight to the point at which concessions or secession can be won. Transient changes in political opportunities often are the immediate precipitants—the accelerators, to use Barbara Harff's concept—of ethnorebellion. An abrupt change in the composition of the state elite may signal temporary indecision; a mutiny implies a weakening of the security apparatus; the outbreak of international or civil war diverts elite attention and state resources that might otherwise be focused on ethnic rebels.[34] The prospects for ethnorebellion in a strong state, in the absence of transient changes in opportunity structures, can be increased by external support, especially the provision of military material and cross-border sanctuaries. The Kurdish PKK was able to sustain a rebellion against a strong Turkish state from 1984 through

1998 because of support from Syria and the Kurdish diaspora in Europe and the availability of safe havens in Syria and, sometimes, northern Iraq.

Institutionalized Democracies

Democratic institutions and elites are the other durable opportunity factor that weighs heavily in the strategic calculus of ethnonationalists. Western European democracies and India afford more than a dozen illustrations in the past twenty-five years of the principle that democratic elites can be persuaded to extend autonomy when enough political resources are brought to bear by communal leaders (see the Naga example on pp. 78–79 and chapter 6). Ethnonationalists have used a mix of conventional and violent tactics in these conflicts, but with a couple of Indian exceptions the winners have been the organizations capable of sustained mobilization and participation in conventional politics and protest, not armed rebellion. The practice of *democratic accommodation under pressure* is evident in the ways democratic governments process all kinds of ethnopolitical demands.

The management of ethnopolitical conflicts in institutionalized democracies depends most fundamentally on two principles. The first is implementing universalistic norms of equal rights and opportunities for all citizens, including ethnoclasses. The second is pluralistic accommodation of indigenous and regional peoples' desires for separate collective status. The application of these norms to national and minority peoples is, however, relatively new and imperfect. The century-long delay between the freeing of slaves in the United States and effective civil rights legislation is only the most obvious example. Australian policy toward Aborigines for most of this century emphasized assimilation, advanced in some instances by forcibly removing Aborigine children from their parents and placing them in English-only boarding schools. The federal government did not grant full citizenship rights to Aborigines until 1967, and states with large Aborigine populations, especially Queensland and Western Australia, continue to resist grants of land rights and other "privileges" to Aborigine communities.[35] The Israeli government continues to discriminate against the country's Arab Israeli minority, despite a shift in the early 1990s that gave Arab Israeli communities somewhat more equitable treatment in the allocation of public funds.

Despite the imperfect application of democratic norms to ethnic identity groups, empirical comparisons made in the Minorities at Risk study show that national and minority peoples in contemporary industrial democracies face few political barriers to participation and are more likely to use the tactics of protest than of rebellion.[36] The reasons are inherent in the political cultures and policies of modern democratic societies. In the past half century most political leaders of these societies have become more responsive to the interests of politicized ethnic groups, in particular to groups able to mobilize large constituencies and allies in persistent campaigns of protest—another example of the principle of *democratic accommodation under pressure* at work. Groups using violent protest and terrorism, by contrast, have risked backlash and loss of public support. Thus, the calculus for ethnopolitical action in democracies favors protest over rebellion.

The advanced industrial democracies also have ample resources to respond favorably to grievances pursued within the democratic framework. On this count also, the opportunity structure for ethnopolitical groups in democracies provides incentives for protest and disincentives for rebellion.[37] India, the world's largest democracy, seems to contradict the argument. At the end of the 1990s it had seven ongoing ethnopolitical rebellions, more than any other country—in fact, more than all the Western and Latin American democracies combined. The essential reason, I suspect, is the relative weakness of the Indian central government combined with its political elite's commitment to norms of accommodation. The relative weakness of the government has made it difficult to contain ethnorebellions in peripheral regions, especially in Assam and Kashmir. This weakness, combined with democratic norms, has prompted Indian governments to attempt to reach accommodation—especially by creating new ethnically and linguistically demarcated states, controlled by communal moderates willing to cooperate with the Congress Party at the center. In this situation the political opportunities have sometimes favored rebels because fighting holds out real promise of gains in the form of regional autonomy and access to resources and influence in New Delhi.[38]

Transitions to Democracy

The process by which many formerly autocratic states in the Second World and Third World have sought to establish more participatory and responsive political systems has problematic consequences for ethnic mobilization and conflict. Successful democratization means the establishment of regimes in which ethnic and other interests are accommodated by peaceful means.[39] But the *process* of transition creates threatening uncertainties for some groups and opens up a range of transitory political opportunities for ethnic entrepreneurs.[40]

In heterogeneous new states democratization poses still greater risks of conflict. James Fearon analyzes them as commitment problems. The key problem (not the only one) in postcommunist states such as Croatia, he says, was that the majority (Croats in this example) could not give minorities (Serbs) convincing guarantees that their status would be protected. The advent of majoritarian politics posed the risk that the new state would abuse minority rights, and nationalistic rhetoric and restrictions by majority politicians increased minorities' insecurity. The strategic question for Serbian leaders was whether to fight for autonomy at the onset of statehood or wait and see. But the risk of waiting was that armed resistance would become more costly, maybe impossible, once the new state consolidated control of the military and the police. Therefore, in the absence of credible and externally guaranteed commitments to respect minority rights, the onset of democratization and independence provoked immediate separatist rebellions in Croatia and other postcommunist states.[41]

Postcommunist regimes relaxed coercive restraints on nationalism and interethnic rivalries at a time when the institutionalized means for their expression and accommodation did not yet exist or were fragile and distrusted. The problem of postrevolutionary communist states was diagnosed by Milovan Djilas, the Yugoslav revolutionary turned critic, in an essay written shortly before his death in 1995: "When revolutions occur, ethnic identities get hammered down, only to bounce back with elemental force unless precisely defined relationships have developed in a society: democratic institutions, a free economy, a middle class. In this regard communism left behind it a desert."[42] The result, in Yugoslavia and elsewhere, was a resurgence of communal activism, both protest and rebellion. Similar consequences can be expected to follow from democratization in multiethnic Third World autocracies. The most dubious expectation of all is that authoritarian states such as Sudan, Iraq, Burma, and Burundi might be able to defuse ethnopolitical wars by moving toward democracy. Democratic institutions in societies riven by ethnic rivalries are more likely to increase incentives and opportunities for more fighting than to provide pathways to peaceful accommodation.[43]

Two general propositions about the effects of state institutions and power on political action by ethnopolitical groups are incorporated in figure 3.1. In established democracies the opportunities for ethnic mobilization are substantial and so are potential gains—for cohesive groups that rely largely on nonviolent tactics. The proposition is that institutionalized democracy facilitates nonviolent ethnopolitical action and inhibits communal rebellion. This tendency is reinforced in strong states, those that have ample power and resources to respond to pluralist interests.

In democratizing autocracies, by contrast, national and minority peoples ordinarily feel a loss of security simultaneously with a transient increase in opportunities for mobilization and action. New democratic regimes usually lack the resources or institutional means to make and guarantee the kinds of accommodations that typify the established democracies. Therefore, democratization in its early stages facilitates both ethnically based protest and rebellion. The worst-case scenario is that the rejection of accommodation by one or all contenders will lead to civil war and the reimposition of autocratic rule by the strongest contender.

It is worth repeating that both the USSR and the Federal Republic of Yugoslavia faced such conditions in 1990–91. The majority of Soviet and Russian leaders chose democracy and decentralization. They accepted the independent statehood of fourteen constituent republics of the USSR and subsequently negotiated autonomy arrangements with many regional entities within the Russian Federation whose leaders were toying with secession. Serbian nationalists chose to fight rather than switch, with devastating short-term consequences. Ethiopia is a state that reached the same choice point by a different path: protracted regional rebellions culminated early in 1991 in the seizure of power in Addis Ababa by a coalition of contending groups led by Tigreans. In the short run the revolutionary leaders acted on the principles that brought them victory. They governed by a transitional constitution that recognized ethnic units as constituent parts of the Ethiopian state and gave them the right, in principle, to self-determination. When Eritreans overwhelmingly voted to act on the principle, Ethiopia's new leaders accepted Eritrea's independence. But they have been more recalcitrant about responding to claims of other communal groups—Oromos and Somalis, in particular—for some combination of greater regional autonomy and shared power in Addis Ababa. In Ethiopia, as in the postcommunist world, there will be for a long time the risk that those who inherit the wreckage of multinational empires will attempt to re-create them.

The International Context of Ethnopolitical Action

Myriad international factors help shape the aspirations, opportunities, and strategies of ethnopolitical groups. They also affect state policies toward minorities. Moreover, the nature of international engagement is a major determinant of whether ethnopolitical conflicts are of short duration or long and whether they end in negotiated settlements or humanitarian disasters. These connections are discussed in this section and summarized, some of them, in figure 3.1.

FOREIGN SUPPORT FOR CONTENDERS

Foreign sympathizers can contribute substantially to an ethnopolitical group's cohesion and political mobilization by providing material, political, and moral support. Indigenous rights organizations such as the American Indian Movement (in the 1970s) and the World Council of Indigenous Peoples (in the 1980s and 1990s) have promoted the establishment of numerous indigenous peoples' movements, provided strategic guidance for their leaders, and pressured governments to respond positively. The Palestine Liberation Organization organized and supported opposition activity by Palestinians in Jordan, Lebanon, and Israel's Occupied Territories. Rebellious Iraqi Kurds have at various times had the diplomatic and material support of the Shah of Iran, the Iranian revolutionary regime, Israel, and Great Britain and the United States (1972–75 and 1991–present).

External support for ethnonational groups also may provoke responses that offset opportunities. Weak regimes facing ethnopolitical challengers frequently seek bilateral military assistance and political support that enhance their capacity to counter ethnopolitical challenges. The most tragic and destructive consequences occur when competing powers support different sides in ethnopolitical wars. Such proxy wars are usually protracted and very deadly, and they are not likely to end in negotiated settlements unless and until it is in the interest of the external powers.

Withdrawal of external support may open up possibilities for settlement, as happened in Afghanistan and Angola in the early 1990s. In both these instances, however, international efforts at settlement failed, quickly in Afghanistan and slowly in Angola, because one or more contenders could not be persuaded that participation in coalition governments was preferable to fighting for complete victory. In Afghanistan the cessation of Russian and U.S. support in 1991 led to a new phase of civil war, fought this time not between Marxists and Islamists but among communal rivals for power. Despite UN-led support for a succession of coalition governments, the country was rent by another seven years of armed conflict among political movements based on Tajiks, Uzbeks, Hazaris, and Pashtuns. The Taliban Islamist movement, which consolidated control in 1998, derived its support almost exclusively from the Pashtuns. More exactly, the Taliban represents the political and religious interests of mullahs from Qandahar, in southern Afghanistan. Qandahari Pashtuns in 1998 made up virtually all the members of the country's supreme *shura,* or consultative assembly, while the *shura* in Kabul included a handful of members of other groups. Thus the Taliban is a vehicle by which one element of the Pashtuns has reestablished the group's historic hegemony.[44]

The resumption of protracted communal conflict, despite international efforts to broker a political settlement, is another manifestation of the commitment problem analyzed by James Fearon. Angola affords a clear example. The Angolan government's main challenger since 1975 has been the Union for the Total Independence of Angola (UNITA), based mainly on the Ovimbundu people of southern Angola. During the Cold War the United States and South Africa gave UNITA ample material and political assistance in a proxy war against the Cuban-supported government in Luanda. Near the end of the Cold War, after Cuban troops had withdrawn and the government had shed its Marxist trappings, an internationally brokered peace plan led to multiparty parliamentary and presidential elections in 1992. In the absence of mutual trust and international guarantees, neither party acted in good faith. UNITA rejected the election results, and many UNITA supporters in the capital were massacred. Another round of international pressure led in 1997 to formation of a coalition government with UNITA's Jonas Savimbi as head of the now-legal opposition. But UNITA did not demobilize its fighters and continued to acquire new arms from old friends. The government expelled some of the UNITA parliamentarians and prompted the others to establish a new, "tame," UNITA. While politicos maneuvered in the capital, UNITA expanded its military control, and since late 1998 a full-fledged civil war has been under way, this time with little international means or will to check it.[45]

The general proposition is that foreign material and military support for contenders in ethnopolitical wars increases group capacities and opportunities for action but also makes it likely that conflicts will be protracted, deadly, and highly resistant to settlement.

INTERNATIONAL SPILLOVER OF ETHNOPOLITICAL CONFLICT

Group incentives, capacities, and opportunities are amplified by the contagious example of successful political action elsewhere and by diffusion of ethnopolitical conflict from nearby regions.

Contagion and *communication* refer to the processes by which one group's actions provide inspiration and guidance, both strategic and tactical, for groups elsewhere. Though some observers have argued that civil or ethnic conflict is in general contagious, a closer reading of the evidence suggests that the strongest contagion effects occur within networks of similar groups.[46] Informal connections and influences have long existed among disadvantaged peoples, so that, for example, one finds Australian Aborigines in the early 1960s organizing freedom rides in rural New South Wales, and Dayaks in northern Borneo in the 1980s resisting commercial logging of their forests with rhetoric and tactics remarkably similar to those used by native Canadian peoples in the early 1990s. By century's end thickening webs of connections among like-minded groups were in place.

More precisely, networks of communication, political support, and material assistance have developed among similar groups that face similar circumstances. The two densest networks of the late twentieth century link Islamic communities and indigenous peoples, respectively. Their connectivity depends on international conferences, transcontinental travel by activists, and fax, phone, and Internet exchanges. Organizations in these networks gain access to expertise on leadership, communications, and mobilization. Their appeals gain plausibility because they resonate with sentiments held by similar peoples elsewhere. Equally important, groups in the networks benefit from the inspiration of successful movements elsewhere, successes that provide the images and moral incentives that help motivate activists.

Contagion effects are not automatic. First, as suggested in the discussion of empowering ideas, frames and victories are contagious only for people who have a preexisting sense of collective identity and some notion of common interests. Second, contagion presupposes some degree of leadership and networks of communication within the group, not just images and rhetoric from outside. Stephen M. Saideman makes a persuasive argument that contagion is most likely to affect groups whose economic and political circumstances are similar to those of ethnonational groups that initiate a successful movement, especially other groups in the same country.[47]

Diffusion refers to the direct "spillover" of conflict from one region to another, either within or across international boundaries. The contagion of conflict is indirect; diffusion is direct. For example, more than twenty national peoples in the Caucasus have been caught up in ethnopolitical tumult in the 1990s through the diffusion (and contagion) of proactive and reactive nationalism. The Association of the Peoples of the Caucasus, which represents most of the peoples of the North Caucasus, was founded after riots between Georgians and Abkhazians in July 1989 to help Abkhazians and other North Caucasus peoples provide assistance to threatened kindred. Since then activists and fighters have moved fluidly from one regional conflict to another and so have arms and supplies.[48] Governments also are active players: in the early 1990s Russians promoted the Abkhaz war of independence and North Ossetia (in the Russian Federation) supported autonomy-minded South Ossetians (in Georgia), while the Armenian government has given political, material, and military support to secessionists in Azerbaijan's Nagorno-Karabakh region throughout the 1990s.

The most intense and complex spillover effects in ethnopolitical conflict happen among groups that straddle international boundaries—intense and complex, because they draw in a multiplicity of ethnic and state actors. Of the 275 groups currently in the Minorities at Risk study, nearly two-thirds have kindred in one or more adjacent countries. Political activists in one country often find sanctuary with and get support from their transnational kindred. Generations of Kurdish leaders and *peshmergas* (warriors) in Turkey, Syria, Iraq, and Iran have provided safe havens for one another's political movements. The Miskitos of Nicaragua mounted a rebellion against the Sandinista government in the 1980s from bases across the Coco River in Honduras, where they were supplied and trained by the CIA.[49] Diasporas also are a substantial and growing source of support. Since the 1970s, Kurdish rebels in Turkey have raised substantial funds from Kurdish workers in Western Europe. Chechen communities in the Middle East, descendants of exiles and political refugees from past conflicts, in the1990s sent fighters and material support to their rebellious cousins in the Caucasus.

If a disadvantaged group's kindred are a favored or dominant group in a neighboring state, they often can count on their diplomatic, political, and sometimes military support. The Republic of Armenia's support for Armenians in Nagorno-Karabakh, cited earlier, is a case in point. The ethnonationalist Moros in the Philippines had the political and material support of the Malaysian government during the early phase of their 1970s civil war against the Marcos regime, partly because Malaysians sympathized with their Muslim coreligionists, partly because Malaysia wanted a counter to Philippine claims to the Malaysian province of Sabah. Global comparative studies confirm that these are instances of general patterns that were already evident in the 1970s and 1980s. Conflict between two neighboring states is higher than average in situations where one state has a disadvantaged ethnic minority and members of the same group hold power in the other. Moreover, if the disadvantaged minority in a dyad of this kind has mobilized for political action, the interstate relationship is even more conflictual.[50]

National peoples also may be able to take risky advantage of interstate warfare to pursue their own interests. At the end of World War II, help from the USSR enabled the Kurds to establish the Mahabad Republic in northwestern Iran; it was soon suppressed by the Iranian government and its leader publicly executed. The Iran-Iraq War and the 1991 Gulf War both provided opportunities for Kurdish parties to mount rebellions for autonomy. In this and most other examples noted in the Minorities at Risk studies, spillover effects contribute to communal rebellion, not protest.

These observations suggest three general propositions about contagion and diffusion effects. (1) An ethnopolitical group's incentives for political action are increased by successful mobilization and political action by similar groups elsewhere. Contagion effects are strongest among similar groups (e.g., ethnonationalists) in the same country, weaker in adjoining countries, and weakest for more distant kindred. Contagion is enhanced by the existence of transnational networks linking similar groups. (2) Group capabilities for political action are increased by political and material support from segments of the group elsewhere, especially from segments that are mobilized (whether as disadvantaged minorities or as a dominant group in control of the state). Political, material, and military assistance from foreign countries also increases capabilities but is likely to prompt the challenged state to seek offsetting support from its own allies. (3) Group opportunities for rebellion are increased by the number of segments of the group in adjoining countries and by their proximity to open conflict (including civil and interstate war). They also are enhanced by power transitions in regional and global alliance structures. These propositions about the effects of state and systemic factors on ethnopolitical action are summarized schematically in figure 3.1.

The Global and Historical Context of Ethnopolitics

This chapter has approached the explanation of ethnopolitical conflict at two levels of analysis. Why and how do particular ethnic groups mobilize to defend and promote their collective interests in the political arena? The general answers have to do with the traits of the group and its relations with state and society, past and present. Second, what determines the timing, strategies, and outcomes of ethnopolitical action? State institutions and policies are crucial, and so are the examples and the support of external actors.

There is a third, world-systems, level of analysis that has not been explored in this chapter. World-level processes, to use Susan Olzak's term, come wrapped in big theories about the dynamics of global economic and political integration, state building, modernization, the communications revolution, the transnational movement of peoples, and world systemic crisis. These and related processes have reshaped the world system during the twentieth century and thus have altered the nature of ethnopolitical identities and conflicts in direct and indirect ways. The first- and second-level dynamics on which this chapter has focused are sometimes the local and specific manifestations of much larger processes. Following is a capsule summary of some world-level processes that are implicated in ethnopolitics.

Fred Riggs thinks that the modern forms of ethnicity are a new phenomenon to which industrialism, democratization, and nationalism have contributed. In premodern societies, he suggests, ethnic diversity was ubiquitous but rarely was the basis for ethnopolitical movements. Modern states create obligations and privileges, giving rise to claims to civic ethnicity by marginalized communities, who seek integration, and to ethnic nationalism among marginalized peoples, who reject the citizenship demands of modern states.[51]

Charles Tilly demonstrates that the concentration and expansion of state and economic power has had profound effects on the nature of collective action. During the past two centuries collective action has shifted from local and private targets to national and public targets. Local grievances about local abuses have given way to national and transnational ideologies of citizens' rights and revolution. The scope of collective action has vastly increased and so has the duration of episodes. The forms of contention have changed from ritual humiliation to demonstrations, from rural arson to guerrilla warfare.[52] These shifts in the scale, repertoires, and objectives of collective action generally are paralleled by similar changes in the shape and content of ethnopolitical action.

Susan Olzak contends that the increasing integration of the world economic and political system has altered the economic status of ethnic and national groups and, along with it, the forms and location of ethnopolitical action. Her conclusion is that

> processes of economic and political integration among the world's states has caused a rise in ethnic protest movements. In core nations, ethnic protest is relatively frequent but it is also temperate. In contrast, in peripheral nations, ethnic protest is likely to be sporadic, but potentially more violent. Whether scattered non-violent protests develop into armed rebellions also depends on a variety of internal processes related to the political opportunities for ethnic inclusion and economic mobility.[53]

Olzak's empirical study of ethnic mobilization across 130 countries from 1965 to 1990 supports this argument and highlights the importance of international ties. Peripheral countries that are more closely tied to international governmental organizations have had more nonviolent ethnic protest but less ethnic violence than countries without such ties.[54]

Finally, Jonathan Friedman analyzes the consequences of decline in global systems for ethnic identity and assertion. This analysis is part of his larger theory that world history is characterized by cycles of hegemonic expansion and contraction. Hegemonic systems are invariably multiethnic and ethnically hierarchic, even if normative weight is given to nonethnic individual and social identifications. When empires and hegemonial state systems decline, *ethnification* occurs. By this Friedman means that disadvantaged groups, who are most susceptible to economic decline and social and psychic insecurity, reassert ethnic and national identities and use them as the basis for political movements.[55]

Juxtaposing these and similar arguments about world-level processes suggests the following general sketch. The construction of the modern state system and a global economy—and all that these processes entail—has altered the meaning and consequences of ethnic identity for nonstate peoples everywhere. Some peoples have gained by these processes—sovereign statehood in some instances, incorporation in civic states in others—whereas others have been marginalized. The frameworks and repertoires of collective action of peoples who want to resist or renegotiate the terms on which they are being incorporated into the world system have diversified. Most modern identity groups have gained greater capability for political action because organizational skills and connectivity have increased for them just as they have for associational groups, corporations, and states. On the other hand, opportunities for collective action within states have narrowed as state powers and resources have increased. When states and hegemonic systems are in transition or decline, windows of opportunity open for many groups. International war, the breakup of empires, and waves of democratic transitions have this effect. In the interdependent world of the twentieth and twenty-first centuries, these crises are transnational; consequently, the tracings of ethnopolitical movements and wars, past and future, can be expected to resemble the ebbs and flows of a tide chart.

In Summary

The foregoing section sketches a framework within which a macro-theory of ethnopolitical conflict might be constructed. Such a theory would help account for the long-term shifts in the character and political consequences of ethnic identity, but it is beyond the reach of this chapter. The origins and dynamics of ethnopolitical conflict at the levels of group and state are complex enough. To summarize, the heart of this chapter is a midrange theory that identifies four sets of factors. Ethnopolitical action presupposes an identity group that shares valued cultural traits and some common grievances or aspirations.

These sentiments and interests provide the essential bases for mobilization and shape the kinds of claims made by group leaders. Shared identity and interests are the elements from which skillful leaders forge a group's capacity for political action. The timing of action and the choice of strategies of participation, protest, or rebellion depend largely on political opportunities external to the group, principally its relationship to the state and external actors.

This framework is used later, in chapter 7, to identify groups at risk of future ethnopolitical conflict. One general implication can be highlighted here. Understandings of ethnopolitical conflict that emphasize the supposedly crucial role of a single factor, such as historical animosities or cultural differences between groups, should be avoided. Such explanations usually become significant because they are invoked by contemporary ethnopolitical leaders seeking to mobilize support, not because cultural or historical differences generate a primordial urge to conflict.

Indigenous Peoples of Amazonian Ecuador

A Little Help from Their Friends

Pamela L. Burke

The indigenous movement in Ecuador illustrates how shifts to democratic governance and support from transnational actors have transformed the strategies and outcomes of ethnopolitical action for peoples who a generation ago were powerless.

ECUADOR'S INDIGENOUS PEOPLES are the most impoverished ethnic group in a heterogeneous country. Approximately 40 percent of the Ecuadoran population is indigenous, most of them Quechua, but the population also includes the Shuar, Achuar, Siona, Secoya, Cofan, and Huaorani ethnolinguistic groups. The highland Indians are about 37.5 percent of the total population, and the lowland, Amazonian, Indians make up about 2.5 percent. The highland peoples are politically coordinated by Ecuador Runacunapac Riccharimui (ECUARUNARI); the Amazonian peoples have a separate regional political organization, the Confederation of Indigenous Nationalities of the Ecuadoran Amazon (CONFENIAE). These groups, along with an association of coastal peoples, are united in a national political action organization, the National Confederation of Indigenous Peoples of Ecuador (CONAIE).

Prior to Ecuador's transition to democracy in 1979, its social landscape was dominated by military leaders and large landowners who operated a *hacienda* system in which indigenous peoples were incorporated, if at all, as textile and agricultural laborers. A literacy requirement that barred most indigenous peoples from voting was not lifted until 1978, when a new democratic constitution was introduced.[1] Thus, indigenous peoples' opportunities for mobilization and political action under the pre-democratic oligarchic governments were almost nonexistent. The transition to democracy prompted mobilization among indigenous peoples. A shift in government priorities was evident when the Roldos administration (1979–84) created the Office for Indigenous Affairs, which funded bilingual education. During this period indigenous organizations also established linkages with international nongovernmental organizations (INGOs), intergovernmental organizations (IGOs), multinational corporations (MNCs), and associations of anthropologists. The opening of a combination of both national and transnational political opportunities prompted indigenous political mobilization that spread from regional and national to transnational levels.

Transnational collective action is illustrated by the Amazonian peoples' engagement in negotiations with multinational oil companies. From the beginning of oil exploration in the 1920s and Texaco's first oil production site in 1972, transnational actors have been present in the upper Amazon. However, indigenous peoples and their interests were not represented in the first negotiations for oil exploration and production. With support from INGOs and the opening of democratic political opportunities, indigenous peoples since the 1980s have succeeded in reconfiguring the bargaining process. Not only are they consulted; they have gained enough leverage to affect the political and social outcomes. There are ten or more political organizations in Amazonian Ecuador;[2] this sketch highlights two of them.

Though Texaco began oil production in 1972 on Cofanes' traditional lands jointly with Petroecuador, the state-owned oil company, it was not until 1993 that the Cofanes, with the aid of the Natural Resources Defense Council (NRDC) in Washington, D.C., and other environmental INGOs filed a class-action suit in New York federal court against Texaco, seeking $1.5 billion in damages to be invested in a cleanup project.[3] This lawsuit was accompanied by a transnational campaign against Texaco, including a 1994 international boycott against Texaco organized by the Cofanes, the NRDC and its allies, and two regional Amazonian social movement organizations, the Coalition for Amazonian Peoples and Their Environment, and Coordinator for Indigenous Peoples of the Amazon Basin (COICA).[4] The case was still pending in April 1999; Petroecuador has initiated a cleanup program with Texaco that is awaiting funding.[5] Since this action the Cofanes have been included in governmental and Texaco negotiations. Moreover, the Cofanes and Petroecuador have signed an agreement that requires the Cofanes' permission for further oil development in their region. Thus, not only have Cofan strategies changed, but they also have gained political access and a say in policy decisions.

Learning from the Cofan experience and encouraged by INGOs, the Organization of Indigenous Peoples of Pastaza (OPIP) initiated negotiations with ARCO, which operated in their region, to integrate indigenous concerns about their environment. OPIP uses international environmental frames to justify its claims, for example, by interpreting indigenous peoples as part of the Amazonian environment, and has drawn support from the Rainforest Action Network, the Coalition, the European Union, IBIS Denmark, Oxfam America, and the Inter-American Foundation.[6] Its repertoire of political action draws heavily on strategies used by other members of the global indigenous rights movement. In April 1992, for example, OPIP organized a march of some ten thousand Quechua, Achuar, and Shiwiar peoples from the Amazon to the capital city of Quito to honor indigenous peoples. OPIP representatives have traveled to California and Texas to negotiate with ARCO representatives and now sit on a committee within the company to develop environmentally safe production strategies. Thus, OPIP has professionalized its role via its transnational networks.

These examples of the mobilization of indigenous peoples in the Ecuadoran Amazon show how opening political opportunities via transnational resources and democratic governance have transformed the actions and status of indigenous peoples. Their strategies for collective action and framing incorporate the "green" ideas and discourse adopted from INGOs. Indigenous organizations have not only changed the process but also made significant gains, including land grants (the largest Amazonian land grant was made to OPIP after the 1992 march), community health and education centers (Occidental Oil Company has a comprehensive community relations plan to provide infrastructure, health, and education for the Quechua, Siona, and Secoya peoples), and inclusion in governmental and MNC negotiation committees. Thus, once-marginalized indigenous peoples now participate in national and transnational policy processes and have a measurable impact on outcomes that affect their immediate environment and well-being.

NOTES

The author did field research on indigenous peoples' movements in Ecuador from 1996 to 1998. This sketch is drawn from her dissertation, "The Globalization of Contentious Politics: The Amazonian Indigenous Rights Movement" (University of Maryland, Department of Government and Politics, 1999). She is a member of the Politics and Geography faculty at Coastal Carolina University.

1. Enrique Ayala Mora, *Resumen de historia del Ecuador* (Quito: Corporacion Editora Nacional, 1993), 93–107.

2. Each region of the Amazon has an indigenous political organization based on ethnolinguistic identities. In the region of Pastaza, for example, the Quechua Indians are the majority people and have formed the Organization of Indigenous Peoples of Pastaza (OPIP). In Sucumbios, the Cofanes have formed a political organization in their name. Similarly, the Siona and Secoya, also in the province of Sucumbios, have formed political organizations. Although these groups are highlighted in this sketch, there are other politically active provincial indigenous organizations in the Amazon representing the Shuar, the Achuar, the Huaorani (ONHAE), the Quechua of Napo (FOIN), and the Quechua of Sucumbios (FOISE).

3. The other transnational organizations supporting the Cofanes included Accion Ecologica, Rainforest Action Network (RAN), the National Wildlife Federation (NWF), and Fundacion Natura.

4. Transnational social movements are defined here as "sustained interactions with opponents based on the claims of connected networks of challengers organized on the basis of collective interests and values across national boundaries." See Sidney Tarrow, *Power in Movement: Social Movements and Contentious Politics,* 2d ed. (New York: Cambridge University Press, 1998), 414.

5. The 1998 Ecuadoran administration under Jamil Mahuad experienced a "state of emergency" due to economic and social duress and has stalled funding for many government programs. See Melina Selverston, ed., "Coalition Office News," in *Amazon Update* 41 (Coalition for Amazonian Peoples and Their Environment, November 15, 1998), 1.

6. Material resources include $25,000 from RAN for the April 1992 march and a $2 million grant from the European Union and IBIS Denmark to create a sustainable development program in the region.

Afro-Brazilians
Poverty without Protest

Pamela L. Burke and Ted Robert Gurr

Brazilians of African descent are a large and disadvantaged ethnoclass who have never organized in support of a common political agenda. This sketch documents their status and suggests why most have acquiesced to it.

THE EIGHTY-TWO MILLION Afro-Brazilians (1998 estimate) are the largest group of African descent outside the continent of Africa and one of the two most numerous groups in the Minorities at Risk study. Social and economic discrimination are widespread, and the group is underrepresented in electoral politics. Yet the salience of collective identity is surprisingly low. Despite rapid and effective political mobilization of indigenous peoples in Latin America and of African Americans in North America, mobilization and collective action by Afro-Brazilian organizations are virtually nil.

IDENTITY AND DISADVANTAGE

Brazil's census report by the Instituto Brasileiro de Geografia e Estatistica (IBGE) identifies five categories of racial and ethnic background—white, black, yellow, brown, and indigenous. Individuals of African ancestry may check the category black or brown. In common discourse those of mixed racial heritage are referred to as *mulattos* or *morenos*. Of the total population the IBGE reports that 5.6 percent, or about 9.5 million, are black and 42.8 percent, or about 72.7 million, are brown.[1] However, social prejudice favors light-skinned features over dark.[2] The IBGE has reported incidents of people from families of mixed racial heritage who check "white" rather than the brown or black category. Thus, no exact count of persons of part-African descent can be determined. This sketch defines Afro-Brazilians as all those who self-identify on the census as black or brown.

Most Afro-Brazilians are poor and undereducated by comparison with Brazilians of European descent. Almost 90 percent live in urban areas, but only 22 percent have completed a middle-school level of education. Moreover, 32 percent of all Afro-Brazilians are illiterate, compared with 14 percent of the white population. The average Afro-Brazilian male worker earns 48 percent as much as his white counterpart, and the average female worker earns 46 percent as much as her white counterpart. Disparities also are evident in the penal system, which convicts more Afro-Brazilians than white citizens. Of five hundred recent criminal cases in São Paulo, 60 percent of whites who could afford their own attorney were acquitted, but only 27 percent of blacks who could do the same were acquitted.[3]

Although inequalities are pervasive, social discrimination is prohibited by law. Legislation passed in 1989 that prohibited discrimination based on race was amended in 1997, adding jail terms for the "incitement of racial discrimination or prejudice and the dissemination of racially offensive symbols and epithets." However, there have been no official reports of convictions based on the new law.[4]

History of an Ethnoclass

Beginning in the 1530s tens of thousands of African slaves were brought to Brazil by Portuguese colonizers to work the sugar plantations. The slave trade was ended in 1831; however, according to Abdias do Nascimento (note 2), informal trading of former slaves persisted into the late nineteenth century. The institution of slavery was officially abolished in 1888.

It was several generations after abolition that the first interest groups were formed by Afro-Brazilians. In 1925 some African residents of São Paulo called for the creation of a racial pressure group and two years later founded the Palmares Civic Center, which sponsored meetings and lectures and campaigned against legislation that prohibited blacks from enlisting in the state militia. However, this movement failed due to limited participation and internal squabbling.[5]

The 1930s witnessed a surge of interest in Brazil's racial diversity. In 1930, under the leadership of President Getulio Vargas, a program of "racial democracy" was instituted that celebrated the mixed racial origins of the Brazilian people. In 1931, Arlindo Veiga dos Santos took the lead in founding the Brazilian Black Front, devoted to fighting the injustices experienced by persons of

African descent. Like other Afro-Brazilian movements, then and later, it had its roots in the emergent black, urban middle class and reflected their interests more than those of impoverished blacks or the black majority population of the northeast. The movement spread throughout the south of the country, and in 1933, dos Santos ran unsuccessfully for the São Paulo city council. The Front ceased activities in 1937 when all political parties were banned by the Vargas administration.

In 1951 the Brazilian government passed the Afonso Arinos Law prohibiting racial discrimination. In 1964 a military-backed revolt ousted the ineffective populist government of João Goulart and replaced it with an autocratic regime that banned most political parties and movements and governed until 1985. This period coincided with the peak of civil rights activism among African Americans in the United States, which might otherwise have inspired a similar movement among Afro-Brazilians. Afro-Brazilian activism during the years of authoritarian rule took nonpolitical forms. The Unified Black Movement (MNU), founded in 1978, held meetings with the goal of raising Afro-Brazilian consciousness but in the 1990s had only six thousand members. Another example is Olodum, founded in 1979 as a musical group, which has developed free education, arts, and theater programs for Afro-Brazilians. Its most famous program, however, is its contribution to Carnival, Brazil's celebration of its African history.

THE EFFECTS OF DEMOCRATIZATION

The restoration of democracy in 1985 provided a supportive environment for expression of Afro-Brazilian cultural and political interests. Democratization in Bolivia and Ecuador in the 1980s had a catalytic effect on the mobilization of indigenous peoples, as illustrated in sketches elsewhere in this book. Not in Brazil: no broad-based political organization has emerged. As one consequence Afro-Brazilians are substantially underrepresented in political offices, military offices, and police positions. Since 1983, an estimated twenty-nine Afro-Brazilians have been elected to the National Congress, including Benedita da Silva, who in 1986 became the first Afro-Brazilian woman member of the Congress.[6] Afro-Brazilian members make up about 5 percent of the 503-member Congress, compared with their 47 percent share of the country's population, and some of them are reluctant to be associated with Afro-Brazilian issues.

In the absence of political activism by Afro-Brazilians, efforts to address their disadvantages have been mainly top-down. Henrique Cardoso, who won the 1995 presidential election, campaigned with a theme of racial equality, noting that he was of mixed racial ancestry. In May 1996 Cardoso announced a broad human rights policy that included the African population. Under his administration the Brazilian government has issued reports on racial discrimination and instituted measures aimed at combating the problem. In November 1996 Cardoso also took the symbolic step of meeting with Afro-Brazilian leaders in response to a thirty-thousand-person march honoring Zumbi, a seventeenth-century Afro-Brazilian. Another sign of change occurred in 1996 when the citizens of São Paulo, Brazil's largest city, elected their first Afro-Brazilian mayor. And recently the Afro-Brazilian members of Congress, although from different political parties, have established an informal caucus to discuss Afro-Brazilian questions.

THE MYTH OF RACIAL DEMOCRACY

The Brazilian political system affords opportunities for Afro-Brazilians, but they have not used those opportunities to mobilize a broad-based movement with an Afro-Brazilian agenda. Rather, to the extent that there is an Afro-Brazilian political agenda, it is pursued within existing political parties. The lack of collective identity and the perception of common interests is due, most fundamentally, to the way in which race is perceived in Brazilian society. There is no sharp social divide between black and white as there is in North America, no history of racial segregation. Most Brazilians accept what Anthony Marx calls "the persistent myth of racial democracy." Those of African descent may claim the identity of black or brown, and at times white, and indeed are encouraged to cross over racial categories. This creates a fluid identity rather than one that supports the emergence of a broad, ethnically based movement with common vision and goals. The weakness of collective identity, combined with discriminatory social and economic practices that are subtle rather than overt, has divided the Afro-Brazilian population rather than united it. As Benedita da Silva observes, appeals to racial identity and interests have little political effect. "In Brazil, it doesn't help to use race; the identity is not strong. . . . Even blacks say we have no racism. . . . [They say] we are poor, not because we are black. . . . In my campaign it was the intellectuals who raised the question of race."[7]

From the theoretical perspective of the Minorities at Risk study, Brazil's lack of a substantial Afro-Brazilian political movement illustrates the importance of coherent identity, common goals, and political mobilization as the basis for political movements and organizations. From the perspective of public policy, it illustrates the stabilizing effects of the myth of racial nondiscrimination. If most people, including disadvantaged minorities, believe that ethnicity does not matter, the political consequence is that truly it does *not* matter.

NOTES

The first author is a Latin American specialist who prepared profiles of Latin American groups for the Minorities at Risk project in 1994–95. She received her doctorate from the University of Maryland's Department of Government and Politics in 1999 and is on the Politics and Geography faculty at Coastal Carolina University. The second author directs the Minorities at Risk project.

1. The percentages are from the Instituto Brasileiro de Geografia e Estatistica (IBGE) report on the 1991 census applied here to the U.S. Census Bureau's 1998 country population estimate of 169,806,000.

2. Abdias do Nascimento, *O Negro revoltado* (Brazil: Editora Nova Frontera, 1982).

3. Data from *Human Rights Practices for 1998 Report: Brazil* (Washington, D.C.: U.S. Department of State, February 1999).

4. *Human Rights Practices,* 19.

5. George Reid Andrews, *Blacks and Whites in São Paulo Brazil: 1888–1988* (Madison, Wis.: University of Wisconsin Press, 1991).

6. Ollie Johnson, "Racial Representation and Brazilian Politics: Black Members of the National Congress, 1983–1999," *Journal of Interamerican Studies and World Affairs* 40, no. 4 (1998): 103.

7. Anthony W. Marx, *Making Race and Nation: A Comparison of the United States, South Africa, and Brazil* (Cambridge: Cambridge University Press, 1998), quotation from da Silva on p. 259.

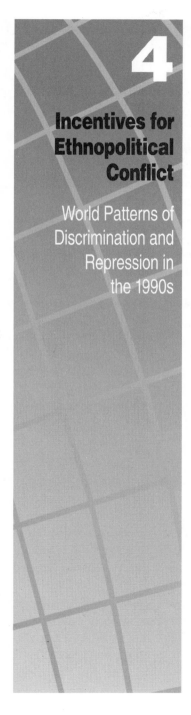

4

Incentives for Ethnopolitical Conflict

World Patterns of Discrimination and Repression in the 1990s

FOR DISADVANTAGED GROUPS, invidious treatment and repression are primary incentives for ethnopolitical action. Discrimination against members of ethnic groups contributes to poverty, powerlessness, and resentment of advantaged groups. When governments use repression to maintain ethnic stratification and to deter organized resistance, they sharpen people's desires for redress and revenge. As proposed in chapter 3, discrimination and repression increase the strength of most peoples' identification with their kindred and motivate them to seek collective remedies. Skillful leaders build on these psychological dispositions to mobilize support for new and renewed campaigns of protest and ethnorebellion.

The first part of this chapter looks at evidence on global and regional patterns of economic, political, and cultural discrimination, the second section at some consequences of discrimination. The third section reports on strategies of state repression in the decade from 1986 to 1995 and some of their consequences.

World Patterns of Economic, Political, and Cultural Discrimination in the 1990s

Of the 275 communal groups covered in the Minorities at Risk survey in the mid-1990s, all but 33 were affected by discrimination based on their culture, ethnicity, or beliefs. The exceptions include politically advantaged groups like the Alawites in Syria and the Tutsis in Burundi and Rwanda (after they regained power in 1994) plus autonomy-seeking peoples like the Quebecois in Canada and German-speakers in the Italian Tyrol who do not now experience any economic, political, or cultural disadvantages—according to the criteria used in the Minorities project.

In 1994–95, 177 groups were disadvantaged economically and 201 were disadvantaged politically because of past or present discrimination. Cultural discrimination affected a smaller proportion, 114 groups.[1] Two questions are addressed here: In what regions was discrimination most severe? And with what prospects for improvement? The global trend in the 1990s, as shown in chapter 5, is toward policies of nondiscrimination. But the data also suggest that the malign consequences of past discrimination are deeply resistant to change.

In the Minorities study *group discrimination* refers to *political, economic, and cultural restrictions that are invidiously imposed on members of ethnic, religious, and other communal minorities as a matter of public policy or social practice.* This working definition differs from that used in the International Convention on the Elimination of All Forms of Discrimination (1965) in two respects. The convention defines racial discrimination as "any distinction, exclusion or preference based on race, colour, descent, or national or ethnic origin which has the purpose or effect of nullifying or impairing the recognition, enjoyment or exercise, on an equal footing, of human rights and fundamental freedoms in the political, economic, social, cultural or any other fields of public life."[2] The working definition used here focuses on discrimination as it affects collectivities, not only their individual members, and it includes discrimination based on peoples' culture and religious beliefs in addition to race, descent, nationality, and ethnicity.[3] A number of aspects of the working definition need elaboration.

First, restrictions are "invidious" if they are specific to group members and not to others in a society. A societal standard of comparison is used to judge the presence of group discrimination, not a universal one. For example, if religious observance is denied for all people in a society, this is not discrimination —though it is a violation of a widely held principle of human rights. But if one group's observance of religion is selectively restricted, or if the economic and political activities of adherents of one faith are restricted but not those of others, this constitutes discrimination.

The Minorities project uses a local standard of comparison partly in response to critics from Asia, Africa, and the Islamic world who question the use of what they claim are Western standards of human rights to judge their own societies. Even if they reject Western standards, they can be held accountable for failures to apply common standards to all peoples in their own societies. Moreover, from an analytic point of view, resentment against locally imposed inequalities is probably a more potent incentive to political action than resentment about local failures to observe abstract international principles.

Second, group discrimination may be the result of either public policy or social practice, or both. Explicitly discriminatory policies include segregation as practiced in the southern United States toward African Americans until the 1960s and the restrictions imposed by the government of Turkey on the expression of Kurdish cultural and political interests.[4] Officially sanctioned policies of discrimination have become gradually less common in most world regions since the 1960s, due in part to international promotion of uniform standards of human rights and social justice. Group discrimination as a matter of social practice nonetheless is widespread and often persists despite public policies that guarantee freedom from discrimination. In most countries in the Americas, for example, indigenous peoples are guaranteed the full protection of laws, and in some states they have gained recognition of collective rights. Yet when people of indigenous speech, dress, and behavior interact with members of European-American societies, they repeatedly encounter prejudices and social barriers whose net effect is to restrict indigenous peoples' access to education, public services, and good jobs and to limit their participation in political life.

Third, discrimination may affect the attainment of a group's collective goals more than the well-being of its individual members. Discrimination and repression against Kurds in Iraq do not reflect widespread Arab aversion to Kurdish language and culture; rather, they are based mainly on the state's opposition to the Kurds' rebellious pursuit of political autonomy. The Hungarian minorities in Romania and Slovakia reportedly encounter little day-to-day discrimination; instead, they live and work within politically imposed restrictions on instruction in Hungarian and use of their language in dealings with local and national governments.[5] In most societies, though, individual and collective discrimination reinforce each other. Individual acts of discrimination have cumulative effects on collectivities, and policies that restrict group rights are widely felt and resented by individuals who identify with those collectivities.

Fourth, inequalities among groups are not necessarily the result of discrimination. Some economic and political inequalities among ethnic and other communal groups in contemporary societies are the cumulative result of malign or neglectful social practices with deep historical roots. Others may not be the result of deliberate agency at all but simply become evident when traditional peoples on the periphery of modernizing societies are drawn into closer contact with more powerful and technologically proficient groups. The indigenous, or "tribal," peoples who live in the uplands of the Indian subcontinent and Southeast Asia are impoverished on virtually all indicators of material well-being compared with the dominant groups in their societies. Outside observers may reasonably debate whether their economic disadvantage is due to (1) the fact that most live in remote areas lacking in educational or wage-labor opportunities, (2) a lack of "cultural capital" for taking advantage of opportunities, (3) debilitating cultural and political conflicts, or (4) pervasive discrimination by the dominant society. The answer probably lies in the complex interaction of all four factors. The Minorities project treats as group discrimination all instances in which a people's disadvantages are judged (by informed observers) to be a consequence of discriminatory treatment, in whole or part, past or present.

Fifth, discrimination often is a manifestation of historically rooted cycles of conflict. Most "minorities" were once autonomous people who were colonized, conquered, or otherwise forcefully subordinated by more powerful peoples and states.[6] Many groups resisted subordination; their resistance justified the imposition of restrictions; the restrictions laid the basis for persistent inequalities. Cycles of resistance and repression can be restarted whenever political opportunities arise, as they do, for example, whenever domestic or international power alignments shift. When an ethnic group resumes a dormant rebellion, repression usually is ratcheted up, leaving a residue of new, more discriminatory policies and practices that often provide justification for future rebellions.

Finally, the Minorities study includes advantaged as well as disadvantaged minorities. Some advantaged minorities have a disproportionate share of political power and use it to protect their collective interests. The risk is that they will be displaced by rival groups and become subject to retaliatory restrictions in turn. This is one of the alternative paths to discriminatory policies, one for which a number of African examples can be cited. Kikuyu politicians dominated the Kenyan state and used it to their collective advantage until 1978, but since then they have been displaced and subjected to increasing restrictions by Kalenjin political leaders and their allies. Another kind of advantaged minority is typified by the so-called overseas Chinese communities in Malaysia, Indonesia, and other Southeast Asian countries, most of whom have relative economic advantages but are subject to countervailing political, and sometimes cultural, restrictions imposed on them by dominant majorities. The sketches of Chinese in Malaysia (pp. 133–137) and of Kenya (pp. 261–265) provide more detailed illustrations. There is an inherent potential for conflict in all situations in which a dominant communal group uses state power to maintain its advantages or to impose disadvantages on other groups.

The global and regional incidence of economic, political, and cultural dis-crimination in 1994–95 is summarized in tables 4.1 through 4.3. The indica-tors used to rate discrimination and the specific results are summarized in the text. The codes assigned to a dozen groups described in the sketches through-out this book are used to illustrate the tables. Four other groups are also used to illustrate the tables but are not discussed in detail: the Francophones of Quebec, African Americans, Arab citizens of Israel, and South African Zulus. Some groups cited in the tables face little or no discrimination, for example, the Gagauz in Moldova and the Russians in Ukraine.[7] Others, such as Tibetans in China, Muslims in India, and the indigenous peoples of Latin America, are subject to discrimination in almost all spheres of life. Most others experi-ence differential discrimination, low or none in some realms and medium to high in others.

ECONOMIC DISCRIMINATION

Roma in some Eastern European countries have been driven out of their homes by villagers or involuntarily resettled by local authorities. Virtually all in-digenous peoples in the Americas have high infant mortality rates due in part to limited pre- and post-natal health care. In Vietnam a Communist Party decree of 1982 excluded ethnic Chinese (the "Hoa people") from various occu-pations, including the armed forces.[8] In Sri Lanka university admission poli-cies have been tilted against Tamils. In Burundi Tutsis have blocked Hutu entry into the armed forces, in part by imposing a "girth-by-height" require-ment on recruits. In South Africa under apartheid nonwhites were excluded from most skilled and professional occupations. These are instances of the diverse kinds of practices and policies that create, maintain, or reinforce mate-rial inequalities between dominant and minority groups.

In the Minorities project groups are said to be subject to economic dis-crimination to the extent that their members are or have been systematically limited in access to desirable economic goods, conditions, or positions that are open to other groups in their society. Two dimensions of economic discrimi-nation are distinguished and compared across groups: first is the *extent* of discriminatory practices toward them; second is the *severity* of their relative economic disadvantage. Because precise data on the economic status of minori-ties are seldom available, we devised the following categorical scales to codify information about the status of each group so that general comparisons could be made across groups and world regions. Note that both scales also have a "none" or zero category, not shown here.

Extent of Economic Discrimination

Low 1 = Substantial poverty and underrepresentation in desirable occupations due to historical marginality, neglect, or restrictions. Current
public policies are designed to improve the group's relative material
well-being.

2 = Substantial poverty and underrepresentation due to historical marginality, neglect, or restrictions. No social practice of deliberate
exclusion. No formal exclusion from economic opportunities. No
public policies aimed at improving the group's material well-being.

3 = Substantial poverty and underrepresentation due to prevailing
social practice by dominant groups. Formal public policies toward
the group are neutral or, if positive, inadequate to offset active and
widespread practices of discrimination.

High 4 = Public policies (formal exclusion or recurring repression or both)
substantially restrict the group's economic opportunities in contrast with other groups.

Severity of Economic Disadvantage

Low 1 = Group is slightly disadvantaged/somewhat below the societal
average.

2 = Group is substantially disadvantaged by comparison with other
societal groups.

High 3 = Group is very seriously disadvantaged, the poorest in society.

In 1994–95 we find that 177 of the 275 groups experienced some degree
of economic discrimination. The discriminatory burden was greatest for the
111 groups at the highest two levels of severity, categories 3 and 4 in the first
part of table 4.1. World regions differ substantially in the relative severity of
economic discrimination. Comparisons in the second part of table 4.1 show
the number of groups subject to low and high economic discrimination in each
region. Disadvantages were by far the greatest in Latin America and the
Caribbean, mainly due to prevailing social practices of economic discrimination that maintain and reinforce the poverty of indigenous peoples and
those of African descent. Few formal discriminatory barriers exist anywhere
in Latin America, and Latins of European descent often express pride that
they are "color-blind." But in fact indigenous peoples and blacks are consistently the poorest and least empowered peoples in these societies. It is likely

that public denial of responsibility for ethnic inequality has contributed to its persistence.

Disadvantages in Asia and the Middle East approximate the global average. In Asia economic discrimination is due mainly to invidious treatment of "hill tribes" and other indigenous peoples. In the Middle East it is mainly a consequence of officially sanctioned discrimination (political and cultural as well as economic) against religious and ethnoreligious minorities like Arabs in Israel, Copts in Egypt, Baha'is in Iran, and Ahmadis in Pakistan. The lowest mean level of economic discrimination is found in the postcommunist states, where it is a legacy of the policies of socialist states that sought to equalize economic opportunities among national and minority peoples.

POLITICAL DISCRIMINATION

The German federal government until the late 1990s imposed stringent legal and procedural barriers to citizenship on Turkish immigrants. In Turkey governments have repeatedly banned and restricted political parties that sought to represent Kurdish interests in municipal and parliamentary elections. Afro-Brazilians make up more than 40 percent of the country's population but hold less than 5 percent of seats in the national congress. When Fiji's 1987 elections were won by an East Indian–dominated coalition, the military ousted the government, abrogated the country's constitution, and established a new one that ensured Fijian political dominance. Disappointed at the outcome of Angola's 1992 elections, Jonas Savimbi pulled his Ovimbundu-based UNITA party out of the peace pact that was supposed to have ended Angola's long civil war. In retaliation, government supporters hunted down and massacred more than a thousand of his followers in the capital city of Luanda. These are all instances of discriminatory restrictions on political rights and participation of minorities.

This is the general definition used by the Minorities project: ethnic and communal groups are subject to political discrimination to the extent that their members are or have been systematically limited in the exercise of political rights or access to political positions by comparison with other groups in their societies. As with economic discrimination, two dimensions of political discrimination are identified and compared across groups. The first is the *extent* of politically discriminatory practices, indexed in the same way as the extent of economic discrimination. The second is the *severity* of a group's relative political disadvantage, indexed using a list of specific political rights and activities that may be infringed. The two elements can be analyzed separately or combined in a single composite indicator of political discrimination. Information about the political status of each group is coded using the following scales.

Table 4.1. Economic Discrimination in 1994–95 with Numbers and Examples of Groups at Each Level of Discrimination and Details for Groups in Each World Region

A. Global Distribution of Groups

Category	Number	Percentage	Examples
0 = No economic discrimination	92	33.4	Quebecois in Canada, Gagauz in Moldova, Russians in Ukraine, Chinese in Malaysia, Copts in Egypt, Kikuyu in Kenya
1 = Past neglect or restrictions, remedial policies	38	13.8	Turks in Germany, African Americans in the United States
2 = Past neglect or restrictions, no remedial policies	28	10.2	Hungarians in Slovakia
3 = Prevailing social practice of discrimination	83	30.2	Roma (Eastern Europe), Hutus in Burundi, Afro-Brazilians, indigenous peoples in Latin America
4 = Public policies of exclusion or repression	28	10.2	Tibetans in China, Sri Lankan Tamils, Arabs in Israel
Could not be coded	6	2.2	

B. Regional Distribution of Groups

World Region	None (0)	Low (1, 2)	High (3, 4)
Western democracies and Japan (31 groups)	4	14	12
Eastern Europe and the newly independent states (59 groups)	32	7	18
East, Southeast, and South Asia (59 groups)	16	18	25
North Africa and the Middle East (27 groups)	10	7	10
Africa south of the Sahara (67 groups)	28	17	19
Latin America and the Caribbean (32 groups)	2	3	27
Global totals	92	66	111

Note: The categories of discrimination are described more fully in the text. Codings of a cross-section of sixteen groups are used as examples in this and the following tables: African Americans in the United States, Quebecois in Canada (Francophones only), Turks in Germany, Hungarians in Slovakia, Roma in Eastern Europe (median values), Gagauz in Moldova, Russians in Ukraine, Tibetans in China, Chinese in Malaysia, Sri Lankan Tamils, Copts in Egypt, Arab citizens of Israel, Hutus in Burundi, Kikuyu in Kenya, Afro–Brazilians, and indigenous peoples in Latin America (median values). Most of these groups are described in the sketches elsewhere in this book.

Extent of Political Discrimination

Low 1 = Substantial underrepresentation in political office holding or participation or both, due to historical neglect or restrictions. Current public policies are designed to improve the group's political status.

2 = Substantial underrepresentation due to historical neglect or restrictions. No social practice of deliberate exclusion. No formal exclusion. No evidence of protective or remedial public policies.

3 = Substantial underrepresentation due to prevailing social practice by dominant groups. Formal public policies toward the group are neutral or, if positive, inadequate to offset active and widespread practices of discrimination.

High 4 = Public policies (formal exclusion or recurring repression or both) substantially restrict the group's political participation in contrast with other groups.

Severity of Political Restrictions

Each of the political rights and activities listed below is coded for the extent to which the activity is restricted:

0 = The activity is not significantly restricted for any group members.

1 = The activity is slightly restricted for most or all group members or sharply restricted for some of them.

2 = The activity is prohibited or sharply restricted for most or all group members by comparison with other groups.

Restrictions on freedom of expression

Restrictions on free movement or place of residence

Restrictions on rights in judicial proceedings

Restrictions on political organization

Restrictions on voting

Restrictions on recruitment to the police and military

Restrictions on access to the civil service

Restrictions on attainment of high office

Nearly three-quarters of the 275 groups experienced political discrimination and restrictions in 1994–95, most often due to prevailing social practice (29 percent), somewhat less often because of explicit public policies (20 percent). As shown in the lower part of table 4.2, eight of thirty-one minorities in the Western democracies and Japan are subject to high levels of political discrimination. The targets are mainly immigrant groups, such as Turks in Germany and immigrant workers in Switzerland, and take the form of barriers to citizenship. More than one-third of the minorities in postcommunist states face serious political discrimination, but the groups affected are mainly in the Yugoslav successor states. Political discrimination is most severe in Latin America, the Middle East, and Asia, for reasons similar to those to which we attributed economic discrimination in the preceding section.

Careful comparison of tables 4.1 and 4.2 shows that political and economic discrimination in Africa south of the Sahara are lower than elsewhere in the global south, despite the severe disadvantages imposed on a few groups such as southerners in Sudan, Hutus in Burundi, and, until recently, black South Africans. In most African societies group discrimination is a consequence of rivalries among communal contenders, rivalries that often began during the colonial period or the struggle for independence. The groups that are disadvantaged in these rivalries typically have limited access to political positions and the material benefits associated with office holding but seldom are subject to widespread political or economic restrictions that affect most members of the group. The Hutus in Burundi, the subject of a sketch on pages 188–194, are an exception to this generalization. A more common pattern is that in which one generation's disadvantaged communal group wrests advantages from its rivals at a later stage and uses political power to redress old communal grievances. The disadvantages of the Kikuyu and Luo in contemporary Kenya are the result of this kind of reversal at the hands of the once-marginalized, now-dominant Kalenjin and their allies (sketch on pp. 261–265). The main challenge that group discrimination poses for most African states is how to restrain successful contenders from imposing crippling disadvantages on their rivals that could precipitate civil and communal warfare.

CULTURAL DISCRIMINATION

Muslim girls attending French secondary schools have been prohibited from wearing their traditional head scarves. Principals of Hungarian-language secondary schools in Slovakia have been dismissed for not speaking Slovak at Hungarian teachers' meetings. Until the 1990s the Egyptian government rarely authorized Coptic Christian congregations to build or repair churches. Bolivians of European descent once expected *indios* to walk on the opposite side of the street so as not to offend the sensibilities of "decent people." These are instances of the myriad ways in which dominant groups have sought to impose their

Table 4.2. Political Discrimination in 1994–95 with Numbers and Examples of Groups at Each Level of Discrimination and Details for Each World Region

A. Global Distribution of Groups

Category	Number	Percentage	Examples
0 = No political discrimination	74	26.9	Quebecois in Canada, Russians in Ukraine
1 = Past neglect or restrictions, remedial policies	39	14.2	African Americans in the United States, Gagauz in Moldova, Hutus in Burundi
2 = Past neglect or restrictions, no remedial policies	26	9.4	Hungarians in Slovakia
3 = Prevailing social practice of political discrimination	80	29.1	Roma (Eastern Europe), Chinese in Malaysia, Arabs in Israel, Muslims in India, indigenous peoples in Latin America, Afro-Brazilians
4 = Public policies of exclusion or repression	55	20.1	Turks in Germany, Tibetans in China, Copts in Egypt, Kikuyu in Kenya
Could not be coded	1	0.4	

B. Regional Distribution of Groups

World Region	None (0)	Low (1, 2)	High (3, 4)
Western democracies and Japan (31 groups)	13	10	8
Eastern Europe and the newly independent states (59 groups)	26	12	21
East, Southeast, and South Asia (59 groups)	7	16	36
North Africa and the Middle East (27 groups)	7	2	17
Africa south of the Sahara (67 groups)	20	19	28
Latin America and the Caribbean (32 groups)	1	6	25
Global totals	74	65	135

Note: See note to table 4.1.

own cultural values on minorities. Such restrictions often seem petty, but symbolically their effects can be far-reaching and enduring.

In the Minorities study, groups are subject to cultural discrimination to the extent that their members are restricted in the pursuit of their cultural interests or expression of their customs and values. As is the case with economic and political discrimination, cultural restrictions may be the result of either public policy or social practice. Restrictions imposed by public policy generally are more extensive than those imposed by social practice, but no separate indicator of *extent* is used in this study. Instead, a single indicator of *severity* of cultural restrictions is constructed, indexed by reference to a list of specific cultural rights and activities that may be infringed.

Severity of Cultural Restrictions

Each of the cultural practices listed below is coded for the extent to which the activity is restricted using these four weights. The severity of restrictions for the group is indexed by summing the weights.

0 = The activity is not significantly restricted.

1 = The activity is restricted by widespread but informal social practice, for example, by job discrimination against people who observe group customs or use the group's language.

2 = The activity is somewhat restricted by public policy.

3 = The activity is prohibited or sharply restricted by public policy.

Restrictions on observance of the group's religion(s)

Restrictions on speaking or publishing in the group's language or dialect

Restrictions on instruction in the group's language

Restrictions on celebration of group holidays, ceremonies, cultural events

Restrictions on dress, appearance, behavior

Restrictions on marriage or family life

Restrictions on organizations that promote the group's cultural interests

Interpretations are needed to code these categories. For example, public restrictions that apply to all citizens because they are necessary for the common good, such as the requirement that families have only one child, or that all children be vaccinated, are not "restrictions" even if they violate the cultural norms of the communal group under study. By a similar logic, lack of public support for group cultural activities is not "restriction" unless public support *is* provided for similar activities by other groups. For example, if a group seeks but is denied public funds for elementary instruction in its language, even though funding is provided for instruction in the majority language, this is an instance of "sharp restriction." If a group is given funding for elementary instruction but limitations are placed on the language of instruction or examination at higher levels (examples include the Chinese in Malaysia and Hungarians in Slovakia), the policy is coded as "somewhat restrictive."

Sixty-five groups encounter medium to high cultural discrimination, as shown in table 4.3 They are disproportionately concentrated in Latin America and the Middle East: half the Latin American groups and twelve of twenty-seven Middle Eastern minorities face medium or high cultural discrimination. Several such groups are the subject of sketches in this book, including the Copts in Egypt, indigenous peoples in Ecuador, and Afro-Brazilians. Cultural discrimination is on average lowest in Africa south of the Sahara, mainly because cultural differences among groups in most African countries are minor and, except in countries that have both Islamic and Christian communities, have seldom figured in intergroup conflict. The sketches of Hutus in Burundi and Kikuyu and others in Kenya illustrate this point: these groups are subject to substantial economic and political discrimination but no cultural restrictions. Cultural discrimination is equally low in the Western democracies, but for different reasons. Restrictive practices once were prevalent in heterogeneous Western societies—Roman Catholics and Jews were targets of public and private hostility, native Australian and American children were sent to boarding schools where they were forbidden to use indigenous languages. But these practices and the prejudices that animated them have been reduced and discredited by several decades of public policies that protect and promote equal rights, pluralism, and in some cases multiculturalism.

The Impact of Group Discrimination

Some of the consequences of discrimination against minorities are readily measured; most are not. These are some spheres of collective life in which pervasive consequences are evident and, in principle, subject to comparative assessment.

MATERIAL INEQUALITIES

Groups subject to discrimination usually are poorer and subject to greater demographic stress than others. There is extensive evidence (not examined

Table 4.3. Cultural Discrimination in 1994–95 with Numbers and Examples of Groups at Each Level of Discrimination and Details for Each World Region

A. Global Distribution of Groups

Category	Number	Percentage	Examples
No cultural discrimination (index score 0)	158	57.4	Quebecois in Canada, African Americans in the United States, Hutus in Burundi
Limited cultural discrimination (index scores 1–2)	51	18.6	Turks in Germany, Russians in Ukraine, Gagauz in Moldova, Chinese in Malaysia, Arabs in Israel, Kikuyu in Kenya
Medium cultural discrimination (index scores 3–5)	41	14.9	Roma (Eastern Europe), Muslims in India, indigenous peoples in Latin America, Afro–Brazilians
High cultural discrimination (index scores 6+)	24	8.7	Hungarians in Slovakia, Copts in Egypt, Tibetans in China
Could not be coded	1	0.4	

B. Regional Distribution of Groups

World Region	None (0)	Limited (1, 2)	Medium or High (3–5, 6+)	Mean Score
Western democracies and Japan (31 groups)	22	5	4	0.71
Eastern Europe and the newly independent states (59 groups)	28	16	15	2.00
East, Southeast, and South Asia (59 groups)	32	13	14	1.85
North Africa and the Middle East (27 groups)	12	2	12	3.27
Africa south of the Sahara (67 groups)	53	9	5	0.75
Latin America and the Caribbean (32 groups)	11	6	15	2.50
Global totals and mean score	158	51	65	1.70

Note: See note to table 4.1.

Peoples versus States

Table 4.4. Economic Discrimination in 1994–95 and
Relative Severity of Group Material Disadvantage

Level of Discrimination	Number of Groups	Extent of Relative Material Disadvantage (percentages of groups)		
		None or Slight	Substantial	Severe
None	89	100	0	0
Past neglect, remedial policies	37	49	30	22
Past neglect, no remedial policies	25	40	20	40
Prevailing social practice	84	10	43	46
Public policies of exclusion or repression	25	8	48	44

Note: Includes 260 groups with coded data on both variables. Rows do not necessarily add to 100 percent because of rounding errors.

here) of a near-universal association among poverty, high birth rates, and high infant mortality rates. Table 4.4 provides comparative evidence on the relation between the severity of economic discrimination in 1994–95 and the extent of material disadvantage for the 275 groups in the survey. The table shows that as severity of discrimination increases, the extent of a group's collective economic disadvantage also increases: the correlation between the two indicators is 0.79.[9]

Group poverty tends to be reproduced over time by mechanisms that are reasonably well understood in advanced industrial societies. Children growing up in poor communities usually have less access to good schooling and must travel further, in social and geographic terms, to get the jobs and careers that enable them to raise their own children out of poverty. Remedial public policies, such as improved educational opportunities and affirmative action programs for ethnoclasses, may eventually erode the cycle of poverty. Public policies and pervasive social practices of economic discrimination, however, reproduce poverty in the future. The global survey identified 111 groups subject to these more severe forms of discrimination in the mid-1990s (see table 4.1), including most indigenous peoples in the Americas, the Roma in European countries, and Muslim minorities in most European societies, including the Kosovar Albanians in the former Yugoslavia. The accompanying sketches illustrate some effects of severe economic discrimination on the Roma in Eastern Europe (pp. 143–150) and the Hutus in Burundi.

LACK OF EMPOWERMENT

Political discrimination means, by definition, that minorities encounter restrictions on political participation and access to decision-making positions. Table 4.5 provides details on the specific restrictions associated with the levels of political discrimination summarized in table 4.2. Voting rights and freedom of expression are least likely to be restricted, affecting less than one-eighth of all groups, whereas restrictions on access to higher political office affect more than one-third of the 274 groups for which we have coded information.

Groups at the highest two levels of political discrimination—through pervasive social practice or deliberate public policies—are much more likely than others to experience each of the eight types of restriction. Among the fifty-five groups that were subject to political discrimination as a matter of official policy in the mid-1990s, more than half were subject to invidious restrictions on political rights and recruitment to security forces. However, they were somewhat less likely to be barred from recruitment to the civil service and higher political office. This seeming inconsistency in public policy is mainly a reflection of the practice, common in stratified plural societies, of recruiting able and compliant representatives of minorities to public office at the same time that barriers are maintained against political activities by others. For example, the Indonesian government for a long time recruited cooperative East Timorese and Papuans into the regional governments of both provinces at the same time that it restricted and repressed Timorese and Papuan political activists and organizations that were regarded as threats to state security. The militia that terrorized and drove out independence supporters before and after the 1999 UN-monitored referendum in East Timor were recruited in the province.

Political restrictions affect two different dimensions of people's lives, their participation in political life and their access to public positions. Restrictions on political participation are most pervasive in Latin America, Asia, and the Middle East, as exemplified in the sketches of indigenous peoples in Ecuador, Tibetans, and Egyptian Copts. Restriction of minorities' political rights has two perverse effects. One is to reinforce the invidious cultural differences and material inequalities that distinguish them from majorities; the other is to deny them conventional political means to seek remedies that are open to others. Such restrictions are uncommon in advanced democratic societies (see table 4.2). Minorities' attainment of political rights in Western societies since the 1960s has given their organizations and leaders the means to challenge discrimination in other spheres. But these societies continue to maintain barriers to citizenship for immigrant ethnoclasses such as the Turks in Germany, Maghrebins in France, and Koreans in Japan.

Table 4.5. Types of Political Restrictions Associated with Different Levels of Political Discrimination in 1994–95

Types of Restrictions	Number and Percentage of All Groups Subject to Restriction		Percentage of Groups at Each Level of Political Discrimination Subject to Restriction		
	Number	Percentage	0, 1, or 2 None or Neglect	3 Social Practice	4 Public Policy
Restrictions on freedom of expression	34	12	9	32	50
Restrictions on freedom of movement	5	18	16	32	52
Restrictions on rights in judicial proceedings	42	15	5	36	60
Restrictions on political organizing	70	25	3	37	59
Restrictions on voting rights	36	13	8	22	69
Restrictions on recruitment to military, police	62	23	8	32	60
Restrictions on recruitment to civil service	81	29	9	42	49
Restrictions on access to higher political office	98	36	17	38	45
Number of groups	274		139	80	55

Note: Includes 274 groups with coded information on restrictions and level of political discrimination. The first two columns of data show the numbers and percentages of 274 groups on which restrictions of each type are imposed. The remaining three columns show the percentages of groups at each level of discrimination whose members are subject to restrictions of each type.

Restrictions on access—to the police and military, the civil service, and higher political office—have two kinds of effects that are especially burdensome for minorities in poor and nondemocratic societies. In poor countries the public sector usually is relatively large and often the main source of professional employment. Discriminatory barriers to minority recruitment thus restrict the economic opportunities of individual members of the group and help perpetuate its material disadvantages. The impact of postcolonial discrimination against Hutus in Burundi is illustrative. The second effect is to reduce opportunities to pursue group interests through the military or civilian political hierarchies. It is a fact of political life in many African and some Asian societies that communal groups' leaders use their positions in the military and in governing coalitions to advance collective interests.[10] When some groups are selectively denied access, not only are inequalities perpetuated, but the ground is prepared for opposition movements and potential rebellions. The Eritrean war of independence, civil war in Sudan, and the thus-far-unrecognized secession of Somaliland from the Somali Republic all were preceded by exclusion or marginalization of these groups' leaders from national politics.

CULTURES UNDER SIEGE

The language and lifeways of a minority in a society with a dominant, culturally distinct majority are inevitably under pressure. Of the 275 groups included in this survey, about half speak a common language different from that of the majority, and another quarter speak multiple languages or dialects.[11] For all these linguistically distinct groups, and especially those who speak a single language, its preservation is one of the keys to maintaining the collectivity's viability as a social entity. Communication in a common language helps maintain networks among group members, reinforces the sense of shared identity, and contributes to the perpetuation of social practices and discourse that give life to the group.

In technologically advanced societies, where dense networks of social interaction cut across groups, the pressures to assimilate to the dominant culture and use its language are especially intense. Bilingualism and trilingualism are strategies of compromise in which, typically, linguistically distinct minorities preserve their language for communication in their family and community but are expected to use another language in exchanges with other groups, and sometimes yet another in dealings with public officials.

David Laitin contends, based on substantial comparative evidence, that linguistic diversity is not intrinsically a source of violent interethnic conflict. Probably not, but governments' use of language policies to reinforce invidious distinctions among groups is a recurring source of friction in multilingual societies.[12] Until the early 1990s the Turkish government proscribed all public use of Kurdish, an everyday reminder to Kurds that Turks denied them a separate identity. Slovak nationalist policies aimed at curbing the public use of Hungarian have exacerbated Slovak-Hungarian relations, as illustrated in the sketch on pages 183–187. Restrictions on communication and instruction in a minority's language may contribute to demands for substate autonomy or complete independence, as they have for the Tamils in Sri Lanka. It is worth repeating the prescient observation of a Sinhalese scholar during the 1950s debate over legislation that made Sinhalese the only official language, to the disadvantage of Tamil-speakers: "One language, two nations or two languages, one nation."[13] Sinhalese nationalists prevailed on this and other policies that disadvantaged the Tamils, and the two nations have been at war since 1975. The principle is equally applicable in other countries, especially for national minorities such as the Russians in the post-Soviet successor states and Hungarians in Romania, Ukraine, Slovakia, and the former Yugoslavia—peoples who share a literary and cultural tradition with kindred who control a neighboring state.

Language policy is also related in complex ways to the perpetuation of economic and political disadvantages. The educational opportunities and attainments of impoverished minorities are usually less than those of other groups. The use of their own language in schooling is particularly problematic. If instruction is not permitted at all, minority children's school performance tends to lag behind that of children who speak the dominant or common language. If the minority language is used at elementary but not higher levels, minority students tend to be disadvantaged in access to higher education in the dominant language. If their language is used at all levels, the risk is that university and technical school graduates will be more proficient in their own language than that of dominant groups and therefore will face barriers to employment and perform less effectively than those schooled in the dominant language. There are creative approaches to dealing with these problems, but the underlying principle remains: members of a disadvantaged group who are not fluent in the common or dominant languages in a society are liable to remain disadvantaged across generations.

SOCIAL VICTIMIZATION

Discrimination is commonly associated with high levels of social pathology among the most severely disadvantaged minorities, especially indigenous peoples and ethnoclasses. Examples from the accompanying sketches include the Roma of Eastern Europe, the indigenous peoples of Ecuador, and Afro-

Brazilians. Members of such groups in advanced industrial societies are disproportionately liable to have high infant mortality rates, to be more susceptible to disease, to engage in substance abuse, and to have high rates of arrest and incarceration for offenses against property and person. Members of dominant societies often explain away such victimization as a consequence of culturally or even genetically determined weaknesses. It is more plausible to regard high levels of social victimization as a cumulative and persistent consequence of poverty, powerlessness, and the erosion of group culture. Poverty and powerlessness, when they are reinforced by invidious social practices, reproduce not only themselves but also a range of social pathologies among those who cannot escape.

Repression and Its Legacies

A government's use of force against people who think they have a just cause is likely to inspire fear and caution in the short run, but in the longer run repression provokes resentment and enduring incentives to resist and retaliate. This general argument is outlined in chapter 3. The sketches of Tibetans and of Hutus in Burundi illustrate the ways in which cycles of resistance and repression perpetuate themselves over time.[14] Here we summarize comparative information from the Minorities study on the severity with which governments have responded to ethnopolitical challenges in the recent past.

Ethnopolitical groups that challenge governments with rebellions or large-scale protest campaigns almost always elicit repressive responses. Even if political elites want to reach accommodation, their first priority usually is to reestablish public order. In principle they can use tactical alternatives that range from intensified policing to counterinsurgency techniques. The most extreme response was chosen by the Iraqi regime when, in June 1987, it set in motion the genocidal *al Anfal* campaign against Kurdish civilians. An area encompassing more than a thousand villages was declared a killing zone by the Iraqi defense minister, whose orders concluded with these two points:

- The corps commanders shall carry out sporadic bombardments using artillery, helicopters and aircraft at all times of the day or night, in order to kill the largest number of persons present in those prohibited zones, keeping us informed of the results.

- All persons captured in those villages shall be detained and interrogated by the security services and those between the ages of 15 and 70 shall be executed after any useful information has been obtained from them.[15]

For the Minorities project we developed a scale with seven categories representing different degrees of regime repression. The scale is reproduced here.[16] Note that actions in the highest three categories are strategies that may be taken proactively by government, regardless of whether a group is in open conflict with a government. Actions in categories 1 through 4 are used almost entirely against groups engaged in open conflict with the government.

High Severity

7 = *Genocide and politicide:* sustained campaigns aimed at physical elimination of a substantial proportion of members of a communal group regardless of their combatant or noncombatant status. *Examples:* the *al Anfal* campaign against Iraqi Kurds; systematic killings of Tutsis by militant Hutus in Rwanda in 1994.[17]

6 = *"Dirty war":* substantial numbers of communal group members are the target of arbitrary arrests, executions, and/or sporadic massacres carried out by regular forces, paramilitary units, vigilantes, or death squads. *Examples:* the Russian campaign to suppress rebellion in Chechnya, 1994–96; tactics used by Mali and Niger in response to the first stages of Tuareg rebellions in 1989–94; extrajudicial killings of suspected guerrilla supporters in Guatemala, 1960–94.[18]

5 = *Preemptive control:* policies of proactive control and deterrence such as forced assimilation, confiscation of property, forced resettlement, criminalization of ethnopolitical activities, systematic domestic spying, large-scale arrests and detention of communal activists. *Examples:* Chinese policies in Tibet since the 1950s; Israeli policies toward Palestinians in the Occupied Territories from 1967 to the early 1990s; Iranian policies toward Baha'is since 1979.

4 = *Counterinsurgency:* near-exclusive reliance on military and counterterror operations targeted at communal combatants. *Examples:* Indonesian military tactics used against Papuan rebels in Irian Jaya, 1964 to the early 1990s; Iranian tactics used against Kurdish rebels, 1981–94.

3 = *Counterinsurgency and accommodation:* reliance on coercive means paralleled by constructive efforts at conflict management, for example, cease-fires, negotiations, amnesties, policy reforms, development programs. *Examples:* policies of democratic Spanish governments toward Basque separatists; Mexican policies toward rebels in Chiapas in 1994–96; tactics used by Mali and Niger in the late stages of Tuareg rebellions in 1989–94 (see 6).

2 = *Emergency policing:* reliance on emergency law enforcement means, including the use of military and armed police to patrol affected areas or to control crowds; suspension of due process for purposes of investigation, detention, and/or trial of communal activists. *Examples:* U.S. responses to racial violence, 1965–72; Pakistan's efforts to control communal conflict by Sindhis and Mohajirs in the 1980s and 1990s.

1 = *Conventional policing:* reliance on conventional law enforcement means, including nonviolent crowd control, standard investigative techniques, arrests and trials of communal activists for criminal offenses. *Examples:* France's policies toward Corsican and Basque separatists; Ecuador's policies toward mass protests by indigenous peoples in 1990–94.

This scale was used in Phase III of the Minorities project to code ethnopolitical groups that engaged in major campaigns of protest or rebellions (including campaigns of terrorism) at any time between 1955 and 1995 or that were targets during those years of state policies of genocide, repression, or forced resettlement, whether or not they openly challenged state authorities. The highest level of repression used against each group was coded for three periods: 1955–85, 1986–90, and 1991–95. Some results are summarized in table 4.6.

Almost 60 percent of the 268 groups surveyed were targets of state repression during the period surveyed, 40 percent of them (106) in 1991–95.[19] With a handful of exceptions, repression was a response to ethnopolitical challenges —protest campaigns, terrorism, or rebellion. The exceptions include the Lhotshampas (Nepalese) in Bhutan, Royhinga Muslims in Burma's Arakan state, Baha'is of Iran, and Ache indigenous people of Paraguay, groups that posed no organized challenge to governments when repression began.[20] The most common strategy of repression in the decade from 1986 to 1995 was counterinsurgency, used against 50 groups. In all but eleven of these ethnopolitical conflicts governments followed dual strategies of "fight and talk," waging war on the one hand and offering negotiations and concessions on the other. The most severely victimized groups were targets of preemptive control (13 groups), "dirty war" (18 groups), or genocide/politicide (3 groups).[21]

World regions differ dramatically in patterns of repression. The Western democracies and Japan rely almost entirely on policing. In Asia counterinsurgency is by far the most common strategy, whereas African regimes are most likely to employ arbitrary violence. The postcommunist and Latin American governments' choices of strategies resemble those of the Western democracies more than those of Asia or Africa. Strategies of repression are in part a reflection of

Table 4.6. Strategies of Repression Used in Ethnopolitical Conflicts by Region, 1955–95

World Region (number of groups in 1995)	Number of Groups Targeted 1955–95[a]	Number of Groups Targeted at Each Level of Repression, 1986–95[b]			Mean Level of Repression by Period[c] (number of groups)		
		Policing (1, 2)	Counter-insurgency (3, 4)	Arbitrary Violence (5, 6, 7)	Before 1986	1986–90	1991–95
Western democracies and Japan (30)	13	12	1	0	1.7 (11)	1.3 (13)	1.1 (8)
Eastern Europe and the newly independent states (59)	16	7	5	3	—[d]	2.8 (6)	2.8 (15)
East, Southeast, and South Asia (57)	40	4	24	6	4.2 (33)	3.2 (32)	3.3 (32)
North Africa and the Middle East (26)	17	3	4	5	3.8 (16)	4.1 (8)	3.5 (11)
Africa south of the Sahara (66)	43	9	12	19	5.3 (24)	3.8 (23)	4.1 (32)
Latin America and the Caribbean (30)	12	4	4	1	5.0 (8)	2.6 (7)	1.5 (8)
Global totals (268)	141	39	50	34	4.2 (92)	3.1 (89)	3.2 (106)

[a] The number of ethnopolitical groups in 1995 (a) that were involved in episodes of open conflict with states at some time between 1955 and 1995 and (b) for which regime coercive responses could be coded. The analysis was done for 268 groups.

[b] Groups are classified according to the highest level of repression used against them between 1986 and 1995, using the eight-category ordinal scale shown in the text. Numbers in parentheses are the coding categories combined in each column.

[c] Average of coded values on the eight-category ordinal scale shown in the text. The number in parentheses is the number of groups targeted by repression during the period.

[d] Insufficient data; most ethnopolitical groups in this region in 1995 are those that became active in the Soviet and Yugoslav successor states. Few were active or subject to repression prior to the late 1980s.

the nature of ethnopolitical challenges. In Western democracies the challenges usually take the form of protest movements, which powerful democratic states usually are able to contain with minimum force. In Asian societies local and regional ethnorebellions are common; however, most Asian states have the government infrastructure and military resources for sustained campaigns of counterinsurgency. In Africa, by contrast, most states are weakly institutionalized, and their armies lack the manpower and restraint that are necessary for successful counterinsurgency. Instead they tend to rely on indiscriminate violence. A dozen of the eighteen "dirty wars" targeted at ethnopolitical rebels during the 1986–95 decade were fought in Africa.

Some noteworthy time trends in strategies of repression are evident when we compare across the three periods shown in the three right-hand columns of table 4.6. The mean level of repression used against ethnopolitical groups in Western democracies and in Latin America has decreased over time, very sharply so in Latin America. A less pronounced downward trend also is evident in Asia, though the region's mean levels of repression remain at the global average. There are no clear trends in other world regions. There are, however, instructive short-term comparisons to be made. In the postcommunist states, the number of ethnic wars increased sharply between the late 1980s and the early 1990s (see chapter 2), but the average severity of repression remained the same, slightly below the global average. The inference is that, despite catastrophic conflicts in the former Yugoslavia and Chechnya, most postcommunist states have exercised restraint toward ethnopolitical challengers. The next two chapters provide additional evidence of this pattern. In Africa south of the Sahara, by contrast, the increase in numbers of ethnopolitical conflicts between the 1980s and the 1990s was accompanied by a significant increase in severity of response to an average of 4.1, the highest level observed in any world region. Even in Africa, however, there are promising examples of restraint and accommodation, cited in chapter 6.

What are the legacies of state repression against ethnopolitical minorities? A detailed answer requires case studies. We can use the Minorities data to sketch a comparative answer for the 1986–95 decade. In the first half of the decade, twenty-eight groups were targeted by the four most severe forms of state repression: counterinsurgency without accommodation, preemptive control, "dirty war," and genocide or politicide. These were the outcomes as of 1996:

Conflict by five groups intensified after 1990.

Conflict by seven groups persisted without significant change in intensity.

Conflict by ten groups declined after negotiated settlements (eight) or rebel victories (two).

Conflict by three groups declined without any settlement or concessions.

Three groups subject to preemptive control did not openly resist.

This evidence suggests that severe state repression is more likely to prolong and intensify conflict than to suppress it, by a ratio of two to one. That is, twelve episodes of ethnoconflict in which severe repression was used continued or intensified, in contrast with six episodes in which repression achieved a short-term increase in security for the government that used it. The comparison suggests that the most effective strategy during the survey period was a negotiated settlement. Such settlements helped de-escalate the Palestinian-Israeli conflict, the Gagauz attempt to secede from Moldova, and Tuareg rebellions in Niger and Mali. They also helped to resolve racial conflict in South Africa. These and other strategies of accommodation are the subject of chapter 6.

Chinese in Malaysia
Balancing Communal Inequalities

Deepa Khosla

The Chinese, Malays, and East Indians are communal contenders in a polity with democratic institutions. The Malay political elite has used majority rule to check the potential for divisive communal conflict, to improve Malays' economic status, and, not least, to stay in power. The result is a trade-off in which prosperity and stability have been achieved for Malaysia as a whole but at some cost to the political rights and cultural interests of the Chinese minority.

THE 5.7 MILLION CHINESE in Malaysia are economically advantaged in relation to the Malay majority population and also to the Indian minority. Under Malaysia's laws all minorities, including the Chinese (who make up 27 percent of the population) and the Indians (8 percent of the population), are guaranteed equal protection. But the Chinese also are subject to restrictive political and cultural policies whose aim is to minimize intercommunal conflict and, not incidentally, to ensure continued Malay dominance of the state and society.

BACKGROUND

Although some Chinese have resided in Malaysia for centuries, most are descended from immigrants who arrived from southern China in the late nineteenth century. Some Malays still regard the Chinese as outsiders whose primary loyalties are to their homeland, China. The role of the Chinese during World War II and the subsequent guerrilla insurgency known as The Emergency (1948–60) contributed to the Malay perception of the Chinese. During the war the Chinese sided with the British and fought against Japanese occupation of what was then known as British Malay. Some Malays chose instead to work with the Japanese; following Japan's defeat, however, they became targets of violent retaliation by the Chinese-dominated Malayan Peoples'

Anti-Japanese Party (MPAJP), which sought to gain political control over the former British colony. The British, upon their return, opted to support the Malays, partly due to the MPAJP's communist ideology. During the twelve-year Emergency period, many rural Chinese who were suspected of supporting the MPAJP's successor, the Malayan Communist Party, were subject to government persecution and forcible relocation. By 1960, three years after Malaysia gained full independence, the communist insurgency had been quashed.

ECONOMIC POLICY

Failure to incorporate Singapore, with its majority-Chinese population, into the Malay federation during the mid-1960s, coupled with the rising political influence of the Chinese and Indian communities, prompted widespread inter-ethnic riots in Malaysia during the summer of 1969. In order to reduce tensions and grievances between the Malay and Chinese communities, the next year the government instituted its New Economic Policy (NEP). Its provisions included subsidies to establish businesses owned by *bumiputra* (groups indigenous to Malaysia), job quotas, and requirements that large new ventures include non-Chinese directors or partners. The net effect was to tilt the economic playing field against the Chinese. Although the NEP and its successor, the 1990 National Development Plan, were established to redress the disadvantages of all *bumiputra*, in effect, they have provided remedial advantages only to Malays. In 1998, Malays, who constitute over half the population, were reported to have achieved the NEP target of 30 percent ownership in the corporate sector, a significant improvement from their status at the establishment of the NEP, when the Malay share of corporate wealth was only 2.4 percent.[1]

Some restrictions on the ownership of Malay enterprises by non-Malays and foreigners were relaxed in 1997 as Malaysia sought to avoid the disastrous effects that the Asian financial crisis had wrought on its neighbor, Indonesia. Limited foreign ownership was allowed in any sector, but regulations remained in effect on non-Malay equity in areas such as manufacturing. It is unlikely that these restrictions will be reinstated, inasmuch as Malaysia is starting to rebound from its first recession in thirteen years.

The urban Chinese still maintain their dominance of Malaysia's economy; however, the rise of a new Malay business and professional elite, who are actively supported by the government, can potentially undermine the long-term economic standing of the Chinese community.

POLITICAL RESTRICTIONS

The Chinese are active participants in Malaysia's limited multiparty democracy, but their political influence has been circumscribed due to the dominance of Malay-majority, National Front governments and the various legal restrictions those governments have adopted, ostensibly to promote interethnic harmony. Primary among these are restrictions on the freedom of expression and the occasional use of preventive detention, measures that have limited the ability of the Chinese-dominated political parties, the Democratic Action Party (DAP) and the Malaysian Chinese Association (MCA), to press more vigorously for the protection of Chinese economic and cultural interests.

In 1995, the National Front coalition government of Prime Minister Mahathir Mohamad, which includes the Malaysian Chinese Association, won a landslide victory in federal elections. However, public opposition to limits on political participation, expressed in various protests and riots in 1997–98, has resulted in both greater support for opposition parties such as the Islamic Parti Islam (PAS) and the emergence of anti-Mahathir coalitions, which include both the PAS and the Chinese-dominated DAP. Since 1990, the Parti Islam has formed the state government in Kelantan. The PAS platform includes provisions to govern Muslims according to shari'a law, while Chinese and Indians would be subject to the current legal system. The November 1999 federal elections were the toughest that Mahathir, the longest-serving elected leader in the world, has faced; however, he won a decisive victory.

CULTURAL RESTRICTIONS

The provision that Malay is the country's official language is a particular source of concern for the Chinese community. Malay is the medium of instruction, along with English, in all public schools and universities. Although there are about sixty secondary schools where Mandarin is the language of instruction, these schools depend on private donations. Further, in 1995, the government initiated a program aimed at eventually merging all the country's public and private (Chinese and Tamil) schools.[2] At institutions of higher learning, limitations on Chinese enrollment in the 1970s alone (the first decade of the NEP) led to a 20 percent drop in Chinese enrollment. By 1995, around 64 percent of all the available openings at the university level were reserved for Malays.[3] Today, there are more Chinese Malaysians studying at universities and colleges outside the country than inside Malaysia.

PROSPECTS

Malaysia is in some respects a model of effective management of ethnic conflict in a plural society whose communities have unequal advantages. But success has been achieved at the cost of discriminatory restrictions on the Chinese. The restrictions are substantially less onerous than those imposed on Chinese minorities in Vietnam and Indonesia. Nonetheless, they are inconsistent with international principles of equal treatment and are sharply resented by many Chinese, especially restrictions that affect their rights of political expression and instruction in Chinese.

The rapid growth of the Malaysian economy during most of the 1980s and 1990s, coupled with the New Economic Policy and public and private efforts to promote cooperation between the two communities, have helped to reduce Malay discontent about Chinese economic advantages. Malaysia did not witness the widespread anti-Chinese violence that occurred in Indonesia in 1997–98 in the wake of its stock and currency collapses. To the contrary, in 1999 Prime Minister Mohamad publicly commended the Chinese community for its role in supporting the country's economy during the crisis.[4] While the Malaysian economy was expected to grow by more than 4 percent in 1999, a prolonged downturn could generate greater tension. Further, with China's emergence as a major economic power, the Malaysian Chinese are more actively promoting their identity and culture and increasing their economic and social contacts with the People's Republic. Chinese-majority states such as Singapore and Taiwan, and China itself, have also become increasingly vocal about the treatment of their kin in Southeast Asian countries.

Increasing Chinese and Muslim assertiveness, along with other factors, indicate that the conditions for future ethnic conflict remain.

NOTES

The author is senior research assistant and Asian regional specialist for the Minorities at Risk project. In 1998–99 she held a United States Institute of Peace dissertation fellowship.

In addition to the sources cited below, the following works were used for this sketch:

Gurr, Ted Robert, and Barbara Harff. *Ethnic Conflict in World Politics*, chaps. 4 and 6. Boulder, Colo.: Westview Press, 1994.

Lim, Linda, and Peter Gosling. "Economic Growth and Ethnic Relations: The Chinese in Southeast Asia." Draft paper, United States Institute of Peace, Washington, D.C., February 1993.

Minority Rights Group International. *The Chinese of South-East Asia.* London: Minority Rights Group, November 1992.

1. Agence France Presse, February 26, 1998; *Financial Times,* November 28, 1995.

2. *Straits Times,* Singapore, August 28, 1995.

3. Sumit Ganguly, "Ethnic Policies and Political Quiescence in Malaysia and Singapore," in *Government Policies and Ethnic Relations in Asia and the Pacific,* ed. Michael E. Brown and Sumit Ganguly (Cambridge, Mass.: MIT Press, 1997), 259.

4. *Asia Pulse,* February 26, 1999.

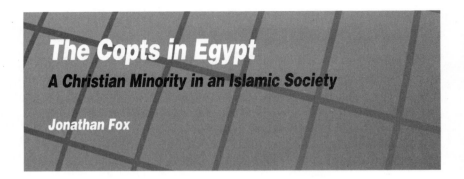

The Copts in Egypt
A Christian Minority in an Islamic Society

Jonathan Fox

Egypt's Copts are subject to long-standing political and cultural restrictions and have been targeted by Islamist militants, but their status is relatively secure and far better than that of religious minorities in most other Islamic societies.

THE SIX MILLION COPTS are indigenous Egyptian Christians who make up about 10 percent of the country's population and 95 percent of its Christians. They live throughout the country, with concentrations in Alexandria, Cairo, and the urban areas of Upper (southern) Egypt. Physically and linguistically they are indistinguishable from the rest of Egypt's population, though they pray in Coptic, which is believed to be a derivative of the ancient Pharaonic language. They have long been subject to political and cultural restrictions because they are non-Muslims in an Islamic society, and during the 1990s they were especially targeted by Islamist militants.[1]

ORIGINS

The Copts believe themselves to be descendants of Egypt's ancient Pharaonic people, who were converted to Christianity in the first century A.D. The first Muslims arrived in A.D. 640 but did not constitute a majority until about three centuries later, mostly due to the conversion of the Egyptian populace. Under Muslim rule the Copts were alternately treated with tolerance and repressed. As *dhimi*, or "peoples of the Book," Copts, like Jews, are recognized in Islamic law; however, Islamic law can be interpreted to support different degrees of tolerance and, in any case, *dhimi* have always been subject to some restrictions.

In the nineteenth century, the influx of Western influence gave Copts opportunities to improve their status. This also led to increasing conflict with the Muslim political community, which intensified when the Copts began demanding equality in the new Egyptian state. The resultant cycle of violence did not end until Colonel Nasser's "bloodless coup" in 1952 and his government's suppression of sectarian violence. The Copts in the 1990s are advantaged in some respects but in other spheres of life are subject to restrictions.

ECONOMIC AND EDUCATIONAL DISCRIMINATION

The Copts are economically advantaged in the sense that relatively large numbers are city dwellers engaging in commerce and the professions, including medicine, law, and accountancy. They tend to be better educated than Muslims and are well represented in the bureaucracy and military (a proportionally higher number of Copts than Muslims are drafted). However, they confront a number of offsetting disadvantages. There is petty discrimination against Copts throughout the job market, and they are underrepresented in the upper levels of government and the military. Moreover, Christian institutions receive a disproportionately small share of public spending. One indicator of the impact of economic discrimination is that a number of Coptic university graduates reportedly convert to Islam for economic reasons. Note also that conversions from Islam to other religions are illegal under article 98f of Egypt's penal code.[2]

According to Egypt's constitution, Copts and Muslims should have equal educational opportunities. In practice, however, Egyptian universities are reluctant to admit Copts, and there have been accusations of discrimination in the allocation of scholarships for study abroad. Muslims have the additional advantage of the state-funded Al Azhar Islamic University, whereas the government has thus far refused to authorize construction of a privately funded Coptic university. Copts are also not accepted into schools that train Arabic teachers, because the curriculum includes the study of the Koran. Copts are underrepresented in both the teaching and research faculties at universities, and there are few or no Copts in the highest-level university administrative positions. There are no Coptic-related studies in university curriculums, and the Coptic era of Egyptian history is omitted from school curriculums. Though Copts do have access to free primary schooling, in some rural areas, especially in Upper Egypt, female students, Muslim as well as Coptic, have been coerced into wearing veils by Islamist militants.

CULTURAL DISADVANTAGES

Although the Egyptian state is avowedly secular, the Copts are also subject to official and unofficial religious discrimination. The government restricts Christian broadcasting, public speech, holiday celebrations, and the number of Coptic institutions. In 1952 some Coptic hospitals and schools and fifteen hundred acres of church land were confiscated by public authorities. In 1996 a government committee was formed to address the issue; as of 1998 it had returned five hundred acres of the church land and continues to study the issue.[3]

Moreover, the government strictly enforces an 1856 law that makes it illegal to build or repair a church without presidential approval. This is supplemented by 1934 Ministry of the Interior regulations dictating several factors that must be considered before a permit may be issued. A provision of these laws, that churches may not be built too close to a mosque, has often been used by Muslims, who have built mosques close to proposed church sites in order to prevent building permits from being issued. In the past, these rules forced Copts to build churches in secret, under the guise of building factories or other, less regulated, structures. Often, the state has reacted by closing or destroying the illicit churches and punishing the offenders. However, attacks by Islamic militants against Coptic churches are not tolerated by the government, which provides armed guards for the churches when deemed necessary.[4]

The Egyptian government is highly sensitive to international criticism that it discriminates against Copts and in the 1990s took steps to moderate public policy. For example, President Mubarak has approved all requests presented to him for permits to build and repair churches. The number of permits issued has increased steadily since the 1980s, when it averaged 5 per year, to 237 in 1998, due in part to President Mubarak's January 1998 delegation of authority to provincial governors to approve such permits. Nonetheless, Christians maintain that the Interior Ministry delays—in some instances indefinitely—submission of their requests to the president. They also say that security forces sometimes block them from utilizing permits that have been issued. Despite shifts in official policy, the singling out of Christian churches for special governmental supervision is indicative of the second-class status of Christianity in Egypt. In addition, the building of many new churches and the general rise in importance of the Coptic Church signals the increasing importance of religious and communal identities in Egypt, and this, in turn, may be increasing the separation between Copts and Muslims.[5]

POLITICAL DISCRIMINATION

There is no Coptic political party or movement. Copts can and do vote in Egyptian elections, but few are elected to significant posts. In the 1995 elections, thousands of Copts were left off voting registers in districts in which Coptic candidates were running for office. Because no Copts won parliamentary seats, President Mubarak appointed 6 Copts to serve in the 454-member body. Copts also are underrepresented in the upper echelons of government and usually are relegated to minor ministries where they have little impact on policy making. They are excluded from the judiciary even in courts that deal with marriage, divorce, and inheritance; however, Christians are subject to church law in most matters concerning the family.

The greatest threat to the Copts' security at the end of the twentieth century is posed by harassment by Islamist militants, which began in earnest in 1972 and increased considerably during the early 1990s. Actions include spreading false rumors, extortion, and violence up to and including murder, sometimes carried out with the tacit approval of local officials. For example, in February 1997, nine Copts were massacred in an attack on a church in Minya province in southern Egypt by Islamic militants who then continued their rampage by killing another fourteen, nine of them Copts. In 1998 a total of eight Copts were killed by Islamic militants.[6]

Islamic extremists clearly want to marginalize the Copts. They demand that Christians be purged from the Egyptian army and that they pay a special religious tax. Some Copts go so far as to accuse Islamist extremists of plotting to "cleanse" the Middle East of non-Muslims. The government's campaign against the Islamic militants has had some success, though the campaign probably is inspired by the challenge the militants present to the secular government rather than by a desire to protect Copts. Islamic militant violence peaked in 1995 and, with the exception of a few dramatic incidents, is dropping.[7]

PROSPECTS

President Mubarak's government has sought to respond to criticisms that Copts are subject to discriminatory treatment. Authorities are more responsive to complaints from Coptic Church officials about religious discrimination, it is much easier to get permission for building and renovating churches, and some confiscated church lands have been returned. Violence by Islamists also is being checked, prompted by the threat they pose to state power as much as or more than their targeting of Copts.

In general, government-imposed restrictions on the Copts are moderate rather than severe and have lessened slightly in the 1990s. They are notably less severe than restrictions on religious minorities in some other Islamic societies, for example, those imposed on the Baha'is in Iran and the Ahmadis in Pakistan. Nonetheless, the Copts are non-Muslims in a society where Islamic identity is increasingly salient, especially among the urban poor. Their future security depends upon the secular government's success in curbing militant Islam. In a state dominated by Islamists, the Copts' situation would worsen substantially.

NOTES

Jonathan Fox was a graduate research assistant for the Minorities at Risk project from 1994 to 1997 and was awarded a doctorate in 1997 by the University of Maryland's Department of Government and Politics for his dissertation, "Religion, Ethnicity, and the State." He is assistant professor of political science at Bar Ilan University in Israel.

Sources for this sketch include journalistic accounts and the works cited in the following notes.

1. See Mark Purcell, "A Place for the Copts: Imagined Territory and Spacial Conflict in Egypt," *Ecumene* 5, no. 4 (1998), for details on Coptic residence patterns and on Egyptian Islamic attitudes toward them, 435–437 and 439–441.

2. On evidence of discrimination, see U.S. Department of State, "Egypt Country Report on Human Rights Practices for 1998," *Country Reports on Human Rights Practices for 1998,* www.state.gov/www/global/human_rights/hrp_reports_mainhp.html; and "The Danger of Foreign Meddling," *Economist,* May 23, 1998.

3. U.S. Department of State, "Egypt Country Report" (note 2).

4. See Purcell, "A Place for the Copts" (note 1); and Virginia N. Sherry, "The Predicament of Egypt's Christian Minority," *Christian Century* 110, no. 21 (July 14–21, 1993).

5. See Saad E. Ibrahim, *The Copts of Egypt: Freedom of Worship?* (London: Minority Rights Group International, 1996); U.S. Department of State, "Egypt Country Report" (note 2); and "Danger of Foreign Meddling" (note 2).

6. Ibrahim, *The Copts of Egypt* (note 5); U.S. Department of State, "Egypt Country Report" (note 2); Jonathan Wright, "Egypt Names Suspects in Church Attack," Reuters, February 15, 1997; and Douglas Jehl, "Killings Erode Cairo's Claim to 'Control' Militants," *New York Times,* March 15, 1997.

7. "Egyptian Christian Killed in Ongoing Strife," *Christian Century* 16, no. 114 (May 14, 1997); John Lancaster, "Fundamentalists Step Up Attacks on Egypt's Coptic Minority," *International Herald Tribune,* May 19, 1997.

The Roma in the Postcommunist Era

Jonathan Fox and Betty Brown

The situation of the Roma, who were already Europe's most disadvantaged minority, has worsened in the 1990s. Socialist policies aimed at incorporating them have been abandoned, and new democracies' policies designed to protect Roma's rights are widely subverted because of local prejudice and resistance. Politically the Roma are fragmented and, except in Macedonia, have little or no leverage on public policy and practice. They are likely to remain the pariahs of Europe.

THE ROMA, also known as the Romani, are a dispersed, numerically significant minority in a dozen Eastern European countries: Albania, Bosnia, Bulgaria, Croatia, the Czech Republic, Hungary, Macedonia, Romania, Slovakia, Russia, Ukraine, and Yugoslavia (Serbia and Montenegro). Population estimates vary wildly.[1] A reasonable estimate is five million to six million in East Central Europe, including Russia and Ukraine; another two million to three million live elsewhere in Europe. Throughout the region the Roma are seriously disadvantaged and usually experience active discrimination with respect to education, living conditions, employment, treatment by the authorities, and relations with non-Roma. They are, at the onset of the twenty-first century, the most economically, politically, and socially disadvantaged group in Europe.

HISTORY AND BACKGROUND

The pariah status of the Roma throughout Europe and the stereotypes associated with them in modern times date back to their arrival in Europe during the thirteenth century from the Punjab. Their arrival coincided with the Seljuk incursions into Europe, the Mongol invasion of Russia in the east, Tatar excursions into the Byzantine Empire in the south, and the Moors' occupation

143

of parts of Western Europe. Fearful and suspicious of all foreign arrivals, many Europeans mistook the Roma for Muslims and labeled them Saracens, Tatars, heathens, or Egyptians (from which the term *gypsy* is derived). Because of the threat from Turkey, the Roma were suspected of being Turkish soldiers or spies and were subject to increasing political, economic, and social discrimination. Some authorities forbade the Roma to do business with shopkeepers; some were denied the use of village water supplies. By 1400 state laws against the Roma had begun to appear, and in Wallachia and Moldova the Roma were enslaved, a status that did not change officially until 1864.[2] These restrictive policies and suspicious attitudes reinforced the Roma's seminomadic way of life, separate and exclusive from the non-Roma world. Over time, their isolation and the discriminatory practices of states and societies left the Roma living as outcasts on the edge of society.

This pattern of discrimination and isolation has persisted to the present, reaching its highest level during World War II, when many Roma—estimates range from 250,000 to four million—were murdered by the Nazis and their allies. Later the state socialist regimes of Eastern Europe followed policies of forced assimilation and settlement that were intended to improve the Roma's economic status. However, these policies often were thwarted by local authorities. In Czechoslovakia, for example, many local authorities refused to provide housing and employment for Roma, undermining the state's plans for assimilation. In Bulgaria, segregation undermined assimilation policies by producing "ghetto" schools, attended exclusively by Roma children. Policies favoring the Roma also were resented by other citizens of the socialist states, and evidence of rising prejudice and discrimination already was evident in the 1980s.

On balance the status of Roma in East Central Europe has not improved since 1990. Postcommunist regimes in Hungary and Macedonia have devised positive policies toward the Roma. Croatia, by contrast, has increased restrictions on them. Even in states where public policies toward the Roma have improved, societal discrimination and resistance by local governments to implementation of those policies have generally had negative effects.

POVERTY AND ECONOMIC DISCRIMINATION

The Roma generally have the least education and highest rates of illiteracy in Eastern and Central European societies. First, if the Roma speak the language of the country in which they live at all, it is generally as a second language. Because education is rarely provided in any of the numerous Roma dialects, many are functionally illiterate. Second, the seminomadic lifestyle of many Roma makes it difficult for their children to attend school regularly. Third, many governments provide Roma with segregated, substandard schools, and some with no schools at all. In Hungary, for example, many villages populated by the Roma have no schools at all; in Bulgaria most Roma attend segregated schools, where they lack equal opportunity to learn the Bulgarian language and have little or no chance at higher education. Fourth, because mandatory education is not enforced to the extent that it was under the state socialist regimes, where social workers often actively brought Roma children to the schools, the Roma's already low mean levels of education are getting lower. In the Czech Republic and elsewhere, they are sometimes sent to schools for the handicapped due to their lack of mastery of the national language.[3]

The low level of education among the Roma contributes to the highest levels of unemployment for any group in Eastern Europe, averaging 30–40 percent and rising in some areas close to 100 percent. Their poverty is reinforced by societal discrimination, which limits most Roma to menial and low-paid jobs. Many of them eke out a living in traditional ways as itinerant craftsmen, casual laborers, and beggars; in Romania, some have taken over the houses and farms of German villagers who have emigrated to Germany.

The Roma in Eastern Europe also suffer substandard housing, health, and living conditions. Their high levels of unemployment and low levels of education contribute to these conditions. Ineffective public policies, lack of resources, and societal discrimination compound these conditions.

STEREOTYPING AND VIOLENCE

The widely held stereotype of the Rom as a lazy, unclean, uneducated, habitual thief remains intact. It often is perpetuated by the media and nationalist politicians and thus reinforces the vicious circle that has contributed to the Roma's historical disadvantage. The negative stereotype is used to justify discrimination, which reinforces the generational poverty of the Roma, which contributes to the high level of crime and poor living conditions among the Roma that explain the stereotype.

This stereotype is also responsible for a sharp increase in violent attacks against Roma, attacks that generally were restrained by state socialist regimes. Attacks by skinheads have been particularly common in Bulgaria, Slovakia, and the Czech Republic. Between 1990 and 1997, over four hundred Roma in the Czech Republic were seriously injured in racially motivated attacks, and as of April 1998, twenty-nine had been killed. In Serbia in October 1997, a fourteen-year-old Roma girl and a pregnant Roma woman were both beaten to death, in two separate incidents. In Romania there have been repeated incidents of rioting by villagers attempting, sometimes successfully, to burn Roma homes and drive out their inhabitants. Central governments in these countries have had little success in curbing such activities or in arresting and prosecuting the perpetrators.[4]

POLITICAL RESTRICTIONS AND REMEDIATION

European doctrines of minority rights have not been of much help to the Roma. The general trend in Europe, Eastern and Western, is that concern for the plight of the Roma is greatest among European institutions, human rights NGOs, and national governments, especially heads of state. Legislative bodies are less likely to enact remedial policies. And even when they do, local governments are generally the least likely to be concerned about the status of the Roma and sometimes actively attempt to undermine central government initiatives.[5]

The Czech Republic provides an instructive example. President Havel has shown considerable interest in improving the situation of his country's Roma. He took the rare step of intervening in a November 1997 cabinet meeting held by a reluctant prime minister to push through a "long delayed" plan to improve the situation of the Roma. However, local governments seem to be paying little heed to these directives. For example, in the northern town of Usti nad Labem, town councilors sought to build a thirteen-foot-high wall to seal off tenements populated by Roma. Another town, Plzen, attempted to resettle hundreds of "socially unacceptable people," a code name for the Roma, in a fenced-in area outside the town. The walls in both places were to be policed around the clock. These local governments reflect the general dislike of the Roma by the Czech population. Roma are banned from many restaurants, bars, swimming pools, and other public places. In a 1997 poll in the Czech Republic, 43 percent of respondents said that it never would be possible for Czechs and the Roma to exist happily, 25 percent said Czechs should be more tolerant of the Roma, and only 6 percent thought relations would improve in the next few years.[6]

Similarly, central governments in Hungary and Macedonia have enacted legislation designed to protect Roma rights and improve their status, but implementation has been made difficult due to prevailing prejudices and social discrimination against Roma and resistance by local governments whose officials often share the same prejudices. Poor economic conditions in most of Eastern Europe also constrain the enforcement of Roma rights and the improvement of their material condition.

In some cases even the central government practices overt discrimination against the Roma. The most egregious example comes from Croatia, where Roma are not recognized as a national minority and therefore are denied "nationality certificates," a policy that effectively denies them the right to attend school, the right to employment, and sometimes the right to an apartment.

Regardless of central government policies, local authorities in most of Eastern Europe have been criticized for their lack of response to violent attacks against the Roma. Police have reportedly failed to prevent attacks that occurred in their presence, authorities do not always investigate attacks, and when perpetrators are apprehended their punishment may be disproportionately light. For example, in 1993 in the Czech Republic a group of eighteen skinheads drowned a Roma boy. Only two were eventually convicted, and they received light sentences. Czech president Havel has accused the police of "hiding around corners to avoid such cases."[7] Also, in Hungary in 1993, the Supreme Court ruled that attacks against Roma, foreigners, and other ethnic minorities were not covered in a section of a law dealing with racially motivated crimes. In light of this pervasive pattern of state-tolerated discrimination and insecurity, it is unsurprising that many Roma have sought political asylum in Western states.

THE ROMA IN POLITICS

Political action by communal groups, the sovereign remedy for ethnic discrimination in democratic states, has not been of much help for the Roma, either. They have organized political parties in most postcommunist countries, but their mobilization has had little impact. Although they have won seats in some local councils and several national legislatures, almost invariably they are represented in small or token numbers.

There are several reasons for their lack of political impact. First, almost everywhere the Roma suffer from deep internal divisions. These divisions are based to some extent on clan or tribal differences but also are reinforced by differences in occupation, language or dialect, lifestyle, geographic location, socioeconomic status, and religion. The salience of their identification as Roma is therefore weak, and the cohesion necessary for mobilization is lacking. Second, the Roma, being among the poorest minorities in Europe, lack many of the resources that facilitate mobilization. Third, the Roma lack political experience and therefore have a low sense of political efficacy. Few Roma political organizations existed before the 1990s, and those few had little or no effect on state policy. Fourth, the Roma in most states lack a centralized organization and authoritative leadership; rather, they have proliferated many organizations with contentious leaders. The leaders rarely have authority outside their own community and are generally more interested in pursuing rivalries with other leaders than in working toward common goals. Fifth, they lack a mother state to protect or promote their interests. Finally, they lack public sympathy. As a result the Roma have spawned a large number of political organizations—240 are registered in Hungary, for example—that are unable to mount any large-scale, coherent, and sustained political effort.[8]

The goals of Roma political movements tend to be the same in most places: the full recognition of their rights as a distinctive nationality; effective enforcement of their civil rights; schools with instruction in Romani; affirmative action policies; broadcast time in the state-run media; economic aid; and other social programs. We have observed an interesting dynamic in the patterns of these types of demands. For most ethnic minorities, discrimination in a particular issue area generally results in the articulation of grievances over that particular issue. However, in both qualitative and statistical analyses, we find that the economic plight of the Roma has no effect on whether they make demands over economic issues. Economic issues are raised only as an add-on to Roma demands over political and social issues, which, in turn, follow from discrimination in these areas. That is, it is political and social discrimination that fuels Roma political movements, not the economic discrimination that most Roma endure. Perhaps this is because poverty has been a constant in Roma history and at some level has been accepted as inevitable. However, especially in an era when human rights are a central issue in European politics and discourse, it is likely that political and social discrimination have become more unacceptable to the Roma. And, once such issues are raised, economic issues are included in their demands.[9]

State policies and public attitudes are the main constraints on attainment of the Roma's political goals. Only where the government has the political will to do something *and* ordinary citizens are willing to accept this has any real progress been made. Macedonia is the one East Central European example where this conjunction is present. Roma are identified in the constitution as a state minority and acknowledged by leading politicians as one of Macedonia's major nationalities. They also have had some local-level success in forming political organizations, electing Roma to the country's parliament, and participating effectively in municipal government. It helps that almost all

Macedonian Roma vote. The first reason for this success is the willingness of governmental leaders to go beyond rhetoric and enact concrete measures to aid the Roma. The second is that negative stereotypes of the Roma are not as strong in Macedonia as elsewhere. In fact, it is argued that the Roma have a better relationship with the Macedonian population because the Macedonians themselves have been subject to discrimination and are, accordingly, more sympathetic. The fact that the Roma crime rate is low may also be a contributing factor. Finally, the divisions among Macedonian Roma are comparatively few.[10]

THE ROMA IN 2000

The situation of the East Central European Roma has worsened since the fall of the Eastern European communist governments. Some governments have imposed new discriminatory policies on them. Others have sought to improve their status, but most such efforts have been ineffective due to high levels of societal discrimination and a lack of political will and resources. Unfortunately, many Eastern Europeans have used their newfound democratic freedoms to act out deep-rooted prejudices against the Roma. Divisions among the Roma themselves, along with their poverty and limited education, have constrained their ability to challenge effectively governmental and societal discrimination. The prospects are faint in the short or medium term that the favorable conditions that have contributed to the Roma's improved status in Macedonia will be replicated elsewhere. Hungary might prove an exception. Elsewhere the Roma are likely to remain the pariahs of Europe.

NOTES

Jonathan Fox was a graduate research assistant for the Minorities at Risk project from 1994 to 1997 and was awarded a doctorate in 1997 by the University of Maryland's Department of Government and Politics for his dissertation, "Religion, Ethnicity, and the State." He is assistant professor of political science at Bar Ilan University in Israel. Betty Brown is a Ph.D. candidate at the University of Maryland

1. Estimates vary for a number of reasons. Roma are not usually enumerated in censuses; if they are, their seminomadic lifestyle makes it difficult to count them accurately; and in any case Roma in Europe and elsewhere often conceal their ethnic identity from outsiders and claim other nationalities. Other groups that follow a seminomadic way of life may be grouped with Roma in population estimates. Governments often have political reasons for underestimating numbers of Roma in their jurisdictions, whereas group advocates have political reasons for making generous

estimates of Roma populations. See Jeremy Druker, "Present but Unaccounted For: How Many Roma Live in Central and Eastern Europe? It Depends on Whom You Ask," *Transitions* 4 (September 1997): 23; also Ali Arayici, "The Gypsy Minority in Europe: Some Considerations," *International Social Science Journal* (1998): 253–262. The largest Roma populations in the region are in Romania (1.8–2.5 million), Bulgaria (700,000–800,000), and Hungary (550,000–600,000). The Minorities at Risk project uses estimates from Jean-Pierre Liegeois and Nicolae Gheorghe, *Roma/Gypsies: A European Minority* (London: Minority Rights Group, 1995), 7, whose source is the Gypsy Research Center, René Descartes University, Paris. We use the midpoint of ranges reported in the source and project them forward, taking account of population growth, to 1998.

2. On the historical sources of prejudices and discrimination against the Roma, see David M. Crowe, *The Gypsies of Eastern Europe* (New York: M. E. Sharpe, 1991); and, by the same author, *A History of the Gypsies of Eastern Europe and Russia* (New York: St. Martin's Press, 1994).

3. On Roma education and illiteracy, see Zoltan Barany, "Orphans of Transition: Gypsies in Eastern Europe," *Journal of Democracy* 9, no. 3 (1998): 142–156. On assignment of Roma children to schools for the learning disabled because they do not speak the national language, see testimony by James Goldston in *Romani Human Rights in Europe, Hearing before the Commission on Security and Cooperation in Europe,* 104th Cong., 2d Sess., July 21, 1998 (Washington, D.C.: U.S. Government Printing Office, 1998), 13.

4. For descriptions of these and many other attacks, see Goldston, *Romani Human Rights in Europe* (note 3), 12–13, 33–34, 42–44, 47–48, and 58–83 passim; and news accounts such as Chris Hedges, "Another Victim, 14, in Serbia's War against Gypsies," *New York Times,* October 22, 1997; Tom Gross, "Persecuted under Vaclav Havel," *Spectator,* November 8, 1997; and "Europe: Sad Gypsies," *Economist,* April 11, 1998.

5. For examples, see Barany, "Orphans of Transition" (note 3), 151–152; and "Romani Human Rights in Europe," passim.

6. See Gross, "Persecuted under Vaclav Havel" (note 4); Jane Perelez, "Havel Lectures Czechs on the Rights of Gypsies," *New York Times,* November 9, 1997; and "Europe: Ghetto for Czech Gypsies," *Economist,* May 30, 1998.

7. Quoted in "Europe: Sad Gypsies" (note 4).

8. See Zoltan Barany, "Ethnic Mobilization and the State: The Roma in Eastern Europe," *Ethnic and Racial Studies* 21, no. 2 (1998): 312–318; and Barany, "Orphans of Transition" (note 3), 148–150.

9. Quantitative and qualitative evidence on this pattern, drawn in part from the Minorities at Risk project, was presented in Betty Brown and Jonathan Fox, "The Roma of Eastern and Western Europe: The Pariahs of Europe" (paper presented at the annual meeting of the Association for the Study of Nationalities, Columbia University, New York, April 1996).

10. Zoltan Barany, "The Roma in Macedonia: Ethnic Politics and the Marginal Condition in a Balkan State," *Ethnic and Racial Studies* 18, no. 3 (1995): 515–531.

5

Democratic Governance and Strategies of Accommodation in Plural Societies

THE QUINTESSENTIAL BARGAIN that builds peace in heterogeneous societies is one in which governments acknowledge and support the rights of subordinate national and minority peoples in exchange for civil peace and their acceptance of the state's superordinate political authority. Such bargains may be reached by different paths. Some are achieved through bargaining, joint problem solving, and electoral competition in democratic political systems.[1] Others are an outcome of negotiated agreements designed to restrain violent ethnopolitical conflict, agreements that in the late twentieth century often were reached during or as a consequence of transitions to democracy. Some societies, however, are wracked by generations of protracted communal conflict because no mutually satisfying bargains are sought or attainable.

Which strategies of peacebuilding are most likely to be acceptable to contending groups in heterogeneous societies depends on the objectives of national peoples and minorities. The most basic distinction is between *access* and *autonomy*. Disadvantaged minority peoples usually want access, that is, greater opportunities to protect and promote their shared cultural, political, and material interests within existing societies. National peoples are more likely to seek greater autonomy, that is, collective governance of their own affairs, usually in an autonomous region of a decentralized state. These objectives are, in principle, subject to compromise. Failure to find a middle ground, however, increases the chances that ethnopolitical conflict will be fought out over nonnegotiable issues, either demands

151

for hegemonic control in an ethnically heterogeneous society or independence in a national people's own state.

The upsurge in ethnopolitical conflict in the late 1980s and early 1990s prompted many creative efforts to contain conflict. The irony is that most observers were so preoccupied with the dynamics of escalating conflict that they overlooked the countervailing tendency to find solutions. In 1999, Western observers and policymakers were focused on security and humanitarian consequences of the Kosovar Albanians' war of independence. On January 24, 1998, the *Washington Post* gave the following account of the negotiated agreement that ended a similar war in Pacific Asia, a decade-long conflict that attracted virtually no attention outside its immediate neighborhood.

> Christchurch, New Zealand: The longest war in the Pacific since World War II came to an end when secessionist fighters for the island of Bougainville signed a cease-fire with Papua New Guinea. Guerrillas had been fighting for independence since 1988. At least 20,000 people were killed and up to 40,000 forced from their homes.

Another recent example is the peace agreement reached in December 1997 between the government of Bangladesh and the representatives of the Chakma rebels of the Chittagong Hill Tracts. This twenty-five-year war of autonomy killed many more than the eight thousand officially recognized victims and made refugees of more than one hundred thousand of the region's six hundred thousand people.[2] The origins, issues, humanitarian consequences, and settlement of this war got not one-hundredth of the attention that Western societies have focused on Kosovo.

This and the next chapter summarize some of the issues and evidence of efforts to resolve potentially deadly and protracted ethnopolitical conflicts. This chapter examines, first, evidence about the effects of democratic governance, including taking a close look at the impact of stable democracy and democratic transitions on trends and patterns of ethnopolitical conflict. Second, it documents a global decline in ethnic discrimination during the 1990s, showing that this decline also was associated with democratic transitions. The next chapter surveys the outcomes of efforts to negotiate an end to ethnonational wars of independence.

Democracy and Ethnopolitical Conflict

The "democratic peace" holds within most long-established democratic states, as well as among them, for reasons discussed in chapter 3. There is much more ambiguity—in evidence and in expert opinion—about the pacifying effects of democratic transitions. Lake and Rothchild observe that "preventing conflict by building democracy is more problematic. . . . Where extremist politicians seek to outflank moderates within their own group and make militant appeals to their ethnic kinsmen for preferential treatment, the fragile ties between elites may snap and the democratic experiment may unravel."[3] The outbreak of ethnic warfare in transitional democracies like Bosnia, Georgia, and Burundi has made some observers skeptical about promoting democratic institutions in any heterogeneous society. Internationally encouraged efforts to build democracy in Burundi in the early 1990s were counterproductive, a recent study by the Center for Prevention Action concludes, because the country's history and society are "a worst-case illustration of a propensity toward national ethnic conflicts." Outsiders unwittingly contributed to Burundi's democratic failure:

> International actors unanimously supported the rushed pseudodemocratization of the country without any attention to the security issues that majoritarian elections under universal suffrage would pose for a divided society like Burundi. They seemed to assume that holding democratic elections would produce democratic politics. . . . [H]owever, the problem of *institutionalizing* politics is key to a successful transition and depends on the construction of many institutions that can wield effective authority, not simply on the existence of political parties and electoral commissions.[4]

On the other hand, democratic transitions during the Cold War period led consistently to a decline in state repression, as Christian Davenport demonstrates in a recent empirical study.[5] They have helped establish civic peace in countries such as South Africa, Lebanon, and Guatemala, where politicized communal warfare once was chronic and supposedly intractable. South Africa and Lebanon are communally divided societies, like Burundi. One key to their successful democratization was the construction (or reconstruction, in Lebanon) of a network of power-sharing institutions that guarantee rights and access to power, national or local, for each major communal contender. In Guatemala effective democratization has meant implementing majoritarian principles that give indigenous peoples more effective participation in institutions long dominated by the *ladino* elite and middle class.[6]

The Minorities at Risk data provide a global vantage point on the issue. They make it possible to assess the impact of all recent democratic transitions, successful and unsuccessful, on trends and patterns in ethnopolitical conflict. The Polity data set is used to distinguish four types of political systems for the comparisons that follow:[7]

Old democracies (twenty-seven countries in 1998): countries with fully democratic political institutions that were established before 1980 and have not reverted to autocratic rule since the 1950s.

New democracies (thirty-three countries in 1998): countries with fully or mostly democratic political institutions that were established between 1980 and 1994 and have not reverted to autocratic rule since then.

Transitional regimes (thirty-two countries in 1998): countries whose regimes have a mixture of autocratic and democratic features or that attempted transitions to democracy after 1970 that ended with temporary or enduring reversion to autocratic rule. This category includes a few mixed political systems of proven durability, as in Singapore and Morocco, but most have a recent history of political experimentation, hence institutional instability. A number of Soviet successor states are in this category, including Belarus, Kazakhstan, and Russia itself.[8] So are post–civil war African countries like Uganda and Ethiopia, whose leaders, as Marina Ottaway points out, are more concerned with statebuilding than democratization.[9]

Autocracies (twenty-six countries in 1998): countries with consistently autocratic institutions that did not attempt democratic transitions between the 1960s and the late 1990s. Autocracies that had incorporated some democratic features before 1996 are classified as transitional.

The four types of regimes have roughly similar numbers of ethnopolitical groups, as shown in table 5.1, but they differ significantly in patterns of ethnopolitical conflict in the 1985-98 period. Three general conclusions can be drawn about the ways in which political institutions structure the nature of ethnopolitical conflict. The subsequent analysis of democratic transitions helps answer the related question of whether and how new democratic institutions alter the trajectories of conflict.

Ethnopolitical groups in democratic societies are more likely to use strategies of protest than rebellion. This proposition was developed in chapter 3 and is confirmed by the global evidence. Old and new democracies have both fewer ethnic wars and lower magnitudes of rebellion than transitional and autocratic regimes. The level of rebellion in the long-established democracies would be even lower were it not for India's inclusion in this group. India accounts for seven of the eleven ethnic wars in the established democracies and about half these countries' aggregate magnitude of rebellion (for reasons discussed in chapter 3, p. 85).

Ethnopolitical groups in nondemocratic societies are more likely to use rebellion as a strategy than protest. This proposition from chapter 3 also is confirmed

Table 5.1. Type of Political Regime and Patterns of Ethnopolitical Protest and Rebellion, 1985–98

Type of Regime[a]	Number of Ethnopolitical Groups	Protest		Rebellion	
		Groups with Major Campaigns[b]	Mean Annual Magnitude[c]	Groups with Ethnic Wars[d]	Mean Annual Magnitude[c]
Old democracies ($n = 27$)	59	22	1.86	11	0.83
New democracies ($n = 33$)	68	22	1.63	12	0.63
Transitional regimes ($n = 32$)	80	16	1.15	32	0.89
Autocracies ($n = 26$)	67	16	1.05	31	1.57

[a] Regime types are defined and countries of each type listed in appendix A.

[b] Number of groups in countries of each regime type with protest scores of 4 or greater at some time during the 1985–98 period. A score of 4 signifies protest activity with 10,000 to 100,000 participants. See table 2.2 for coding categories for protest and rebellion.

[c] Mean levels of protest and rebellion are calculated from the Minorities at Risk data set's annual codes for protest and rebellion for each group. The means are computed by pooling all nonmissing annual values for all groups in each of the four types of regime.

[d] Number of groups in countries of each regime type with rebellion scores of 4 or greater at some time during the 1985–98 period. A score of 4 signifies small-scale guerrilla war.

here, but with some theoretically interesting qualifications. The evidence shows that rebellion is the more common strategy in nondemocracies, used by twice as many groups as used protest.[10] But ethnic protest also is relatively common in nondemocratic societies: about one ethnopolitical group in five in nondemocracies organized major protest campaigns during the fourteen-year period under review compared with one group in three in democratic societies. We infer that the institutions and policies of autocratic regimes do not effectively suppress ethnic protest; rather, they make protest less attractive than rebellion as a strategy for political action.

Transitional regimes have less ethnopolitical conflict than autocracies and only slightly greater ethnopolitical conflict than democracies. There are two bases in table 5.1 for this counterintuitive observation. First, relatively few groups in these regimes used protest in 1985–98; in this respect they resemble the autocracies. Second, although a relatively large proportion of minorities in transitional regimes chose armed conflict, their average magnitude of rebellion was not significantly higher than in the democracies. That is, their rebellions were on average either short-lived or of low magnitude, or both. This is all the more surprising because of theoretical arguments and comparative evidence that countries with mixed and unstable political institutions ordinarily have high levels of civil conflict of all kinds.[11] Before drawing revisionist conclusions, we will look at more direct evidence on how transitions toward democracy affect ethnopolitical conflict.

Thirty-three new democracies were established in states with ethnopolitical minorities between 1980 and 1994 without backsliding toward autocracy by early 1999. Twelve of these transitions took place in postcommunist states; the others were scattered throughout the global South: Latin America (eleven), Asia (five), Africa (four), and the Middle East (one). The empirical evidence, summarized in table 5.2, gives qualified support to proponents of democratic solutions to ethnic conflict. It also is consistent with the thesis that the assertion of ethnopolitical identities and demands was particularly great in the new postcommunist states. The principal findings are as follow.

Successful democratic transitions are often followed by substantial increases in ethnopolitical protest. Half (thirty-four) of the sixty-eight ethnopolitical groups in the new democracies showed a sustained increase in protest during the first five years after transitions by comparison with the five years before the transition; thirty did not. The increases were especially great in the postcommunist democracies, where the annual magnitude of protest increased by an average of 1.1 on the 0–5 scale used in the Minorities project. This is equivalent to a shift from political organizing to small-scale demonstrations or from small-scale (less than ten thousand demonstrators) to large-scale (ten thousand to one hundred thousand demonstrators) political action. In new Third World democracies, by contrast, protest was more likely to decline than to increase.[12] Large increases in protest by some ethnopolitical groups in countries such as Taiwan, Bangladesh, and Guyana were offset by substantial decreases in South Africa and South Korea. In both the latter two countries, democratization was key to the incorporation of historically marginalized groups into the polity.[13]

Successful democratic transitions have inconsistent effects on ethnorebellion. Rebellion was uncommon among the sixty-eight ethnopolitical groups in these countries during the five years before their democratic transitions, a fact that probably contributed to the success of their transitions. In postcommunist Moldova and Georgia, though, transitions were followed by major regional rebellions that were only gradually and partially contained. In the new democracies of the Third World, democratic transitions provoked increased rebellion by eight groups—Mohajirs in Pakistan, for example—and lessened rebellion by eight others—the Cordillera peoples in the Philippines and Miskitos in Nicaragua, for example. Four continued without change. One thin token of support for the "domestic democratic peace" thesis is the observation that the mean level of ethnorebellion declined slightly in the new Third World democracies. No wonder that experts disagree on the potential effects of democratization for destabilizing ethnopolitical conflict: there are roughly an equal number of instances that can be cited in support of each position. The strong inference is that other societal and political factors determine the outcomes of democratic transitions, an issue we return to briefly at the end of this section.

Twenty-five states made partial or abortive transitions to democratic governance between 1980 and 1995. These countries have relatively large numbers of ethnopolitical groups (sixty-seven), of which nearly one-half (thirty-two) were in rebellion during the transitional period. It is plausible, therefore, to infer that ethnopolitical conflict played a part in derailing or delaying democratic transitions. We use the same diagnostic approach applied to new democracies and compare changes in protest and rebellion during the five years before and after these countries' transitions toward democracy.[14]

Partial and failed democratic transitions are usually followed by substantial increases in ethnopolitical protest. The comparative evidence summarized in table 5.3 differs on this point from the consequences observed in full democratic transitions. Forty-six groups in transitional democracies increased protest during the five years after transitions, by contrast with thirteen in which protest remained the same or decreased. The mean increase in protest

Table 5.2. The Effects of Democratization on Ethnopolitical Conflict in New Democracies, 1980–99

	New Postcommunist Democracies: 12 Countries, 25 Groups		New Third World Democracies: 21 Countries, 43 Groups	
	Change in Protest[a]	Change in Rebellion[b]	Change in Protest[a]	Change in Rebellion[b]
	Increased in 20 groups	Increased in 6 groups	Increased in 14 groups	Increased in 8 groups
	No protest by 1 group	No rebellion by 19 groups	No protest by 3 groups	No rebellion by 23 groups
	Unchanged or decreased in 4 groups	Unchanged or decreased in 0 groups	Unchanged or decreased in 26 groups	Unchanged or decreased in 12 groups
	Mean change: +1.1	Mean change: +0.6	Mean change: ±0.0	Mean change: −0.2
	Countries with large increases in protest:[c] Hungary, Romania, Estonia, Latvia, Macedonia, Ukraine	Countries with large increases in rebellion: Moldova, Georgia	Countries with large increases in protest: Taiwan, Bangladesh, Guyana	Countries with large increases in rebellion: Pakistan
	Countries with large decreases in protest:[c] none	Countries with large decreases in rebellion: none	Countries with large decreases in protest: South Korea, South Africa	Countries with large decreases in rebellion: Philippines, Nicaragua

Note: "New democracies" and their transition years are detailed in appendix A. The analysis is limited to countries whose democratic institutions were established between 1980 and 1994. Countries with no politically significant minorities are not included.

[a] The mean level of protest is calculated for each group during the five years before and the five years after the year in which democratic institutions were introduced. Protest in the transition year is not included in the calculation. Protest levels are those coded in the Minorities at Risk data set using the five-category scale described in table 2.2. The mean level of change in protest is determined by summing the before-and-after differences in mean protest scores and dividing by the number of groups engaged in protest. Groups with ongoing protest but no before-and-after difference in means are included in the "unchanged or decreased" counts.

[b] The mean level of rebellion is calculated for each group during the five years before and the five years after the year in which democratic institutions were introduced. Rebellion in the transition year is not included in the calculation. Rebellion levels are those coded in the Minorities at Risk data set using the seven-category scale described in table 2.2. The mean level of change in rebellion is determined by summing the before-and-after differences in mean rebellion scores and dividing by the number of groups engaged in rebellion. Groups with ongoing rebellion but no before-and-after differences in means are included in the "unchanged or decreased" counts.

[c] Countries listed as having large increases or decreases are those in which one or more groups' mean score for protest or rebellion changed by ±1.8 points or more in the before-and-after comparison.

Table 5.3. The Effects of Regime Transitions on Ethnopolitical Conflict in Failed and Partial Democracies, 1980–99

	Failed and Partial Postcommunist Democracies: 9 Countries, 27 Groups		Failed and Partial Third World Democracies: 16 Countries, 40 Groups	
	Change in Protest[a]	Change in Rebellion[b]	Change in Protest[a]	Change in Rebellion[b]
	Increased in 22 groups	Increased in 8 groups	Increased in 24 groups	Increased in 9 groups
	No protest by 1 group	No rebellion by 17 groups	No protest by 7 groups	No rebellion by 18 groups
	Unchanged or decreased in 4 groups	Unchanged or decreased in 2 groups	Unchanged or decreased in 9 groups	Unchanged or decreased in 13 groups
	Mean change: +0.7	Mean change: +1.7	Mean change: +0.2	Mean change: −0.8
	Countries with large increases in protest:[c] Russia, Azerbaijan, Kazakhstan	Countries with large increases in rebellion: Croatia, Bosnia, Russia, Azerbaijan	Countries with large increases in protest: Fiji, Nigeria, Ethiopia, Zambia	Countries with large increases in rebellion: none
	Countries with large decreases in protest:[c,d] Croatia, Bosnia	Countries with large decreases in rebellion: none	Countries with large decreases in protest: Togo	Countries with large decreases in rebellion: Lebanon, Niger, Ethiopia, Zimbabwe

Note: Failed and partial democracies ("transitional regimes") and their transition years are detailed in appendix A. These are countries that made transitions toward institutional democracy between 1980 and 1995 that either subsequently reverted to autocracy or retain mixed democratic and autocratic features. Also included are Fiji and Thailand, in which fully democratic polities shifted to autocracy (in 1987 and 1991, respectively) and back toward democracy several years later. Countries whose partial democratic institutions predate 1980 or were instituted after 1995 are not included in the analysis because reliable before-and-after comparisons of ethnopolitical conflict (see note a) cannot be made for them: they are Singapore, Morocco, Egypt, Senegal, Chad, Guinea, and Mexico. Countries with no politically significant minorities also are excluded from the analysis.

[a] The mean level of protest is calculated for each group during the five years before and the five years after the first post-1980 transition year. The transition year is the year in which full or partial democratic institutions were first attempted, as shown in appendix A, except for Fiji and Thailand, for which the transition year is the year when democratic institutions failed. Protest in the transition year is not included in the calculation. Protest levels are those coded in the Minorities at Risk data set using the five-category scale described in table 2.2. The mean level of change in protest is determined by summing the before-and-after differences in mean protest scores and dividing by the number of groups engaged in protest. Groups with ongoing protest but no before-and-after difference in means are included in the "unchanged or decreased" counts.

[b] The mean level of rebellion is calculated for each group during the five years before and the five years after the first post-1980 transition year. Rebellion in the transition year is not included in the calculation. Rebellion levels are those coded in the Minorities at Risk data set using the seven-category scale described in table 2.2. The mean level of change in rebellion is determined by summing the before-and-after differences in mean rebellion scores and dividing by the number of groups engaged in rebellion. Groups with ongoing rebellion but no before-and-after differences in means are included in the "unchanged or decreased" counts.

[c] Countries listed as having large increases or decreases are those in which one or more groups' mean score for protest or rebellion changed by ±1.8 points or more in the before-and-after comparison.

[d] Serbs in Croatia and Bosnia shifted from protest to rebellion after regime transitions.

was greater in the postcommunist states than in the Third World. This suggests a provocative comparison. Partial and failed efforts at democratization prompt increased protest by ethnopolitical groups (table 5.3), whereas in the Third World successful transitions are most likely to be followed by a decline in ethnopolitical protest (table 5.2). The inference is that increased protest is one of the factors that provokes elites to halt or reverse democratic transitions.

Ethnopolitical rebellions are strongly implicated in the failure of democratic transitions in the postcommunist states. The evidence confirms the conventional wisdom of regional observers. Ethnic rebellions increased in almost all the postcommunist democracies, but the magnitude of their increase was three times greater in failed and partial democracies (+1.7 in table 5.3) than in successful ones (+0.6 in table 5.2). Croatia, Azerbaijan, and Bosnia are among the failed and partial democracies in this world region in which ethnopolitical strife contributed to the failure or postponement of democratic consolidation.

Partial and failed democratic transitions in Third World states tend to be followed by declines in ethnic rebellion. This finding is both counterintuitive and at odds with the pattern observed in the postcommunist states. The magnitude of rebellion decreased for thirteen of the twenty-two warring ethnic groups in these sixteen countries by a significant 0.8 magnitude, equivalent to a shift from intermediate to small-scale guerrilla war or from terrorist campaigns to political banditry. In the partial democracies with the greatest decreases in rebellion, including Lebanon and Ethiopia, the establishment of quasi-democratic regimes was part of a package of political changes that ended protracted communal conflict. Moreover, there are no offsetting examples of partial democratization, or democratic failure, that precipitated serious new ethnorebellions.

The inference is that Third World regimes in heterogeneous societies have had some recent success in containing ethnic warfare through experimental mixes of democratic and autocratic institutions. It is worth pointing out that the main institutional difference between partial and full democracies is an elected chief executive who operates with few constraints on his or her power.[15] A strong executive in a new, quasi-open regime may be able to respond more quickly and effectively to ethnopolitical challenges, whether by force or compromise, than the politically constrained chief executives of Western-model democracies.

Following are some summary observations about the evidence just reviewed. The proposition that democracies are hospitable settings for ethnopolitical protest is generally supported. It is true for old democracies and new postcommunist democracies. Moreover, it is not just a "structural" phenomenon, because most recent transitions toward democracy, successful or not, complete or partial, have been accompanied by increases in ethnopolitical protest.

The one exception is the experience of new democracies in the Third World, where transitions to full democracy tended to reduce protest.

The proposition that democracy inhibits ethnic rebellion has only qualified support. Old and new democracies have less ethnic rebellion than autocracies, but transitions toward democracy have mixed effects. Democratic transitions in the postcommunist states provided incentives and opportunities for increased rebellion, whereas democratic transitions in Third World democracies led on average to a decline in rebellion. Rebellion declined most, not in new full democracies, but in the quasi-democracies and failed democracies categorized here as "transitional." We suspect that, in the Third World, regimes with a mix of democratic and autocratic features are somewhat better able to contain ethnopolitical conflict than new Western-model democracies.

The postcommunist anomaly is open to different interpretations. One kind of explanation emphasizes incentives and threats: democratization provided incentives for ethnopolitical entrepreneurs, encouraged outbidding among rival politicians, and posed a security dilemma for minority peoples. A complementary explanation emphasizes opportunities: when central authority weakened in Moscow and Belgrade, it became possible for peoples to act on long-suppressed ethnic identities and hostilities. A third explanation emphasizes capacities: the USSR and Yugoslavia both gave ethnicity a political and territorial basis, so that when central control was relaxed, titular nationalities had administrative and party structures through which to pursue their own interests. A fourth kind of explanation points to the crucial role of state formation. Ethnic warfare in the postcommunist states was specific to new states: it erupted in Croatia and Georgia, Moldova and Azerbaijan, but not in Romania or Czechoslovakia. Seen from a distance, the pattern of ethnopolitical action in the territorially intact postcommunist states resembles that of new and transitional democracies in the Third World: Protest increased after democratic transitions; rebellion did not. The supposition, therefore, is that the incentives, opportunities, and capacities for ethnic warfare in periods of democratic transition are most pronounced, or least controllable, in new states. *The formation of new states in heterogeneous societies is the primary risk factor for serious ethnopolitical conflict, not the formation of new democracies per se.*

Democracy and Discrimination

The theoretical argument driving the Minorities project asserts that collective disadvantages are the root cause of ethnopolitical action. Discriminatory treatment helps define group boundaries and enhances the salience of group identity. Redress of grievances about invidious treatment and the desire to gain advantages are principal sources of group incentives for action. Cultural restrictions are a challenge to group identity, contribute to group resentment and resistance against advantaged groups, and help perpetuate intergroup prejudices and intercommunal conflict. In the next few pages we consider the connections between democratic governance and discrimination. The initial substantive discussion lays the groundwork for a review of comparative evidence on the effects of regime type and democratization on patterns of discriminatory treatment between 1985 and 1998.

If political and economic inequalities are an essential issue for a disadvantaged minority, as they are, for example, for people of African descent throughout the Americas, then the optimal strategies for minimizing ethnopolitical conflict are the provision of enforceable protections against discrimination complemented by opportunities that compensate for past discrimination. Democratic regimes are most likely to provide such protections and opportunities, but they do so imperfectly. Brazil gives legal protections to its Afro-Brazilian minority but makes little effort to enforce them (see the sketch on pp. 100–104). Enforcement is essential to ending the ingrained social practices that maintain political and economic disadvantages of minorities.

Enforcement of equal rights is seldom enough to reduce the poverty and powerlessness that are the long-term legacies of discrimination. Since the 1960s reformers in many Western and Asian societies have urged positive action to reduce inequalities and have designed public policies that give special opportunities to disadvantaged minorities. Affirmative action and the use of quotas in education and employment, as practiced in democracies as different as the United States and India, have undoubtedly contributed to the reduction of communal inequalities. But they have proven to be costly strategies, not so much in material terms but in political terms, because they have provoked resistance by more advantaged groups who resent "unfair" policies and fear losing their own advantages.[16]

As a general rule, reducing the legacy of past discrimination requires consistent, long-term policies whose basic principles are accepted by all parties. In one respect democracies are at a disadvantage when implementing such policies because public officials are susceptible to electoral pressures from majorities, whereas autocracies have more leeway to follow policies of redistribution —if their leaders choose to do so. Therefore, there is no reason to expect group discrimination and restrictions to be necessarily higher in autocracies than democracies. Both types of regimes may initiate remedial policies. Regardless of the type of political system, however, whenever acceptance of the principle of intergroup equality becomes an issue of serious political contention, the risks of polarization and open conflict across communal lines are substantial.

Recognition and perpetuation of a group's distinctive culture often are an essential issue in majority-minority relations, even in the absence of significant material and political inequalities. Cultural traits, especially language, are highly valued by Hungarians in Slovakia and by Chinese in Malaysia, as shown in our sketches of the two groups. They are intrinsic to maintaining group identity, and their acceptance by government and society at large is symbolic of the group's status vis-à-vis the state and dominant groups. The optimal strategy is to give such peoples the means—legal, political, material—to protect and promote their cultural practices in those regions and spheres of life where they matter to group members. For many this means unimpeded instruction and communication in the group's language, not only within the group but in dealings with others. For other groups, like Egyptian Copts and Tibetans, it means ensuring freedom of religious practice—largely ensured for Copts, sharply constrained for Tibetan Buddhists. One price of multiculturalism is acceptance and even-handed public management of the social friction and inefficiency that often accompany the coexistence of multiple languages, lifeways, and systems of belief.

We showed in chapter 4 that historical and contemporary practices of discrimination against national, ethnocultural, and religious minorities adversely affected all but 33 of the 275 groups covered in the Minorities at Risk survey in the mid-1990s. The impact of different kinds of political institutions on levels of discrimination and restrictions on minorities is summarized in table 5.4. These are some summary observations.

Old democracies. Minorities in long-established democracies face few cultural and political restrictions by comparison with groups living under other kinds of regimes, but they encounter a relatively high degree of economic discrimination and intermediate levels of political discrimination. Explanations of these deviations from democratic norms of equality of status and opportunity are suggested in chapter 4 and worth repeating here. First, virtually all "visible minorities" and indigenous peoples in the older democracies are economically disadvantaged because of historical discrimination and, in the case of new immigrant groups, contemporary discrimination that is highly resistant to change. Second, some recent immigrant groups in European societies, such as Turks in Germany, face substantial barriers to full citizenship—barriers that by definition constitute political discrimination.

New democracies. The sharpest contrast between old and new democracies is that the latter continue to restrict a wider range of political and, especially, cultural activities of minorities. Economic discrimination is somewhat less in

Table 5.4. Type of Political Regime and Ethnic Discrimination in the 1990s

Type of Regime[a]	Number of Ethnopolitical Groups	Discrimination[b]			Restrictions[c]	
		Economic	Political		Political	Cultural
Old democracies (n = 27)	60	2.03	1.92		1.82	1.02
New democracies (n = 33)	68	1.77	2.13		2.24	1.99
Transitional regimes (n = 32)	80	1.06	1.64		2.03	1.47
Autocracies (n = 26)	68	1.99	2.74		4.20	2.60

[a] Regime types are defined and countries of each type listed in appendix A.

[b] Mean scores on the Minorities project's five-category scales of extent of discrimination, as described in chapter 3, pp. 110, 114. Mean levels of discrimination are calculated from the data set's annual and biannual codes for each type of discrimination from 1990–91 through 1998. The means are computed by pooling all nonmissing annual values for all groups in each of the four types of regime.

[c] Mean scores on the Minorities project's indicators of political and cultural restrictions, as described in chapter 3, 114, 118. Mean levels of restriction are calculated in the same way as mean levels of discrimination (note b).

new than in old democracies because many of the new democracies are post-communist states in which long-standing social and economic policies helped level the playing field among minority and national peoples.[17] Political discrimination and restrictions are somewhat greater in new than in old democracies because many of the new democrats are also nationalists who do not trust democratic institutions enough to forgo restrictions on groups that are seen as potential or overt threats to state security—Russians in the Baltic states, Hungarians in Romania (until 1997), Kurds in Turkey.

Transitional regimes. The partial and failed democracies show unexpected results: they have the lowest levels of economic and political discrimination of any regime type and are relatively nonrestrictive of minority political and cultural activities. There is no one obvious explanation for this unexpected pattern, but two observations can be suggested. First, a relatively large number of "transitional" regimes exist in what Donald Horowitz characterizes as unranked plural societies, that is, societies in which ethnic relations are not sharply stratified along economic or political lines. Discrimination and its malign consequences should be less evident in such societies. Second, the institutional instability of many of these regimes may have precluded the development or perpetuation of consistent policies of political and cultural restrictions.

Autocracies. The autocracies exhibit an expected pattern of high discrimination and pervasive restrictions on minorities. Political discrimination and restrictions are markedly more severe, on average, in these regimes than elsewhere. Cultural restrictions are more than twice as severe as in the old democracies, whereas economic discrimination is about equally great in both types of societies. The severe discrimination and restrictions in autocracies have multiple causes. Most Islamic autocracies sharply restrict adherents of religious minorities, such as Baha'is in Iran, Shi'is in Bahrain, and Ahmadis in Pakistan. Dominant groups in African autocracies often use state power to restrict communal rivals, for example, in Mobutu's Zaire, in Moi's Kenya, and in Rwanda before 1994. A number of autocracies have adopted or tightened restrictive policies as a consequence of persistent ethnic challenges. In China, Indonesia, Burma, Iraq, and Angola, restrictions and discrimination are at least partly a consequence of the mutually reinforcing conflict cycle mentioned in chapter 4: ethnic wars prompt leaders to impose greater restrictions, which, in turn, provide incentives that sustain warfare. The existence of such cycles also weighs heavily against efforts to democratize autocratic regimes.

The autocracies and transitional regimes pose the sharpest and most unexpected contrast in patterns and policies of ethnic discrimination. The transitional regimes, despite—or perhaps because of—their partial and failed attempts to adopt democratic institutions, are far less restrictive than autocracies in their policies toward minorities. It is not possible to disentangle cause and effect from macro-level data, but the global contrasts suggest the importance of small-*n* comparative analysis of changing policies toward minorities by regimes that are attempting to negotiate the transition from autocracy to democracy.

What are the post–Cold War trends in political and economic discrimination and cultural restrictions in plural societies? And what are the consequences of democratic transitions for discrimination and restrictions? We did a series of comparative analyses to provide some general answers to these questions. From 1990–91 to 1998 the Minorities project has biannual or annual data on levels of discrimination and restrictions that we use to identify general trends and shifts in policy in each of the four types of regime.[18] The results on trends are summarized in table 5.5 and discussed below.

The status of ethnopolitical groups consistently improved during the 1990s. Substantial overall improvements in group status occurred in the 1990s. Political discrimination declined the most: about 30 percent of groups restrained by political discrimination in 1990–91 had more political rights and greater access by 1998 (60 of 211), gains that were only partly offset by increased political discrimination imposed on 17 groups. One in three groups that experienced cultural restrictions in 1990–91 had greater cultural rights by 1998 (43 of 132), but their gains were offset by increased cultural restrictions on 27 other groups. The net improvements in mean scores on political discrimination and cultural restrictions were similar, about 13 percent each. Economic discrimination overall changed for fewer groups and at a lower magnitude, affirming an observation made in chapter 4. It is easier for governments to give minorities access to political institutions and to eliminate culturally restrictive policies than it is to compensate them for historically derived and structurally rooted economic disadvantages.

Overall more than one-third of the 275 groups in the Minorities survey were better off in 1998 than at the beginning of the decade. Equally important, the improvement was not only or mainly the result of the post–Cold War transition at the beginning of the decade. Year-by-year averages, not reported here, show regular declines from the beginning to the end of the decade in almost all indicators of discrimination and restrictions in most types of regime—but not in autocracies.

There is ample evidence, summarized in tables 5.6 and 5.7, that democratization contributed to much of the improvement in minority group status in the 1990s. New and transitional democracies had better records in reducing discrimination and lifting restrictions than old democracies. Autocracies

Table 5.5. Global Trends in Discrimination and Restrictions, 1990–98

	Economic Discrimination	Political Discrimination	Cultural Restrictions
Number of groups affected in 1990–91[a]	179	211	132
Mean score in 1990-91[b]	1.73	2.26	2.00
Number of groups with better status in 1998[c]	41	60	43
Number of groups with worse status in 1998[d]	15	17	27
Mean score in 1998[b]	1.62	1.95	1.74
Net improvement in status:			
In mean score (%)	6.4%	13.7%	13.0%
In groups affected (%)	14.5%	20.4%	12.1%

[a] Number of groups with non-zero scores on the three indicators of discrimination and restrictions. Political restrictions are not analyzed separately, because their trends are similar to those in political discrimination.

[b] Groups with missing data are excluded when calculating means.

[c] Number of groups out of 275 whose scores on each indicator declined between 1990–91 and 1998.

[d] Number of groups out of 275 whose scores on each indicator increased between 1990–91 and 1998. Some of these groups had zero scores in 1990–91.

show a net decline in economic discrimination, but it was more than offset by increases in political discrimination and cultural restrictions. These are some more specific findings and some examples.

Group status improved most in the new democracies. The introduction of democratic principles and institutions should, in principle, put an end to official policies of political discrimination and, sometimes, lead to remedial policies of political incorporation for minorities. That is, in fact, the experience of the new democracies: of the fifty-seven groups subject to political restrictions in these countries in 1990–91, twenty-four had achieved substantial political gains by 1998, that is, gains of at least one category on the five-category scale of political discrimination. Economic discrimination and cultural restrictions also were alleviated, though to a lesser degree. The sixteen groups that gained most in the new democracies are listed in the right-hand column in table 5.6. Half are in the postcommunist states; the others include non-European

Table 5.6. The Effects of Democratization on Minority Group Status, 1990–98

	Old Democracies: 27 Countries, 59 Groups			New Democracies: 33 Countries, 68 Groups		
	Economic Discrimination	Political Discrimination	Cultural Restrictions	Economic Discrimination	Political Discrimination	Cultural Restrictions
	Decreased in 4 groups	Decreased in 6 groups	Decreased in 5 groups	Decreased in 17 groups	Decreased in 24 groups	Decreased in 15 groups
	No change in 54 groups[a]	No change in 52 groups	No change in 51 groups	No change in 46 groups[b]	No change in 40 groups	No change in 44 groups
	Increased in 1 group	Increased in 1 group	Increased in 3 groups	Increased in 5 groups	Increased in 4 groups	Increased in 9 groups
	Mean change: −.05	Mean change: −.17	Mean change: −.08	Mean change: −.19	Mean change: −.79	Mean change: −.44

Major decreases in discrimination and restrictions:[c] Kashmiris and Sikhs in India, indigenous peoples in Ecuador

Major decreases in discrimination and restrictions: Turks in Bulgaria; Roma in Macedonia; Hungarians in Romania,[d] Gagauz in Moldova;[e] Tatars in Ukraine; Abkhaz, Adzars, and Ossetians in Georgia;[e] Asians, Coloreds, Xhosa, and Zulus in South Africa; East Indians in Guyana; indigenous peoples in Guatemala, Bolivia, and Chile

Major increases in discrimination and restrictions:[f] Sri Lankan Tamils, Muslims in India

Major increases in discrimination and restrictions: Serbs in Macedonia, Hungarians in Slovakia and Romania,[d] Russians in Latvia and Lithuania, Ahmadis and Mohajirs in Pakistan, Africans in Guyana

---

[a] The "no change" category includes groups with no discrimination or restrictions throughout the period and groups with nonzero codes that did not change from 1990–91 to 1998.

[b] Including three groups in which data were insufficient to classify trends.

[c] Declines of two or more categories on the economic or political discrimination scale, or declines in two or more of the eight categories of cultural restrictions.

[d] Political and economic discrimination increased sharply against Hungarians in Romania in the early to mid-1990s but decreased equally sharply after 1996.

[e] Relaxation of restrictions imposed in the immediate aftermath of independence.

[f] Increases of two or more categories on the economic or political discrimination scale, or increases in two or more of the eight categories of cultural restrictions.

Table 5.7. The Effects of Autocracy and Failed or Partial Democratic Transitions on Minority Group Status, 1990–98

	Failed and Partial Democracies: 32 Countries, 80 Groups			Autocracies: 26 Countries, 68 Groups		
	Economic Discrimination	Political Discrimination	Cultural Restrictions	Economic Discrimination	Political Discrimination	Cultural Restrictions
Decreased in	8 groups	20 groups	15 groups	12 groups	10 groups	8 groups
No change in	68 groups[a,b]	56 groups	59 groups	51 groups[c]	50 groups[d]	51 groups
Increased in	4 groups	4 groups	6 groups	5 groups	8 groups	9 groups
Mean change:	−.07	−.34	−.54	−.06	+.18	+.09

Major decreases in discrimination and restrictions:[e] Serbs in Croatia;[f] Muslims in Bosnia;[f] Chechens,[f] Buryats, Karachays, Lezgins, Tuvinians, and Yakuts in Russia; Poles in Belarus; Russians in Kyrghizia;[g] Druze and Shi'i in Lebanon; Malay Muslims in Thailand; Susu in Guinea; Mende in Sierra Leone

Major decreases in discrimination and restrictions: Kachin in Burma, Chinese and Montagnards in Vietnam, East Timorese in Indonesia, westerners in Cameroon, Lunda/Yeke in Zaire, Tutsis in Rwanda,[h] Isaaqs in Somalia,[h] Afars in Djibouti[f]

Major increases in discrimination and restrictions: Russians in Turkmenistan and Uzbekistan; Hazaris, Tajiks, and Uzbeks in Afghanistan;[j] Turkmen and Tibetans in China; Berbers in Algeria; Shi'i in Bahrain; Hutus in Rwanda;[j] Luba of Kasai in Congo (formerly Zaire)

Major increases in discrimination and restrictions:[i] Greeks in Albania, Muslims in Bosnia, Armenians in Azerbaijan, Avars in Russia, Russians and Germans in Kazakhstan, Vietnamese in Cambodia

---

[a] The "no change" category includes groups with no discrimination or restrictions throughout the period and groups with nonzero codes that did not change from 1990–91 to 1998.

[b] Including seven groups for which data were insufficient to classify trends.

[c] Including fourteen groups for which data were insufficient to classify trends.

[d] Including six groups for which data were insufficient to classify trends.

[e] Declines of two or more categories on the five-category economic or political discrimination scale, or declines in two or more of eight categories of cultural restrictions.

[f] After the end of civil wars.

[g] Relaxation of restrictions imposed in the immediate aftermath of independence.

[h] Winners in civil and revolutionary wars.

[i] Increases of two or more categories on the five-category economic or political discrimination scale, or increases in two or more of eight categories of cultural restrictions.

[j] Losers in civil and revolutionary wars.

South Africans and indigenous peoples in Latin America. Offsetting these gains, democratic nationalists in five postcommunist European countries imposed new restrictions on national minorities who were regarded as threats to state security.

Minority gains in new democracies of Latin America, Asia, and southern Africa usually are the result of two complementary processes. One is the commitment of most democratic elites to incorporation of minorities. The second is the effective use many groups have made of the political opportunities provided by newly democratic regimes. This is illustrated in a striking way by the sketch of the indigenous peoples of Bolivia (pp. 178–182). In 1950 they were utterly powerless, in 1980 they had token political representation, in 1994 an indigenous politician was elected vice president, and in 1997 the major indigenous political party slated a woman as its presidential candidate. The Bolivian example also provides a glimpse of what is probably a general tendency: the political openings that empower minorities also may help empower women.[19]

Transitional regimes have been almost as effective as new democracies in improving minority group status. If the success of democratic transitions is judged by improvements in minority status, rather than complete institutional transformation, then the transitional regimes performed just about as well as the new democracies. In fact, they outpaced the new democracies in lifting cultural restrictions. A more cautionary conclusion is suggested by looking at the list of fifteen minorities that gained the most—shown in the left-hand column in table 5.7. Five of them, including Chechens in Russia (whose gains have proven transitory) and Druze and Shi'i in Lebanon, gained only after civil wars were fought over issues of group rights and autonomy. Most groups subject to major new restrictions—shown at the botom of the left-hand column —live in transitional postcommunist states that have mixed records of democratic accommodation. The Bosnian Muslims appear on both lists, victimized from 1992 to 1994 by Serbs and Croats and then restored to precarious equality once the Dayton Accords began to be implemented.

Restrictions on minorities have eased in some autocracies. An appreciable number of minority and national peoples in the autocracies gained in status during the 1990s, for a variety of reasons, some of which can be inferred from the lists of winners and losers shown at the bottom of the right-hand column of table 5.7. Most major gains were concessions aimed at managing ethnopolitical conflict: for example, rebellions by Kachins in Burma, the people of East Timor, and Afars in Djibouti and large-scale protest by the people of Cameroon's Western Region. For Isaaqs in Somalia and the Rwandan Tutsis, group status improved because communal rebels gained power. The downside is that autocratic governments just as often responded to challenges by ratcheting up discrimination, as did the Taliban in Afghanistan and the Beijing government in response to nationalist resistance in Tibet and Xinjiang province. There also may be foreign policy reasons for decreased group discrimination in some nondemocratic states. For example, the Vietnamese government in the 1990s reduced restrictions on the Chinese minority as part of policies aimed at reducing tensions with the People's Republic of China and gaining access to capital investment from overseas Chinese communities.

The old democracies are glacially slow in reducing the historical legacies of discrimination and cultural restrictions. Very few minorities in the old democracies made appreciable gains in the 1990s—not when judged by the indicators applied uniformly to all 275 groups in the Minorities study. We know from comparisons in table 5.4 that the twenty-seven old democracies impose fewer cultural restrictions on minorities than other types of polities; therefore, few such restrictions remain to be lifted. On the other hand, the old democracies have the highest average level of economic discrimination of any type of polity and about the same level of political discrimination as the new democracies. But very few minorities in these countries improved in political or economic status during the 1990s.

All substantial changes in group status in the old democracies, shown in the left-hand column in table 5.6, occurred in the context of major episodes of ethnopolitical conflict. In India the central government restored home rule in the mid-1990s to the Punjab and Kashmir as part of a strategy to defuse ethnonational rebellions, but it also tolerated new infringements by militant Hindu nationalists on the rights of the country's large Muslim majority. In Ecuador nationwide protests by indigenous peoples paid off in more-than-token concessions. In Sri Lanka the Tamil insurgency provoked new restrictions as part of a long-term counterinsurgency strategy.

Finally, we looked for evidence of changes in group status in the advanced industrial democracies, home to thirty groups in the Minorities survey. A few marginal improvements were registered: greater political rights for indigenous peoples in Canada; modest gains in political access for Afro-Caribbeans in Britain, Turks in Germany, and Maori in New Zealand; improved economic opportunities for Muslims in France and Koreans in Japan; and greater language rights for Italy's Sards. The Western democracies have been world leaders in promoting individual and group rights for minorities. Most of them made considerable progress in implementing those rights in the 1960s and 1970s. By the 1990s, however, political resistance to further public action in behalf of minority rights had emerged in most Western societies. Thus these countries have little prospect for substantial gains like those registered in the 1990s in the new and transitional democracies. Resistance to further state-sponsored improvements in group rights may also develop in the new democracies. The worst-case scenario is a possible shift throughout the democratic world to a pattern on which we have already commented in respect of the autocracies: major changes in the status of minority and national peoples are most likely to occur in these countries as a consequence of serious ethnopolitical conflict.

To summarize the findings, the status of ethnopolitical groups was least susceptible to change in the 1990s in long-established, well-institutionalized political systems—whether democratic or autocratic. The changes that did occur in these polities were usually positive in the democracies and negative in the autocracies. Group status was much more subject to change in new and transitional regimes—for the better in new democracies and also in most transitional regimes. Substantial changes in group status in transitional regimes and autocracies were most likely to occur as a response, sometimes positive and sometimes negative, to ethnopolitical rebellions and major protest campaigns.

This discussion's focus on democratic institutions and opportunities may convey the misleading impression that democratic transitions should be regarded as the main cause of positive shifts in states' policies toward national and minority communities. Not so. Three other dynamics also are at work in the post–Cold War era, each of which has an international dimension.

1. *Pressures to implement international principles of nondiscrimination in plural societies.* The United Nations' lead in opposing ethnic and religious discrimination has been complemented and amplified by the policies of regional organizations, especially the Organization for Security and Cooperation in Europe and the Council of Europe, and by a large number of nongovernmental organizations that monitor human rights issues and campaign for observance of international standards of nondiscrimination and recognition of group rights.[20]

2. *Political leaders who are increasingly likely to make cost-benefit assessments that favor strategies of accommodation as low-cost alternatives to strategies of forcible assimilation or repression.* The willingness of governing elites to compromise on issues of rights and access may end or head off costly ethnic wars. It also can enhance elites' support from their own citizens and from outsiders, including regional powers, potential investors, and international lenders. Increased political and economic interdependency among states has substantially increased elites' awareness of successful strategies of conflict

management elsewhere. Interdependencies also have made them more susceptible to outside pressures and inducements.

3. *Politically mobilized minorities that have shifted strategies and tactics to take advantage of new sources of international support as well as political opportunities provided by more responsive states.* The case study of indigenous peoples of Amazonian Ecuador, on pp. 96–99, shows how international support has shaped their strategies and outcomes. In general, the post–Cold War political environment provides incentives to minorities to enlist international support and to state elites to moderate their political actions and seek grounds for accommodation. The incentives for moderation are greater in democracies than autocracies because the former are more open to international influence. The net result of these international factors is this: even if democratic governments face growing domestic political constraints on policies for reducing discrimination, these constraints are likely to be offset by countervailing international support to continue and enhance policies of accommodation.

The Indigenous Peoples of Bolivia
Mobilization and Empowerment in the 1990s

Ted Robert Gurr and Pamela L. Burke

Bolivia's pueblas originarias *gained enough political power in the 1980s and 1990s to determine electoral outcomes and to shape public policy on indigenous rights. They remain the poorest people in an impoverished country, and their political impact is being diluted by factional conflict between highland and lowland peoples and within indigenous organizations.*

B OLIVIA IS THE POOREST COUNTRY of continental South America, and its four and a half million indigenous people, about 55 percent of the population, were historically an impoverished and powerless rural majority. In 1950 they held less than one-tenth of the country's arable land, and many were obliged to work on large estates owned by Bolivians of European descent. The *indios,* as they were called by the dominant group, lacked most political rights, including the right to vote. Moreover, the culture, language, and traditions of the highland Aymara and Quechua and the lowland Guarani and Arawak were socially unacceptable to the dominant group, the *gente decente* ("decent people"). Indigenous languages were rarely taught in the schools. In urban areas indigenous peoples were expected to ride in the backs of buses and to move to the opposite side of the street in the presence of *gente decente.* In social interactions they were referred to in the familiar *tu* form rather than with the formal *usted.* One of the few forms of upward mobility for indigenous men was to join the lower ranks of the army and police. Those admitted to the military academy had to change their names and give up their indigenous language.

Differences of culture, means of livelihood, and collective interest divide the highland indigenous peoples from the tribes of lowland eastern Bolivia. The people of the highlands, mostly Quechua and Aymara, number about 4.4 million, whereas the lowland indigenous tribes, including Guarani and Arawaks, number about two hundred thousand. Another line of cleavage separates indigenous peoples from *cholos,* people of whole or part indigenous descent who have adopted the lifeways and language of Bolivians of European descent. *Cholos* are a middle stratum between *indios* and the *gente decente,* upwardly mobile but nonetheless discriminated against by the dominant group.

RESISTANCE AND MOBILIZATION

In the first half of the twentieth century there were scattered uprisings in which indigenous peoples sought to regain their communal lands from the big estates. In 1952 the National Revolutionary Movement (MNR, a leftist party whose supporters were mainly Bolivians of European descent) seized power in a popularly supported revolution. Most estates were immediately occupied by indigenous communities, a change ratified in the Agrarian Reform Laws passed in 1953. The MNR also gave indigenous peoples citizenship and the right to vote but at the same time followed assimilationist policies and sought to channel indigenous participation through state-sponsored political parties.

The Aymara, who make up nearly half the indigenous highland population, responded to assimilationist pressures in the 1960s and 1970s by founding their own political movements, building on peasants' unions that had begun to form in the 1940s. Most important was the Katarista movement, which identified with Tupac Katari, an Aymara leader who led an anticolonial uprising in 1781. Some of these efforts had violent consequences, including a 1974 protest against rising prices that resulted in the killing of a thousand peasants, and the formation of a peasant guerrilla group that carried out a wave of bombings in the early and mid-1980s. Most indigenous energies, though, were channeled into interest-group activity and electoral politics. Indigenous political parties achieved token representation in congressional elections in 1979 and 1989.

The major political breakthrough occurred after 1989. Carlos Palenque, an Aymara Indian and popular television host, founded a new party, Conciencia de Patria (CONDEPA), to represent indigenous and other rural peoples. In three elections between 1989 and 1991 CONDEPA scored substantial gains, including Palenque's election as mayor of the capital, La Paz. In 1991 and 1992 indigenous groups organized countrywide campaigns of protest, including a seven-hundred-kilometer "March for Territory and Dignity" from the eastern lowlands to La Paz in 1991. At the culmination of a similar but larger march in October 1992, fifty thousand indigenous people formed a human chain around the national capital buildings.

EMPOWERMENT AND REFORM

In 1993, facing national elections and recognizing the political power of the indigenous movement, the MNR, one of three major parties, slated former Katarista leader Victor Hugo Cardenas as its vice presidential candidate. The MNR won, and at the August 6, 1993, inauguration Cardenas spoke in Aymara, Quechua, and Guarani, and he and his wife wore traditional Aymara clothing. The symbolism, and the political change from the years before 1952, when *indios* lacked citizenship rights, could not have been more dramatic.

The material consequences of indigenous political activism began under the previous coalition government. In 1991 national legislation was passed to protect the rights of indigenous peoples; in 1992 they were granted title to large tracts of land in the highlands. The United Nations and the World Bank funded new government-endorsed projects in 1993 aimed at cultural conservation, promotion of bilingual education, and technological and crafts development in indigenous areas.

The MNR victory was followed by constitutional reforms in 1994 that acknowledge Bolivia to be a "multiethnic, pluricultural society" and allow indigenous peoples to assume ownership of traditional lands. A Popular Participation Plan, enacted in 1994, provides for legal recognition for indigenous communities. In 1995, 40 percent of the government's revenue-sharing funds for roads, schools, water development, and other local projects ($255 million) was granted under terms of the Plan to rural indigenous communities; previously virtually all such grants went to the cities. Equally important, local councils were given the authority to carry out the projects. By mid-1997 legal recognition had been extended to 528 indigenous communities. Thirty-three of these communities were in the eastern lowlands, encompassing 150,000 people. The national government continues to allocate substantial resources to implement the principles of the Popular Participation Plan. Observers regard the Plan as a model of decentralization for Latin American countries with large indigenous populations.

PROSPECTS FOR FUTURE REFORM

Empowerment has also brought to the surface divisions within Bolivia's indigenous rights movement. Contention over a controversial land reform bill in 1996 precipitated an open split between highland organizations and lowland peoples, who had nurtured long-standing resentments about the patronizing attitudes of the highlanders. After months of demonstrations in opposition to the bill, the lowland groups, whose own confederations date from the early 1980s, reached a separate accord with the government and received title deeds recognizing the collective ownership of their land. Factionalism among the highland groups erupted in 1997 when Carlos Palenque, the founder of CONDEPA and its presidential candidate, died of a heart attack shortly before national elections. CONDEPA was one of five parties that entered into the new coalition government of President Hugo Banzer Suarez, but a year later he ousted CONDEPA because it had been crippled by factional infighting.

Local disputes also have undercut the cohesion of the indigenous movement. The livelihood of some sixty thousand Quechuas and Aymaras depends on coca cultivation. Between 1995 and 1998 indigenous coca growers in the Chapare area clashed repeatedly and violently with government forces seeking to eradicate coca production. Elsewhere in the highlands Quechua factions had deadly clashes in 1995 over agricultural boundaries.

Empowerment of Bolivia's indigenous peoples has the potential, in principle and in the long run, to overcome the legacy of generations of impoverishment and cultural discrimination. But there are serious obstacles along the way. One is the limited supply of public resources in a poor country. Reducing poverty and providing education in indigenous languages require sustained investment from national and international sources, which depends, in turn, on continued influence of indigenous peoples in national politics and international forums. But the cohesiveness and political effectiveness of indigenous organizations in Bolivia are being crippled by factionalism and the diffusion of their political energies. Given Bolivia's political history of governmental instability, and the presence of other parties with different agendas, optimism about the long-term course of reform needs to be hedged with a large measure of caution.

There is also a more positive conclusion. If South America's poorest country can empower its indigenous peoples at the local and national levels and enact policies aimed at reducing their economic and cultural disadvantages, as Bolivia has, it can provide a powerful model for indigenous peoples and governments elsewhere in the region. Just as the repertoire of conflict diffuses from one society to others, so does the repertoire of reform.

NOTES

The first author directs the Minorities at Risk project. The second author is a specialist on Latin America who prepared profiles of Latin American groups for the project in 1994–95.

She received her doctorate from the University of Maryland's Department of Government and Politics in 1999 and is on the faculty at Coastal Carolina University.

News accounts and the following sources were used to prepare and update this sketch.

Albo, Xavier. "Ethnic Violence: The Case of Bolivia." In *The Culture of Violence,* ed. Kumar Rupesinghe and M. Rubio Correa. Tokyo: United Nations University Press, 1994.

Lagos, Maria L. *Autonomy and Power.* Philadelphia: University of Pennsylvania Press, 1994.

Lobo, Susan. "The Fabric of Life." *Cultural Survival Quarterly* 15 (summer 1991): 40–46.

Queiser Morales, Waltraud. *Bolivia: Land of Struggle.* Boulder, Colo.: Westview Press, 1992.

Smith, Richard Chase. "Indians, Forest Rights, and Lumber Mills." *Cultural Survival Quarterly* 17 (spring 1993): 52–55.

Strobele-Gregor, Juliana. "From Indio to Mestizo . . . to Indio." *Latin American Perspectives* 21, no. 81 (spring 1994): 106–123.

Wood, Bill, and Harry Anthony Patrinos. "Urban Bolivia." In *Indigenous People and Poverty in Latin America: An Empirical Analysis,* ed. George Psacharopoulos and Harry Anthony Patrinos. Washington, D.C.: World Bank, 1994.

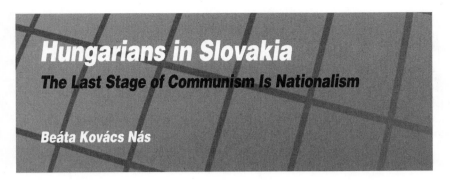

Hungarians in Slovakia
The Last Stage of Communism Is Nationalism

Beáta Kovács Nás

The postcommunist nationalists who came to power in East Central Europe in the early 1990s frequently imposed new restrictions on national minorities such as Serbs in Croatia and Hungarians in Slovakia, Romania, and Yugoslavia. This sketch shows how and why such restrictions were imposed and also illustrates the principle that, though democratic institutions can be manipulated to serve nationalist interests, the democratic process also can undo discriminatory policies.

A FTER SLOVAKIA SEPARATED from the Czech and Slovak Republic in January 1993, its democratically elected but intensely nationalist government increasingly restricted the rights of its ethnic Hungarian national minority. Adopting Slovak nationalism as its legitimating ideology, Slovakia's old communist elite, led by Prime Minister Vladimír Mečiar, took control of Slovak nationalist political parties and manipulated popular nationalist sentiment to gain and hold power through free elections. The economic difficulties of transition from state socialism, a weak opposition, and the Slovak people's historical fear of Hungarian irredentism allowed Mečiar to stay in power for six years in part by invoking the threat of Hungarian secession and blaming Hungarians for the country's problems. As the Slovak elections of September 1998 indicate, however, institutions of democracy potentially provide a corrective against abuses of minority rights. This is true especially when international actors exert economic and political pressure for reform.

According to the 1991 census, the population of Slovakia was 5,274,335, of which 10.8 percent was ethnic Hungarian. Virtually all Hungarians live in geographically contiguous areas of southern Slovakia. This region, bordering Hungary, is approximately thirty-five hundred square miles, and its population is 61.2 percent ethnic Hungarian. Ethnic Hungarians exceed 50 percent of the population in 432 townships. After 1993 Hungarian leaders and parties looked to protect their collective interests by seeking the right to local self-government, whereby democratically elected officials are empowered to decide local issues, including those of language use, education, and culture. The Mečiar-led Slovak government, however, rejected these claims and used democratic institutions to pursue aggressive centralizing and discriminatory policies regarding native language use, control of education, and local politics, to name a few.

RESTRICTIONS ON LANGUAGE AND EDUCATION

On November 28, 1995, the Slovak National Council (parliament) approved and President Michal Kovac signed a new law on state language that established the supremacy of the Slovak language and linguistic identity above all others. The state language law declares that Slovak is the state language (as opposed to "official" language) and enjoys precedence over all other languages used in the territory of Slovakia. It orders the use of Slovak in all official contacts, education, culture, economic activity, health care, and court and administrative proceedings. Paragraph 10 of the state language law, which imposes heavy fines for violations of certain provisions, is enforced through a network of language inspectors at the central, regional, and local levels. The new law does not regulate or protect the use of minority languages, reserving that for separate legislation. The law empowers officials to clamp down on the use of non-Slovak language in schools. Several Hungarian teachers and principals were dismissed on the grounds of having violated the state language law by issuing bilingual documents.

On April 6, 1995, the Slovak government passed a new law on educational administration that shifted the right to appoint and recall school directors from local government councils to the Ministry of Education. Also in 1995 a second law was drafted to require certain subjects, including history, to be taught in the Slovak language in all schools. A number of Hungarians in educational posts were dismissed throughout 1995 for protesting the draft law or not speaking Slovak at Hungarian teachers' meetings.

POLITICAL RESTRICTIONS

At the beginning of 1996 Hungarians were an absolute majority in three of Slovakia's thirty-eight districts and 17 of 121 circuits, first-tier administrative districts with fifteen thousand to thirty thousand inhabitants. In March 1996 the Slovak cabinet adopted a draft bill that aimed at greater centralization by abolishing the circuits and redividing Slovakia into nine regions and seventy-four districts. The functions of the circuits were reassigned to higher-level administrative units at the district or regional level whose chiefs were nominated by the government. The centralization plan was designed to minimize Hungarian influence in local affairs: they were an absolute majority in none of the nine second-tier administrative units (regions, formerly districts) and only two of the seventy-four new first-tier units (districts, formerly circuits). The bill also provided for changing the proportional representation electoral system to a majoritarian one, with the likely consequence of reducing Hungarians' influence in the central government. The redistricting plan was put into effect later that year. The legislation demonstrates how redistricting and changes in electoral systems can be used to restrict a minority's political rights without any explicit reference to the group at which they are targeted. Hungarians, though, saw in them both a threat and evidence of their inferior status.

INTERNATIONAL RESPONSES

Beginning in January 1993, international actors criticized Mečiar's centralizing and antiminority policies. Although the Council of Europe granted Slovakia membership after getting assurances from the Mečiar government that it would remedy the complaints of the Hungarian community, the European Union and NATO refused to consider membership for Slovakia until it rescinded its antiminority politics. Slovakia's resulting isolation from Western Europe has taken a major toll on the country's postcommunist transition in the economic, political, and security spheres.

Since the parliamentary elections of September 1998, won by Slovakia's democratic opposition, the European Union's high commissioner, the OSCE High Commissioner on Minorities, NATO, and influential countries such as the United States have brought renewed pressure on the new Slovak government to modify its minority policy. The new government has taken steps to meet those demands in order to gain acceptance and support from the West.

NEW POLICIES TOWARD MINORITIES

The stagnation and international isolation of Slovakia during nearly six years of postcommunist nationalist-led governance prompted cooperation among members of the democratic opposition. A similar realignment in Romania, less than two years earlier, had ousted the postcommunist nationalist government that had governed there since 1991. In Slovakia the September 1998 parliamentary elections brought to power a coalition of four opposition parties, including the Hungarian Coalition Party. Since then the new government of Prime Minister Mikulás Dzurinda has taken steps to bring policies toward the Hungarian minority in line with prevailing European norms.

There has been some reform regarding language and decentralization issues. The new coalition government's program specifically addresses the issue of bilingualism and proposes establishment of a separate department for minority affairs within the Ministry of Education. It also promises more financial support for minority cultural activities. In response to pressure from the European Union, Prime Minister Dzurinda has declared that adoption of a long-awaited law on national minority languages is on the agenda. The new Slovak cabinet also has demonstrated support for native-language training for teachers, theologians, and ethnographers and proposed issuing a statement declaring that Slovakia is a multinational country. More concretely, the government amended the education law to allow Hungarian-language schools to issue bilingual report cards. As a result, students in Hungarian-language schools received bilingual report cards on January 29, 1999. A number of dismissed Hungarian school principals also have been reinstated. The effects of the 1996 redistricting also are likely to be moderated as part of a long-term process aimed at decentralizing administration and strengthening local self-government.

At the same time, the long-awaited minority language law adopted on July 10, 1999, fails to regulate minorities' native language use beyond official contacts on the level of local government. The law was roundly rejected by the Hungarian Coalition Party.

These declarations and actions are early signs of the new government's intent to correct at least some—if not all—of the minority rights abuses of the nationalist government. A continuation of more equitable and sensitive policies toward the Hungarian minority inevitably would strengthen Slovakia's pluralist political system and complete its postcommunist transition to democracy on the Western European model.

NOTES

The author received her doctorate in 1996 from the University of Maryland's Department of Government and Politics for her dissertation, "Transnational Kindred and Ethnic Conflict:

The Effects of Basic Bilateral Treaties on Domestic Minority Policy." In 2000 she is a Fulbright lecturer at Esztertházy Károly Teacher Training College in Eger, Hungary.

The following Slovakian and Hungarian sources document the policies and issues discussed in the text.

"Alternative Education Is Not Being Postponed," *Sme*, July 26, 1995.

The Forum Institute News, *www.hhrf.org/forum/hirek.htm.*

Minority Protection Association. *The Slovak State Language Law and the Minorities: Critical Analyses and Remarks.* Minority Protection Series no. 1. Budapest: Kossuth Publishing and Trading, 1996.

"Self-Administration Is the Foundation of Self-Determination." Document of the General Assembly of local governments, mayors, and members of parliament of Southern Slovakia, Komárno, January 8, 1994.

"There Will Be Eight Regions and 80–90 Districts," *Bratislava Pravda*, January 17, 1996.

Tornay István. "Kerülgetve a taposóaknákat" [Avoiding the land mines], *Napi Magyarország*, November 8, 1998.

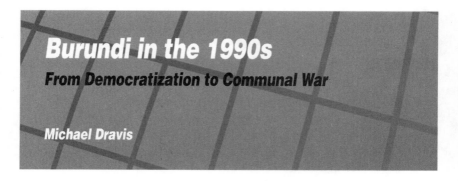

Burundi in the 1990s
From Democratization to Communal War

Michael Dravis

The decade of crisis in Burundi that began in the late 1980s shows how a sustained effort to democratize a plural society prompted a genocidal reaction. The democratic experiment failed essentially because it threatened the ethnocratic power base of a Tutsi minority that controls the army, security forces, and key state bureaucracies.

IN 1989 PRESIDENT PIERRE BUYOYA of Burundi, a Tutsi army officer who had seized power from his cousin a year earlier, initiated a reform process that opened the political system to greater Hutu participation at all levels. In democratic elections held in June 1993 a Hutu, Melchior Ndadaye, was elected with 71 percent of the vote and installed as president. Ndadaye's constituency included few Tutsi voters, and this sign of Hutu ascendancy prompted immediate Tutsi responses. Days after the presidential election, Tutsi students and civil servants demonstrated in the capital and denounced the "ethnic sentiments" manifested in the vote. Tutsi fears intensified later in the month, when President Ndadaye's party swept legislative elections, winning sixty-five of eighty-one seats in the national parliament. Reactionary Tutsi elements acted swiftly. In July, a military coup was thwarted. Three months later army units revolted and assassinated the president.

Both attempts to reassert Tutsi control of the executive collapsed when the conspirators failed to gain the support of moderate Tutsis. However, the death of the president in October 1993 did provoke a long cycle of Hutu-Tutsi clashes that have effectively nullified Burundi's democratic gains. Guerrilla raids, counterinsurgency operations, massacres of civilians, massive refugee flows, political assassinations, and individual vengeance killings have become routine. The scale and intensity of the fighting is indicated by the fact that in May 1996, the U.S. Department of State took the unusual step of publicly declaring that intercommunal violence in Burundi constituted genocide. The symbolic death of Burundi's fledgling democracy occurred in July of the same

188

year when Buyoya retook power in a military coup. Just three years earlier, he had made history by becoming the country's first president to relinquish his office in the wake of open democratic elections.

A History of Communal Conflict

Belgian colonial policy favored the Tutsis and sharpened stratification between the two peoples, making it likely that after independence political mobilization would occur along ethnic lines. Shortly after independence (achieved on July 1, 1962) the leading political party splintered, leaving Tutsis in control of the government. Fearing the example of Rwanda, where initial postcolonial democratization led to the creation of a Hutu power structure and reprisal killings of Tutsis, Burundi's Tutsi elites successfully undermined emerging democratic institutions, judging them an inherent threat to their political and economic dominance. In 1965 the Hutus' sense of separate identity and political interest crystallized in the face of their increasing exclusion from politics. In January, the Hutu prime minister was assassinated. Three months later Hutus won elections that gave them a majority in the legislature, but Tutsi elements were determined to deny them effective power. In October aggrieved Hutus in the army and gendarmerie attacked the royal palace, and civil war ensued. The reigning monarch was toppled, most Hutu members of the army and gendarmerie were killed, and many Hutu politicians were assassinated. The events of 1965 foreshadowed a recurring pattern in Burundi's postindependence history, namely, intermingling streams of communal and political conflict.

From the mid-1960s on, a cycle of coups occurred that undermined democratic norms and led to military-dominated governments. Tutsi control of the military, security, and political structures was strengthened in 1968–69 when Hutu officers were executed and other Hutu notables were arrested. In 1972, royalist and Hutu elements staged an uprising and targeted Tutsi civilians. Killings of Tutsis provoked retaliatory massacres of Hutus by the Tutsi-dominated army. Chillingly, the deliberate nature of the genocide perpetrated by the Tutsis was signaled when younger, educated Hutus were specifically targeted to preempt the emergence of a future Hutu leadership cadre.

Why Democratization?

International factors prompted the Buyoya regime's reformist turn, including pervasive sentiment elsewhere in Africa for democratization and, more immediately, unprecedented international pressure on Burundi in the wake of an outbreak of communal violence in 1988. Previously, as in the 1972 episode of genocide, the world community did virtually nothing to stop, condemn, or apportion blame for the carnage. In contrast, in 1988 Burundi found itself the target of unexpected scrutiny from a variety of quarters. U.S. and European press coverage was far more extensive, both qualitatively and quantitatively. News of the killings reached an international public more attuned to human rights issues. Public opinion prompted governments and international organizations to act: Belgium, Canada, the European Parliament, and the World Bank each advised the Burundi government that positive change was needed.

The response of the United States is illustrative. The House of Representatives voted 415–0 for a nonbinding resolution condemning ethnic violence and urging the government of Burundi to accelerate measures for national reconciliation. Congressional action was followed by considerable State Department pressure. Washington officials shelved previous statements blaming both sides for targeting civilians and specifically charged the Tutsi-controlled army with initiating large-scale killings. To appreciate the cumulative effect of international pressure, it must be placed within the context of Burundi's subsistence economy, which is heavily dependent on agricultural exports (chiefly coffee). Thus, the possibility of restrictions on trade and aid at any time threatens the economic viability of the country. Warnings, especially by Belgium (the former colonial power), the United States, and the World Bank (upon which Burundi relies for loans and technical advice), seem to have convinced Buyoya that reform measures could no longer be avoided.

Domestic imperatives may also have played a role in Buyoya's political calculus. Burundian society has never been divided between a monolithic and repressive Tutsi bloc pitted against a monolithic and vengeance-driven Hutu bloc. The political elite has always included both Hutu and Tutsi notables who preferred accommodation, and presumably they also pushed Buyoya to opt for peaceful change. Also, Buyoya had seized power very recently, in September 1987, which meant that he had to be concerned with factions among the Tutsis, including supporters of the ousted president and hard-liners who favored genocidal policies against Hutus.

THE FAILURE OF THE DEMOCRATIC EXPERIMENT

Despite President Ndadaye's reconciliation efforts after his 1993 electoral victories, by late summer conditions in Burundi were volatile. On the surface, the democracy drive appeared to be a spectacular success. Internationally certified free and fair elections had been held, and the country's long-repressed Hutu majority had expressed its will and captured the executive and legislative branches by means of ballots rather than bayonets. However, world coffee prices were falling, which raised the stakes for access to government posts. Although Burundian society was democratized, at least to the extent of elections and relatively free speech, the state bureaucracies—including the key military and security services—remained under Tutsi control. Tutsi elites had always relied on their official positions as their main source of income and the ultimate guarantors of their power, and the 1993 elections did not change this situation but threatened it.

Two discriminatory policies of the government had long been effective in maintaining Hutu subordination. The first, restriction of Hutu admittance to higher and technical education, ensured an almost exclusively Tutsi pool of talent from which to recruit mid- and upper-level government functionaries. The second was blockage of Hutu entry into the armed forces, in part by means of an unusual "girth by height" enlistment requirement. Thus, Tutsis were ensured control of the civilian bureaucracies and security apparatuses. After 1993, induction of Hutu officers and noncommissioned officers began, but the army remained an overwhelmingly Tutsi organization. The extent of the army's ethnic partisanship is dramatically evident in periods of "fear and flight," when Tutsis rush to military camps for protection and Hutus flee from them. In March 1994, the army leadership refused to furnish an ethnic breakdown of its troops and claimed, absurdly, that the military was a neutral actor in ethnic clashes. Despite such official obfuscation, it is obvious that Burundi cannot end intercommunal conflict unless the security forces are retrained, subjected to civilian oversight and control, and recruited in a fashion that more accurately represents the ethnic composition of the country.

In addition to internal conditions that were inimical to the democratic experiment, international and regional factors proved harmful. Although the attention of the world community has been sustained—in February 1996 the Organization of African Unity credited international pressure with preventing a total collapse in Burundi—it has not been as focused as it was in the late 1980s. Despite the enormity of Burundi's crisis, it has been of secondary concern to international actors preoccupied with transitions and crises in the postcommunist states and the Middle East. Moreover, the international community has opted for the "one size fits all" approach to democratic power sharing, without much sensitivity to Burundi's special vulnerabilities.

Regional instability also diverted international attention from Burundi and helped destabilize the country. Burundi lies within a "crisis zone" characterized by a cycle of deadly civil wars, rebellions, genocides, and enormous refugee flows. At its core, this crisis zone consists of Burundi, Rwanda, and the Democratic Republic of Congo (formerly Zaire). Other states in the region have been drawn into these conflicts by political machinations, strategic imperatives, ethnic affinities, and geographic proximity. The spillover effect of conflict is demonstrated by the lingering effects of the 1994 genocide in Rwanda, carried out by agents of the Hutu government against its Tutsi subjects. The genocide and the subsequent victory of the Tutsi-dominated Rwandan Patriotic Front (RPF), backed by the Uganda government, set in motion a vast diaspora of Hutus. Militants among them became an increasingly effective force that not only operated within the former Zaire but also carried out cross-border raids into Rwanda (against the new Tutsi-controlled government) and into Burundi, in conjunction with the Hutu rebels operating in that country. In retaliation Burundi has taken part in interventions aimed at neutralizing these attacks at their source. In September 1998 the Belgian foreign minister accused Burundi (along with Rwanda) of deploying troops in the Democratic Republic of Congo, a charge that Burundi denied. Such accusations and denials continued into 1999, but by late in the year independent journalists had confirmed the presence of Burundi army contingents in eastern Congo. The destabilizing effect of Burundi's strategy was apparent in October 1999, when a progovernment newspaper in Congo called for a "war on Burundi." This incident confirmed, yet again, the regional nature of conflict in Central Africa. Indeed, in November 1998 a United Nations report listed no fewer than twenty rebel groups active in the area and stated that many of them were linked in a tangled web of alliances and counteralliances.

BURUNDI'S FUTURE

On the cusp of a new century and new millennium, Burundi's prospects are dim. According to press reports, from October 1993 to late 1999 Burundi's spiral of violence resulted in over 200,000 deaths, most of them civilian, and hundreds of thousands of internally displaced people. Spouting familiar bromides about "national unity" and restoring security, Buyoya's praetorian regime has brutally prosecuted the war against Hutu rebels inside and outside the country. Internally, beginning in late 1998 a new and draconian security policy was implemented. Intending to deny the rebels sources of support, in particular a pool of young male recruits, the government has forcibly resettled rural populations into so-called "protection sites" (also referred to as "regroupment camps" in official parlance and denounced as "concentration camps" by the opposition). According to senior government officials, the protection sites are militarily secured safe havens established in response to murderous rebel attacks. International observers, however, have noted that most internees are Hutus, who are forced to live in appalling conditions.

In October 1999 the UN Office for the Coordination of Humanitarian Affairs estimated that more than 300,000 internees were in fifty-three different regroupment camps. That same month, representatives of the UN High Commissioner for Refugees received reports that Hutu rebels—apparently to counter the government's strategy of corralling the Hutu population into protection sites—were attempting to drive Burundi civilians into forced exile in Tanzania by systematically burning homes and destroying crops. Thus, as of late 1999 Burundian civilians (especially rural Hutus) were under threat from government troops, rebel cadres, the natural elements (from which inadequate shelters in the regroupment camps offered scant protection), and malnutrition and starvation. Shortages of food were accentuated by the de facto suspension of all international humanitarian assistance following the United Nations' decision in October 1999 to withdraw its nonessential personnel from the country.

Burundi's future as a viable polity rests upon the outcome of a long series of desultory peace talks held under international mediation in Arusha, Tanzania. In late 1998 there were signs that momentum was building in support of a comprehensive settlement, and in January 1999 regional leaders decided to give a symbolic and substantive lift to the peace process by "suspending"—but not completely removing—the economic sanctions that their countries had imposed on Burundi following Buyoya's seizure of power in 1996. The encouraging mood, however, quickly evaporated. The leading international mediator, Julius Nyerere, died in October 1999, and prospects for reaching a peace settlement in the short and middle term seem to have died with him. Even if the Burundi factions do achieve a domestic peace settlement, it will probably count for little in the absence of a larger regional peace process. An internationally sponsored, monitored, and verified security structure for the entire Great Lakes region would greatly enhance the chances of achieving peace and stability in Burundi, and in February 2000 the UN Security Council authorized deployment of five hundred observers and some five thousand supporting peacekeepers.

Although democratization in Burundi cannot be called a success, that process has established a foundation on which future politicians may be able to build. In theory, Burundi established a constitutional democracy in which political freedom, human rights, and the rule of law were guaranteed. Tutsi military dictatorship and national crisis are constant bedfellows; if normalization is to be achieved, Hutus must be given fair access to political and economic opportunities, state bureaucracies and the army must be reformed, and both Tutsis and Hutus must be convinced that they will be safe from reprisals, from the possibility of economic and political domination, and from a return to genocidal purges.

NOTES

The author, a doctoral candidate in history at the University of Maryland, prepared analyses for the Minorities at Risk project on groups in Rwanda and Burundi. He is now a research associate with the Center for International Development and Conflict Management.

Sources used for this sketch, in addition to standard references and contemporary news reports, include the following.

Daniels, Morna, comp. *Burundi.* Santa Barbara, Calif.: CLIO Press, 1992.

Lemarchand, René. "Burundi: The Politics of Ethnic Amnesia." In *Genocide Watch,* ed. Helen Fein, 70-86. New Haven, Conn.: Yale University Press, 1992.

———. *Burundi: Ethnocide as Discourse and Practice.* New York: Cambridge University Press, 1995.

Lund, Michael, Barnett R. Rubin, and Fabienne Hara. "Learning from Burundi's Failed Democratic Transition, 1993–1996: Did International Initiatives Match the Problem?" In *Cases and Strategies for Preventive Action,* ed. Barnett R. Rubin, 47–92. New York: Century Press for the Center for Preventive Action, 1998.

Minority Rights Group. *Burundi since the Genocide.* London: Minority Rights Group, 1982.

———. *Burundi: Breaking the Cycle of Violence.* London: Minority Rights Group, 1995.

United Nations, Office for the Coordination of Humanitarian Affairs. *Integrated Regional Information Network for Central and Eastern Africa (IRIN-CEA).* Updates for October and November 1999.

U.S. Department of State. *Country Reports on Human Rights Practices.* Washington, D.C.: U.S. Government Printing Office, various years.

6

The Challenge of Resolving Ethnonational Conflicts

MOST OF THE ETHNIC WARS of the last half century have been fought over issues of group autonomy and independence. If a national people seeks independent statehood, accommodation is potentially very costly because governing elites usually give highest priority to preservation of the integrity of the state and its territory. Substate autonomy is the broad middle ground in which solutions are most likely to be found.[1] This chapter reports evidence that more ethnonational wars have been settled or contained through international engagement and negotiations since the early 1990s than in any decade of the Cold War. Examples include the settlement and de-escalation of ethnonational rebellions by the Miskitos and other coastal peoples in Nicaragua (1990), the Gagauz in Moldova (1995), the Moros in the Philippines (the most recent of a series of agreements being signed in June 1996), and the Chakmas in Bangladesh (December 1997).

Autonomy without Warfare?

Many regions and peoples have attained substate autonomy in the twentieth century by peaceful means, as Ruth Lapidoth documents in a wide-ranging comparative study.[2] After World War I interstate agreements established autonomy within the Finnish state for the Swedish-inhabited Åland Islands and the port city of Memel, now part of Lithuania. The Danish government granted extensive home rule powers to the Faroe Islands in 1948 and Greenland (officially Kalaalit Nunaat) in 1979. The USSR,

195

Yugoslavia, and the People's Republic of China all provided something more than paper autonomy to regions inhabited by minority nationalities and peoples. The politically organized tribes in the United States were given substantially broadened control over reservation territory and governance during the Nixon administration. In April 1999 the Canadian government gave self-government to the new territory of Nunavut, 20 percent of the country's land and home to twenty-two thousand Inuits. In none of these examples was autonomy granted in response to ethnic rebellion. Canada's Inuit, for example, "won their territory without any acts of violence or civil disobedience—without even filing a lawsuit."[3]

The examples in the previous paragraph demonstrate that there are a great many alternatives to sovereign statehood for protecting the cultural and security interests of ethnically and nationally distinct peoples. The issue addressed here is whether autonomy agreements also can be an effective instrument for managing ethnopolitical conflicts after they have escalated into open warfare. Many well-grounded analyses document the intrinsic difficulty of halting internal wars once under way. Barbara Walter observes, "Between 1940 and 1990 55 percent of interstate wars were resolved at the bargaining table, whereas only 20 percent of civil wars reached similar solutions."[4] Many reasons for the intransigence of combatants in civil wars are cited by analysts: the lack of security guarantees, the zero-sum nature of conflicts over power, the intensity of animosities generated by protracted conflict, fears of being trapped in a prisoner's dilemma, and so on.[5] Nonetheless, civil wars *are* sometimes settled, and, according to a comparative analysis by Patrick Regan, civil wars driven by ethnic and religious issues are more likely to be settled by third-party intervention than are revolutionary wars.[6] The main reason ethnic wars are more susceptible to settlement is that there is more middle ground for compromise when the issue is group autonomy. It is less threatening to most state elites to negotiate a transfer of regional power to ethnonationalists than to share power at the center with revolutionary challengers. And ethnonationalists are more likely to regard autonomy as an acceptable alternative to independence than are revolutionaries to accept a few seats in the council of state as an alternative to controlling the council.

Outcomes of Autonomy Wars from 1960 to 1999

One can debate endlessly whether and why ethnonational wars can be settled by negotiations. The strength of the study reported here is that it documents the outcomes and current status of virtually all armed conflicts fought by ethno-nationalists seeking autonomy or independence during the past forty years. Table 6.1 lists and sketches the outcomes of fifty-seven ethnonational rebellions fought since 1960. The list is limited to guerrilla and civil wars in independent states in which group autonomy or independence was a primary objective. It excludes wars fought by communal contenders for control of the state, as in Liberia, Sierra Leone, Rwanda, and Zaire. Nor does it include wars of independence fought against European colonial powers or the Belgian-supported secession of Katanga province from newly independent Congo in the early 1960s. It also excludes low-level terrorist campaigns by regional nationalists in Western societies and elsewhere, for example, by South Tyroleans in Italy, Corsicans in France, and Puerto Ricans. And it excludes the secession of Croatia, Slovenia, and Bosnia from Yugoslavia. With these at-the-margin exceptions we think the list is comprehensive, given the scope of the Minorities at Risk project.[7] Following are the principal findings.

Most ethnonational wars since 1960 have led to increased autonomy for the groups that fought them. Successful wars of autonomy outnumber suppressed wars by a ratio of more than three to one. Of the fifty-seven conflicts, thirty led to negotiated extensions of regional autonomy, to power sharing in regional or central governments (Sikhs in Punjab, Tuaregs in Mali and Niger, Afars in Djibouti), or to independence (Bangladesh, Eritrea). Six of the seven wars categorized as "stalemated" in table 6.1 have also secured de facto autonomy or independence for ethnonationalists; in the seventh instance ongoing negotiations in the second Naga rebellion are likely to lead to substantial concessions. On the "suppressed" side of the ledger are eight conflicts ended by military means without significant accommodation. Twelve conflicts continue in early 2000, several of which appear ripe for negotiated settlement.

Autonomy agreements usually de-escalate armed conflict, but fighting sometimes continues during their implementation or resumes years later. Armed conflict often persists after peace agreements are signed. Basques in Spain, for example, gained extensive regional autonomy in 1980 but ETA separatists continued their terror campaign in pursuit of complete independence until 1998. At the end of 1999, low-level attacks persisted in four of thirty "settled" conflicts because some rebel groups, such as Hamas in the West Bank and Gaza and pro-Indonesian militias in East Timor, rejected the terms or implementation of agreements. In another half-dozen instances, serious armed conflict continued at the end of the 1990s despite negotiations and settlements concluded earlier in the decade. In the Southern Philippines, for example, one holdout rebel movement spoils full implementation of an innovative 1996

Table 6.1. Outcomes of Ethnonational Wars of Autonomy and Independence, 1960–99

Group	Country	Serious Conflict[a]	No Armed Conflict[b]	Status at the End of 1999
Negotiated Autonomy or Independence: No Armed Conflict[b]				
Nagas I	India	1952–64		Separate state in federal system, 1963
Bengalis	Pakistan	1971		Independent in 1971 after popular uprising and Indian intervention
Tripuras I	India	1967–72		Separate state in federal system, 1972
Southerners I	Sudan	1956–72		Regional autonomy with power sharing in central government in 1973
Afars	Ethiopia	1975–85		Regional autonomy in 1985
Mizos	India	1962–86		Separate state in federal system in 1986
Miskitos	Nicaragua	1981–88		Autonomous region, 1990
Eritreans	Ethiopia	1961–91		Independent in 1993 by agreement with postrevolutionary Ethiopian government
Gagauz	Moldova	1991–92		Autonomous republic since 1994
Sikhs	India	1978–93		Militants suppressed, Sikh moderates in power in Punjab state since 1992
Kachins	Burma	1961–94		Peace accord with limited concessions led to end of fighting in 1994
Catholics	Northern Ireland	1969–94		Full implementation of 1994 accord blocked in 1999 by dispute over arms
Serbs	Bosnia	1992–95		Autonomy in confederal state since 1995
Croats	Bosnia	1992–95		Autonomy in confederal state since 1995
Tuaregs	Mali	1990–95		Peace accords in 1992, 1995 provided regional development help
Chittagong Hill peoples (Chakma)	Bangladesh	1975–96		Peace accord in 1997 provided for significant regional autonomy
Tuaregs	Niger	1988–97		Peace accord in 1995 provided for decentralization, development help

Trans-Dniester Slavs	Moldova	1991–97	Regional autonomy ratified by 1997 peace agreement
Mons	Burma	1975–97	Cease-fire in 1995 led to limited concessions and an end to rebellion
Bougainvillians	Papua New Guinea	1989–98	Cease-fire, preliminary agreement, and peace monitors ended fighting in 1998

Negotiated Autonomy or Concessions: Low-Level Armed Conflict Continues[c]

Basques	Spain	1959–80	Autonomous region 1980, cease-fire in 1998, negotiations began 1999
Palestinians	West Bank and Gaza	1968–93	Self-rule agreement phased in 1994–99; final-status talks began in November 1999
Afars	Djibouti	1991–95	Autonomy rebellion largely ended by 1995 agreement for power sharing
East Timorese	Indonesia	1974–99	Resistance largely suppressed by 1997; 1999 independence referendum prompted scorched-earth Indonesian withdrawal

Negotiated Autonomy or Concessions: Serious Armed Conflict Continues[d]

Shan	Burma	1962–present	Cease-fire with limited concessions in 1995 rejected by some factions, intense fighting and repression continue
Somali	Ethiopia	1963–present	Regional autonomy in federal state since 1994, major factions continue rebellion
Moros	Philippines	1972–present	Autonomous region 1979; peace agreement in 1996 is rejected by MILF
Oromo	Ethiopia	1973–present	Regional autonomy in federal state since 1994, major factions continue rebellion
Kashmiri Muslims	India	1989–present	Kashmiri moderates elected to regional government in 1996; separatist violence escalated beginning mid-1999
Bodos	India	1989–present	Autonomous Council 1993; rejected by some factions who continue fighting

continued on next page

Table 6.1. *(cont.)*

Group	Country	Serious Conflict[a]	Status at the End of 1999
Stalemated Conflicts: Violence Checked by Cease-Fires, Negotiations, Military Action, or Peacekeeping Forces without Peace Agreements or Decisive Military Defeats			
Isaaqs (Somaliland)	Somalia	1986–90	De facto regional independence since 1991
Kurds	Iraq	1980–92	Internationally supported autonomy compromised by factional fighting between KDP and PUK
South Ossetians	Georgia	1991–93	De facto regional autonomy
Nagas II	India	1972–96	Cease-fire, ongoing peace talks since 1997
Armenians	Azerbaijan	1988–97	Cease-fire in 1997, negotiations continue between Armenia and Azerbaijan
Abkhaz	Georgia	1992–93, 1998	De facto independence
Kosovar Albanians	Serbia	1998–99	Autonomy assured by NATO intervention but ethnic cleansing of Serbs ensues
Conflicts Suppressed without Significant Accommodation			
Tibetans	China	1959–67	Defeated, episodic resistance continues
Papuans	Indonesia	1964–96	Defeated, episodic resistance continues
Ibo	Nigeria	1967–70	Defeated, reincorporated in state
Baluchis	Pakistan	1973–77	Defeated, autonomy lost in 1973, partly restored in 1980
Saharawis	Morocco	1973–95	Defeated, UN referendum on autonomy postponed repeatedly by government

Kurds	Iran	1979–94	Defeated
Serbs	Croatia	1991–95	Defeated, many fled as refugees
Muslims	Thailand	1995–98	Latest episode of local rebellion ended without settlement or serious repression

Conflicts Persisting or Escalating in 1998–99

Karen and Karenni	Burma	1945–present	Continued rebellion despite escalating counterinsurgency campaigns in 1990s
Tamils	Sri Lanka	1975–present	Continued rebellion, Tamil militants reject government proposals for settlement
Acehense	Indonesia	1977–present	Rebellion almost suppressed by 1996–97, resumed in 1998–99; government proposed negotiations in late 1999
Tripuras II	India	1979–present	Continued rebellion
Southerners II	Sudan	1983–present	Government abrogated 1972 autonomy agreement, intense continued rebellion
Kurds	Turkey	1984–present	Severe repression and trial of PKK founder led to de-escalation in 1999
Wa	Burma	1989–present	Fighting resumed in 1994 after rebels rejected earlier cease-fire agreement
Assamese	India	1990–present	Militants reject proposed talks, fight for complete independence
Uighers	China	1990–present	Separatist rebellion in Xinjiang persists despite severe repression
Cabindans	Angola	1991–present	New phase of protracted, low-level separatist rebellion
Casamançais region (Diola)	Senegal	1991–present	Rebellion and repression persist despite episodic negotiations
Chechens	Russia	1991–present	Peace accord and de facto autonomy in 1997, armed conflict resumed in 1999

continued on next page

Table 6.1. *(cont.)*

Note: This table includes all sustained or episodic armed conflicts and mass popular uprisings aimed wholly or mainly at securing national independence or regional autonomy for an ethnopolitical group, or unification with kindred groups in adjoining states, with the exceptions noted in the text on p. 197. It is compiled principally from information on groups included in the Minorities at Risk study. Conflicts are listed under the first three headings in sequence of their termination. Under the other headings, conflicts are listed in the sequence of onset. It has been updated by Deepa Khosla through November 1999. Not included are three low-level separatist conflicts that began in 1997–98 among Mongols in China, Anjouanese in Comoros, and Caprivians in Namibia. At present it appears unlikely that they will lead to sustained armed conflict.

[a] For conflicts under way in 1985, serious conflict ends when rebellion codes in the Minorities at Risk data set decline to 2 or less (terrorism) and remain below that threshold through 1999. For conflicts that ended before 1985, the ending date is determined from political and historical accounts.

[b] Includes wars of autonomy in which autonomy agreements led to five or more years of peace before the resumption of armed conflict. Conflicts with shorter lulls in fighting are listed under subsequent categories.

[c] Groups with low-level antigovernment violence in 1998–99 (rebellion scores of 1 or 2 in the Minorities at Risk data set). Autonomy agreements are in place and partially or fully implemented.

[d] Groups with 1998 rebellion scores of 3 or more in the Minorities at Risk data set. Autonomy agreements are in place and partially or fully implemented.

peace agreement that was accepted by most Muslims in Mindinao.[8] Table 6.1 also includes three historical instances—Nagas I, Tripuras I, and Southern Sudanese I—in which negotiated agreements kept the peace for a decade or so before the onset of new rebellions. Putting these numbers together, armed conflict continued or resumed in thirteen of thirty conflicts that protagonists thought were settled by autonomy agreements. The risk of renewed rebellion thus remains significant where peace pacts are recent and not yet fully implemented, for example, in Bosnia, Bangladesh, and Papua New Guinea.

Ethnonational wars seldom lead to complete independence for the rebels. Only East Bengalis and Eritreans became recognized members of the United Nations club of sovereign states. The "facts on the ground" are that four additional groups have achieved effective independence but have not yet had their status ratified by state or international authorities. The Isaaqs and allied peoples have their own state of Somaliland in what once was northern Somalia. The others are the Abkhaz in Georgia, the Trans-Dniester Slavs in Moldova, and the Kosovars in Yugoslavia. The Kurds in northern Iraq also have established a quasi-independent state, but its continued existence depends on Allied protection that prevents the Baghdad government from reestablishing control of the region.

In the 1990s there has been an unprecedented global increase in negotiated settlements of wars for autonomy. Trends in outcomes are shown in table 6.2 and figure 6.1, which are constructed using information on the inception and outcomes of the fifty-seven conflicts listed in table 6.1. These general important conclusions are worth highlighting.

Ethnonational warfare increased throughout the Cold War and peaked in the early 1990s but then decreased sharply. From the late 1960s through the end of the 1980s, new wars in each five-year period substantially outnumbered wars contained or settled during the period. Since 1990, however, the number of wars contained or settled has increased sharply: three were contained and three were settled in the first three years of the 1990s. Between 1994 and 1996 the balance shifted even more decisively: five ethnonational wars were contained and nine were settled, whereas only one escalated, in southern Thailand, followed in 1998 by Kosovo. At the end of 1999 only eighteen ethnonational wars were being waged—the lowest number since the early 1970s.[9]

Two-thirds of negotiated settlements of ethnopolitical wars in the past forty years have been concluded since the end of the Cold War. Between 1960 and 1990 eight ethnonational wars were ended by negotiated settlements, and three of those settlements failed to prevent renewed warfare some years later. Since 1990, by comparison, settlements have ended or led to de-escalation of sixteen

Table 6.2. Trends in Outcomes of Ethnonational Wars, 1956–99

Period	New Ethnonational Wars[a]	Ongoing Wars at End of Period	Wars Contained during Period	Wars Settled during Period
1956–60	3	5	0	0
1961–65	6	10	0	1
1966–70	4	12	2	0
1971–75	11	20	0	3
1976–80	5	23	1	1
1981–85	3	25	1	1
1986–90	10	32	1	2
1991–93[b]	11	37	3	3
1994–96[b]	1	24	5	9
1997–99[b]	1	18	3	4
Totals	55	—	16	24

Note: Tabulated from cases listed in table 6.1, Outcomes of Ethnonational Wars. "Contained" conflicts include those categorized in table 6.1 as "Stalemated" or "Suppressed." "Settled" conflicts are those that led to negotiated settlements, including those in which low-level armed conflict continues.

[a] Only fifty-five new wars are listed in the first column because two of the fifty-seven wars in table 6.1 began before 1956.

[b] Time periods for the 1990s cover three years rather than the five-year spans used for earlier periods.

wars. This remarkable post–Cold War shift toward reliance on negotiations to settle separatist conflicts is consistent with other researchers' findings that ever-larger numbers of civil wars of all kinds are being terminated at the negotiating table.[10]

Democratic transitions have contributed to the negotiated settlement of a number of ethnopolitical wars. The evidence on this point is summarized in table 6.3. The settled ethnonational wars were only slightly more likely to have begun in autocratic regimes than in full or partial democracies, by a ratio of 15 to 12. But by a ratio of 20 to 7 the settlements were negotiated by democratic or partially democratic governments. Democratic regimes have a good record of negotiating settlements with rebels whose wars began in democratic settings —India is a leading example here but by no means the only one. It is uncommon, however, for autocratic governments to negotiate an end to ethnonational wars that began on their watch. The handful of exceptions include the

Figure 6.1. Trends in Outcomes of Ethnonational Wars, 1956–99

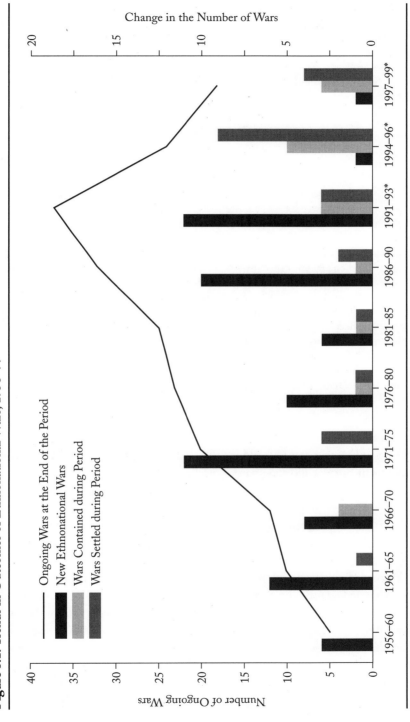

Table 6.3. Effects of Regime Type on Settlements in Ethnonational Wars, 1956–99

---

15 ethnonational wars began in autocracies, of which

> 6 were settled by autocratic regimes
> 5 were settled by democratic regimes
> 4 were settled by partially democratic regimes

10 ethnonational wars began in full democracies, of which

> 1 was settled by an autocratic regime
> 9 were settled by fully democratic regimes

2 ethnonational wars began in partially democratic regimes, of which
> 2 were settled by partially democratic regimes

Note: Based on analysis of twenty-seven ethnonational wars that led to wholly or partly successful negotiated settlements between 1956 and 1999. All conflicts in the first three segments of table 6.1 are included except Bangladesh's secession from Pakistan (because Indian intervention determined the outcome) and civil wars by Serbs and Croats in Bosnia (because no effective regime existed at the onset of the wars). Type of regime is recorded for the year in which serious conflict began and in the year of negotiated settlement, as listed in the first three segments of table 6.1. Democracy minus autocracy scores are used to categorize regimes (see appendix A): full democracies = 8 to 10, partial democracies = 1 to 7, autocracies = 0 to –10.

Afars in Ethiopia and Djibouti in 1985 and 1995, respectively; the Kachins and Mons in Burma; and the Tuaregs in Niger.

The Costs of Secessionist Wars and the Alternatives

The concessions won by the protagonists in most ethnonational wars need to be weighed against the costs. First, many of the conflicts were long and destructive. The median duration of twenty-four settled wars was twelve years, and nine of them lasted more than twenty years. East Timor's capital and towns are devastated; so is much of Bosnia and Kosovo. Chronic warfare has drained public resources and set back social and economic improvement by decades in India's northeast and the hill country of Burma. Second, the "successful" outcomes are offset by a significant number of rebellions that have been suppressed without accommodation or that continue in 2000 with little prospect for settlement. There are twenty such conflicts listed in the last two sections of table 6.1. The raw numbers suggest that ethnonational rebels of the last forty years have a 24:8 won/lost record, with seven ties and eighteen contests still being fought. These are not bad statistics in sports but a grim record when one realizes that many people, in some cases hundreds of thousands, have died in each of the contests.

The third major liability is that negotiated settlements do not necessarily lead to a decisive end to serious conflict. Ethnonationalists seldom have unified leadership, and some among them may reject settlements that provide less than total independence or may seek greater gains for their faction. Violent resistance by militant Palestinians, Oromos, Moros, and Kashmiri Muslims continues despite political accommodations that have been accepted by most of their number. Stephen Stedman describes this as the "spoiler problem" and analyzes a number of internal wars, for example, in Zimbabwe-Rhodesia, Mozambique, and Angola, in which spoilers impaired or derailed the peace process.[11]

Sudan represents the worst possible outcome of negotiated settlements. In 1983 the government's northern leadership defected from the 1972 agreement that gave autonomy to the south. President Jaafar al-Nimieri sought to take advantage of divisions among southerners by dividing the autonomous region into three smaller entities, thus violating a key part of the agreement. Shortly thereafter, to bolster his support from Islamists, he announced that shari'a law was to be imposed throughout the country, including the mainly Christian south. The renewed fighting provoked by these policies has become the most deadly ethnic war of the post-1945 era, cause of nearly two million civilian deaths through starvation and massacres.[12] The rebels have divided and fought among themselves, reunited, and then divided again. Other groups in the east and center of the country have joined the civil war. Some rebels have been discredited because they made separate peace with the Khartoum government. For the most part, warriors determine policy by all parties; the cohesion and trust necessary for a negotiated settlement have long since been destroyed. The 1993 Israeli-Palestinian agreement was at risk in a similar way from 1996 to 1999 because the Likud-dominated government sought to block its implementation. The consequences were to undermine the Israeli government's credibility, the credibility of the Palestinian leadership that negotiated within the framework of the Oslo agreement, and the credibility of negotiations as a means to end the Israeli-Palestinian conflict. After the 1999 election of the Barak government, the downward spiral toward renewed violence was checked when implementation resumed.

By far the less costly alternative to ethnonational war is to negotiate the accommodation of ethnonational claims before the cycle of violence begins. There usually is time, often ample time, for preemptive peacemaking. Evidence summarized in table 2.6 showed that thirty-seven of the fifty-two new ethno-rebellions that began between 1986 and 1998 were preceded by more limited but readily visible forms of political action. The median time span was a decade, a ten-year time horizon in which mutually satisfactory accommodations might have been reached.[13]

Many recent examples can be cited of positive government responses to ethnonational claims pursued nonviolently. Western democracies have been particularly effective in settling claims for autonomy by ethnonationalists and indigenous activists before they escalated into serious rebellions. In the 1970s the French socialist government devised decentralizing policies that checked the escalation of ethnonational movements in Brittany and elsewhere (though they did not satisfy Corsican separatists). The Swiss government put an end to separatism in the French-speaking part of the Jura by partitioning the canton. The U.S., Australian, and Canadian governments have responded to activism by indigenous peoples with reforms that give indigenous leaders greater control over land, resources, and local governance. Not everyone has bought into these arrangements; some indigenous and ethnonational leaders are sharply critical of them. The point is that the accommodations have led to the transformation of these conflicts. Regional and separatist aspirations in these societies are now much more likely to be pursued within the existing framework of political institutions and relationships and less likely to lead to violent confrontations.[14]

Democratic Russia provides a remarkable and little-known set of examples of constructive responses to ethnonational demands. In the early 1990s the Russian Federation was challenged by assertions of sovereignty by the leaders of many of its constituent republics, among them the Tatars, Bashkirs, Yakuts, and Tuvinians. Beginning with Tatarstan, federal and regional officials engaged in protracted negotiations that led to power- and revenue-sharing arrangements that preempted open rebellion. Chechnya was an exception, not because Moscow rejected accommodation, but because the Chechen leadership was militantly nationalistic and refused any compromise short of complete independence. As of early 1999 the Russian government was reported to have negotiated separate power-sharing arrangements with more than forty of the country's eighty-nine regions.[15]

Negotiated autonomy should in principle be less costly than ethnonational war, but it also has costs and poses risks for state elites.[16] Some states are sufficiently secure, domestically and internationally, that they can accept substate autonomy for national minorities without fearing the loss of majority support or dissolution of the state. Others may do so under international pressure or with international guarantees, as was the case in Moldova. A number of states and their elites are far more resistant to substate autonomy as a solution to ethnonational conflict. The nationalist leaders of Ukraine, a state whose policies are in most respects a model of multicultural accommodation, are fundamentally opposed to any local or regional autonomy arrangements, even for numerically small minorities like the Ruthenians and Hungarians in western Ukraine, much less the large Russian population in eastern Ukraine.[17] Ukraine is a new state that lacks a tradition of independent statehood, which helps explain its leaders' aversion to substate autonomy as a strategy for accommodating minorities. Similarly, one can find the origins of the Turkish government's adamant opposition to Kurdish demands for cultural recognition or regional autonomy in the circumstances of the founding of the modern Turkish state, when it was besieged by foreign powers who sought to carve separate states or spheres of influence out of Anatolia. Nationalist leaders of European states with Hungarian minorities, especially Romania and Slovakia, have opposed demands for autonomy of local administration out of concern that autonomy will encourage Hungarian irredentism.

The following principles can be suggested about the process of arriving at successful autonomy arrangements.[18]

1. *Negotiations should begin as early as possible in the conflict, before positions become hardened by protracted warfare.* A settlement was easier to reach in the Gagauz conflict because moderates on both sides acted to preempt armed conflict shortly after mobilization and the first armed clashes occurred.

2. *Ethnopolitical groups whose leaders demand sovereignty and independence usually are willing to settle for more limited forms of autonomy.* Negotiated settlements that grant substate autonomy (and commensurate control of resources) to a widely supported ethnonational movement usually marginalize more militant and uncompromising factions. If a separatist conflict has been protracted and violent, though, some factions are likely to reject any agreement and continue fighting. Planning a coordinated response to postsettlement violence then becomes an important issue in negotiations.

3. *There are infinitely varied ways in which authority can be devolved to an ethnopolitical group.* The abstract possibilities include confederalism, federalism, regional autonomy, regional administrative decentralization, and communal autonomy, or "cantonization." The underlying principle of cantonization is to devolve political power to the smallest possible unit of decision

making and administration. A distinction also can be made between federalism, in which all regional units enjoy equal powers, and *asymmetrical* federalism, in which some units have greater self-governing powers than others. The United States successfully uses both: federalism with limited powers for the fifty states, quasi-sovereignty and more extensive powers for organized Native American tribes and the Commonwealth of Puerto Rico. It is important to recognize that autonomy need not be territorial. Central institutions can be established through which national and minority peoples administer educational and cultural activities. This approach is especially suitable for communities dispersed throughout a larger society.[19]

4. *Autonomy agreements require protracted negotiation and close attention to detail.* There is no model charter for autonomy arrangements, because the essential issues differ across groups and situations. The core questions are how much authority is to be devolved and how it is to be exercised—questions for which there are many alternative answers. Other key issues may include language rights, respect for religious practices, mutual recognition of national symbols, control of land and resources, internal security arrangements, the right to participate in central decisions that affect the group, protection of the rights of minorities within the autonomous region, or any combination of these and others.

5. *Both parties must participate in designing autonomy agreements.* The principle may seem obvious, but it was ignored by the Sri Lankan government when it implemented a regional autonomy plan in 1987 that was supposed to end the Tamil insurgency.[20] Because the principal rebel group was not party to designing the plan, it assumed no obligation to accept it.

6. *International actors—the United Nations, regional organizations, neighboring states—should play a role in the negotiation of autonomy agreements.* International actors have a familiar role as mediators. It is equally or more important, Barbara F. Walter contends (note 4), that they serve as guarantors of the agreement and the security of disarmed contenders. Autonomy agreements are most likely to work if they include incentives for both ethnonationalist leaders and state elites to abide by the agreement's terms. Domestic obligations and incentives should be reinforced by international commitments—to provide diplomatic support and material assistance to parties that abide by agreements and to bring pressure to bear on parties that threaten to defect from agreements.

Concluding Observations

This and the preceding chapter document the existence of strong global trends in the 1990s toward accommodation of the interests of national and minority peoples. The elected leaders of many heterogeneous states are experimenting creatively with policies of nondiscrimination, provision of remedial opportunities for disadvantaged minorities, recognition of cultural pluralism, and negotiated arrangements for substate autonomy. Not all such policy initiatives satisfy aggrieved ethnopolitical groups, and many are too recent for us to speculate about long-run outcomes. The legacies of economic discrimination are particularly persistent. There is also the risk that strategies of accommodation will be subverted by advantaged groups who resist loss of privileges or—what amounts to the same thing—subverted by political entrepreneurs who build political movements that capitalize on resentment against minorities.

There also exist serious structural and ideological barriers to accommodation in some states. Some elites, especially in impoverished African states, use the state as an instrument for maintaining their own group's advantages. When threatened by the demands of communal challengers, they are likely to respond with draconian measures. Other governing elites remain ideologically committed to nation-building projects that require minorities either to assimilate to the dominant group or to accept marginalization. Religious minorities are targets of systematic discrimination in a number of Islamic states, discrimination based on doctrinal justifications that are highly resistant to international arguments about minority rights.

Nonetheless, the overall trend in the last decade of the twentieth century has been promising. Political and cultural restrictions are declining, and so is the incidence of new ethnopolitical conflicts. The positive trends are most pronounced in new democratic societies, including governments that incorporate a mix of democratic and autocratic features. These trends will have to be reinforced by continued international support for nondiscriminatory policies, recognition of group rights, and provision of substate autonomy. And concerted efforts should be made to assess the effects of alternative civil strategies of ethnic accommodation, to identify exemplary policies, and to promote their adoption elsewhere.

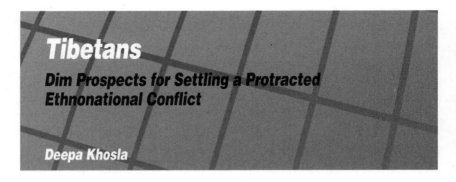

Tibetans
Dim Prospects for Settling a Protracted Ethnonational Conflict

Deepa Khosla

Tibetans' half century of resistance to control by the Beijing government illus-
trates the dynamics of ethnonationalism in a conquered people. The Chinese
government has tried policies of repression and accommodation, Sinification
and assimilation, without extinguishing the underlying desire of many Bud-
dhist Tibetans for restoration of their independence.

T HE PEOPLE'S REPUBLIC OF CHINA invaded the mountainous Buddhist
kingdom of Tibet in 1950, reasserting China's historical claim to the
region. Since then successive governments of the People's Republic have generally relied on repression, with occasional periods of liberalization, in an effort
to incorporate Tibetans into the Chinese polity and society. The Tibet Autonomous Region (TAR) is autonomous in name only. Because of long-term and
pervasive political, economic, and cultural discrimination, many Tibetans
inside and outside China continue their campaign for independence or, at a
minimum, for effective substate autonomy. An estimated 5.4 million Tibetans
live in the TAR and in neighboring regions—Qinghai, Gansu, Sichuan, and
Yunnan—that are administered separately from the TAR. Around one hundred thousand exiles live in Dharamsala, India, the political and spiritual center established by the Dalai Lama upon his flight from Tibet in 1959.

POLITICAL RESTRICTIONS

Explicit policies of the Chinese government severely restrict freedom of expression and the freedom of political organization for all citizens. These policies are imposed with special force on those who are perceived as *splittists*,
the Chinese term for supporters of independence. Therefore, campaigns of

suppression and detention of activists are a recurring fact of political existence in Tibet. The Tibetan government-in-exile in Dharamsala estimates that over three hundred thousand Tibetans have been killed by Chinese forces and twice as many have died due to famine and imprisonment since the occupation. The Chinese government is equally unyielding in Xinjiang, where Muslim Uighurs have waged a violent independence campaign since the early 1990s, and in Inner Mongolia, where a segment of China's Mongol population is demanding independence or reunification with Mongolia.

In 1990, following a year of martial law prompted by demonstrations in Lhasa, the government loosened its grip on the region, only to tighten it again during 1994 after Tibetans launched protests against a new round of restrictions on the practice of Buddhism. The number of political prisoners in Tibet has at least doubled since the mid-1990s; over twelve hundred Tibetans, mostly monks and nuns, were reported to be in custody in 1998.[1] Various human rights and pro-Tibetan nongovernmental organizations have reported an increase in the use of torture, forced labor, and killing of political prisoners in Tibetan jails. Due to Chinese restrictions on access to the region, these reports have not been independently verified.

POVERTY AND DEVELOPMENT

Although political restrictions have remained relatively constant, in the 1980s the government launched an economic liberalization campaign to provide some relief for Tibetans, one of the poorest groups in the country. Acknowledging that minorities lack even basic necessities, China proposed to spend over $1.6 billion by the end of the century to provide Tibetans with adequate food and clothing and to promote economic growth in the isolated region.[2]

The government's economic development plans have included sponsoring large-scale settlement of Han Chinese in Tibet. Tibetans are now reported to be a minority in Lhasa, whereas the Chinese constitute around 60 percent of the capital's population.[3] The Han immigrants work as agriculturalists and miners and also hold most professional and technical positions. The Tibetan government-in-exile claims that the migrants have been the prime beneficiaries of the government's economic programs. Further, many Tibetans interpret the Han influx as an attempt to overwhelm their culture and make them a minority in their own region.

CULTURAL RESTRICTIONS

Tibetan cultural identity is very closely intertwined with Buddhism. There-fore, attempts by the Chinese government to restrict cultural and religious practices in Tibet have on several occasions been the impetus for a resurgence in the struggle for autonomy. During the Cultural Revolution (1966–76), au-thorities destroyed nearly all Buddhist monasteries and religious symbols and outlawed all manifestations of Tibetan culture. In the 1980s the government relaxed its restrictions on the practice of Buddhism and provided funds to rebuild some monasteries, but it tightened restrictions again in the mid-1990s. In 1994 authorities banned the display of photographs of the Dalai Lama, except inside temples, and a campaign was launched to eliminate the tradi-tional Tibetan practice of polyandry. In 1995 new regulations limited the number of monks in each temple. These measures were probably an effort to dampen the Tibetan independence campaign; monks and nuns have been at the forefront of nonviolent protest in the past. The government reported that 87 percent of those arrested in Tibet in 1994 were monks and nuns.[4]

The most recent and controversial attempt by the Chinese government to regulate Tibetan cultural and religious life began in mid-1995, when it directly challenged the religious authority of the Dalai Lama. According to Tibetan custom, the Dalai Lama is responsible for choosing the successor for the sec-ond most senior religious position, the Panchem Lama. Denouncing the Dalai Lama's choice as another effort to split the country, the Chinese government instead appointed its own successor. Repeated protests and hunger strikes in both Dharamsala and Tibet have resulted in further clamp-downs on the Himalayan region.

The ban on the display of pictures of the Dalai Lama was extended in 1996 to encompass temples, schools, and even private homes. Moreover, Tibetan language schools have been closed and the use of Tibetan in postsecondary institutions eliminated. Major religious centers are now controlled by gov-ernment work teams. A 1996 patriotic reeducation campaign that requires monks and nuns to denounce the Dalai Lama and sign a pledge of allegiance to China was extended in 1998 to include ordinary citizens.[5] Some twenty-three hundred nuns and monks sought refuge in India in 1998 after refusing to sign these declarations.[6] Chinese officials reported that as of March 1998 some thirty-five thousand out of its estimate of forty-six thousand monks and nuns had been "rectified" by its reeducation campaign.[7]

The death of a Tibetan activist by self-immolation in New Delhi in 1998 has been referred to as a watershed by the ten-thousand-member Tibetan

Youth Congress (TYC), which advocates an armed struggle for independence. The TYC, the largest political organization representing the exiles, states that respect for the Dalai Lama and his nonviolent approach, among other factors, has ensured that so far only symbolic violence has occurred. Since 1996 at least four bombs have been set off in Tibet, and the Tibetan Youth Congress contends that future violence is likely, especially if authorities in Tibet continue their repression.[8]

Thus far Chinese officials have refused to hold direct negotiations with the Dalai Lama until he renounces his support for independence. Since the late 1980s, the Dalai Lama has repeatedly stated that he is only seeking to protect Tibetan culture in an autonomous Tibet within the People's Republic. The most recent effort to bring the sides to the negotiating table ended in November 1998 after some eighteen months of informal contacts.[9] So far, the Dalai Lama has been very successful in keeping Tibet on the international agenda despite efforts by Chinese authorities to limit information about and access to the region.

PROSPECTS FOR SETTLEMENT

The Tibetans' long-term quest to reestablish the political and cultural freedom they lost in the early 1950s is similar to the objectives of ethnonationalists in many other countries. The fact that it has seldom been manifest in armed rebellion is probably testimony to the effectiveness of Chinese policies of containment. Episodes of Tibetan resistance have provoked and served to justify high levels of discrimination and repression by the central Chinese government. The large-scale influx of Han settlers who have taken a central place in the economy has further marginalized Tibetans and added a new dimension to the conflict.

Chinese policies have not extinguished Tibetan resistance. On the contrary, the salience of Tibetan identity and the collective interest in autonomy seem as strong as ever. Whenever the authorities have eased restrictions, Tibetans have seized on the opportunity to mobilize and press their claims. In many similar separatist conflicts, as shown in chapter 6, governments and ethnonationalists have settled for substate autonomy. Not so in China. How the Tibetan quest for effective political and cultural autonomy will be pursued and whether it achieves positive results will be determined by a mix of domestic and international factors.

Most prominent is the future status of the institution of the Dalai Lama. If the current Dalai Lama were to die in the near future, it is not clear how his successor would be chosen. In Tibetan practice the Panchem Lama, who is second to the Dalai Lama, is responsible for determining the next incarnation. But the current Panchem Lama was appointed by Beijing, and the whereabouts of the Dalai Lama's choice are unknown. A leadership void would be likely to deflate support for a free Tibet both within the Tibetan community and among its international supporters.

A rapprochement between Chinese authorities and the Dalai Lama could lead to a negotiated settlement. But the present government of the PRC is unlikely to meet even minimal Tibetan demands for broad autonomy within a Greater Tibet. Moreover, factionalism among Tibetan exiles over the Dalai Lama's nonviolent approach is already threatening to weaken the movement. The lack of prospects for a negotiated settlement may prompt some Tibetans within and outside Tibet to use violence to increase the costs of China's occupation. There is little reason to think that the government of the PRC will respond to rebellion with anything other than repression. Nor is there any evidence that the PRC has learned lessons about the utility of negotiated autonomy agreements as an instrument for managing ethnonational conflicts.

NOTES

The author is senior research assistant and Asian regional specialist for the Minorities at Risk project. In 1998–99 she held a United States Institute of Peace dissertation fellowship.

In addition to the news items cited in the notes, the following sources were used for this sketch.

Barnett, Robert, ed. *Resistance and Reform in Tibet.* Bloomington and Indianapolis: Indiana University Press, 1994.

Bowers, Stephen. "Tibet since Mao Zedong." *Journal of Social, Political, and Economic Studies* 19, no. 4 (1994): 409–432.

Bray, John. "China and Tibet: An End to Empire." *World Today,* December 1990, 221–224.

Goldstein, Melvyn C. "The Dalai Lama's Dilemma." *Foreign Affairs* 77, no. 1 (1998): 83–97.

Gurr, Ted Robert, and Deepa Khosla. "Domestic and Transnational Strategies for Managing Separatist Conflicts: Four Asian Cases." In *Journeys through Conflict: Narratives and Lessons,* ed. Hayward Alker, Ted Robert Gurr, and Kumar Rupesinghe. Lanham, Md.: Rowman & Littlefield, forthcoming.

International Alert. *Tibet: An International Consultation.* London: International Alert, July 6–8, 1990.

James, Craig G. "Fanning the Flames of Desire: China's Failing Policy in Tibet." *Fourth World Bulletin* 5 (spring-summer 1996): 43–49.

1. *Economist,* August 29, 1998.

2. United Press International, March 1, 1995.

3. *International Herald Tribune,* November 12, 1998.

4. Reuters News Agency, June 17 and 22, 1995.

5. *Economist,* August 29, 1998.

6. *Christian Science Monitor,* October 29, 1998.

7. Deutsche Press-Agentur, May 15, 1998.

8. *Asiaweek,* September 11, 1998.

9. *Christian Science Monitor,* March 11, 1999.

The Gagauz of Moldova
Settling an Ethnonational Rebellion

Ted Robert Gurr and Michael L. Haxton

The Moldovan government was the first Soviet successor state to negotiate and implement a comprehensive autonomy agreement with a rebellious ethnonationalist movement. Enthusiasm about the agreement's applicability elsewhere needs to be tempered by recognition that its success has depended on an unusual conjunction of circumstances.

THE 160,000 GAGAUZ OF MOLDOVA are a small minority, less than 4 percent of the population of a small country, but their demands for greater autonomy parallel those of eighty other national peoples in the Minorities at Risk survey. Moreover, the autonomy agreement reached between Gagauz leaders and the Moldovan government in 1994, after two years of negotiation, has been praised as a model for resolving similar conflicts elsewhere.

BACKGROUND TO SEPARATISM

The Gagauz are Turkic-speaking Christians whose ancestors fled from persecution in Bulgaria in the early nineteenth century to Bessarabia, a province that was then under Romanian domination but is now divided between Ukraine and Moldova. Most live in a relatively small area of southern Moldova, not in exclusively Gagauz settlements but rather in districts that have significant Moldovan and Slavic minorities. Moldovans, in turn, are culturally and linguistically Romanians, who are the dominant group in a post-Soviet republic, most of which was carved out of pre-1945 Romania. Under Soviet rule the Gagauz were encouraged both to retain their Gagauz heritage and to learn Russian, thus serving as a counterweight to Moldovans' identification with Romania. The Soviets followed similar policies toward the mainly Slavic population of easternmost Moldova, the Trans-Dniester region—the site of another ethnonational rebellion that continued until the late 1990s.

MOLDOVAN NATIONALISM AS A THREAT TO
GAGAUZ IDENTITY

In the late 1980s Moldovan nationalists took a series of mostly symbolic steps that were widely seen as moves toward unification with Romania. Most threatening to non-Moldovans was legislation passed by the Moldovan Supreme Soviet (legislature) in 1989 that made Romanian the only official state language and required all officials to demonstrate proficiency in Romanian, even if serving in Gagauz- and Russian-speaking communities—a law whose implementation was repeatedly postponed. Largely in response to the language law, the Gagauz formed the Gagauz Khalk (Movement). At their first congress, in November 1989, they established an autonomous republic within Moldova, and in August 1990 they proclaimed the independence of the Republic of Gagauzia, announced their intention to remain within the Soviet Union, and called for presidential elections in October.

In response the Moldovan legislature declared the Gagauz Khalk illegal, and the Moldovan Popular Front, a nationalist movement, ordered some tens of thousands of young Moldovan "volunteers" to enter Gagauz towns to block the elections. Busloads of Russian "volunteers" arrived to help the Gagauz "republican guard" repel Moldovan "volunteers." Moldovan president Mircea Snegur, a moderate nationalist, forestalled mass bloodshed with a last-minute recall of the Moldovan volunteers, though not before clashes resulted in the deaths of a few Gagauz. Troops of the Soviet Interior Ministry were sent in and a compromise worked out whereby the Moldovan parliament agreed to reconsider Gagauz autonomy and the Khalk went ahead and elected Stepan Topal president of the still-unrecognized Gagauz Republic.

In August 1991, following the failed coup against Mikhail Gorbachev, the Moldovan legislature declared its independence from the USSR. Moldovan troops were sent to arrest leaders of the Gagauz Republic on charges that they had supported the coup attempt in Moscow, an act that prompted demonstrations in Komrat (the Gagauz capital) and threatened to jump-start the simmering civil war. Four months later presidential elections were held in Moldova, and Snegur, the only candidate, was reelected.

The Slavic peoples of the Trans-Dniester region also declared their own republic in 1990, and, like separatists in Gagauzia, they boycotted the December 1991 presidential elections. Later that winter Trans-Dniester leaders began a low-level military campaign for complete independence with the tacit support of Russian troops stationed in the region. The Gagauz leaders, by contrast, chose to pursue negotiations with the Moldovan government.

TOWARD ACCOMMODATION

During the next two years the Moldovan and Gagauz governments both sought to reach agreement on Gagauz autonomy within the Moldovan state. President Snegur gained leeway to do so as a result of early 1993 elections in which the moderate Agrarian Party gained a legislative majority over pro-Romanian nationalists. As the nationalists lost ground, Gagauz fears of being incorporated in Romania ebbed. At the same time support declined for militants who opposed Gagauz president Topal's low-key discussions with representatives of the Moldovan government.

External factors had a major effect on negotiations. The Moscow government was no longer readily able to manipulate Moldovan politics (though Russian support for an independent Trans-Dniester republic continued). The Turkish government persistently encouraged the Gagauz to accept autonomy within Moldova, offered to assist economic development in the region, and later carried through on the offer. The Council of Europe also gave its backing to a limited autonomy plan. The nationalist Romanian government was opposed, on grounds that it might impede eventual Moldovan unification with Romania, but to little effect.

THE AUTONOMY PLAN AND ITS IMPLEMENTATION

In July 1994 the Moldovan legislature adopted a new constitution that provided a framework within which effective substate autonomy could be implemented. Among other provisions, it guaranteed parents' rights to choose the language of their children's instruction and provided for the autonomy of the Gagauz and Trans-Dniester regions. Separate legislation passed later in 1994 established Gagauz-Eri (land) as a "national-territorial autonomy unit." The new entity was to have its own elected legislative and executive authorities, would use three official languages (Russian as well as Gagauz and Romanian), and was entitled to secession in the hypothetical event that Moldova merged with Romania. The legislation also gave Gagauz-Eri control of its own internal security affairs and gave its chief executive the right to determine the basing and movement of Moldova's military units on Gagauz-Eri's territory.

The implementation of agreements for substate autonomy is critical to their success. If governments defect or delay, as they have in Sudan and Israel, fighting may resume. Not in Moldova. During the first year after the 1994 agreement was reached, virtually all its provisions were implemented. Districts with a majority Gagauz population were automatically made part of Gagauz-Eri. In March 1995 referenda were held in thirty-six other districts with substantial Gagauz populations, and thirty of them voted to join the new entity, mostly with percentages that far exceeded the number of local Gagauz. The first *bashkan*, or leader, of Moldovan-recognized Gagauz-Eri was elected in June 1995, a former communist functionary turned businessman. During summer 1995 the Moldovan prime minister declared an end to the conflict, and Gagauz militia turned in their arms and were incorporated into the Moldovan security forces.

There have been technical problems in implementing some terms of the autonomy agreement, but during its first five years it has met the main political objectives of both parties. Renewed conflict is possible, but only in the very unlikely event that hard-line Romanian nationalists win control of the Moldovan presidency and legislature. In a March 1997 referendum, 95 percent of voters throughout the country favored continued independence from both Russia and Romania. The main threat to civil peace in Moldova is chronic economic decline, but because all parts of the country are similarly afflicted, it is not likely to provoke a revival of militant separatism. Rather, continued international economic assistance is contingent on internal stability.

CAN THE AUTONOMY PLAN BE EXPORTED?

The Gagauz agreement has been heralded as the first in East Central Europe to resolve a nationality conflict by negotiating ethnic-territorial autonomy. Observers regard it as a potential model for dealing with nationality conflicts elsewhere, for example, in Georgia, in Romania, and in Moldova's own Trans-Dniester region. It also might have been applied to Chechnya as an alternative to full-scale civil war. But for some it is a threatening model. The Romanian nationalist government, before its electoral defeat in late 1997, opposed the Gagauz settlement in part for fear that it might inspire demands for substate autonomy among the Hungarian minority in Romania. The separatist government in Trans-Dniester for a long time rejected the Gagauz model because it would leave them short of complete independence. Yet in 1998 the Trans-Dniester leadership reached an agreement with the Moldovan government for regional autonomy that was inspired by the successful implementation of the Gagauz agreement. A new territorial and administrative system that includes provisions for both autonomous regions was to be implemented throughout the country in summer 1999.

There are reasons for caution about the exportability of the Gagauz model. First, there was no history of intergroup conflict or discrimination between Moldovans and Gagauz, nor are Gagauz economically disadvantaged vis-à-vis Moldovans: thus, mutual hostilities and grievances were muted. Second, both peoples were fortunate to have moderate political leaders who eschewed appeals to exclusive nationalism. Third, it can be inferred that the Moldovan leadership was eager to resolve one ethnopolitical challenge the better to deal with the threat of more militant, Russian-backed Trans-Dniester separatism. Finally, by 1992–93 the international environment favored a settlement, and international actors promised material incentives once the conflict was settled. This seems a relatively uncommon conjuncture of favorable circumstances and not one often repeated.

NOTES

Ted Robert Gurr directs the Minorities at Risk project. Michael L. Haxton was Minorities project coordinator in 1994–96, received his doctorate at the University of Maryland in 1996, and is a senior analyst for the Joint Warfare Analysis Center of the U.S. Department of Defense.

This sketch is based on regional news sources and newsletters, including detailed coverage in publications of Radio Free Europe/Radio Liberty.

7

Assessing Risks of Future Ethnic Wars

Ted Robert Gurr and Monty G. Marshall

THE EBB IN NEW ethnopolitical conflicts since the early 1990s and the expanding repertoire of strategies for managing them do not mean that communal violence is about to disappear as a challenge to global or regional order. Ethnic rioting in Indonesia, communal and civil war in eastern Congo, and ethnic cleansing in Kosovo illustrate the ever-present possibility that ethnic conflicts can recur and morph in unexpected and deadly ways. For example, forty-one groups were in rebellion at the beginning of 1999, including contenders in protracted and deadly conflicts in Afghanistan, Sudan, and Africa's Great Lakes region that in the aggregate have cost hundreds of thousands of lives and put millions of refugees to flight.[1] Most of these conflicts are likely to continue; some of them may escalate. Moreover, other groups match the risk profile of ethnopolitical groups that *have* initiated serious rebellions in the recent past. Some high-risk groups, such as the peoples of the Niger delta, Tibetans in China, and Kachins in Burma, have little to show other than repression and resentment for protracted conflicts. Shifts in their political opportunities, domestic or international, are likely to set off new rebellions. Other high-risk groups are communal contenders in poor and potentially unstable states in Africa, Asia, and the Caucasus. New regimes are especially susceptible to ethnic challenges, as we showed in chapter 5.

This chapter identifies a set of risk factors for ethnopolitical rebellion, derived from the theory of ethnopolitical conflict in chapter 3, and applies them to recent data on the 275 groups surveyed in the current phase of the Minorities at Risk project. The approach is analogous to the procedure used by physicians to assess an individual's risk of heart disease or breast cancer. Epidemiological and clinical studies have identified factors—genetic, environmental, dietary, life-style—that increase susceptibility to disease. An individual's chances of getting a disease are assessed by the presence or absence of risk factors in his or her personal history and experience. In the case of ethnopolitical conflict, the empirical basis for assessing risk factors comes from 1990s data on the 275 groups. Logistic regression analysis is used to identify factors measured in the early 1990s most closely linked to the presence of protest and rebellion in 1996–98. The groups that are highest on the risk factors at the end of the 1990s are identified, and the kinds of political circumstances in which they might initiate or escalate rebellion are discussed briefly.

From Risk Assessment to Early Warning to Preventive Action?

The procedure applied in this chapter is a response to the need, often expressed by people who design and implement development and humanitarian programs, and by practitioners of preventive diplomacy, for better foreknowledge of serious ethnopolitical conflicts and humanitarian crises. Early warning is the first step in the "ladder of prevention" for post–Cold War conflicts proposed by Jan Elliason, the United Nations' first undersecretary for humanitarian affairs and later Sweden's secretary of state for foreign affairs. The next steps after early warning are fact-finding, peaceful settlement of disputes, and peacekeeping operations.[2]

Policymakers usually think of early warning as a flow of near-real-time information that contains signals of the imminent outbreak of conflict. Systems for compiling and evaluating such information are usually transnational in scope and designed to serve national foreign policy interests. They also can be local and designed to provide warnings and assessments to domestic officials, the media, and nongovernmental organizations. Domestic networks designed to provide early warnings of ethnic tension have been established in South Africa and the former Soviet Union, for example.[3]

Whereas early warners focus on signals of immediate crises, analysts are more concerned with identifying and profiling high-risk situations.[4] The two activities are interdependent: risk assessment provides the context in which policymakers and activists interpret the significance of political events; in the absence of risk assessments, early warning signals cannot reliably be picked

out of the "noise" of political reportage. In the absence of near-real-time monitoring of potential crisis situations, risk assessments may provide useful inputs
for those who plan policies and humanitarian assistance but do not signal an
imperative need for preventive action.

Several assumptions undergird the contemporary interest in conflict risk
assessment and early warning. One is that policymakers, when convincingly
forewarned, have means at their disposal for heading off violent conflicts within
states. The cumulating evidence on preventive diplomacy is impressive.
Michael Lund has catalogued its instrumentalities, the Center for Preventive
Action has compiled case studies of effective and ineffective preventive action,
and many experts are examining the conditions in which preventive action
should be attempted.[5]

A second assumption is that preventive action is less costly than the costs of
emergency aid and peacekeeping once serious conflicts have begun. There is
a small but telling body of confirming evidence on this point. A recent study
for the Carnegie Commission on Preventing Deadly Conflict estimates the
direct and indirect costs of recent conflicts in Bosnia and elsewhere and then
projects what the costs would have been if remedial programs had been in place
and peacekeeping forces on the ground before the outbreak of fighting. For
example, the "total measurable cost to the international community" of the
Bosnian conflict from 1992 through 1996 is estimated at $48.7 billion,
whereas the four-year cost of a 45,000-member peacekeeping force, deployed
in early 1992, would have been about $10 billion—and a great many lives
would have been saved.[6]

A third assumption is that comparative assessments add substantially to
what is already known by country specialists and people on the ground. This
assumption is challenged by some. Many, perhaps most, area specialists and
diplomats believe that their own "understanding" of situations and actors provides a better basis for risk assessments and early warnings than regularities
identified in quantitative comparative analyses. Another basis for skepticism
about all early warning research is that there are abundant early warnings of
any crisis—that is, the task is not to warn but to create the political willingness to take action. Donald Krumm, formerly of the U.S. Department of
State, writes,

> In the information age, the problem is not so much early warning, but urgently
> engaged early action by governments and international organizations based on
> having received warning. Many would argue that, had warnings been matched
> with decisive action, the disintegration of the former Yugoslavia and the geno-
> cide in Rwanda could have been averted.[7]

Analysts and policymakers who are convinced that risk assessments and early warnings based on the analysis of one case are superior to those derived from statistical analysis of multiple cases might be asked these essential questions: On the basis of what criteria do you assess the risks of conflict escalation, using what kinds of evidence? And are the criteria explicit enough, and the evidence precise enough, that decision makers can be persuaded to take *early* action? Our view is that theory and comparative evidence can provide a guide to gathering and interpreting information about impending conflicts in a reliable and convincing way. Comparative statistical research will never supplant conventional methods of risk assessment and early warning, but it is imperative that systematic methods be used to complement conventional methods.

The optimal test of whether empirical studies can reinforce or improve on the judgments of area experts and on-the-ground observers is to carry out such studies and test their results against expert assessments and real-world outcomes. There is a small but expanding body of systematic risk assessment and early warning studies that might be tested in this way.[8] Unfortunately, their utility is limited by several factors. Most of them use complex statistical techniques that area specialists and policymakers seldom understand. They are applied after the fact to information on past crises and conflicts, which raises doubts about whether their results are applicable to future conflicts. And we know of no efforts by either researchers or policymakers to compare model-based forecasts of political conflicts against other assessments or against outcomes. These liabilities could be overcome, as they have been by researchers who use macroeconomic models to generate forecasts of countries' economic performance. At present, however, empirically based forecasting of political crises is at the Wright brothers stage: test flights are promising, but cargo- and passenger-carrying capabilities remain to be demonstrated.

This chapter is concerned with risk assessment, not with early warnings. Risk assessments, as suggested, identify situations in which the conditions for a particular kind of conflict—in this study, ethnopolitical rebellion—are present. They are not predictions in the sense that is usually meant by the terms *forecast* and *early warning*, because risks are assessed on the basis of background and intervening conditions—the conditions that establish the potential for conflict. Whether or not risks are realized depends on whether the preconditions remain unchanged *and* on accelerating or triggering events. Early warnings, by contrast, are derived from monitoring the flow of political events, with special attention to actions that are likely to precipitate the onset of conflict in high-risk situations. Risk assessments provide the context. Early warnings are interpretations that the outbreak of conflict in a high-risk situation is likely and imminent.[9]

Risk Assessment Model of Ethnopolitical Protest and Rebellion

The method used to derive risk assessments in this chapter builds on previous studies that correlated characteristics of ethnopolitical groups in the early and mid-1990s with their levels of political protest and rebellion. Those studies were good enough to pinpoint such high-risk groups as southerners in Chad, Banyarwandans in Zaire, Rwandan Hutus, Palestinians in Israel, Uzbeks in Afghanistan, Sindhis in Pakistan, and Kosovar Albanians, but they also gave false alarms of new or escalating rebellion for Avars in Russia, Russians in Lithuania, and Maya in Guatemala.[10] The methodological approach used here is rigorous and uses data that are current through 1998. The procedures are described in sufficient detail in appendix B that other researchers, using the Minorities at Risk data, can reproduce and attempt to improve on our results. The most interesting challenge, in our view, is to follow political developments during the next several years in the high-risk cases. Do risky situations have disruptive consequences, and if not, why not?

RISK ASSESSMENTS OF WHAT? THE DEPENDENT VARIABLES

Protest is less disruptive and more susceptible to accommodation than rebellion. Protest also is a leading indicator of rebellion, as demonstrated in chapter 2: most new ethnorebellions of 1986–95 were preceded by a decade or more of protest. These are two good reasons for assessing the risks of protest and rebellion separately. We used two measures, one based on each group's observed level of *protest in 1996–98*, the other on *rebellion in 1997–98*. The Minorities data set includes roughly calibrated data on both variables. Our decision to use logistic regression required that we reduce this information to dichotomies, as described in appendix B, section I.1.

Rebellion 1997–98 is scored 1 if a group engaged in any kind of antigovernment rebellion in either year, including terrorism, local rebellions, or guerrilla or civil wars (see table 2.2); otherwise, it is scored 0.[11]

Protest 1996–98 is scored 1 if a group used any kind of organized protest in the three years *and* if its rebellion score was less than 3 in those years; otherwise, it is scored 0.[12] The second criterion excludes groups for which protest is incidental to armed conflict. By focusing on groups for which protest is the principal form of political action, we are more likely to identify the factors that lead to protest *before* the onset of rebellion and the characteristics of the political process that make nonviolent protest a preferred alternative to open and armed rebellion.

Rebellion rarely occurs in the absence of nonviolent political action; in fact, the two forms may be best understood as symbiotic in the sense that they present important information and clarify alternatives to government decision makers concerning group strength, commitment, values, priorities, resolve. Such information helps decision makers to judge their ability to leverage negotiated outcomes. If conventional organizations gain important concessions, support for militant organizations and tactics should recede in the short term, while the group pursues prioritiy goals, and diminish over the medium term if accommodations regarding essential group goals are realized and confidence in conventional tactics is reestablished. But if "working within the system" fails or gains only symbolic, minor, or short-term concessions, support for militancy will likely increase and grow even more resolute. Forecasting dynamic increases and decreases in the strategic use of protest and rebellion is a more difficult research task than identifying the structural risk factors that determine whether each tactic is present or absent. Most risk factors that can be constructed from the Minorities data set are not sensitive to the kinds of short-term changes that are likely to precipitate shifts in strategies of group action. The analysis of accelerators and decelerators is a more precise approach to this "early warning" issue (see note 9). But we tried anyway, using the following three indicators:

Increase in Protest 1995–98 is scored 1 if a group registered an increase of two or more categories on the protest scale at any time between 1995 and 1998; otherwise, 0.

Increase in Rebellion 1995–98 is scored 1 if a group registered an increase of two or more categories on the rebellion scale at any time between 1995 and 1998; otherwise, 0.

Decrease in Rebellion 1995–98 is scored 1 if a group registered a decrease of two or more categories on the rebellion scale at any time between 1995 and 1998; otherwise, 0.

THE RISK FACTORS

The chance that a communal group will initiate political action depends on four kinds of conditions: *salience of group identity, collective incentives, capacity for joint action,* and *external opportunities.* Collective decisions about whether to use strategies of protest or rebellion depend jointly on these conditions and on the nature of group interests, *access* or *autonomy*. These concepts, most of which were developed in chapter 3, are the template for the risk assessment models tested here. Each concept is represented by binary indicators constructed from data coded in the most recent phase of the Minorities project. The process of constructing and validating indicators is reported in appendix B. What follows is an overview of the indicators tested and a summary of how they contributed to the risk assessments presented in the last section of this chapter.

Salience of Group Identity

The salience of identity to members of ethnopolitical groups is not easily indexed using coded or aggregate data. Theory suggests that collective identity should be most important for peoples who experience discrimination and have recently been involved in substantial conflict. Five indicators of these conditions were tested with these outcomes, as detailed in appendix B, section III.

Persistent protest during the previous decade has a consistent leading relationship with future rebellion and is one of the six factors in the final risk assessment model for rebellion (table 7.2).

Persistent rebellion during the previous decade correlates with future rebellion but is not used in the risk models, because it tells us only what we already know, that once rebellions have begun they tend to persist.

Economic and political discrimination are correlated with future increases in protest but do not contribute independently to the risk models. This result parallels evidence from analysis of Minorities data from the 1980s that showed that discrimination has an indirect rather than a direct impact on political action. Discriminatory treatment precedes the articulation of group grievances; grievances prompt mobilization; mobilization leads to political action.[13]

Cultural restrictions prove to be a significant risk factor in the model for protest (table 7.1).

Group Incentives for Collective Action

The greater the disadvantages imposed on a people and the greater their sense of injustice, the easier it is for group leaders to convince them that they have something to gain from collective action. Opposition to new discriminatory policies (cultural restrictions are an example), anger about state repression, and hopes for redress of past wrongs, such as loss of collective autonomy, therefore, are among the precursors of sustained political action by ethnopolitical groups. Three such conditions are tested as risk factors:

Lost autonomy is correlated with ongoing rebellions and is used in our index of domestic conditions that facilitate future rebellions (summarized in table 7.3).

Government repression is a very strong leading indicator of both protest and rebellion. Any inhibiting effect repression might have on ethnopolitical action is more than offset by the mutually reinforcing spiral of attack and counter-attack. Repression is an instrument of government policy; policies can be changed. The repression indicator, therefore, is included in both risk models (tables 7.1 and 7.2).

Increased political restrictions is a leading indicator of rebellion, probably for the same reason as repression. Governments often respond to rebellions by imposing new restrictions that provide fresh incentives for continued resistance. The indicator has no independent effect on risks of future rebellion and is not included in any of the models used.

Group Capacity for Collective Action

The greater a people's sense of common identity, the greater their potential for joint action. Identity alone is not sufficient; it needs organizational expression. The argument is similar to Charles Tilly's contention that group mobilization is the precursor to collective action.[14] Two structural indicators of ethnopolitical groups' capacity for political action were tested as well as two indicators of change in capacity.

Territorial concentration has been established in other studies as a precondition for most ethnorebellions. It proves to be the second-strongest risk indicator in our rebellion model (table 7.2).

Group organization is the third-strongest risk indicator in the rebellion model (table 7.2) but, like territorial concentration, is not a leading indicator of protest (table 7.1).

Increases in support for conventional and for militant ethnopolitical organizations are two of the time-sensitive indicators we tested in an effort to forecast imminent changes in collective action. We did not expect either one to contribute to the risk models (tables 7.1 and 7.2), nor did they. However, we found that increased support for *conventional organizations,* other things being equal, reduces the likelihood of future rebellion. The implication is that strengthening conventional ethnopolitical organizations, by either increasing their capabilities or enhancing their success in gaining concessions, increases the utility of noncoercive strategies of political action. Therefore, we use the indicator as one of five domestic facilitating factors (inversely, because it reduces the risks of rebellion) in table 7.3.

Domestic Opportunities for Collective Action

Group leaders make strategic decisions about when to initiate, escalate, and terminate collective action. They do so in the context of changing political environments that shape the chances of successful political action. A great many factors might provide, or increase, the opportunities for successful ethno-rebellion. We tested how characteristics of political systems affect the likelihood of protest and rebellion.

Democratic, autocratic, and incoherent polities: As expected, democratic polities have above average protest but below average rebellion. Democracy proves to be a significant risk factor in the protest equation (table 7.1). By contrast, autocracies and incoherent polities (regimes with a mix of democratic and autocratic features) had less than average protest. Incoherent regimes are especially susceptible to increased rebellion; therefore, we use the incoherence indicator as one of five domestic facilitating factors (table 7.3).

Regime instability: Consistent with evidence examined in chapter 5, the risk analysis showed that ethnic protest and rebellion increase during the first five years after an abrupt change in political regime. Regime instability is the strongest risk indicator in the protest model (table 7.1) and also enters the rebellion model (table 7.2).

International Opportunities for Collective Action

We distinguish between direct and diffuse international factors that encourage ethnopolitical activism. Direct support includes diplomatic, material, and military assistance from kindred groups, sympathetic states, and international organizations. Diffuse factors include the effects of armed conflicts being fought in adjoining countries. Their spillovers—arms, refugees, militants looking for safe havens—may give ethnic contenders incentives and opportunities to press their claims. They also contribute to a general climate of insecurity that can provoke preemptive action by communal groups and state authorities alike.[15]

Support from kindred groups: Ethnopolitical groups supported by kindred in neighboring states are more likely to openly challenge state authority through protest and rebellion. Cross-border access to support, resources, and refuge gives groups a broader array of strategic and tactical options; these social networks also provide a conduit for spillover, demonstration, and amelioration effects. This indicator appears in the protest risk model (table 7.1) as a factor that significantly enhances the chances of protest. It also is one of four international factors that facilitate future rebellion (table 7.3).

Support from foreign states: Support from foreign states predicts to future rebellion in the risk model in table 7.2.

International political support: Whereas bilateral support for ethnopolitical groups (from kindred or states) increases the risks of violent conflict, our statistical analyses show that in the 1990s sustained engagement by international organizations reduced the risk of future rebellion. We use international political support as one of four external facilitating factors (inversely, because it reduces the risks of rebellion) in the index described in table 7.3.

Spillover effects of regional conflicts: Protest is significantly less likely and rebellion is more likely in countries in "bad neighborhoods." Two indicators of regional conflict are used as external facilitating factors in the index described in table 7.3.

Effects of Group Type on Political Action

The six types of ethnopolitical groups defined in chapter 2 have different objectives and different relationships with state authorities. They also tend to rely on different strategies of political action. We tested the effects of group type on risks of future protest and rebellion with the following results.

Ethnonationalists are more likely than any other type of group to use strategies of rebellion. Ethnonationalist aims, therefore, are one of the factors used in the index of facilitating domestic conditions (table 7.3).

Indigenous peoples and ethnoclasses, by contrast, were unlikely to rebel in the 1990s—indigenous peoples because they have come to rely more heavily on strategies of protest, ethnoclasses because they are, in general, less politically active than any other group type.[16] This information also is incorporated in the index of facilitating domestic conditions (table 7.3).

Religious sects often use protest strategies but are no more or less likely than others to engage in rebellion. Most of the groups so categorized in the Minorities project are in or on the borders of the Islamic world. Readers are free to speculate about the implications of this finding for debates on civilizational conflict and the supposed relationship between Islam and communal conflict.[17] The only conclusion drawn here is that religiously defined communal groups are not a relevant factor in a risk model of ethnorebellion.

THE RISK MODELS AND FACILITATION INDICATORS

The optimal risk models for protest in 1996–98 and rebellion in 1997–98 are summarized in tables 7.1 and 7.2. In the protest model five risk factors make

Table 7.1. Risk Factors for Ethnopolitical Protest in 1996–98

A. Logistic Regression Results

Key Variables	Groups at Greater Risk	Groups at Lesser Risk	Relative Risk of Protest[a]
Cultural restrictions 1994–95	Subject to restrictions	Not subject to restrictions	2.3
Government repression in 1996	Subject to repression	Not subject to repression	2.6
Democratic polity in 1995	In democratic states	In nondemocratic states	2.2
Regime instability 1992–95	No regime instability	Regime instability	3.8
Support from kindred groups 1995	No kindred support	Kindred support	2.0

B. Accuracy of Classification of 254 Groups[b]

Observed	Predicted		Percentage Correct
	No Protest	Protest	
No protest	66	40	62.3
Protest	30	118	79.7
Overall percentage			72.4

[a] Based on beta weights. All weights are significant at the 0.01 level except kindred support, significant at the 0.05 level.

[b] Data on one or more variables were missing for twenty-one groups.

it possible to classify correctly 72 percent of the groups. The model is especially good at correct classification of groups with protest (and minimal rebellion) in 1996–98. It correctly identifies 118 of the 148 protest groups and produces only 30 "false negatives" (groups with observed protest that the model predicts should not have protested).

In the rebellion model six risk factors provide an even higher overall level of accuracy, correctly classifying 88 percent of groups. This model does exceptionally well at distinguishing groups that did not rebel in 1997–98. It correctly classifies 186 of the 203 nonrebellious groups and produces only 17 "false positives" (groups that were predicted to rebel but did not). We experimented with alternative sets of variables to arrive at these results, taking into account both theoretical expectations and empirical results. The model provides a solid empirical basis for forecasts of future protest and rebellion based on risk factors measured in the late 1990s.

A few general comments about the factors in the two risk models. Each of the five clusters of theoretical variables is represented in the models, all of them in the rebellion model and all except *capacity for political action* in the protest model. The strongest predictive factors for protest are *incentives* (government repression) and *domestic opportunities*. The most potent risk factors for rebellion are *incentives* (government repression again), *group capacity* (territorial concentration and group organization), and *domestic opportunities* (regime instability). We also note that two of the five factors in the protest model are, in effect, measures of the *absence* of conditions that otherwise predict to rebellion. If regimes are stable and democratic, ethnopolitical groups are likely to protest; in unstable and autocratic regimes, they are likely to rebel. Bilateral support from kindred groups and foreign governments has a similar "switching" effect. If such support is absent, groups are likely to protest; if it is present, rebellion is more likely.

Other factors also predicted increased rebellion but not strongly or consistently enough to be included in the risk equations. We use these factors, as described in appendix B, sections II.7 and II.8, to construct two composite indicators of conditions, domestic and external, that facilitate or dampen a group's future resort to rebellion. Some of these facilitating and dampening factors (listed in table 7.3) are invariant or structural conditions, whereas others can change quickly. Structural conditions include general group identity characteristics and historical changes in the group's autonomy. More transitory structural factors involve the context within which groups make decisions regarding their relationship with the state: the structures of state authority (coherent or incoherent) and the more general conditions characterizing the

Table 7.2. Risk Factors for Ethnopolitical Rebellion in 1997–98

A. Logistic Regression Results

Key Variables	Groups at Greater Risk	Groups at Lesser Risk	Relative Risk of Rebellion[a]
Persistent protest 1985–94	Five or more years' protest	Less than five years' protest	3.7
Government repression 1996	Subject to repression	Not subject to repression	16.4
Territorial concentration	Concentrated	Dispersed	7.0
Group organization 1990–95	Has political organizations	No political organizations	5.7
Regime instability 1992–95	Regime instability	No regime instability	4.1
Support from foreign governments 1995	Foreign support	No foreign support	3.4

B. Accuracy of Classification of 275 Groups

Observed	Predicted		Percentage Correct
	No Rebellion	Rebellion	
No rebellion	186	17	92
Rebellion	18	54	75
Overall percentage			88

[a] Based on beta weights. All weights are significant at the 0.01 level.

Table 7.3. Domestic and External Factors That Facilitate Future Rebellion

Factor	Effect
Domestic Factors That Facilitate Future Rebellion	
History of lost political autonomy	Increases risks of rebellion
Increased group support for conventional	Decreases risks of rebellion organizations
Incoherent polity (mix of democratic and	Increases risks of rebellion autocratic traits)
Group is a communal contender	Increases risks of rebellion
Group is an indigenous people or ethnoclass	Decreases risks of rebellion
Group is ethnonationalist in type	Increases risks of rebellion
External Factors That Facilitate Future Rebellion	
Transnational support from kindred groups	Increases risks of rebellion
Transnational support from regional or	Decreases risks of rebellion international organizations
High level of armed civil conflict in neighboring states	Increases risks of rebellion
High level of armed civil conflict in wider region	Increases risks of rebellion

Note: These factors amplify or dampen the effects of the risk factors in table 7.2. Indicators of the factors in this table are described in appendix B, sections II.7 and II.8.

international "neighborhood," especially the degree of insecurity—armed conflict—in bordering states and in the broader region. The most transitory factors concern group capacity and access to viable alternatives to violence: increased support within the group for its conventional organizations, and the nature of transnational support. The most immediate and accessible influences for managing and transforming minority group conflicts are these support factors. States can reduce the risk of rebellion by establishing constructive relations with the group's conventional organizations. Engagement by regional and international organizations provides greater latitude for managing the tensions between peoples and states and thus reduces the risks of armed conflict. The factors that make up the domestic and external composite indicators of rebellion facilitation are summarized in table 7.3 and used to interpret the risk estimates in tables 7.4 through 7.9.

Minorities at Risk of Rebellion at the Beginning of the Twenty-First Century

The basic assumption of this analysis is straightforward: groups that are highest on the risk factors that predicted to protest and rebellion in the late 1990s have the greatest prospects of initiating future conflicts or of escalating from lower to higher levels of rebellion. The ninety-four highest-risk groups are listed by region in tables 7.4 to 7.9. For each group we report first their predicted likelihood of rebellion from the "1995 model," which uses information from the early to mid-1990s to predict to conflict in 1997–98. All groups with likelihood estimates greater than –0.54 are included in the tables—in other words, the tables include both high- and medium-risk groups. Also listed are each group's observed levels of protest and rebellion in the late 1990s and an indicator of whether its magnitude of rebellion increased or decreased during the 1990s. Note that the estimates predicted from the 1995 model are probability factors that violent tactics will be used by the group, not predictions of the magnitude of rebellion; therefore, they are not directly comparable with the observed conflict scores. Actual and eventual magnitudes of armed conflict depend upon escalatory dynamics; once started, armed conflicts tend to escalate and become protracted. The decisive test of the adequacy of the likelihood estimates is that they correctly discriminate 88 percent of the rebellious versus nonrebellious groups, as was shown in table 7.2. It is the threshold of interactive violence that is critical in the management of minority group conflicts. The model is especially useful because it is parsimonious; it closely approximates the necessary and sufficient conditions for the outbreak of violence. Of the six factors that make up the model estimates, at least four of the factors must be present for a prediction that a group is at risk.

The four right-hand columns of tables 7.4 to 7.9 summarize the evaluations of risks of future rebellions for these ninety-four groups. First is the predicted likelihood of future rebellion. No specific time frame is given to these estimates of likelihood, because they are valid (within the limitations of the model and data used) as long as the risk factors themselves remain unchanged. The next column compares the predicted risks of rebellion using the 1995 and 1998 models. If the risks increased, the sign is positive. The last two columns summarize our information on the domestic and external factors listed in table 7.3 that facilitate or dampen the risk of future rebellion. We interpret positive scores as evidence that an ethnopolitical group's risk of future rebellion is greater than predicted by the 1998 model. Negative scores suggest that a group's risk of future rebellion is inhibited by some combination of domestic or international factors, or both. Bold type is used in tables 7.4 to 7.9 to highlight thirty-one groups with positive changes in two out of three of the right-hand columns and no offsetting factors that might minimize conflicts. These are the groups at greatest risk of future rebellion.

One important issue needs to be addressed before surveying the regional results: how to interpret the risk assessments for groups already in rebellion. The ninety-four medium- to high-risk groups include all forty-one groups involved in armed conflict at the beginning of 1999. They also include another fifty-two groups with no significant armed conflict in 1997–98. "High risks" for groups already fighting ethnic wars, such as Kashmiris in India and Hutus in Burundi, means that armed conflict is likely to continue or escalate.[18] "High risks" for other groups, such as Russians in Crimea, Tibetans, and Ogani in Nigeria, means that they are likely to initiate rebellions unless their circumstances change.

Another diagnostic tool is provided by the indicators of facilitating factors —the two right-hand columns in tables 7.4 to 7.9. Where negative, they suggest shifts away from the conditions that sustain ongoing rebellions. They point, for example, to potential de-escalation of rebellions by Armenians in Azerbaijan, Moros in the Philippines, and the people of East Timor. They also signal the presence of domestic and external factors that inhibit the potential for future rebellions by Palestinians in Gaza and the West Bank, Yugoslavia's Sandzak Muslims, Hungarians in Romania, and indigenous peoples in Ecuador, Bolivia, Guatemala, Venezuela, and Peru.

WESTERN DEMOCRACIES AND THE POSTCOMMUNIST STATES

Western Europe

Risks of rebellion among the thirty-one groups in this region are small. The Basques head the list of five medium-risk groups (likelihood of future rebellion between −0.54 and +1.00), mainly because authorities in both France and Spain have recently arrested group leaders, a factor that in other political contexts would be likely to provoke escalated rebellion. In Spain, though, the militant Basque organization ETA declared a 1998 cease-fire in order to participate in regional elections. The risk of rebellion for Turks in Germany increased during the 1990s due to repression—arrests of some activists—and external support. These risk factors are more than offset by another development that does not yet show up in the Turks' risk profile, namely, the passage of federal legislation that grants German citizenship to all persons born in the Federal Republic.

The Balkans

Alarms that rebellion and ethnic cleansing in Kosovo foreshadow a new wave of destabilizing European ethnic wars seem inconsistent with our finding that only five out of fifty-nine ethnopolitical groups in the postcommunist states have a high risk of rebellion (predicted risks greater than 1.00). However, spillover from the Kosovo conflict may itself increase the risk factors, especially for groups in the Balkans already at medium risk, such as Yugoslavia's Sandzak Muslims and Vojvodina Hungarians. The risk profiles also suggest medium potentials for renewed fighting among Serb, Muslim, and Croat contenders in the Yugoslav successor states. Massive international engagement has not yet changed the underlying risk factors for these groups.

Russians in the Near Abroad

Russians in Estonia, Crimea, and Kyrgyzstan are in the medium- to high-risk range and several other elements of the Russian diaspora are just below it, due in part to external support. Russians in Crimea have engaged in sustained protest during the 1990s, one of the leading indicators of future rebellion. The key issue for all Russians in the "near abroad" is their status and rights as citizens of the Soviet successor states. Most have had the safety valve of emigrating to Russia. The future threat is that nationalists in Moscow, bent on reestablishing Russian hegemony, will promote irredentist activity that could escalate into rebellions.

Ethnonationalists in the Caucasus

The most serious ethnonational rebellions in the Soviet successor states were fought in the Caucasus and in Moldova. Virtually all have subsided, some of them ending in negotiated settlements, as documented in chapter 6. Four groups in the region remain at substantial risk. The greatest risk in the region is that full-fledged warfare will resume over the status of Nagorno-Karabakh. The inhibiting factors are international pressures on all governments concerned to conclude a negotiated settlement that recognizes the sovereignty of Nagorno-Karabakh but stops short of ratifying its incorporation into Armenia. The risks for the Ingush and Avars in Russia are due to their political activism and ethnonationalism, intensified by potential spillover effects from conflicts in their immediate neighborhood. Most ethnonational groups in Russia have negotiated autonomous status within the Russian Federation. Moscow's accommodation of demands for greater local control makes rebellion unlikely under present circumstances. But ethnonationalists' control of regional governments enhances their capacity to defend their interests, and

Table 7.4. Groups at Highest Risk of Rebellion in the Western Democracies and Japan

Country	Group	Mean Annual Conflict in 1997–98[a]				Risks of Future Rebellion			
		Predicted Rebellion from 1995 Model	Observed Rebellion	Observed Protest	Trend in Rebellion in the 1990s[b]	Predicted from 1998 Model[c]	Change in Predictions 1995–98[d]	Changes in Facilitating Factors[e]	
								Domestic	External
France	Basques	-0.54	2.0	2.0	0	0.77	1	1	1
Spain	Basques	0.77	2.0	3.0	0	0.77	0	1	0
United Kingdom	Catholics in Northern Ireland	0.03	1.0	2.0	-1	0.03	0	0	0
Germany	Turks	-3.98	0.0	3.5	0	0.03	1	-2	1
France	Corsicans	0.77	3.0	2.0	1	-0.54	-1	2	0

Note: Groups are listed in descending order of predicted risks from the 1998 model. Only five groups, whose predicted rebellion scores are greater than or equal to –0.54, are included; twenty-five other groups in these countries are below this threshold, i.e., have low or very low risks of future rebellion. Groups in bold are those with positive changes in two out of three of the right-hand columns and no offsetting conflict-minimizing factors.

[a] The predicted scores for rebellion are those generated by the logistic regression model summarized in table 7.2. Observed scores are the means of annual coded values of rebellion and protest for 1997 and 1998 on the scales given in table 2.2.

[b] The trend in observed rebellion between 1990 and 1998. Groups whose rebellion scores in the last three years of the decade increased by 2 or more over previous years are coded +1; groups whose scores declined by 2 or more are coded –1; others are coded 0.

[c] The predicted scores for future rebellion are generated by applying the logistic regression model in table 7.2 to 1998 data on the independent variables. Similar analyses were done to generate predicted scores for 1996 and 1997.

[d] The direction of change in predicted rebellion scores from 1995 to 1998.

[e] In addition to the six variables in the model summarized in table 7.2 we identified a number of other domestic and international factors that correlate with increases or decreases in rebellion, listed in table 7.3. These variables are used to construct the composite scores reported here, which indicate the net effects of, respectively, domestic and international factors that increase or decrease the likelihood of future rebellion. See appendix B, section IV, for details.

Table 7.5. Groups at Highest Risk of Rebellion in Eastern Europe and the Former USSR

Country	Group	Mean Annual Conflict in 1997–98[a]			Trend in Rebellion in the 1990s[b]	Risks of Future Rebellion			
		Predicted Rebellion from 1995 Model	Observed Rebellion	Observed Protest		Predicted from 1998 Model[c]	Change in Predictions 1995–98[d]	Changes in Facilitating Factors[e]	
								Domestic	External
Azerbaijan	Armenians	2.10	3.5	1.5	−1	2.10	0	0	−2
Yugoslavia	Kosovars	1.98	4.0	3.5	1	1.98	0	0	−1
Estonia	Russians	−0.82	0.0	1.5	0	1.98	1	0	−1
Ukraine	Crimean Tatars	0.67	0.0	3.0	0	1.98	1	2	−1
Ukraine	Crimean Russians	−2.13	0.0	2.0	0	1.98	1	1	0
Bosnia	Serbs	−0.70	0.5	2.0	−1	0.89	1	2	−1
Yugoslavia	Sandzak Muslims	−0.54	0.0	2.0	0	0.77	1	−2	0
Russia	Ingush	0.67	0.0	2.0	−1	0.77	1	1	0
Croatia	Serbs	0.67	0.5	1.0	−1	0.67	0	1	−1
Yugoslavia	Hungarians	−2.13	0.0	2.0	0	0.67	1	−1	1

Moldova	Slavs	2.10	3.0	0	2.5	0	0.67	−1	1	0
Bosnia	**Muslims**	**−2.65**	**0.0**	**−1**	**0.0**	**−1**	**0.15**	**1**	**2**	**0**
Romania	Hungarians	−4.08	0.0	0	1.5	0	0.15	1	−1	−2
Kyrgyzstan	**Russians**	**−4.08**	**0.0**	**0**	**2.0**	**0**	**0.15**	**1**	**2**	**1**
Russia	Avars	−3.34	0.0	0	1.0	0	−0.54	1	3	0

Note: Groups are listed in descending order of predicted risks from the 1998 model. Only fifteen groups, whose predicted rebellion scores are greater than or equal to −0.54, are included; forty-four other groups in these countries are below this threshold, i.e., have low or very low risks of future rebellion. Groups in bold are those with positive changes in two out of three of the right-hand columns and no offsetting conflict-minimizing factors.

[a] The predicted scores for rebellion are those generated by the logistic regression model summarized in table 7.2. Observed scores are the means of annual coded values of rebellion and protest for 1997 and 1998 on the scales given in table 2.2.

[b] The trend in observed rebellion between 1990 and 1998. Groups whose rebellion scores in the last three years of the decade increased by 2 or more over previous years are coded +1; groups whose scores declined by 2 or more are coded −1; others are coded 0.

[c] The predicted scores for future rebellion are generated by applying the logistic regression model in table 7.2 to 1998 data on the independent variables. Similar analyses were done to generate predicted scores for 1996 and 1997.

[d] The direction of change in predicted rebellion scores from 1995 to 1998.

[e] In addition to the six variables in the model summarized in table 7.2 we identified a number of other domestic and international factors that correlate with increases or decreases in rebellion, listed in table 7.3. These variables are used to construct the composite scores reported here, which indicate, respectively, the net effects of domestic and international factors that increase or decrease the likelihood of future rebellion. See appendix B, section IV, for details.

any future effort to reassert Moscow's authority over the autonomous regions is highly likely to provoke armed resistance. The same generalizations hold for the Slavs in Moldova and the Abkhaz and South Ossetians in Georgia. All gained de facto regional autonomy as a result of rebellions in the early 1990s and have a high capacity to resume fighting if their autonomy is not ratified in negotiated settlements—which has happened in Moldova but not Georgia.

The absence of Chechens from the risk list may be puzzling. The reason is that, according to our risk factors, the withdrawal of Russian forces from Chechnya following the 1994–96 war reduced the Chechens' potential for future rebellion below the medium-risk threshold. The decision to resume the war was made in Moscow in response to conditions and events that do not register in the risk model. Once the Russians did invade and push Chechen fighters out of their cities and villages, the risk factors for continued rebellion went to the maximum.

Asia

Asia has a larger absolute and proportional number of high-risk groups than any other world region. More than half the region's fifty-nine ethnopolitical groups are at medium to high risk of future rebellions. In 1998 fourteen of them were fighting serious rebellions; four others supported low-level armed conflicts. The following specific assessments move from South to Southeast Asia and then to China.

Afghanistan and Pakistan

The highest-risk groups in all Asia are the Hazari, Tajik, and Uzbek organizations that have lost out to the Pashtun-dominated Taliban movement that now controls most of Afghanistan. The cycle of repression and resistance in that country seems likely to continue indefinitely with minimal international engagement. In Pakistan the Pashtuns, Baluchi, and Sindhis have used mainly strategies of protest in the 1990s, but all are at medium risk of future rebellion. Pakistan's endemic communal conflict could easily escalate into more serious separatist rebellions, especially among the Sindhis and Baluchi.

India

Seven of India's eight medium- and high-risk ethnopolitical groups are fighting ongoing rebellions. The risk factors for future rebellion are highest for the Kashmiris in the northwest and the Tripuras in the northeast, which suggests that these conflicts will be most resistant to settlement. The risks are lowest for

Table 7.6. Groups at Highest Risk of Rebellion in Asia

Country	Group	Mean Annual Conflict in 1997–98[a]				Risks of Future Rebellion			
		Predicted Rebellion from 1995 Model	Observed Rebellion	Observed Protest	Trend in Rebellion in the 1990s[b]	Predicted from 1998 Model[c]	Change in Predictions 1995–98[d]	Changes in Facilitating Factors[e]	
								Domestic	External
Afghanistan	Hazaris	2.10	7.0	0.0	1	2.10	0	1	0
Afghanistan	Tajiks	2.10	7.0	0.0	1	2.10	0	1	-1
Afghanistan	Uzbeks	2.10	7.0	0.0	1	2.10	0	1	-1
China	Uighurs and Kazakhs	1.98	5.5	4.0	1	1.98	0	-1	3
India	**Kashmiris**	**1.98**	**6.0**	**5.0**	**1**	**1.98**	**0**	**1**	**1**
India	Tripuras	1.98	5.0	4.0	1	1.98	0	-1	2
Indonesia	Timorese	1.98	3.0	4.0	-1	1.98	0	1	-2
Taiwan	Aboriginal Taiwanese	-3.65	0.0	1.5	0	0.77	1	-1	1
India	Scheduled tribes	0.77	5.0	2.5	1	0.77	0	-1	2
China	**Tibetans**	**1.98**	**0.5**	**2.5**	**0**	**0.67**	**-1**	**2**	**3**
India	Sikhs	0.67	0.0	0.5	-1	0.67	0	0	3
India	Assamese	0.67	4.0	4.0	0	0.67	0	0	2
India	Bodos	0.67	4.5	1.5	1	0.67	0	-1	2

continued on next page

Table 7.6. (cont.)

| Country | Group | Mean Annual Conflict in 1997–98[a] | | | | Risks of Future Rebellion | | | |
| | | Predicted Rebellion from 1995 Model | Observed Rebellion | Observed Protest | Trend in Rebellion in the 1990s[b] | Predicted from 1998 Model[c] | Change in Predictions 1995–98[d] | Changes in Facilitating Factors[e] | |
								Domestic	External
Bhutan	Lhotshampas	0.67	1.0	2.0	0	0.67	0	-1	1
Bangladesh	Chittagong Hill peoples	0.67	1.0	2.5	-1	0.67	0	0	1
Burma	Rohingya	0.67	0.5	1.0	-1	0.67	0	-1	1
Burma	Zomi (Chin)	0.67	0.0	2.5	-1	0.67	0	0	2
Burma	Karen	0.67	4.5	1.5	-1	0.67	0	2	1
Burma	Shan	0.67	4.0	1.5	0	0.67	0	2	0
Sri Lanka	Sri Lankan Tamils	0.67	7.0	2.5	0	0.67	0	1	1
Thailand	Malay Muslims	2.10	4.5	1.5	1	0.67	-1	1	1
Laos	Hmong	0.67	1.5	0.0	-1	0.67	0	0	0
Vietnam	Montagnards	-0.54	0.0	0.0	0	0.67	1	-1	0
Philippines	Moro	0.67	6.0	3.5	0	0.67	0	1	-2
Indonesia	Papuans	0.67	1.0	1.5	0	0.67	0	0	0
Indonesia	Acehense	0.67	1.5	1.5	-1	0.67	0	2	-1

India	Muslims	0.03	1.5	3.5	1	0.03	0	0	2
Bangladesh	Biharis	0.03	0.0	2.0	0	0.03	0	0	1
Sri Lanka	Indian Tamils	-4.08	0.0	4.0	0	0.03	1	-1	1
India	Nagas	1.98	1.5	5.0	-1	-0.54	-1	-1	2
Pakistan	Baluchi	-3.34	0.0	3.0	0	-0.54	1	-2	2
Pakistan	Pashtuns	-0.82	0.0	2.5	0	-0.54	1	-1	2
Pakistan	**Sindhis**	**-0.82**	**0.5**	**2.5**	**0**	**-0.54**	**1**	**0**	**2**
Burma	Kachin	-0.54	0.0	1.5	-1	-0.54	0	0	2

Note: Groups are listed in descending order of predicted risks from the 1998 model. Only thirty-four groups, whose predicted rebellion scores are greater than or equal to –0.54, are included; twenty-five other groups in these countries are below this threshold, i.e., have low or very low risks of future rebellion. Groups in bold are those with positive changes in two out of three of the right-hand columns and no offsetting conflict-minimizing factors.

[a] The predicted scores for rebellion are those generated by the logistic regression model summarized in table 7.2. Observed scores are the means of annual coded values of rebellion and protest for 1997 and 1998 on the scales given in table 2.2.

[b] The trend in observed rebellion between 1990 and 1998. Groups whose rebellion scores in the last three years of the decade increased by 2 or more over previous years are coded +1; groups whose scores declined by 2 or more are coded –1; others are coded 0.

[c] The predicted scores for future rebellion are generated by applying the logistic regression model in table 7.2 to 1998 data on the independent variables. Similar analyses were done to generate predicted scores for 1996 and 1997.

[d] The direction of change in predicted rebellion scores from 1995 to 1998.

[e] In addition to the six variables in the model summarized in table 7.2 we identified a number of other domestic and international factors that correlate with increases or decreases in rebellion, listed in table 7.3. These variables are used to construct the composite scores reported here, which indicate, respectively, the net effects of domestic and international factors that increase or decrease the likelihood of future rebellion. See appendix B, section IV, for details.

the non-Kashmiri Muslims, who lack a regional base, and for the Nagas, who in early 1999 were close to reaching a new negotiated settlement.

Arakanese Muslims in Burma and Lhotshampas in Bhutan

Both these groups have been targets of state repression, and as a result both have high incentives for action. Exiles from both groups have established externally based opposition movements. The Rangoon government has relied mainly on military means to ensure security in the Arakanese region, and the risks of future rebellion are substantial. The government of Bhutan, by contrast, has sought to defuse conflict by reducing discriminatory policies and investing substantially in development in areas where the Lhotshampas (ethnic Nepalese) live, but the underlying risk factors remain high.

Regional Minorities in Burma

Government concessions to moderate factions of Zomi, Shan, and Kachin rebels checked their armed resistance in the mid-1990s but did not eliminate their capacity to fight or their external sources of support. Most Karen rejected compromises and continued to fight throughout the decade; by 1998 the Shan rebellion had resumed. The risk factors of future rebellion are substantial for all Burma's regional rebels except the Mon, and any weakening of the military government, or increase in foreign support, is likely to intensify armed conflict. An alliance with students and others who have sought a revolutionary transformation of the Rangoon regime since the late 1980s is a possible alternative to renewal of old-style regional separatism supported by the drug trade and other illicit activities.

East Timorese, Acehense, and Papuans in Indonesia

By the mid-1990s Indonesian repression, with token concessions, had largely ended protracted rebellions by these three regional peoples. The methods used to suppress resistance, however, provided incentives for the revival of rebellions in Ache and East Timor after the Suharto government collapsed in 1998. The Papuans of Irian Jaya are the only one of these three peoples who have not yet taken advantage of the opportunities inherent in an unstable regime.

Tibetans and Uighurs in China

These non-Han peoples have been subject to recurrent repression, the Tibetans more than the Uighurs, and to marginalization by Han settlers. Both groups have been flagged in our previous analyses as high-risk cases.[19] Beginning in 1996 violent protest and terrorism increased sharply among the Uighurs and other Muslims in Xinjiang province, reportedly encouraged by exile groups in the Central Asian republics. Risks are substantial for similar resistance by militant Tibetans, some of whom have begun to challenge the Dalai Lama's advocacy of nonviolent strategies (see the sketch of Tibet on pp. 212–217).

NORTH AFRICA AND THE MIDDLE EAST

Despite this region's history of intense and protracted communal conflict, only eight of its twenty-eight ethnopolitical groups have substantial risks of future rebellion.

Kurds

The rebellions of Kurds in Turkey and Iraq are the most intense conflicts in the Middle East in the late 1990s. The Turkish Kurds' rebellion is at very high risk of escalation. In Iraq the risks also are high: a decline in international support for the Kurdish autonomous region or another shift in relations among the Kurdish factions and the Baghdad regime will almost certainly precipitate a new round of armed conflict. In Iran, by contrast, the chances of renewed fighting by Kurds, whose rebellion apparently ended in 1994, appear to be low. Iranian Kurds and almost all the half-dozen other politically significant groups in Iran have far below average predicted risks of rebellion. We think that both the Iranian Kurds and the Baluchi have substantially higher risks of rebellion than is indicated by our risk model, first because of their recent history of rebellion, and second because much of the data needed to assess risks for groups in Iran is missing.

Palestinians in Israel, the West Bank, and Gaza

The Israeli government's glacially slow approach to implementing the Oslo Agreement has added to incentives for rebellion that are already high among Palestinians in Gaza and the West Bank. Their capacity to act is equally great, which means that the risks of renewed fighting are among the highest in the region. The Palestinian Arab citizens of Israel also have medium probability of future rebellion, but most of their risk factors point to continued protest rather than rebellion.

Shi'i

The risk model estimates that Shi'i minorities are at high risk in Iraq (where their 1991 rebellion was harshly suppressed) and in Lebanon, where they are at greater risk than any of the other communal contenders in the Lebanese civil war that ended at the beginning of the 1990s. Two other politically active Shi'i

Table 7.7. Groups at Highest Risk of Rebellion in North Africa and the Middle East

Country	Group	Mean Annual Conflict in 1997–98[a]			Trend in Rebellion in the 1990s[b]	Risks of Future Rebellion			
		Predicted Rebellion from 1995 Model	Observed Rebellion	Observed Protest		Predicted from 1998 Model[c]	Change in Predictions 1995–98[d]	Changes in Facilitating Factors[e]	
								Domestic	External
Turkey	Kurds	1.98	7.0	3.0	0	1.98	0	1	–1
Iraq	Shi'i	1.98	3.5	1.0	0	1.98	0	0	1
Lebanon	Shi'i	–0.70	2.0	3.0	0	1.98	1	2	0
Israel	Palestinians[f]	1.98	1.0	4.0	–1	1.98	0	2	–2
Iraq	Kurds	1.98	4.0	2.0	0	0.77	–1	1	1
Israel	Arabs[g]	0.77	0.0	3.0	0	0.77	0	0	0
Morocco	Saharawis	0.67	0.0	1.0	–1	0.67	0	1	0
Algeria	Berbers	–0.60	0.0	4.0	0	0.62	1	0	0

Note: Groups are listed in descending order of predicted risks from the 1998 model. Only eight groups, whose predicted rebellion scores are greater than or equal to –0.54, are included; twenty other groups in these countries are below this threshold, i.e., have low or very low risks of future rebellion. Groups in bold are those with positive changes in two out of three of the right-hand columns and no offsetting conflict-minimizing factors.

a The predicted scores for rebellion are those generated by the logistic regression model summarized in table 7.2. Observed scores are the means of annual coded values of rebellion and protest for 1997 and 1998 on the scales given in table 2.2.

b The trend in observed rebellion between 1990 and 1998. Groups whose rebellion scores in the last three years of the decade increased by 2 or more over previous years are coded +1; groups whose scores declined by 2 or more are coded –1; others are coded 0.

c The predicted scores for future rebellion are generated by applying the logistic regression model in table 7.2 to 1998 data on the independent variables. Similar analyses were done to generate predicted scores for 1996 and 1997.

d The direction of change in predicted rebellion scores from 1995 to 1998.

e In addition to the six variables in the model summarized in table 7.2 we identified a number of other domestic and international factors that correlate with increases or decreases in rebellion, listed in table 7.3. These variables are used to construct the composite scores reported here, which indicate, respectively, the net effects of domestic and international factors that increase or decrease the likelihood of future rebellion. See appendix B, section IV, for details.

f Palestinians in the West Bank and Gaza.

g Arab citizens of Israel.

Table 7.8. Groups at Highest Risk of Rebellion in Africa South of the Sahara

Country	Group	Mean Annual Conflict in 1997–98[a]			Trend in Rebellion in the 1990s[b]	Risks of Future Rebellion			
		Predicted Rebellion from 1995 Model	Observed Rebellion	Observed Protest		Predicted from 1998 Model[c]	Change in Predictions 1995–98[d]	Changes in Facilitating Factors[e]	
								Domestic	External
Nigeria	Ogani	0.67	0.0	2.5	0	2.10	1	1	1
Congo (former Zaire)	Tutsis (Banyamulenge)	-2.28	6.0	0.0	1	2.10	1	-1	1
Angola	Ovimbundu	-1.91	3.0	1.0	-1	2.10	1	1	0
Nigeria	Yoruba	-1.07	0.0	3.0	0	1.68	1	2	0
Burundi	Hutus	1.47	4.5	2.0	1	1.47	0	2	2
Sierra Leone	Temne	-0.54	5.5	0.0	1	0.89	1	2	0
Ethiopia	Afar	0.89	3.0	2.0	0	0.89	0	1	2
Ethiopia	Somali	0.89	2.0	0.0	-1	0.89	0	0	2
Angola	Bakongo	-1.91	3.0	1.0	1	0.89	1	3	0
Angola	Cabinda	-0.70	4.0	0.0	-1	0.89	1	2	0
Zambia	Lozi	-0.54	0.0	2.0	-1	0.89	1	0	1
Chad	Southerners	3.42	1.5	1.5	-1	0.77	-1	2	0
Senegal	Diola (Casamance)	0.67	4.0	2.5	1	0.67	0	2	0

Sudan	Southerners	0.67	7.0	1.5	0	0.67	0	2	0
Kenya	**Kikuyu**	**-0.97**	**0.0**	**2.0**	**0**	**0.37**	**1**	**2**	**2**
Kenya	**Luo**	**-3.77**	**0.0**	**2.0**	**0**	**0.37**	**1**	**2**	**2**
Kenya	**Luhya**	**-5.08**	**0.0**	**2.0**	**0**	**0.37**	**1**	**2**	**2**
Cameroon	Westerners	0.25	0.5	2.0	0	0.25	0	0	0
Rwanda	Hutus	0.15	5.5	0.0	1	0.15	0	1	0
Zimbabwe	**Ndebele**	**-3.34**	**0.0**	**2.5**	**0**	**-0.54**	**1**	**2**	**0**

Note: Groups are listed in descending order of predicted risks from the 1998 model. Only twenty groups, whose predicted rebellion scores are greater than or equal to –0.54, are included; forty-seven other groups in these countries are below this threshold, i.e., have low or very low risks of future rebellion. Groups in bold are those with positive changes in two out of three of the right-hand columns and no offsetting conflict-minimizing factors.

a The predicted scores for rebellion are those generated by the logistic regression model summarized in table 7.2. Observed scores are the means of annual coded values of rebellion and protest for 1997 and 1998 on the scales given in table 2.2.

b The trend in observed rebellion between 1990 and 1998. Groups whose rebellion scores in the last three years of the period increased by 2 or more over previous years are coded +1; groups whose scores declined by 2 or more are coded –1; others are coded 0.

c The predicted scores for future rebellion are generated by applying the logistic regression model in table 7.2 to 1998 data on the independent variables. Similar analyses were done to generate predicted scores for 1996 and 1997.

d The direction of change in predicted rebellion scores from 1995 to 1998.

e In addition to the six variables in the model summarized in table 7.2 we identified a number of other domestic and international factors that correlate with increases or decreases in rebellion, listed in table 7.3. These variables are used to construct the composite scores reported here, which indicate, respectively, the net effects of domestic and international factors that increase or decrease the likelihood of future rebellion. See appendix B, section IV, for details.

minorities in the region, in Saudi Arabia and Bahrain, are not at high risk of rebellion.

AFRICA SOUTH OF THE SAHARA

Twenty of Africa's sixty-seven ethnopolitical groups have relatively high risks of rebellion in the early years of the twenty-first century. Seven of them were fighting ethnic wars in 1998, and five others were protagonists in low-level insurgencies, one of which—UNITA's war with the Angolan government— had shifted back into full gear by 1999. Eight other groups are at significant risk of future rebellion, including the Ogani and Yoruba in Nigeria, three groups in Kenya, and communal contenders in Zambia and Zimbabwe.

Future risks of ethnic warfare in Africa are probably worse than these numbers suggest, for several reasons. First, the risk factors in the rebellion model tend to be high throughout Africa. Many African regimes are incoherent or have had recent, abrupt regime transitions—factors that both predict to future rebellions. Most of their politically active groups are communal contenders, which our analyses show are increasingly likely in the 1990s to engage in armed conflict. Support for rebellious groups from kindred and neighboring states is common. International engagement in African conflicts is selective and not nearly enough to offset the "bad neighborhood" effects of regional warfare. Furthermore, a review of the indicators of facilitation, listed in the two right-hand columns of table 7.8, shows virtually no evidence of inhibiting domestic or external factors that, in other world regions, check the propensity to rebellion. In short, virtually all the risk factors of escalating rebellion are present in Africa.[20]

Risks of new and sustained rebellion are particularly high in two zones of regional conflict that have had destabilizing spillover effects on nearby countries and communal groups. Sudan and Ethiopia have been the center of one such conflict region since the early 1960s. Four of the highest-risk groups at the end of the 1990s are in or on the periphery of this region. The second zone of insecurity and conflict is centered on Hutu-Tutsi rivalries in the Great Lakes region. Its spillover effects have spread more widely and quickly, interacting with protracted conflicts in Angola, Congo (former Zaire), and Congo-Brazzaville. Six of the highest-risk Africa groups are in or on the periphery of this region, and more are likely to be drawn into ethnic wars in the short-term future. Congo (former Zaire) and Angola provide examples.

Congo (former Zaire)

The highest-risk group in Congo is the Banyamulenge, kindred to Tutsis in Rwanda and Burundi, who were the objects of Zairian government repression and displacement in the early 1990s. Military support from Rwanda and Uganda prompted them in 1996–97 to initiate a rebellion (in alliance with other political forces) that ousted Mobutu's ineffective government and brought to power the equally ineffective government of Laurent Kabila. Since 1998 they and regional allies have wrested control of most of eastern Congo from Kabila's supporters. The key to Congo's future depends on which long-standing regional and ethnic rivalries will erupt in communal and separatist warfare. One group likely to be drawn into communal conflict in circum-stances of general insecurity and instability is the Lunda, the dominant group in Shaba province (Katanga), a region with a secessionist past. Another is the Luba of Kasai, who suffered from a violent government-provoked ethnic cleansing campaign in the early 1990s at the hands of the Lunda and who have established effective regional autonomy in the eastern province of South Kasai. Laurent Kabila is a Luba by origin. In these two cases the risk model underestimates the chances of future armed conflict.

Angola

The country was wracked by an ethnicized civil war from the mid-1960s to the mid-1990s. Intensive international mediation efforts to end the war seemed to pay off in spring 1997 when Savimbi, who led the Ovimbundu-based UNITA rebellion, agreed to lead the opposition in Angola's parliament—and then walked out. The Cabindans, minor players in the civil war, continue a low-level insurgency for autonomy or independence of their oil-rich enclave. The risk analysis suggests that, in addition to the Ovimbundu and Cabindans, the Bakongo of northwestern Angola are at significant risk of rebellion. Spillover effects from revolution and civil war in Angola and Congo (former Zaire) have increased the chances of new or renewed rebellion by communal groups throughout Central Africa.

Some of the high-risk groups identified in table 7.8 lie outside the conflict regions identified above, three of them in Kenya. The risk model results con-firm our assessment, in the sketch on pages 261–265, that the Kikuyu, Luo, and other peoples who were attacked by Kalenjin and Maasai, with the gov-ernment's complicity, are likely prospects for future rebellion. Two others are in Nigeria, the Yoruba and Ogani. Each has strong incentives for collective action; both were targets of repression by the military-dominated Nigerian government during the 1990s. Their risks of future rebellion depend very much on the outcome of Nigeria's latest transition to democracy, being implemented in 2000.

Absent from the list in table 7.8 are some groups that regional observers might expect to be at high future risk of rebellion. The Tuareg in Mali and Niger are examples. These seminomadic people fought localized rebellions in the early 1990s, responding to privation and drought and helped by support from cross-border kindred. Cease-fires and negotiations in the early 1990s, sketched in chapter 6, halted the rebellions and held out prospects for reform and local development. Risks of future rebellion in both countries have since declined significantly, especially in newly democratic Mali. A similar scenario may eventually bring an end to the rebellion of the Diola and other peoples of Senegal's southern Casamançe region. The risk factors of future rebellion are medium rather than high, and the government and rebels have on several occasions attempted to find a successful peacemaking formula.

LATIN AMERICA AND THE CARIBBEAN

Twelve of the thirty-two ethnopolitical groups in Latin America and the Caribbean, most of them indigenous peoples, are at significant risk of future rebellion. By contrast with Africa, however, the facilitating domestic and external factors in Latin America—summarized in the last two columns of table 7.9—almost all indicate a dampening of risks. Moreover, the only serious ethnic conflict in the region in the late 1990s was a local rebellion by indigenous Maya in Chiapas, a people who have relied mainly on nonviolent collective resistance to local and federal authorities. Two other cases are worth closer attention.

The risk model indicates that the Miskitos of the eastern Nicaraguan lowlands, a people whose rebellion in the 1980s was ended by a negotiated autonomy agreement, have the region's highest risks of future rebellion. There have been persistent problems with implementation of the terms of the agreement due to some combination of lack of political will on the government's part and its very limited resources.

The Maya in Guatemala also have relatively high risks of rebellion, mainly because of the lingering effects of a protracted ethnic and revolutionary war that began in the 1960s and was fought in alliance with the left. Because of their alignment with revolutionaries, the Maya were targets of genocidal repression during the 1970s and 1980s. Fighting ended in the 1990s, due in part to democratic reforms that improved the status of indigenous Guatemalans and to a December 1996 political peace pact between the government and the left. The risks of future conflict depend above all on the implementation of these reforms. If they are reversed, the Maya's risk factors for rebellion are high, including resentment about past repression (strong incentives), territorial cohesion, and political organization (high capacity for political action).

Incentives for political action are relatively high for indigenous peoples elsewhere in Latin America because of resentment about past discrimination and repression. One consequence of democratization during the 1970s and 1980s is that many indigenous peoples have developed political organizations and secured external assistance, which have significantly enhanced their capacity for conventional political action. This combination has been especially effective for indigenous peoples in Bolivia and Ecuador, as illustrated in the sketches of indigenous activism in those two countries on pages 178–182 and pages 96–99. Indigenous organizations also have had some measure of success in Colombia and Venezuela.

In other Latin American countries where indigenous peoples are numerous, especially Mexico and Peru, there has been less movement toward accommodation of indigenous interests. The risks of rebellion by groups in these countries probably are greater than is indicated by the data in table 7.9.

Groups of African descent are notably absent from the roster of high-risk groups in Latin America. The Haitian blacks in the Dominican Republic are mostly illegal immigrants who are at risk mainly because they are periodically targeted for expulsion by authorities. As pointed out elsewhere in this study, for example, in the sketch of Afro-Brazilians, most Afro–Latin Americans have few or none of the traits that predict to rebellion. Though disadvantaged, they are rarely if ever targets of state repression, have few and weak political organizations, lack the territorial base of indigenous peoples, and have attracted little or no external support. To the extent that they do have collective interests, those interests can be pursued by conventional political means.

Conclusions

To summarize the argument of the first part of this chapter, systematic risk assessments of ethnopolitical conflict precede and complement early warning in four respects. First, they identify the background and intervening conditions that establish the potential for conflict and crises. By doing so they make it more likely that preventive actions can be focused on "root causes." Second, they focus monitoring and analytic attention on high-risk situations at an early stage. Third, as demonstrated in Barbara Harff's work (note 9), they help structure the analysis of accelerating and triggering events that are likely to precipitate particular kinds of conflict. Finally, risk assessment models

Table 7.9. Groups at Highest Risk of Rebellion in Latin America and the Caribbean

Country	Group	Mean Annual Conflict in 1997–98[a]				Risks of Future Rebellion		Changes in Facilitating Factors[e]	
		Predicted Rebellion from 1995 Model	Observed Rebellion	Observed Protest	Trend in Rebellion in the 1990s[b]	Predicted from 1998 Model[c]	Change in Predictions 1995–98[d]	Domestic	External
Nicaragua	Miskitos	1.98	0.5	0.0	−1	1.98	0	−2	−1
Mexico	Maya	2.10	2.5	3.5	−1	0.77	−1	−1	1
Ecuador	Indigenous highlanders	−0.82	0.0	3.0	0	0.77	1	−3	−2
Bolivia	Indigenous highlanders	−0.54	0.0	3.0	−1	0.67	1	−1	0
Bolivia	Indigenous lowlanders	−0.54	0.0	4.0	−1	0.67	1	−3	0
Guatemala	Maya	1.98	0.0	0.5	−1	0.62	−1	−3	−2
Dominican Republic	Haitian blacks	−1.07	0.0	1.5	0	0.37	1	−1	−2
Colombia	Indigenous peoples	−0.54	0.0	0.5	−1	−0.54	0	−1	0

Venezuela	Indigenous peoples	-0.54	0.0	3.0	0	-0.54	0	-1	0
Peru	Indigenous highlanders	2.10	0.0	0.0	0	-0.54	-1	-1	0
Peru	Indigenous lowlanders	2.10	0.0	2.0	0	-0.54	-1	-1	0
Brazil	Indigenous Amazonians	-0.54	0.0	2.0	-1	-0.54	0	-1	0

Note: Groups are listed in descending order of predicted risks from the 1998 model. Only twelve groups, whose predicted rebellion scores are greater than or equal to −0.54, are included; twenty other groups in these countries are below this threshold, i.e., have low or very low risks of future rebellion. Groups in bold are those with positive changes in two out of three of the right-hand columns and no offsetting conflict-minimizing factors.

[a] The predicted scores for rebellion are those generated by the logistic regression model summarized in table 7.2. Observed scores are the means of annual coded values of rebellion and protest for 1997 and 1998 on the scales given in table 2.2.

[b] The trend in observed rebellion between 1990 and 1998. Groups whose rebellion scores in the last three years of the decade increased by 2 or more over previous years are coded +1; groups whose scores declined by 2 or more are coded −1; others are coded 0.

[c] The predicted scores for future rebellion are generated by applying the logistic regression model in table 7.2 to 1998 data on the independent variables. Similar analyses were done to generate predicted scores for 1996 and 1997.

[d] The direction of change in predicted rebellion scores from 1995 to 1998.

[e] In addition to the six variables in the model summarized in table 7.2 we identified a number of other domestic and international factors that correlate with increases or decreases in rebellion, listed in table 7.3. These variables are used to construct the composite scores reported here, which indicate, respectively, the net effects of domestic and international factors that increase or decrease the likelihood of future rebellion. See appendix B, section IV, for details.

provide a framework that analysts can use to interpret the results of real-time monitoring.

The systematic risk assessments developed in the second part of this chapter gain credibility from political developments of the late 1990s. Serious conflict has begun or escalated in a half-dozen groups that are and have been high on our risk profiles, including the Kosovar Albanians, Uighurs in China, Palestinians in Gaza and the West Bank, and Banyamulenge in eastern Congo. These developments add to the credibility of the assessments but they are not and cannot be definitive. The incentives and especially the capacities and opportunities that provide the basis for these risk assessments can and do change. Old regimes are overthrown; democratic leaders are installed; international patterns of support and engagement change. Regardless of such changes in political context, policymakers in office make their own assessments of risk and often attempt to forestall ethnic challenges by manipulating risk factors, for example, by reducing incentives or opportunities or initiating reforms. As suggested in chapters 5 and 6, a number of high-risk situations have been managed in these ways. The ultimate test of the adequacy of systematic risk assessments is not whether or not a rebellion occurs but whether the risk assessments help international actors and local policymakers design strategies that reduce the preconditions for rebellion.

Political Rivalries and Communal Vengeance in Kenya

Anne Pitsch

Kenyan politics in the 1980s and 1990s illustrates how a government based on communal minorities has used its powers to marginalize larger groups. In response to pressures to open up the political system, the government of President Moi, a Kalenjin, encouraged communal violence against the Kikuyu and the Luo, contributing to polarization and animosities that contain the seeds of future instability and violence.

FOR A NUMBER OF YEARS after Kenya's independence in 1963, the country was recognized as one of Africa's most developed and stable countries. Like the late Mobutu Sese Seko of Zaire (now the Democratic Republic of Congo), President Daniel arap Moi, a Kalenjin, has deftly manipulated ethnic groups within Kenya, fomenting distrust and sometimes violence among them, in order to maintain his hold on the state while ruling through a minority-led coalition that largely excludes the largest ethnic groups. His KANU (Kenya African National Union) party has been particularly keen to keep political power out of the hands of the Kikuyu, the dominant minority in the post-colonial period. In 1991, President Moi, under pressure from international donors and human rights groups to improve Kenya's human rights record, agreed to introduce a system of multiparty democracy in the country. Ethnic violence soon erupted in the Rift Valley Province as the politically dominant Kalenjin (11 percent of the population) and their allies the Maasai (1.5 percent) sought to force Kikuyu (21 percent of the population), Luo (11 percent), and members of several other communal groups, including the Luhya and Kisii, out of the rich agricultural lands of the province.

There is much evidence that the fighting was deliberately instigated by the government and was an escalation of previous policies that restricted the political and economic status of the Kikuyu and Luo. In Kenya, as in a number of other African societies, invidious inequalities are not usually a matter of explicit public policy. Rather, they result from the use of state power and repression by one communally based political group to advance its interests at the expense of others.

BACKGROUND TO COMMUNAL CONFLICT

The Maasai and Kalenjin were pastoral, seminomadic peoples indigenous to the fertile Rift Valley when the area was colonized by the British. In the early 1900s, the British pushed the pastoral peoples onto reserves in order to develop the area's agricultural potential and brought in agriculturalists, including Kikuyu from the east and Luo and Luhya from the west, to work the land.

During the transition to independence, the Kikuyu and Luo gained power through their control of the Kenya African Democratic Union (KADU), the country's dominant party at independence and, after 1969, its only legal party. These ethnic groups held a disproportionate share of political offices and benefited economically as well through business contracts with the government and access to land in the Rift Valley that had formerly been held by Europeans. The Kalenjin pastoralists who originally inhabited the area regained little if any of the land of which their ancestors had been dispossessed.

The governing coalition split in 1966, and Daniel arap Moi became the vice president. When he assumed the presidency in 1978, Moi began appointing his Kalenjin supporters to political positions, gradually turning the tables on the Kikuyu and Luo. The extent of their political dominance is reflected by the fact that the Kikuyu and Luo, though they account for more than a third of the country's population, had only two members in Moi's twenty-five-member cabinet in the early 1990s. Kalenjin and Maasai politicians also have advocated a policy of Majimboism, meaning federalism based on ethnicity, and called for the expulsion of all nonindigenous people in the Rift Valley.

DEMOCRATIZATION: MANIPULATING THE POLITICAL SYSTEM

The process of democratization in Kenya was instituted in 1991 largely because of external pressure on Moi's government to respect human rights and allow a more open political system. As Donald Horowitz points out, however, "purely procedural conceptions of democracy are inadequate for ethnically divided polities, for the procedure can be impeccable and the exclusion complete."[1] At the same time that Moi allowed the opposition to organize legally for the first time since parties were banned in 1982, Majimbo rallies were held to oppose multipartyism and politically motivated violence began in the Rift Valley. Between 1991 and 1994, armed bands of Maasai and Kalenjin repeatedly attacked and burned villages, killing some fifteen hundred and prompting three hundred thousand to flee. Most of the victims were Kikuyu, Luo, Luhya, or Kisii.

Evidence suggests that leading Kalenjin politicians, in order to demonstrate that a multiparty system in Kenya would be destabilizing, were the main instigators of the violence. Local politicians in the Rift Valley openly acknowledged their collusion with Kalenjin and Maasai attacks aimed at forcing non-natives from the region. Kenyan security forces did little to protect the victims of Kalenjin and Maasai attacks and, according to a number of reports by villagers, sometimes took part in them. Reportedly police sometimes stood by and watched the attacks occur, rejected statements from witnesses, and refused to investigate acts of intimidation. The Kenyan judiciary was also implicated. The Moi government has long been criticized for lacking an independent judiciary and for using it to punish political foes. The judiciary took little or no action against Kalenjin and Maasai warriors but was quick to prosecute non-Kalenjin for obtaining weapons to defend themselves against attacks.

By 1995, the violence in the Rift Valley had largely diminished, though there continued to be occasional clashes up to early 1996, resulting in injury and death. The Moi government never admitted complicity in the violence, nor did it fully condemn the perpetrators of the violence. Violence flared again in 1997 in the run-up to national elections. Pro-democracy demonstrations were harshly broken up on several different occasions, resulting in scores of injuries and more than a dozen deaths. Pro-democracy activists in Kenya demanded changes in electoral laws that favor the incumbent president. Opposition leaders and outside observers reported election irregularities, including bribing and intimidation of voters, and bias on the part of presiding election officers. In addition, as early as 1996, it was reported that identity cards needed for registration were withheld from some opposition strongholds and from Kikuyu youth in the Rift Valley. Moi was able to manipulate the electoral system to his advantage and won the December 1997 presidential election with only 40 percent of the vote.

In addition to general unrest in the country, ethnic violence broke out in August 1997 in the Mombasa region and again in the Rift Valley in January 1998. As in the 1991–94 violence in the Rift Valley, the main victims in the ethnic violence in Mombasa and the Rift Valley were Kikuyu, Luo, and Luhya. Once again, the government did little to stop the violence, and radical government supporters are thought to be the main perpetrators of the conflict.

There is compelling evidence that the initial attacks in the Rift Valley were organized from outside the communities.

THE HERITAGE OF COMMUNAL VIOLENCE

Agriculture in the Rift Valley was severely affected by the 1991–94 violence and continues to suffer as a result of subsequent episodes of conflict. The government was criticized for inadequate relief aid to refugees and other victims of the violence. For example, most of the forty thousand refugees who fled fighting in the Nakuru District in the southwest Rift Valley after February 1992 settled in Elburgon and Kamwuara camps in appalling living conditions and received no government assistance. In another incident, some three thousand refugees from Enosupukia who were promised resettlement were dumped along a roadside in their "ancestral homeland." The government also was said to have obstructed relief efforts by outside and local agencies, including churches, and harassed journalists who sought to report on the conflict. For example, the staff of outspoken magazines faced threats, arrests, charges, and seizures for reporting on the violence. Church workers were harassed or arrested by local police, and clash victims also reported police harassment.

The 1990s conflict in the Rift Valley also altered land-ownership patterns in the province, with Kikuyu, Luo, Luhya, and Kisii losing lands to Kalenjin and Maasai. This outcome has helped to consolidate President Moi's support by firmly entrenching the loyalty of those who gained from the violence. Moreover, Moi has deftly manipulated the democratic opposition by denying opposition groups freedom to organize, violently repressing democratic rallies and meetings, and offering government perks to those who defect from the opposition and join the KANU government. Communal relations are polarized in Kenya, and the resentment of the victimized groups is highly likely to precipitate a future round of retribution against those who support the present government. The history of ethnic politics in Africa has shown that, eventually, even the strongest leaders fall from power. Unfortunately, where leaders of a minority ethnic group have controlled the state by excluding larger ethnic groups from power, the costs of subsequent intense interethnic conflict have proved high.[2]

The next occasion for intensified political conflict with ethnic overtones will be provided by the 2002 general elections. Indeed, the by-elections of January 1999 provide a warning of the problems that could occur in 2002. Opposition MPs were beaten at the counting house in Makueni, where elections were needed to replace the opposition MP who died in November 1998. In addition to protesting the validity of the elections in Makueni and the subsequent police beatings, opposition MPs across the country have also been voicing their concern over the constitutional reform process currently under way in Kenya. Because parliamentarians have been relegated to mere observers in the reform process and because KANU controls the review team at both the party and district levels, opposition leaders fear the new constitution will further consolidate KANU's dominant political power and give Moi the opportunity to remain head of state beyond his current constitutional limits. Yet, Moi's attempts to manipulate the political process cannot last forever. Indeed, violence between subclans of the Kalenjin, pitting those who support Moi against those who oppose him, occurred during 1998, suggesting that the foundation of Moi's political power is shaky.

NOTES

Anne Pitsch has been Project Coordinator of the Minorities at Risk project since 1996 and is a doctoral candidate in the Department of Government and Politics at the University of Maryland. She served as a Peace Corps volunteer in Mauritania and has done fieldwork in Ghana and Rwanda.

This sketch draws upon regional and international news sources, including Africa News Service, Inter Press Service, Reuters World Service, the Washington Post, and the United Nations Integrated Regional Information Network for Eastern Africa. Also used were the following publications and the works cited in the notes.

Africa Watch. *Divide and Rule: State-Sponsored Ethnic Violence in Kenya.* New York: Human Rights Watch, 1993.

Kahl, Colin H. "Chaos and Calm in East Africa: Population Growth, Land, and State-Sponsored Violence in Kenya, 1991–1993." Environment and Security Project. Cambridge, Mass.: Harvard University, 1997.

Spence, Glenys. "Caught in the Crossfire: The Maasai and Majimboism in Kenya." *Fourth World Bulletin* 5, no. 1–2 (spring/summer 1996): 22–27.

   1. Donald L. Horowitz, "Democracy in Divided States," in *Nationalism, Ethnic Conflict, and Democracy,* ed. Larry Diamond and Marc F. Plattner (Baltimore: Johns Hopkins University Press, 1994), 48.

   2. Donald Rothchild, *Managing Ethnic Conflict in Africa: Pressures and Incentives for Cooperation* (Washington, D.C.: Brookings Institution Press, 1997).

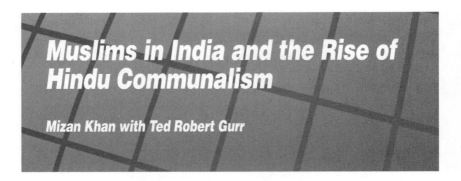

Muslims in India and the Rise of Hindu Communalism

Mizan Khan with Ted Robert Gurr

The secular political principles that have helped protect India's disadvantaged Muslim minority for half a century have been eroded by the rise of Hindu fundamentalism and communal politics. The risks of anti-Muslim policies and violent communal attacks increased sharply in the late 1990s.

INDIA'S 112 MILLION MUSLIMS are at greater risk than at any time since the massacres that followed the 1947 partition of the subcontinent into India and Pakistan. The stage was set by the rise of Hindu communalism in the 1980s. During the 1990s a group of Hindu fundamentalist organizations, the Sang parivar, contributed to a climate of hate that justified the exclusion of, and attacks on, Muslims.[1] Two political events of 1999 amplified the threat. In April 1999 the thirteen-month-old coalition government led by the Hindu nationalist Bharatiya Janata Party (BJP) lost a no-confidence vote in the lower house of the Indian parliament, and it was widely feared that the BJP would campaign for October elections by emphasizing its agenda of *Hindutva* (cultural nationalism). Second, in June 1999 the aborted Pakistani invasion across the Line of Control in Kashmir prompted Hindu fundamentalists to spread allegations, widely reported in the tabloid and vernacular press, that Indian Muslims supported the Pakistani cause. Attacks on Muslims intensified and included the partial destruction of an Islamic seminary in Lucknow.

What does this situation of escalating communal tensions portend for India's largest minority community, and what is their future role in Indian politics? This sketch reviews the status of Muslims in Indian society and the changing nature of Hindu-Muslim communal politics.

THE STATUS OF INDIAN MUSLIMS

Muslims make up 11.4 percent (1981 census) of India's population. At an estimated 112 million, they are numerically the largest group in the Minorities

266

project survey. This also means that India has the fourth-largest Muslim population in the world, after Indonesia, Pakistan, and Bangladesh. Most Muslims live in India's northwest, which was the path of Muslim conquest in past centuries, and the northeast, where large-scale conversion of Hindus to Islam occurred. Currently about 97 percent of the Muslim population is concentrated in thirteen of India's thirty-two states and territories, one of which—Jammu and Kashmir—has a Muslim majority. But only 11 of the 544 constituencies of the Lok Sabha (the Indian parliament) have a Muslim majority, 3 each in Jammu and Kashmir and West Bengal, 2 in Kerala (south-central), and 1 each in Assam, Bihar, and Lakshadweep (a Union territory).

The marginalization of Muslims in Indian politics is illustrated by the fact that there are only twenty-nine Muslim members in the Lok Sabha, less than half their proportion in the general population. Moreover, their share of Lok Sabha seats has decreased from 9.2 percent in 1980 to the present 5.3 percent. The decline in Muslim representation has been paralleled by a meteoric rise of the BJP in national politics as well as in parliamentary representation.

There are many other indicators of Indian Muslims' political and socioeconomic disadvantages. Muslims make up less than 2 percent of the government's Administrative Service and only a fraction of 1 percent of the Defense Forces. More than half of the Muslim population is illiterate, well below the national average. In higher education the picture is still more dismal. In Calcutta, once the capital of British India and currently capital of West Bengal, for example, Muslims make up 16 percent of the population but only 2.2 percent of total school enrollment and only 0.5 percent of enrollment in higher education. Calcutta University has no Muslim employee at any level.

In the private sector Muslims also face widespread discrimination. As a result, most earn their livelihood in small, self-employment enterprises. The lack of economic opportunity has encouraged an exodus of labor to the Gulf countries. This exodus causes further social problems: prosperity among a segment of Muslims because of remittances from the Gulf fuels resentment by poor Hindus. There also have been clashes in some states between Hindu middlemen who market handicrafts and Muslims who produce them.

The failure of successive Congress Party governments in New Delhi to increase the Muslims' share of the pie contributes to their sense of deprivation. However, Muslims' disadvantages are less the result of deliberate government policies than of the ethos prevailing in a society dominated by a Hindu majority. The 1947 partition of the subcontinent on the basis of the "two nations theory" prompted a large-scale exodus of Muslims to Pakistan, including much of their political elite. Large-scale communal riots instilled a fear psychosis among the Muslims who opted to remain in India, a fear psychosis that still inhibits Muslims from asserting themselves as a collectivity lest such efforts be interpreted as communal.

During the Congress Party's long periods of governance, it relied on the Muslims as a "vote bank," that is, as a reliable bloc of electoral support. For many decades Muslims aligned politically with lower-caste Hindus. But the dispersion of Muslims across constituencies has always made it difficult even for secular parties to nominate candidates for elective office from other than the majority community. Moreover, Muslim support and the Congress Party's avowed secularism did not translate into remedial concessions to Muslims in the form of reserved quotas in government jobs, social services, or political representation. Such policies were widely used to reduce the disadvantages of other communal groups, including the lowest castes, but were not applied to Muslims.

THE RISE OF HINDU COMMUNALISM

Although there is a deep-rooted cultural conflict between the polytheistic and monotheistic natures of Hinduism and Islam, little communal violence occurred during seven hundred years of Muslim rule over the subcontinent. Muslim rulers were mostly tolerant of communal diversity. Still, Hindus welcomed colonial rule by the British, who encouraged the formation of separate identities among the two communities. After the violent separation of India and Pakistan, the Indian preoccupation with the security threat posed by Muslim Pakistan distorted perceptions of Muslim societies and adversely conditioned Hindus' attitudes toward the Muslims who remained in India.

Secularism was an avowed goal of the postcolonial Indian government under Nehru, who warned that the greatest danger to India was not communism but right-wing Hindu communalism cloaked by nationalism. Nonetheless, Hindu nationalism and communalism have long been present within the ruling Congress Party, and secular principles have eroded. As leaders of India, both Indira Gandhi and Rajiv Gandhi, daughter and grandson of Nehru, compromised the Congress Party's secular ideology by wooing the electorate with promises of establishing a Ram Rajya (Hindu state). In early 1999 the Congress Party's leadership redefined secularism, equating it with Hinduism as both a philosophy and a way of life. As a result, the ideological distance between the two parties with countrywide clout, Congress and BJP, has lessened.

The rise of Hindu communalism is a result of changes in Indian society, not party politics. It began in the 1980s as an urban-based, upper-caste, and white-collar phenomenon. Three factors can be cited. First, some secular Indians contend that Hindus, though a majority religious community, suffer from a minority complex because Hinduism has no unifying creed or priesthood and because "mainstream" Hindu culture is based on the upper caste, who make up only 15 percent of the Hindu population. The entrenched socioeconomic position of this group has been challenged in recent years by the majority Hindu Dalits (Oppressed) and the Scheduled Caste Hindus. The revolution in information technology and the Congress government's economic liberalization program of the 1990s, with its prospect of huge Western investment, also were seen as threats by many of the elite. In response some upper-caste Hindu leaders began to use religious appeals to unite the majority community against non-Hindu values.

A second factor contributing to the Hindu perception of threat has been the ascendance of Islamist movements in the Middle East and the growing power of petrodollars. Most Muslims, in India and elsewhere, think of themselves as part of the global Islamic *umma* (community) and express solidarity with their coreligionists elsewhere. Hindus also resent the growth of Islamic charity and conversions of Scheduled Caste Hindus to Islam, allegedly funded by petrodollars. In reaction the World Hindu Council has launched a program to reconvert Muslims and Christians to Hinduism. Some Hindu leaders in Bombay have even proposed sending Muslims to Pakistan or Bangladesh.

Finally, the perception that successive Congress Party governments have pandered to Muslims and other minorities who constitute vote banks has fueled a Hindu backlash. This perception is far from the truth, as is evident from the extent of Muslim disadvantages in all spheres of life.

DISUNITY AMONG MUSLIMS

Muslims outside Jammu and Kashmir have never articulated or pursued a distinctive political agenda, not in the past and not yet in response to rising Hindu communalism. Several reasons are mentioned earlier, including Muslims' fear psychosis and their dispersion across political constituencies. More immediately, Muslims are divided along political and ideological lines. In every constituency Muslim votes tend to be split among rival candidates from various parties and sects, some of them funded by anti-Muslim forces in order to neutralize Muslim votes. Divisions in the disputed state of Jammu and Kashmir illustrate the crosscutting forces that splinter Muslim cohesion. There are cleavages between Indian Muslims and Kashmiri Muslims, Muslims with modern education and the religiously orthodox. The English-educated Muslim elite tends to distance itself from commoner Muslims. Politically there are pro-Indian and anti-Indian parties, pro-independence and pro-autonomy forces. The Muslim-based National Conference, the state's ruling party since the 1996 elections, appears to have overcome its ideological repugnance for Rastrya Swayansevak Sangh (RSS), a cadre-based Hindu organization closely linked to the BJP. Farook Abdullah, the state's Muslim chief minister, has angered many of his supporters by openly supporting the RSS, saying it is not anti-Muslim, and by accepting a National Amity Award from the country's prime minister.

Disunity is compounded by an absence of Muslim leaders with national or even regional standing. Even senior Muslim members of the Congress Party are at odds with one another. A Muslim journalist and former parliamentarian, M. J. Akar, has called Joyti Basu, the Hindu chief minister of West Bengal, "the biggest leader of Indian Muslims" because "more Muslims trust him than any Muslim leader."

Even the rise of Hindu fundamentalism and the demolition of the Babri Mosque in 1992, after more than forty years of communal squabbles about the site, have failed to increase cohesion in the fractious Muslim community. Hindu militants demolished the 464-year-old mosque because Mogul emperor Babar allegedly built it on the spot where the Hindu god Rama was born. The daytime demolition by thousands of Hindu militants was facilitated by the Congress government's inaction. It plunged the country into a grievous communal crisis with a wave of riots and attacks that left about two thousand dead and five thousand injured. Records show that casualties from communal riots have increased throughout the 1990s by comparison with previous decades. The problem is all the more ominous because security forces sympathetic to Hindu militants are reported to have participated in some killings and attacks on Muslim properties.

Growing frustration with the political and electoral system among Muslims has not led to greater mobilization. On the contrary, although electoral turnout among the poor and minorities—including Muslims—had traditionally been higher than the national average, Muslims recorded a lower turnout than average in the 1996 Lok Sabha elections. Moreover, in a survey conducted after those elections, 49 percent of Muslims (highest among religious groups) said their community no longer voted for Congress. Alienated from the Congress Party by the Babri Mosque demolition, they shifted support toward left-of-center regional parties. The process seems to have been checked in state elections in 1998, when most Muslims again supported Congress. And in 1999 the Congress Party, under the leadership of Sonia Gandhi, a Christian, actively sought Muslim support for national elections.

One hesitant step to activate the Muslim community's political potential began in October 1998 when the first-ever meeting of Muslim parliamentarians was convened. At this and subsequent meetings, recommendations were put forward for greater Muslim representation by secular parties, the use of proportional representation, and the gerrymandering of electoral boundaries to increase the number of Muslim-majority districts. Notably absent from political discourse is advocacy of protest or civil disobedience campaigns of the sort widely used by disadvantaged communal minorities elsewhere.

THE DYNAMICS OF CONTEMPORARY POLITICS

One might expect that the Hindu nationalist BJP would act against Muslims, in keeping with the sentiments of its most militant supporters. In fact, when the BJP came to power in March 1998 at the head of a coalition government, its leaders began to woo Muslims for practical political reasons. For example, the BJP sought Muslim support by projecting the Muslim nuclear scientist Abul Kalam as the quintessential new Muslim Indian. BJP also held several state-level conferences on minority issues and placed on the back burner controversial issues such as the construction of Ram Temple on the site of the demolished Babri Mosque, the promulgation of a uniform civil code, and the deletion of secular principles from the Constitution. The party followed the same strategy of downplaying communal issues during the 1999 electoral campaign, which ended with a victory for the BJP-led coalition.

On the other hand, there has been a simultaneous drive to Hinduize moral education and culture. During BJP rule at the center, Hindu rituals have been introduced in formal events in schools, particularly in north-Indian Uttar Pradesh, the state with the largest Muslim population. Muslim parents reacted by withdrawing their children, until it was agreed that Muslim students would be exempted from such rituals. The non-Hindi-speaking states in the east and south appear more liberal and accommodative, eschewing sweeping approaches such as Hinduization of school curricula.

The political events of 1999 suggest that in a highly diverse democracy such as India, despite all its weaknesses, communal politics may not succeed. The April 1999 no-confidence vote that toppled the BJP-led government indicated that the ideology of *Hindutva* alone was not enough for the BJP's political survival. Ordinary voters hoped for political stability and economic progress rather than antiminority rhetoric, a round of nuclear tests, and the launch of an Indian-made missile, none of which had any nutritional value. The Indian political system appears to be moving toward the Italian model, with frequent changes in weak coalition governments. In such a system, parties, big or small, downplay their ideologies in order to embark on the horse trading needed to reach or retain power. This was precisely the winning strategy followed by the BJP in the fall 1999 electoral campaigns.

For the foreseeable future, having no political platform or clout of their own outside Jammu and Kashmir, Muslims' electoral support is likely to be split among Congress, the center-left Swamajbadi Party, which governs the large state of Uttar Pradesh, and other regional parties. One possible outcome is a strengthening of the historic electoral alliance between Muslims and lower-caste Hindus. Should this happen, it may offset or even eclipse the rise of Hindu communal politics at the national level. But it is not likely to diminish the threat that Hindu fundamentalism poses to social peace. Irrespective of electoral outcomes, the risks are high that Hindu militants will continue to direct provocative rhetoric and attacks against Muslim Indians.

NOTES

Mizan R. Khan was a senior researcher with the Minorities project from 1993 to 1995 and again in 1997. He received a Ph.D. from the University of Maryland's School of Public Affairs in 1997 for a fieldwork-based dissertation on community management of forest resources. In 1998 he resumed his position at the Bangladesh Institute of International and Strategic Studies (BIISS) in Dhaka, where he now holds the post of research director.

The following sources were used in the preparation of this sketch.

Constable, Pamela. "With BJP, Indian Masses No Longer Get Religion." *Washington Post*, September 16, 1999.

D'Monte, Darryl. "Another Election: The Italianization of Indian Politics." *New Leader*, May 17–31, 1999.

Haqqi, S. A. H., ed. *Democracy, Pluralism, and Nation-Building*. New Delhi: N. B. O. Publishers, 1984.

Imtiaz, Ahmed. "Facing the Will of the Majority: Muslim Minority in De-secularized Modern India." *Journal of Muslim Minority Affairs* 15, no. 1 (January 1994) and no. 2 (July 1994).

Ishtiaq, Ahmed. *State, Nation, and Ethnicity in Contemporary South Asia*. London and New York: Pinter, 1996.

Islam, Syed S. "The Tragedy of the Babri Masjid: An Expression of Militant Hindu Fundamentalism in India." *Journal of Muslim Minority Affairs* 17, no. 2 (October 1997): 345–351.

Kholi, Atul. *Democracy and Discontent: India's Growing Crisis of Governability.* Cambridge: Cambridge University Press, 1991.

Malik, Yogendra, and D. K. Vajpeyi. "The Rise of Hindu Militancy: India's Secular Democracy at Stake." *Asian Survey* 29, no. 3 (March 1989): 308–325.

Mishra, Panjak. "A New, Nuclear India?" *New York Review,* June 25, 1998, 55–64.

Sabur, A. K. M. A. *Challenges of Governance in India: Fundamentals under Threat.* Dhaka: Bangladesh Institute of International and Strategic Studies, Paper no. 15, July 1995.

1. The term *climate of hate* was used in a public statement issued in New Delhi by the president and general secretary of the National Council of Churches in India on July 29, 1999. The statement's purpose was to call on voters to support secular rather than communal parties in the upcoming elections.

8

Conclusions

Managing Conflict in Heterogeneous Societies

THE BREAKUP of the international system into warring ethnic statelets, which many feared in the early 1990s, has been checked by more effective international and domestic strategies for managing ethnopolitical conflict. Relations between communal groups and states in heterogeneous societies changed in the 1990s in ways that suggest that a new regime governing minority-majority relations is under construction. This chapter begins with a summary of evidence about the transformation of ethnopolitical conflict in the 1990s. It then outlines the basic principles of an emergent "regime of managed ethnic heterogeneity." Finally, it identifies the main challenges to global implementation of these principles: reluctant states and prospective communal conflicts that will require sustained transnational efforts at conflict management.

The Tide Changes: From Ethnic Warfare to Accommodation in the 1990s

A global shift from ethnic warfare to the politics of accommodation is amply documented in previous chapters. In the late 1990s the most common political strategy among the 275 ethnopolitical groups surveyed in the Minorities at Risk study was not rebellion; it was symbolic and organizational politics, as shown in chapter 2. Equally important, the number of groups using armed violence has been declining after decades of increase. The eruption of ethnic warfare that seized observers' attention in the early 1990s was actually the culmination of a long-term general trend of increasing communal-based protest and rebellion that began in the 1950s and peaked immediately after the end of the Cold War. The breakup of the USSR and Yugoslavia provided opportunities for new ethnonational claims and the eruption of a dozen new ethnic wars between 1988 and 1992. In the global south more than two dozen ethnic wars began or restarted in roughly the same period, between 1988 and 1994 (see table 2.5).

By mid-decade a worldwide shift in strategies of ethnopolitical action was taking place. When we compare the early with the late 1990s, we observe a modest decline from 115 to 95 groups in open conflicts, those in which the parties included coercion and violence among their tactics. More important is the balance between escalation and de-escalation: examination of 59 armed ethnic conflicts under way in 1998 shows that de-escalating conflicts outnumbered escalating ones by 23 to 7, with the remaining 29 having no short-term trend.

Another way of documenting trends is to time the onset of new episodes of ethnopolitical conflict. When this is done over the thirteen years from 1986 to 1998, in chapter 2, we find that two-thirds of all new campaigns of protest and new armed rebellions began in the five years from 1989 to 1993. Few new ethnopolitical conflicts began after 1994, neither protest movements nor rebellions. The decline in numbers of new protest movements is especially hopeful. We observed that a median of ten years of nonviolent political action preceded the new rebellions of 1986 to 1998. Because the number of new ethnopolitical protest campaigns is declining—from a global average of ten per year in the late 1980s to four per year since 1995—the pool of potential future rebellions is shrinking.

A third way to look at trends is to examine secessionist wars—ethnonational conflicts whose protagonists aim at establishing a new ethnic state or autonomous region. These wars are among the most deadly and protracted of all ethnopolitical conflicts, and spillovers from them pose serious threats to regional security. Secessionist wars are in especially steep decline. Between 1991 and 1999 sixteen were settled and eleven others were checked by cease-fires and negotiations, as shown in chapter 6. It is not only ethnic conflict that spreads by example; the successes of conflict management also are contagious.[1] By the end of 1999 fewer secessionist wars were being fought—eighteen by our count—than at any time since 1970. Revolutionary wars that had begun during the Cold War also were being settled, especially in Africa.[2] The trends help put the rebellion of Kosovar Albanians in perspective. It was the only new ethnic war in Europe since 1993 and one of only two ethnic wars to begin anywhere in the world in 1997–98.[3]

Less visible than the shift toward settlement of ethnonational wars in the 1990s is a parallel trend toward accommodation of ethnopolitical conflicts that have not yet escalated to protracted rebellion. Examples are cited in chapter 6, including a sketch of negotiations that preempted an ethnic rebellion by the Gagauz in Moldova. One remarkable and little-noticed achievement of democratic Russia has been the successful negotiation of substate autonomy agreements with Tatarstan, Bashkiria, and some forty other regions in the Russian Federation.[4] These agreements provide models that could and should have been employed to head off ethnic wars in Chechnya and Kosovo. Accommodation failed because of the intransigence of one or both parties to the disputes. Studies of failed efforts to forestall ethnic wars provide poignant glimpses of paths not taken. Knowing the tragic outcomes, one reads such studies with a sense of impending disaster.[5]

If cultural restrictions and denial of political rights are essential incentives for political action by disadvantaged minorities, as they usually are, then implementation of international standards of individual and group rights should reduce the potential for conflict. This is precisely what happened in the 1990s, as shown in chapter 5. Discrimination eased for more than one-third of the 275 groups in the Minorities project between 1990 and 1998, mainly because of shifts in public policies and practices that lifted restrictions on their political and cultural rights. Groups gained most in the new democracies of Europe, Asia, and Latin America. This trend was only partially offset by autocratic governments' imposing new restrictions in the name of exclusive nationalism or in response to security threats, as the Yugoslav government did in Kosovo after 1989. A number of autocratic governments, especially in Asia, reduced restrictions on their minorities in the 1990s.

The Emerging Regime of Managed Ethnic Heterogeneity

The global decline in open ethnic conflict during the 1990s is the result of concerted efforts by a great many people and organizations, including domestic and international peacemakers and some of the protagonists themselves. The term *regime* is used in international politics to refer to "a framework of rules, norms, principles, and procedures" that facilitate the negotiation of substantive agreements among states.[6] I use the phrase *regime of managed ethnic heterogeneity* as shorthand for a bundle of conflict-mitigating doctrines and practices. It consists of a widely articulated set of principles about intergroup relations in heterogeneous states, a repertoire of strategies for institutionalizing the principles, and agreement on both domestic and international policies for how best to respond to ethnopolitical crises and conflicts.

These are the outlines of the emerging global regime governing the status and rights of national and minority peoples. The first and most basic principle is the recognition and active protection of the rights of minority peoples: freedom from discrimination based on race, national origin, language, or religion, complemented by institutional means to protect and promote collective interests. A corollary principle is the right of national peoples to exercise some degree of autonomy within existing states to govern their own affairs. This principle is a logical consequence of the first. That is, it follows that if minority peoples who constitute a majority in one region of a heterogeneous democratic state have the right to protect and promote their collective interests, then they should have the right to local or regional self-governance.

Contemporary democracies have been most consistent in articulating, promoting, and implementing such policies. After World War II a human rights regime evolved in the Atlantic democracies that emphasized the protection of individual rights.[7] During the early 1990s the emphasis of Western advocates shifted from individual rights to protection of collective rights of national minorities. The effect of standard-setting texts adopted in 1990–95 by the Organization for Security and Cooperation in Europe and the Council of Europe was to establish what Preece calls "an international regime for protection of national minorities in Europe—however limited." The texts embody several principles. One is prohibition against forced assimilation and population transfer; another is endorsement of autonomy for minority communities within existing states; a third is recognition that national minority questions are "once more legitimate subjects of international relations both at the United Nations and within European regional organizations."[8]

Virtually all European democracies have implemented these principles. In the first stage of democratization in postcommunist Europe, at the beginning of the 1990s, some ethnonational leaders manipulated the democratic process to serve nationalist interests at the expense of national minorities such as the Russians in the Baltic states, Hungarians in Slovakia and Romania, and Serbs in Croatia. In most of these countries a combination of diplomatic engagement by European institutions and the democratic process led to a reversal of discriminatory policies by the late 1990s, as shown in chapter 5 and in the case study of Hungarians in Slovakia.

The principle of substate autonomy for national minorities is more difficult to implement than policies of nondiscrimination, for two reasons. One is the resistance of most governing elites to devolution of central authority; the other is the necessity to negotiate situation-specific arrangements that satisfy both parties. The best-known models for substate autonomy agreements have been reached through negotiated settlements of ethnonational rebellions. Such rebellions usually begin with demands for complete independence—and usually end with negotiated or de facto autonomy for the ethnonationalists. What can be discerned is a growing disposition of parties to these conflicts to work toward accommodation in early stages rather than after prolonged warfare. Nationalist Serbia became the pariah state and bombing range of Europe precisely because of its blatant violation of principles about group rights and autonomy that elsewhere are widely accepted.

The recognition and protection of collective rights is one of the three elements of the regime or doctrine of managed ethnic heterogeneity. Political democracy is another. It provides the institutional means by which national peoples and minorities in most societies secure their rights and pursue collective interests. There are other institutional mechanisms for the protection of communal groups' interests, for example, the hegemonic exchange system (the term is Donald Rothchild's) found in many nondemocratic African states. Nonetheless, democracy, in one of its European variants, is widely regarded as the most reliable guarantee of minority rights. It is inherent in the logic of democratic politics that all peoples in heterogeneous societies should have equal civil and political rights. Democratic governance also implies acceptance of peaceful means for resolving civil conflicts.[9]

A third element of the new regime is the principle that disputes between communal groups and states are best settled by negotiation and mutual accommodation. The principle is backed up by the active engagement of major powers, the United Nations, and some regional organizations (especially in Europe and Africa), which use various mixes of diplomacy, mediation, inducements, and threats to encourage negotiated settlements of ethnic conflicts. Connie Peck characterizes the United Nations as a dispute settlement system and points to human rights issues and the resolution of conflicts within states as two of the UN system's principal post–Cold War obligations.[10] The notion of preventive diplomacy has great current popularity, not only because early engagement is potentially cheaper than belated responses to ethnic and other internal disputes, but also because it is the preferred instrument of the new regime. Coercive intervention, as in Serbia, is the international system's response of last resort to gross violations of human rights and to ethnic wars whose spillover effects threaten regional security.[11]

Four general—that is, regional and global—forces reinforce the application of principles of accommodation in heterogeneous societies. First is the active promotion of democratic institutions and practices by the Atlantic democracies. There is near-conclusive evidence that modern democracies rarely fight one another and are tempered in their use of repression against internal opponents. Before-and-after comparisons of national and minority peoples in new democracies, in chapter 5, show that their political and cultural status improves substantially during democratic transitions.

The second source of reinforcement is proactive action in behalf of the rights of national peoples and minorities by the United Nations and its constituent organizations, by regional bodies, and by interested nongovernmental organizations. In a number of instances, bodies such as the Organization for Security and Cooperation in Europe, the Council of Europe, the Organization of African Unity, and the Organization of the Islamic Conference have used diplomatic initiatives and mediation to temper the policies of member states toward minorities and to move open conflicts toward agreement. The empirical analysis of risk factors for future ethnic rebellions, reported in chapter 7, showed that whereas bilateral engagement by kindred groups and external states increases the risks, engagement by regional and international organizations has a dampening effect.[12]

Third is the virtually universal consensus among the international political class—the global foreign policy elite—about the goal of reestablishing and maintaining global and regional order. Empire building is out of fashion; interstate rivalries in the 1990s focus mainly on increased productivity and competition for markets; wars of any stripe are a threat to regional order and stable economic relations. Thus the United Nations, the United States and regional powers, and the regional organizations of Europe, Latin America, and Africa give high priority to containing local conflicts by preventive measures where possible, by mediation and peacekeeping operations where necessary.

Finally, whatever the nature of the political system, the costs of violent ethnopolitical conflict have become evident to both governing elites and the leaders of ethnopolitical movements. The costs of civil war have been acknowledged with deep regret in countries where postwar settlements are taking hold—in Bosnia, the Philippines, Mozambique, and elsewhere. The lesson drawn by outside observers of the 1994–96 war in Chechnya was the inability of the Russian military—as earlier in Afghanistan—to defeat highly motivated guerrilla opponents. The lesson the protagonists should have learned was that the war was not worth fighting, because neither side gained anything that could not have been achieved by negotiations before the Russian invasion. Caution about the likely costs of war and the unlikely chances of victory on either side probably have helped check ethnic rebellions elsewhere on the periphery of Russia and in most of the Soviet successor states. NATO's spring 1999 campaign against Serbia conveys a similar message to other states whose leaders have not been willing to compromise with ethnonationalists. The lesson has reached as far as China, where the Kosovo crisis reportedly prompted Communist Party officials to begin drafting alternative policies for dealing with Tibetans and Uighurs.[13]

In summary, international doctrines specify the rights of minorities and national peoples within states and stipulate international responsibilities for promoting those rights. These doctrines are invoked by representatives of minorities and nongovernmental organizations as well as public and international officials. Democratic governance, power sharing, and devolution are widely advocated as institutional means for securing group rights. Although the principles and institutions are mainly of Western democratic origins, they are articulated and applied in many other places, including Latin America, much of Asia, and some parts of Africa and the Middle East. They underlie two global trends documented above: first, the crisscrossing trends of declining ethnic warfare and increasing numbers of negotiated settlements (in chapter 6), and second, the reduction of political and cultural restrictions on minorities in virtually every world region (chapter 5). Both are sustained and reinforced by the emergence of democratic norms and institutions in heterogeneous societies in most postcommunist states, in Latin America, in much of Asia, and in parts of Africa.

Challenges to the Peaceful Management of Heterogeneity

The claim that there is an emerging global regime for managing ethnic heterogeneity challenges the conventional wisdom of policymakers and foreign affairs analysts in Western societies. What about communal warfare and genocide in central Africa, ethnic cleansing in Kosovo, Muslim and Hindu fundamentalism, and regional rebellions in Indonesia? The answer is a paradox. Objectively we have shown that there were substantially fewer such conflicts in the mid- to late 1990s than in previous years, but subjectively they received far more public attention—precisely because they challenged the emerging norms of recognition for group rights and peaceful accommodation of communal conflicts and the comforting assumption that the "international community" is capable of guaranteeing local and regional security.

The heterogeneous world system that is emerging from the settlement of ethnic and regional conflicts is more complex than its Cold War predecessor. It is a multilayered system with three interdependent sets of political actors: states; ethnopolitical movements, some situated within existing states, others that transcend them; and regional and international organizations that are assuming greater responsibility for managing relations among the other two. States remain the paramount actors in this heterogeneous system, but they are constrained by a growing network of mutual obligations with respect to identity groups and supranational actors.

This heterogeneous world system is not fully developed and faces violent challenges from states and ethnopolitical movements that do not accept its principles. Few states in the Islamic world are prepared to grant full political and cultural rights to religious minorities. A number of protracted ethnopolitical conflicts are highly resistant to regional and international influence. Conflicts in Afghanistan and Sudan seem to be intractable unless and until one party or coalition wins a decisive victory. Odds are against settlement of protracted conflicts between Kurdish nationalists and governments in Iraq and Turkey or containment of communal conflict between Hutus and Tutsis. Some ethnoconflicts are being held in check by cease-fires and promised reforms that can easily come apart: examples from Africa, Asia, and the Caucasus are cited in chapter 6. South Asia has a dozen serious ethnopolitical conflicts whose chances for settlement are highly problematic. Since the 1950s the central government of India has faced a series of secessionist challenges; no sooner has one movement been checked than another emerges. Other problematic conflicts are those that have been "settled" in the traditional way, by overwhelming force, for example, by the governments of Burma, Indonesia, and China. Repression without accommodation leads with some regularity to renewed resistance and rebellion, as has happened in Indonesia since the fall of Suharto's government.

The theory and data of the Minorities project provide a means for systematically identifying groups at high risk of future rebellion. A risk model is developed along the lines used by medical researchers to assess the risks that individuals will suffer from heart disease. Risk factors are measured for past cases of ethnorebellion, and then the 275 groups in the Minorities study are profiled on these factors in 1998 and statistical models used to assess each group's probability of new or escalating rebellion. The procedures and results of risk assessment are detailed in chapter 7 and appendix B. The risk model starts with the premise, based on empirical evidence, that incentives for future conflict are inherent in discriminatory treatment and policies of repressive control. Other major factors in the risk equations are groups' capacity for action, their domestic opportunities—especially regime instability—and international support. About 90 of the 275 groups in the study, including those already fighting ethnic wars, had medium to high predicted risks of future rebellion.

The risk assessments come in two parts. The first is a probability estimate for each group generated by a statistical risks model; the numbers of high and medium-risk groups in each region are shown in the middle column of table 8.1. The second is a data-based set of indicators that show whether domestic and external factors that facilitate rebellion are increasing or decreasing. The highest-risk groups in each region are listed in the right-hand column of table 8.1; the net escalating and dampening effects for each group are summarized in the pluses and minuses.

The risk assessment approach gives some perspective on the Kosovo conflict. In no sense was it unprecedented; it was the most warned-about crisis in Europe during the 1990s. A group's loss of political autonomy is one of the strong leading indicators of future rebellion: the Yugoslav government led by Slobodan Milosevic dissolved the Kosovo regional government in 1989. A decade of political activism and protest typically precedes the onset of ethnic wars: the Kosovars resisted their loss of autonomy by forming a parallel government, but the first terrorist attacks did not begin until 1997, and large-scale rebellion in 1998. Milosevic's ultranationalist policies fundamentally contradict European and international principles about minority rights: no significant concessions were offered to the Kosovars.[14] Preventive international responses to the situation were not carried through: the Bush administration warned the Yugoslav government against the use of repression in Kosovo in December 1992, but the issue was not addressed in the Dayton Accords in 1996 (negotiated by the Clinton administration) and the preparatory steps in the ethnic cleansing campaign in October 1998 elicited no international response.

The ninety medium- to high-risk groups are the most likely protagonists in new and escalating ethnic wars early in the twenty-first century. They are most numerous in the postcommunist states, West and South Asia, and Africa south of the Sahara. Risks of ethnic war are minimal in the Western democracies and only slightly greater in Latin America and the Caribbean. In Europe risks are highest in the Balkans. Spillover from the Kosovo conflict is likely to increase risks for groups such as the Sandzak Muslims and Vojvodina Hungarians in Serbia and Albanians in Macedonia. A new democratic government in Serbia is the best antidote for these risks. Our analysis also points

Table 8.1. Risks of Future Ethnic Wars

Region and Number of Groups	Groups in Ethnic Wars in 1998 and at Future Risk	Highest-Risk Groups and Facilitating Factors in 1998
Western democracies: 31 ethnopolitical groups	No groups in ethnic wars; 5 groups at medium risk	Basques in France + + Basques in Spain +
Eastern Europe and former USSR: 59 ethnopolitical groups	2 groups in ethnic wars; 8 groups at high risk; 7 groups at medium risk	Armenians in Nagorno-Karabakh – – Kosovars in Yugoslavia – Russians in Estonia – Crimean Tatars + Crimean Russians + Bosnian Serbs +
Southeast and Pacific Asia: 34 ethnopolitical groups	5 groups in ethnic wars; 3 groups at high risk; 12 groups at medium risk	Uighurs in China + + Timorese in Indonesia – Aboriginal Taiwanese 0
West and South Asia: 25 ethnopolitical groups	11 groups in ethnic wars; 6 groups at high risk; 13 groups at medium risk	Hazaris, Tajiks, and Uzbeks in Afghanistan 0 Kashmiris in India + + Tripuras and Scheduled tribes in India +

North Africa and Middle East: 28 ethnopolitical groups	3 groups in ethnic wars; 6 groups at high risk; 2 groups at medium risk	Kurds in Turkey 0 Shi'i in Iraq + Shi'i in Lebanon + Palestinians in Gaza and the West Bank 0 Kurds in Iraq + + Arabs in Israel 0
Africa south of the Sahara: 67 ethnopolitical groups	11 groups in ethnic wars; 12 groups at high risk; 8 groups at medium risk	Ogani in Nigeria + + Tutsis in Congo (former Zaire) 0 Ovimbundu in Angola + Yoruba in Nigeria + + Hutus in Burundi + + Afars in Ethiopia + +
Latin America and the Caribbean: 32 ethnopolitical groups	No groups in ethnic wars; 1 group at high risk; 11 groups at medium risk	Miskitos in Nicaragua – – Maya in Mexico 0 Indigenous highlanders in Ecuador – –

Note: Ethnic wars in 1998 are conflicts between rebels and states with magnitudes of 4 or greater. No more than six highest-risk groups in each region are listed here. For details and information on other groups, see tables 7.4 to 7.9.

to medium potentials for renewed fighting among Serb, Muslim, and Croat contenders in the Yugoslav successor states. In the Caucasus preventive diplomacy and peacekeeping efforts have paid off in the containment and settlement of most ethnic wars of the early 1990s. Risks remain high, however, for intensification of warfare over the status of Nagorno-Karabakh and armed conflict by the Ingush, who live on Chechnya's western border.

Outside Europe, prospects for ethnopolitical peace are best in Latin America. Almost all domestic and external facilitating factors indicate a dampening of risks in this region. Most high-risk protagonists are indigenous peoples whose demands for recognition and local autonomy are being substantially addressed by democratic governments. The Nicaraguan and Mexican governments face the greatest risks of rebellion. In Nicaragua this is due to lack of resources for implementing an autonomy agreement for the coastal peoples, in Mexico because of lack of political will to respond with real reforms to political action by indigenous peoples in Chiapas, Oaxaca, and elsewhere.

Four other zones of ethnopolitical conflict pose greater present and future challenges. One is the Middle East, where the central issues are the unsatisfied ethnonational aspirations of Palestinians and Kurds. Farther east is the West and South Asia zone, characterized by communal contention for power in Afghanistan and Pakistan and ethnonationalist rebellions by Kashmiris and Sri Lankan Tamils. The largest number of ongoing and prospective ethnic wars anywhere in the world occur in the Central Asian uplands, stretching from the hill country of Bangladesh, Assam, and Burma to Tibet and China's Xinjiang province.

Africa's situation is the most grave. Twenty African groups are at medium to high risk of future rebellion; half of them live in or on the periphery of the eastern and middle African conflict zone (or two zones) ranging from Sudan and Ethiopia through the Great Lakes region to the Congo basin and the Angola highlands. There is also a less threatening West African conflict zone, where revolutionary and ethnic wars have been brought under control in Niger, Mali, and Liberia but continue in Sierra Leone and Chad. The greatest risk in this region has been the possibility of internal war in Nigeria along the north-south, Muslim-Christian divide. The Ogoni minority of the Niger delta[15] and the much more numerous Yoruba both are high on the factors that elsewhere predict to ethnic war. The prospects of ethnic war in Nigeria are very much dependent on the current transition to democracy. Civil war in Nigeria would have spillover effects far beyond its borders.

The primary purpose of the risk analysis is to highlight situations that should have the highest priority for remedial and preventive action. By whom and how? The answers depend on which actors have the will, the political leverage, and the resources to act. The Kosovo and East Timor cases illustrate that the reach of the new doctrine of managed ethnic heterogeneity depends on whether it is accepted by those whose conflicts are to be managed and on the willingness of regional and international organizations to enforce it. International and regional organizations are more likely to pursue effective preventive strategies in areas where the Western powers have vital interests, which means Europe, Latin America, and the Middle East. Asian and African conflicts are more remote and resistant to external influence. When preventive strategies fail, or are not pursued in the first place, the international challenges are different: how to provide humanitarian aid and how to contain the regional dispersion of conflict.

The evidence of this study shows decisively that group rights and interests are being protected and promoted more effectively in the decade since the Cold War ended than they were before 1989. The norms, institutions, and practices of managed ethnic heterogeneity have strong international support, but their application is ultimately a local matter, the result of decisions taken by societies and governments. Many of the principles are embodied in democratic doctrine, and democracy is in the ascendance in all world regions. However, ultranationalists can impose majoritarian tyranny. Islamist leaders reject the validity of groups' claims based on dispensations of religious doctrine other than their own. Probably the greatest threats to claims of a universal regime of group rights come from predatory, hegemonic elites who use the state as an instrument to protect and promote the interests of their own people at the expense of others. These and other sources of communal warfare and repression remain in many corners of the world and will continue to cast up challenges to those who would contain ethnic violence.

The zones of ethnopolitical conflict will pose a critical set of tests of whether regional and international actors will act to strengthen the regime of managed ethnic heterogeneity. The regime is most likely to operate in the more developed and democratic regions. Regional powers in Asia can be expected to evolve and promote their own responses to ethnopolitical conflict, especially when and where it threatens economic development and regional stability. The most severe new challenges probably will come in Africa, particularly in the broad middle belt of Africa where resource constraints and economic decline are severe, failures of governance are endemic, and the international will and ability to act have been weakest.

No one strategy is likely to contain deep-rooted communal conflicts in Central Africa or any other high-risk regions. What's needed is coordinated effort by international actors and major powers to facilitate negotiated settlements, guarantee local and regional security, promote democratic power sharing, and assist economic development. If policies of managed ethnic heterogeneity are to succeed, they have to be devised in partnership with elements of civil society, those local people and organizations who are committed to the nonviolent and democratic reconstruction of their societies. And they require sustained effort. Building civil peace in divided societies depends not just on peace settlements and institutional engineering but on consistent, long-term engagement to ensure that agreements are implemented and that institutions work.

Appendix A
Classification of Countries
by Regime Type in the Late 1990s

Table A.1 includes 116 countries with politically significant minorities. The countries are classified by type of regime and transition years identified mainly on the basis of time-series data on democracy and autocracy indicators in the 1996 update of the Polity III data set, as described in Keith Jaggers and Ted Robert Gurr, "Tracking Democracy's Third Wave with the Polity III Data," *Journal of Peace Research* 32 (November 1995): 483–488. These indicators are constructed from annually coded information on political institutions. Highly democratic regimes have competitive political participation, elected chief executives, and significant checks on executives' exercise of powers. The annually coded Democracy indicator ranges from 0 to 10. In highly autocratic regimes, by contrast, citizens' participation is sharply restricted or suppressed; chief executives are selected within the political elite; and, once in office, chief executives exercise power with few or no institutional constraints. The annually coded Autocracy indicator ranges from 0 to 10. Many regimes have a mix of autocratic and democratic features and thus have low positive scores on both indicators. They are classified here as transitional. The most recent update of the Polity data set is available from *www.bsos.umd.edu/cidcm/polity*. The following variables and categories are used in the table:

Old democracies (*n* = 27): Countries whose democratic political institutions were established before 1980 and that have not reverted to autocratic rule (Democracy – Autocracy scores < 0) since the 1950s. All but two of the twenty-five countries in this group are full democracies, with Democracy – Autocracy scores of 8 or more in 1996. The exceptions are Malaysia and Sri Lanka, both at 5.

New democracies (*n* = 33): Countries whose democratic institutions were established between 1980 and 1994 and that have not reverted to autocratic rule since 1980. All but six of the countries in this group were full democracies in 1996; the others were slightly below the threshold of full institutional democracy with Democracy – Autocracy scores of 6 or 7. Countries with mixed political systems in which democratic traits outweighed autocratic traits only slightly are classified as transitional.

Autocracies (*n* = 26): Countries with consistently autocratic institutions that did not attempt democratic transitions (Democracy – Autocracy scores > 0) at any time between the 1960s and the late 1990s. Autocracies that had incorporated some democratic features by 1996 are classified as transitional.

Transitional regimes (*n* = 32): Countries with regimes that have a mixture of autocratic and democratic features plus countries that have had one or more transitions to democracy after the 1970s that subsequently failed. Most countries are in the former category. Years in which democratic features were incorporated in these regimes are shown in italics. The odds are high that countries with mixed institutions like these will either revert to autocratic rule or shift toward fully institutional democracy, as reported in Daniel C. Esty, Jack A. Goldstone, Ted Robert Gurr, Barbara Harff, Marc Levy, Geoffrey D. Dabelko, Pamela T. Surko, and Alan N. Unger, "State Failure Task Force Report: Phase II Findings," in *Environmental Change and Security Project Report* (Washington, D.C.: Woodrow Wilson Center), no. 5 (summer 1999), 59–62.

Transition year(s): For democracies, the year that current democratic institutions were established, if the transition occurred after 1950. For transitional regimes, the year or years (if any) since 1975 in which the regime underwent significant shifts toward or away from democracy. Shifts toward democracy in transitional regimes are italicized.

Table A.1. Countries by Regime Type in the Late 1990s

Country	Polity Type	Transition Year(s) (if after 1950)	Democracy Score 1996	Autocracy Score 1996	Democracy Minus Autocracy
United States	Old democracy		10	0	10
Canada	Old democracy		10	0	10
United Kingdom	Old democracy		10	0	10
France	Old democracy	1969	8	0	8
Switzerland	Old democracy		10	0	10
Spain	Old democracy	1978	10	0	10
Germany[a]	Old democracy		10	0	10
Italy	Old democracy		10	0	10
Greece	Old democracy	1975	10	0	10
Cyprus[b]	Old democracy	1973	10	0	10
Nordic countries[c]	Old democracy		10	0	10
Japan	Old democracy	1952	10	0	10
Australia	Old democracy		10	0	10
Papua New Guinea	Old democracy	1976	10	0	10
New Zealand	Old democracy		10	0	10
India	Old democracy		8	0	8
Sri Lanka	Old democracy		6	1	5
Malaysia	Old democracy	1957	5	0	5
Israel	Old democracy		10	0	10
Botswana	Old democracy	1966	10	0	10
Dominican Republic	Old democracy	1978	8	0	8
Costa Rica	Old democracy		10	0	10
Colombia	Old democracy	1957	8	0	8
Venezuela	Old democracy	1958	8	0	8
Ecuador	Old democracy	1979	9	0	9
Hungary	New democracy	1990	10	0	10
Czech Republic	New democracy	1990	10	0	10
Slovakia	New democracy	1993	7	0	7
Macedonia	New democracy	1991	8	0	8
Bulgaria	New democracy	1990	8	0	8
Moldova	New democracy	1991	7	0	7
Romania	New democracy	1990	8	0	8
Estonia	New democracy	1991	8	0	8

continued on next page

Table A.1. *(cont.)*

Country	Polity Type	Transition Year(s) (if after 1950)	Democracy Score 1996	Autocracy Score 1996	Democracy Minus Autocracy
Latvia	New democracy	1991	8	0	8
Lithuania	New democracy	1991	10	0	10
Ukraine	New democracy	1991	8	0	8
Georgia	New democracy	1991	6	0	6
Taiwan	New democracy	1991	8	0	8
South Korea	New democracy	1988	9	0	9
Pakistan	New democracy	1988	7	0	7
Bangladesh	New democracy	1991	8	0	8
Philippines	New democracy	1987	8	0	8
Turkey	New democracy	1984	9	0	9
Mali	New democracy	1992	9	0	9
Madagascar	New democracy	1993	9	0	9
Namibia	New democracy	1990	9	0	9
South Africa	New democracy	1994	9	0	9
Guatemala	New democracy	1986	8	0	8
Honduras	New democracy	1982	7	0	7
El Salvador	New democracy	1984	9	0	9
Nicaragua	New democracy	1990	8	0	8
Panama	New democracy	1990	9	0	9
Guyana	New democracy	1992	6	0	6
Brazil	New democracy	1985	9	0	9
Bolivia	New democracy	1982	9	0	9
Paraguay	New democracy	1989	7	0	7
Chile	New democracy	1990	8	0	8
Argentina	New democracy	1983	8	0	8
Albania	Transitional	*1992*, 1996	1	4	−3
Croatia	Transitional	*1991*, 1993	2	3	−1
Bosnia	Transitional	*1992, 1995*	3	2	1
Russian Federation	Transitional	*1991*	5	1	4
Belarus	Transitional	*1991*, 1996	1	6	−5
Azerbaijan	Transitional	*1991*, 1993	0	7	−7
Tajikistan	Transitional	*1991*, 1992	0	6	−6
Kyrgyzstan	Transitional	*1991*	3	1	2
Kazakhstan	Transitional	*1991*, 1992	1	5	−4
Cambodia	Transitional	*1993*, 1996	3	2	1
Thailand	Transitional	*1975*, 1991, *1992*	9	0	9
Singapore	Transitional		2	4	−2
Fiji	Transitional	1987, *1990*	6	2	4

Table A.1. *(cont.)*

Country	Polity Type	Transition Year(s) (if after 1950)	Democracy Score 1996	Autocracy Score 1996	Democracy Minus Autocracy
Morocco	Transitional	*1977*	1	5	−4
Egypt	Transitional		1	4	−3
Lebanon	Transitional	*1990*	1	4	−3
Jordan	Transitional	*1993*	4	1	3
Senegal	Transitional	*1978*	3	2	1
Niger	Transitional	*1993*, 1995	0	6	−6
Guinea	Transitional	*1996?*	1	4	−3
Sierra Leone	Transitional	1971, *1995*, 1997	6	0	6
Ghana	Transitional	*1979*, 1981, *1992*	4	1	3
Togo	Transitional	*1993*	1	4	−3
Nigeria[d]	Transitional	*1979*, 1984, *1994*	0	6	−6
Chad	Transitional	*1996?*	3	3	0
Uganda	Transitional	*1994*	2	4	−2
Burundi	Transitional	*1993*, 1996	0	7	−7
Ethiopia	Transitional	*1994*	3	2	1
Zambia	Transitional	*1991*	3	2	1
Zimbabwe	Transitional	*1980*, 1987	0	6	−6
Mexico	Transitional	*1996*	4	2	2
Peru	Transitional	*1980*, 1992	3	1	2
Serbia and Montenegro	Autocracy		0	7	−7
Turkmenistan	Autocracy		0	9	−9
Uzbekistan	Autocracy		0	9	−9
Afghanistan[e]	Autocracy		—	—	—
China	Autocracy		0	7	−7
Bhutan	Autocracy		0	8	−8
Burma	Autocracy		0	9	−9
Laos	Autocracy		0	7	−7
Vietnam	Autocracy		0	7	−7
Indonesia	Autocracy		0	7	−7
Algeria	Autocracy		0	7	−7
Iran	Autocracy		0	6	−6
Iraq	Autocracy		0	9	−9
Syria	Autocracy		0	9	−9
Saudi Arabia	Autocracy		0	10	−10
Bahrain	Autocracy		0	10	−10
Mauritania	Autocracy		0	6	−6
Cameroon	Autocracy		0	6	−6

continued on next page

Table A.1. *(cont.)*

Country	Polity Type	Transition Year(s) (if after 1950)	Democracy Score 1996	Autocracy Score 1996	Democracy Minus Autocracy
Congo (former Zaire)[f]	Autocracy				
Kenya	Autocracy		0	6	−6
Rwanda	Autocracy		0	4	−4
Somalia[f]	Autocracy				
Djibouti	Autocracy		0	6	−6
Eritrea	Autocracy		1	3	−2
Angola	Autocracy		0	7	−7
Sudan	Autocracy		0	7	−7

[a] Federal Republic of Germany.

[b] Greek Cyprus only. The political institutions of autonomous political entities that have not gained widespread international recognition are not included in this analysis.

[c] Norway, Sweden, and Finland are combined in this table because their Saami minorities are treated as a single aggregate group in the Minorities at Risk data set. The count of old democracies in this appendix, above, and in chapter 5, counts them separately.

[d] Nigeria's military rulers conducted a series of elections leading to a transition to democracy in 1993–94 but rejected the results of the presidential election and resumed autocratic military rule.

[e] Insufficient data; Afghanistan is classified as an autocracy on the basis of the rule imposed by the Taliban on those parts of the country it controls.

[f] Congo (former Zaire) and Somalia were failed states in 1996; that is, they had no effective central governments. Congo (former Zaire) is classified an autocracy by reference to the regime led by President Mobutu prior to his overthrow by Laurent Kabila in May 1997. Somalia is classified as an autocracy by reference to the regime led by President Siad Barre before it collapsed in 1991.

Appendix B
The Analytic Basis of Risk Assessments

Ted Robert Gurr and Monty G. Marshall

The first two parts of this appendix describe the indicators of risk factors used in chapter 7. The third part summarizes the results of their statistical analysis.

I. Indicators Used to Estimate Risk Assessment Models of Protest and Rebellion

Indicators for the risk analysis, described in section I, were constructed from coded data in the Minorities at Risk data set for 275 groups. Indicators with *italicized* labels are the binary variables tested to develop the risk models reported in tables 7.1 and 7.2. Y... labels identify dependent (conflict) variables, and X... labels identify independent variables. Labels in capital letters are the indicators from the Minorities at Risk and other data sets used to construct these binary variables. Section II lists indicators used to estimate risks of future conflict in tables 7.3 ff. Unless otherwise specified, all indicators are included in the Minorities data set at *www.bsos.umd.edu/cidcm/mar.*

I.1 INDICATORS OF ETHNOPOLITICAL PROTEST AND REBELLION

These binary indicators were constructed from data coded on the scales described in table 2.2.

Protest 1996–98 (YLEVPROT):
1 if group protest scores in 1996, 1997, and/or 1998 (PROT96, PROT97, PROT98) were greater than 0 *and* if rebellion 1996, 1997, and 1998 (REB96, REB97, REB98) scores were all less than 3; otherwise, 0.

Note that groups with substantial rebellion are scored 0 on this indicator even if they also engaged in some protest.

Rebellion 1997–98 (YLEVREB):
1 if group rebellion scores in 1997 and/or 1998 were greater than 0; otherwise, 0.

Increase in protest 1995–98 (YINCPROT):
1 if there was any increase of two or more categories on the protest scale at any time between 1995 and 1998; otherwise, 0.

Increase in rebellion 1995–98 (YINCREB):
1 if there was any increase of two or more categories on the rebellion scale at any time between 1995 and 1998; otherwise, 0

Decrease in rebellion 1995–98 (YDECREB):
1 if there was any decrease of two or more categories on the rebellion scale at any time between 1995 and 1998; otherwise, 0.

I.2 INDICATORS OF SALIENCE OF GROUP IDENTITY

Persistent past protest 1985–94 (XPERPROT): This binary indicator was constructed from annually coded data on protest from 1985 through 1994.
1 if the group engaged in at least five years of protest at the 3 or higher level; otherwise, 0.

Persistent past rebellion 1985–94 (XPERREB): This binary indicator was constructed from annually coded data on rebellion from 1985 through 1994.
1 if the group engaged in at least five years of rebellion at the 3 or higher level; otherwise, 0.

Economic and political discrimination (XECDISC, XPOLDISC): Binary indicators of discrimination were constructed from biennially coded information on the four-category scales described in tables 4.1 and 4.2 (ECDIS94, POLDIS94).
1 if the group in 1994–95 was subject to discrimination as a result of social practice or public policy; otherwise, 0.

Cultural restrictions (XCULRES): Constructed from biennially coded information on discriminatory cultural restrictions as described in table 4.3 (CULRES94).
1 if the group in 1994–95 was subject to any restrictions; otherwise, 0.

I.3 INDICATORS OF INCENTIVES FOR POLITICAL ACTION

Lost autonomy (XLOSAUT): The binary indicator is derived from a complex six-category index of a group's historical loss of autonomy, derived from codings of the magnitude of loss and the group's status prior to loss, and weighted by length of time since loss (AUTLOST).
1 if AUTLOST is coded 0 or 1; otherwise, 0.

State repression (XREP): The latest Minorities coding system records twenty-three different categories of repressive action used by governments against

ethnopolitical groups (REP961 through REP9623). The binary indicator is based on whether any of these actions were coded in 1996.
1 if any repression category was coded for 1996; otherwise, 0.

Increase in political and cultural restrictions (XINCPRES, XINCCRES): Increased political and cultural restrictions from 1994–95 to 1996.
1 if any increase is registered on any category of political restrictions in 1996 (POLREX96); otherwise, 0.
1 if any increase is registered on any category of cultural restrictions in 1996 (CULRESX96); otherwise, 0.

I.4 Indicators of Capacity for Political Action

Territorial concentration (XGRCON): Extent to which the group has a territorial base.
1 if the group is coded on GROUPCON as "majority in one region, others dispersed" or "concentrated in one region"; otherwise, 0.

Group organization (XGORG): Character of group organization for joint political action in 1990–95.
1 if the group is coded on GOJPA95 as having its own conventional or militant political movements, parties, or organizations; 0 if the group has no such organizations or if its interests are promoted by umbrella organizations only.

Increase in support for conventional organization 1995–96 (XCHCORG): This and the following indicator were not coded until 1996; analytic results suggest that they are significant leading indicators of future conflict.
1 if the group is coded as having any positive change on support for conventional political organizations between 1995 and 1996 (CONOR#96); otherwise, 0.

Increase in support for militant organizations 1995–96 (XCHMORG):
1 if the group is coded as having any positive change on support for militant organizations between 1995 and 1996 (MILOR#96); otherwise, 0.

I.5 Indicators of Domestic Opportunities for Political Action

These indicators are derived from coded data from the latest update of the Polity data set on democracy, autocracy, and regime transitions; see chapter 5. The data set is available on the Polity project's Web site: *www.bsos.umd.edu/cidcm/polity*

Democratic polity 1995 (XDEM):
1 if the regime is greater than or equal to 6 on the 0–10 scale of institutional democracy for 1995 (DEMOC); otherwise, 0.

Autocratic polity 1995 (XAUT):
1 if the regime is greater than or equal to 6 on the 0–10 scale of institutional autocracy for 1995 (AUTOC); otherwise, 0.

Regime incoherence 1995 (INCOHR95):
1 if the regime has a mix of democratic and autocratic features in 1995, that is, if DEMOC minus AUTOC is less than 5 and more than −5.

Regime instability 1992–95 (XDUR): Derived from information on the number of years since the last abrupt change in polity.
1 if DURAB95 is less than 4 (that is, a new polity was established in 1992 or later); otherwise, 0.

I.6 INDICATORS OF INTERNATIONAL OPPORTUNITIES FOR POLITICAL ACTION

The first three indicators summarize information on the main sources of external support for ethnopolitical groups. They are derived from coded information in the Minorities at Risk profiles on types and sources of transnational support for ethnopolitical groups. The last two indicators represent immediate and more diffuse international spillover effects. They are derived by summing magnitudes of civil conflict in nearby states. They are derived from the Major Armed Conflict data set, which is available from the Center for Systemic Peace Web site: *www.bsos.umd.edu/cidcm/csp.*

Transnational support from kindred groups in 1995 (XKSUP):
1 if the group received any support from exile organizations or organized kindred groups in neighboring countries in 1995 (KSUP5); otherwise, 0.[1]

Transnational support from foreign governments in 1995 (XSSUP):
1 if the group received any support from foreign governments in 1995 (SSUP5); otherwise, 0.[2]

Political support from regional and international organizations in 1995 (XIPOLSUP):
1 if the group received any political support from regional and international organizations in 1995 (IPOLSUP5); otherwise, 0.[3]

Civil conflict in neighboring states in 1995 (XTOTCIV):
1 if the total magnitude of civil conflict in neighboring states in 1995 (TOTCIV95) is greater than 8; otherwise, 0.

Civil conflict in the region in 1995 (XREGCIV):
1 if civil conflict in the larger region in 1995 (REGCIV95) is greater than 22; otherwise, 0.

For definitions of regions see the Center for Systemic Peace Web site, cited above.

I.7 INDICATORS OF TYPES OF COMMUNAL GROUPS

Binary indicators are used to identify the type of communal group. Group type is a determinant of political objectives, strategies, and state responses. Indicators of group type were used in the final risk analyses.

Communal Contenders (XCOMCONT)

Ethnonationalists (XETHNAT)

Ethnoclasses (XETHCLA)

Indigenous Peoples (XIND)

National Minorities (XNATMIN)

Religious Sects (XRELSEC)

II. Indicators Used to Identify Groups at Highest Risk of Future Rebellion

The following are the indicators of variables for the mid- to late 1990s used in the forecasting equations whose results are reported in tables 7.4 to 7.9. The independent variables used in the forecasting analysis to generate values of PRED98 are labeled *F* to distinguish them from the indicators used to estimate the risk equations. The source variables in the Minorities and other data sets are the same as those listed in section I, except that the most recent coded values are used.

II.1 PREDICTED REBELLION IN 1997–98 FROM 1995 MODEL (PRED95)

The logistic regression equation used to postdict 1997–98 values of rebellion, based on circa 1995 values on the independent variables, is summarized in table 7.2. The range of predicted values of the logistic regression equation is –7.03 to 3.42. Any positive predicted value represents a substantial risk of rebellion; negative values indicate that the group, barring any change in its current status, is unlikely to use systematic violence. There is no identified association between the magnitude of predicted values (PRED95) and the actual magnitude of rebellion (REB9798).

II.2 Observed Rebellion in 1997–98 (REB9798)

The averaged values of the group's rebellion scores for 1997 and 1998 on a scale of 0 to 7. If one year's score is missing, the single-year score is used. If both values are missing, the missing-value code is used.

II.3 Observed Protest in 1997–98 (PROT9798)

The averaged value of the group's protest scores for 1997 and 1998 on a scale of 0 to 5. If one year's score is missing, the single-year score is used. If both values are missing, the missing-value code is used.

II.4 Trend in Rebellion in the 1990s (TREND90S)

An indicator of the general trend in a group's rebellion scores from 1990 to 1998. Groups whose rebellion scores in the last three years of the decade increased by 2 or more over previous years are coded +1; groups whose scores declined by 2 or more are coded −1; others are coded 0.

II.5 Predicted Future Rebellion from 1998 Model (PRED98)

The logistic regression equation in table 7.2 is applied to 1998 values on six independent variables and used to estimate likely levels of future rebellions. The range of estimated values is −7.03 to 3.42 (the highest observed value is 2.10). Groups with values of −0.54 and higher are assumed to have significant risks of future rebellion and are included in tables 7.4 through 7.9. The following six independent variables are used in the predictive equation.

Persistent past protest 1989–98 (FPERPROT) is an updated variable: 1 if the group engaged in at least five years of protest at the 3 or higher level between 1989 and 1998, PROT(89 . . . 98); otherwise, 0.

Government repression in 1998 (FREP) is derived from coded data on repressive state actions in 1998, REP98(1 . . . 23).

Territorial concentration (FGRCON) is the same as XGRCON; group concentration is invariant over time for almost all groups.

Group organization in 1998 (FGORG) is derived from GOJPA98.

Regime instability 1995–98 (FDUR) is derived from the 1998 value of DURABLE (Polity).

Transnational support in 1998 from foreign states (FSSUP) is derived from coded data on transnational state support in 1998, F(11 . . . 42)SPRT8.

II.6 TRENDS IN PREDICTED REBELLION 1995 TO 1998 (CHPRED)

This variable is based on a comparison of the values of rebellion predicted using the 1995 model and the 1998 forecasting model.

−1 = Value for 1998 (PRED98) is less than 1995 value (PRED95).

 0 = No change in predicted values.

+1 = Value for 1998 (PRED98) is greater than 1995 value (PRED95).

II.7 INDICATOR OF DOMESTIC FACTORS THAT FACILITATE OR DAMPEN REBELLION (XDOMFAC)

Bivariate and multivariate analysis identified five domestic factors that in the late 1990s facilitated or inhibited a group's choices of strategies of rebellion, in addition to the six variables in the predictive model. They are used to construct a composite indicator by combining values on the following five indicators using this formula:

XDOMFAC = LOSTAUT + INCOHR98 + COMCONT + SEPID − CORG9698

LOSTAUT is described in section I.3 as an indicator of incentives for political action.

INCOHR98 is the 1998 value of INCOHR95, described in section I.5 as an indicator of domestic political opportunities.

COMCONT is the same as XCOMCON, described in section I.7 as a type of communal group (for example, Communal Contender).

SEPID is a composite indicator of group orientation to state authority as described in section I.7, type of communal group.
+1 if the group is classified as ethnonationalist (separatist orientation).
−1 if the group is classified as either indigenous or an ethnoclass (nonseparatist or autonomy orientation).

CORG9698 is an indicator of increase in support for conventional political organizations (see XCHCORG in section I.4, Capacity for Political Action) constructed from information on CONOR#96, #97, and #98:
0 = No change in support for conventional political organizations.
1 = Increase in support coded in one of three years.
2 = Increase in support coded in more than one year.

II.8. Indicator of External Factors That Facilitate or Dampen Rebellion (XEXTFAC)

Bivariate and multivariate analysis identified four international factors that in the late 1990s facilitated or inhibited a group's choice of strategies of rebellion, in addition to the six variables in the predictive model. They are used to construct a composite indicator by combining values on the following four indicators using this formula:

XEXTFAC = KSUP98 + TOTCIV98 + REGCIV98 - IPOLSUP

KSUP98 is the 1998 value of *XKSUP.* This and the following three variables are described in section I.5 as indicators of international opportunities.[4]

TOTCIV98 is the 1998 value of *XTOTCIV.*

REGCIV98 is the 1998 value of *XREGCIV.*

IPOLSUP is an indicator of political support for a group from regional and international organizations between 1996 and 1998 and is constructed from information on IPOLSUP6, IPOLSUP7, and IPOLSUP8.

0 = No support from regional or international organizations.

1 = Support from regional or international organizations in one year.

2 = Support from regional or international organizations in more than one year.

III. Validation of Risk Indicators

The risk indicators were tested in a number of time-lagged correlation analyses with the four binary measures of protest and rebellion. The bivariate correlations for risk factors that postdict to protest and rebellion in 1996–98 are summarized in table B.1 and discussed here. Other bivariate and multivariate analyses were done to test the stability of these results but are not reported in detail.

III.1 Indicators of Salience of Group Identity

Persistent protest and rebellion. Protest and rebellion between 1985 and 1994 both predict to rebellion in 1997–98, but for different reasons. Rebellion, once begun, is likely to continue (evident from the robust .56 correlation between persistent past rebellion and presence of rebellion in 1997–98) and has a weaker tendency to escalate (persistent rebellion in 1985–94 has a weak leading correlation of 0.13 with increased rebellion in the late 1990s). Most interesting, both theoretically and for purposes of risk assessment, is the leading relationship (correlation of 0.26) between persistent past protest and the level of 1997–98 rebellion. This relationship is consistent with the finding reported in chapter 2 that a decade or more of protest preceded most rebellions that began between 1985 and 1995. Another dynamic also is at work, as suggested by the substantial negative correlation (–.31) between persistent rebellion and protest in the late 1990s: persistent rebellion also tends to inhibit protest.

Discrimination and restrictions. Most indicators of discrimination are not good predictors of future protest or rebellion. Cultural restrictions in 1994–95 are the only indicator of salience (or of incentives for action) with a significant leading relationship to the level of protest in 1995–98. On the other hand, all three indicators of discrimination have weak but significant correlations with *increases* in protest in the late 1990s. These are, in fact, the only risk factors out of twenty-six that we tested that predict to increased protest. These three variables do not give us enough leverage to build a reliable risk model for increased protest. The theoretical implications of the lack of strong correlations between discrimination and political action are discussed in chapter 7. The finding may also be due, in part, to selection bias in the Minorities project. That is, "minorities at risk" are a subset of all ethnic groups, most of which are included because they have been subject to discrimination. In a study that assessed the risks of political action for *all* communal groups, discrimination would be likely to have stronger effects.

III.2 INDICATORS OF INCENTIVES FOR POLITICAL ACTION

History of lost political autonomy. Virtually all national and indigenous peoples and most communal contenders—groups that make up more than two hundred of the 275 groups tracked by the Minorities project—once were politically independent or were part of political entities other than the states that now govern them. The loss of autonomy is an historical fact around which myths and grievances are formed. Appeals to those myths and grievances are a potent source of mobilization for present political action. "Lost autonomy" is derived from a complex indicator that takes into account both the extent of autonomy lost and how recently the loss was incurred. The greater and more recent the loss, the higher a group's score on the indicator. The dichotomous version of the indicator correlates significantly with level of rebellion in 1997–98 (with $r = .18$).

Government repression in the 1990s. The use of force against people who think they have a just cause may provoke fear and caution in the short run, but it also increases resentment and enduring incentives to resist and retaliate. Evidence

Table B.1. Risk Factors of Ethnopolitical Protest and Rebellion in the 1990s

	Logistic Correlations with Ethnopolitical Conflict			
Theoretical Variables and Indicators	Protest 1996–98	Increase in Protest 1995–98	Rebellion 1997–98	Increase in Rebellion 1995–98
Salience of group identity				
Persistent protest, 1985–94	.04	-.01	.26[b]	.08
Persistent rebellion, 1985–94	-.31[b]	.03	.56[b]	.13[a]
Economic discrimination, 1994–95	.08	.25[b]	.12	-.02
Political discrimination, 1994–95	.09	.12[a]	.11	.07
Cultural restrictions, 1994–95	.17[b]	.15[a]	-.06	-.01
Incentives for political action				
Lost autonomy	-.03	.02	.18[b]	.02
Government repression, 1996	-.11	.04	.54[b]	.25[b]
Increased political restrictions, 1996	-.06	-.01	.24[b]	.05
Increased cultural restrictions, 1996	.01	.04	.06	.02
Capacity for political action				
Territorial concentration	-.09	.04	.25[b]	.07
Group organization, 1990–95	-.01	-.04	.27[b]	.11
Increased support for conventional organization, 1995–96	.07	.01	.00	.00
Increased support for militant organization, 1995–96	-.07	-.07	.02	.12
Domestic opportunities for political action				
Democratic polity, 1995	.25[b]	.01	-.12[a]	-.11
Autocratic polity, 1996	-.15[a]	.03	.08	-.02

Regime incoherence, 1995	-.13[a]	-.03	.06	.13[a]
Regime instability, 1992–95	-.25[b]	-.09	.09	.19[b]
International opportunities for political action				
Support from kindred groups, 1995	-.11	.08	.24[b]	.04
Support from other states, 1995	-.12	.10	.35[b]	.13[a]
Support from regional and international organizations, 1995	.04	.03	.01	.04
Civil conflict in neighboring states, 1995	-.13[a]	.00	.16[b]	.04
Civil conflict in larger region, 1995	-.12	.02	.16[b]	.03
Intercorrelations of protest and rebellion				
Protest, 1996–98	1.00			
Increase in protest, 1995–98	.20[b]	1.00		
Rebellion, 1997–98	-.43[b]	.02	1.00	
Increase in rebellion, 1995–98	-.37[b]	.00	.44[b]	1.00
Type of group				
Ethnonationalists	-.04	-.06	.25[b]	.11
Communal contenders	-.09	-.11	.02	.10
Indigenous peoples	.06	.16[a]	.01	-.07
Ethnoclasses	.04	.04	-.21[b]	-.04
Natonal minorities	-.01	-.03	-.03	-.04
Religious sects	.12[a]	-.01	-.05	-.07

Notes: Indicators are described in appendix B. In logistic regression all indicators are transformed to nominal variables (0 or 1, low or high). The untransformed indicators also were analyzed, with similar but often higher levels of statistical significance. All indicators used in this analysis are included in the full Minorities at Risk data set on the project's Web site or in Web sites linked to it: *www.bsos.umd.edu/cidm/mar.*

[a] $p < .05$

[b] $p < .01$

summarized in chapter 4 showed that severe state repression in the 1980s was more likely to prolong and intensify ethnopolitical conflict than to suppress it. The indicator used as a risk factor is based on profiles of types of state repression first coded in the Minorities project beginning in 1996. The dichotomous version of this indicator (1 for any kind of repression, 0 for none) has a strong short-term relationship with rebellion in 1997–98 and with increases in rebellion 1995–98, but no relationship to protest. The time lag is too short to give decisive support to the theoretical argument. Rebellions tend to persist; they also attract repressive responses. We therefore think that the correlations reported in table B.1 are manifestations of the mutually reinforcing spiral of tit-for-tat coercion during ethnorebellions. When longer time series of data on government repression are available, we expect to do a better job of tracking escalation processes.

Increased political restrictions in 1996. Good time-sensitive measures of changes in political and cultural restrictions were included in the Minorities data set beginning in 1996. We expect that the cumulative effect of new restrictions over several years will provide strong incentives for action, but we have only one year's data to test time-leading relationships. The only significant effect is that increased restrictions in 1996 are correlated with rebellion in 1997–98 (the r is a highly significant .24). Like the results for government repression, this, we think, is a manifestation of the dynamics of ongoing rebellions. Governments often respond to rebellions with new restrictions on rebels as well as with other kinds of repression, both of which add to the rebels' incentives to continue fighting.

III.3 INDICATORS OF CAPACITY FOR POLITICAL ACTION

Territorial concentration. Evidence that territorial concentration is a precondition for most rebellions was summarized in chapter 3. The dichotomous indicator used here distinguishes between groups that are concentrated in one region (whether or not some are dispersed elsewhere), scored 1, and those that are more widely dispersed, scored 0. As expected, concentration is correlated significantly with rebellion in 1997–98 but not with any other conflict indicators.

Group organization 1990–95. The Minorities project has a large but uneven collection of coded information on the kinds of organizations that have acted on behalf of ethnopolitical groups in the 1990s. For the purpose of risk analysis this information is summarized in a dichotomy that distinguishes between groups that are represented by one or more political movements, parties, or organizations and those that have no such organizations or that pursue their interests through umbrella organizations.[5] The indicator has the same effects as territorial concentration: it predicts only to rebellion in 1997–98.

Changes in organizational support. Beginning in 1996 the Minorities at Risk profiles code annual information about changes in support for conventional and militant organizations. Conventional movements and parties are those that rely mainly on noncoercive political techniques including symbolic action, participation in electoral politics, and interest representation. Militant movements and parties rely substantially on coercive political techniques, such as obtaining support by use or threat of force, use of threats or violence against officials and rivals, and campaigns of armed violence. Our expectation is that increased support for these two kinds of organizations should be a short-term leading indicator of increased protest and rebellion, respectively. The correlations in table B.1 show no statistically significant relationships, but multivariate analyses, not reported here, show that when other factors are controlled, increases in support for conventional organizations decrease the likelihood of future rebellion. This finding has important implications for both risk assessments and conflict management.

III.4 INDICATORS OF DOMESTIC OPPORTUNITIES FOR POLITICAL ACTION

Democratic, autocratic, and incoherent polities in 1995. The impact of types of political systems on the forms of ethnopolitical conflict is tested using indicators of institutional democracy and autocracy from the Polity study, described in chapter 5 and appendix A. "Incoherent" polities are regimes with a mix of democratic and autocratic features. The correlations in table B.1 are consistent with theory and other evidence. Democratic polities (regimes that in 1995 had scores greater than 5 on the 0–10 scale of institutional democracy) had more than average protest but less than average rebellion in the late 1990s. Autocratic and incoherent polities, by contrast, had less than average protest but separately were not especially susceptible to rebellion. When these two categories are pooled together, they are seen to have had greater than average rebellion, less than average protest, and greater association with increased rebellion.

Regime instability 1992–95. The "infant mortality" of new political systems is particularly high during their first five years. So are their risks of rebellion, as suggested by some of the evidence developed in chapter 5. That evidence suggested the construction of this indicator: countries with abrupt polity changes in 1992–95 should be at higher risk of rebellion than others. The correlation evidence qualifies this indicator in theoretically interesting ways. Regime instability inhibits protest in 1996–98 but has a leading effect on increases in rebellion. Similarly we find that incoherent polities in 1995 tended ($r = .13$) to have increased rebellion in the late 1990s. We know that incoherent polities are at greater risk of instability than either democracies or autocracies. The implication is that political transformations in incoherent regimes during the 1990s have decreased the strategic value of ethnopolitical protest and increased the utility of rebellion.

III.5 INDICATORS OF INTERNATIONAL OPPORTUNITIES FOR POLITICAL ACTION

Support from kindred groups and foreign states. Coded data from the Minorities project is used to index the presence or absence of support—political, material, military—from kindred groups and from other states in 1995. Both prove to be highly significant leading indicators of rebellion in 1997–98, as shown in table B.1. Support from other states in 1995 also predicts to increases in rebellion from 1995 to 1998. We suspect that the strength of these correlations is amplified by external meddling in ongoing rebellions. These correlations are not irrelevant to risk assessment, however. The implication is that external support, like repressive state responses, may encourage groups to rebel and perpetuate ongoing rebellions and therefore needs to be factored into risk models. A curious finding is that kindred group support is also one of the few factors (with measures of protracted rebellion) associated with decreases in rebellion, indicating that access to cross-border kindred support may make groups more flexible in their relations with the state.[6]

International political support 1995–98. We also want to test the argument that international and regional engagement helps reduce ethnopolitical conflict. Results in table B.1 appear inconsistent with the conventional wisdom, because they show a correlation between international support in 1995–98 and ethno-rebellion in 1997–98. But this says more about effect than cause: international organizations tend to get involved after rebellions have begun. More fine-grained analyses (not reported here) showed that when other factors—including persisting rebellion—were controlled, sustained engagement by international organizations reduced the risks of future rebellion.

Spillover effects of regional conflicts. Two indicators of spillover effects are tested. One is based on the magnitude of civil conflict in 1995 in states that share a common border with the country in which each minority resides; the other takes into account the magnitude of civil conflict in the same year in all states in the larger conflict region. They have similar effects. Protest is significantly less likely and rebellion is more likely in countries in "bad neighborhoods."

III.6 INDICATORS OF GROUP TYPE

Because types of ethnopolitical groups differ in their objectives, they have different propensities to protest and rebellion. To test this argument, the group types (six separate dichotomous indicators) were tested in logistic correlations and in the risk models. Bivariate correlations for five group types are listed in table B.1.

Ethnonationalists were more likely than other types of groups to be in rebellion in 1997–98, with a strongly significant correlation of .25. National minorities have 0-order correlations with all conflict indicators. Indigenous peoples were significantly more likely than any other type of group to have increased protest in the late 1990s but were no more or less likely than any other type of group to engage in rebellion. This finding is consistent with our evidence of sustained increase in activism by indigenous peoples since the 1980s and the observation that the indigenous activists, cooperating through regional and global networks, have developed an effective repertoire of domestic and transnational tactics of protest.[7]

Religious sects were more likely than any other kind of group to use protest in the late 1990s ($r = .12$) but no more or less likely than others to engage in rebellion.

Ethnoclasses are less likely than any other type of group to engage in rebellion; they also are not especially likely to protest. The inference is that ethnoclasses are politically the least active of all group types. Communal contenders do not have any distinctive conflict profile, but a trend analysis (not reported here) showed that they were more likely to engage in rebellion late in the 1990s than earlier.

Appendix C
Additional Groups for the Minorities at Risk Study

Deepa Khosla

New groups are added periodically to the Minorities at Risk case list. This appendix lists groups that have been identified in recent research, and suggested by regional specialists, as meeting the basic criteria for inclusion: they are politically active in defense of group interests or are at risk because of discriminatory policies or escalating challenges from other communal groups. Coded profiles have been prepared and added to the project's Web site. Other new groups also will be posted on the project's Web site.

The groups are listed by region. Population estimates and proportions of country population are for 1998.

Belgium: Flemings and Walloons
Flemings: 5.5 million (57%)
Walloons: 4.0 million (42%)
Politically active since the 1950s
The Dutch-speaking Flemings and the French-speaking Walloons are the principal ethnic groups in Belgium. The Flemings reside in the Flanders region in northern Belgium, and the Walloons are concentrated in Wallonia in the country's south. Since the 1950s, when linguistic-based political parties emerged, Belgium has undergone several constitutional revisions in an effort to balance the interests of the two communities. In 1993, each of the country's three regions (Brussels is the third) were granted further autonomy, including their own governments. Though there has not been any significant intercommunal violence, minority factions in both communities are calling for independence. Residents in the more prosperous Flemish region are resentful that their tax dollars are used to subsidize the poorer Wallonia. The Walloons contend that French-speakers in Flemish areas are discriminated against in seeking employment and housing. In late 1999, Belgium held another round of constitutional talks.

Canada: Anglophones in Quebec
610,000 (2%)

Politically active since 1982

The number of English-speakers in Quebec has steadily declined since the late 1970s as successive pro-Francophone provincial governments have enacted legislation that promotes the use of French over English in the governmental, economic, and educational sectors. Although Canada is officially bilingual, legislation passed in Quebec in 1977 banned the use of English-language signs. Although this law was amended in 1993 to allow for the use of English provided that French was predominant, Anglophones contend that they are second-class citizens in Quebec. They have mobilized politically to press for the equal use of English, including unlimited access to English-language schools and equal visibility for English signs.

United Kingdom: Cornish
480,000 in Cornwall (0.8%)

Politically active since the 1970s

Although there are only a few thousand Cornish-speakers, a resurgence of interest in the Celtic language and culture, coupled with the economic backwardness of the region, has fueled Cornish nationalist demands. During the 1970s, some Cornish pressed for recognition of their separate identity. But a concerted campaign of political lobbying and protest emerged only in the mid-1990s as poverty and unemployment increased due to the closure of many businesses in the region's traditional industries. Cornwall is the poorest region in Britain; this fact has led to Cornish charges of governmental indifference to their economic plight. Since 1997, thousands of Cornish have participated in various demonstrations to press for economic development, recognition of their separate identity, and some form of autonomous status such as that accorded to the Scots and the Welsh.

Tajikistan: Uzbeks
1.4 million (23.1%)

Politically active since 1992

The Uzbeks, who make up around one-quarter of Tajikistan's population, gained political prominence during the 1992–97 civil war between government forces and Tajiki Islamic rebels. The Uzbeks supported the government but by the mid-1990s some group members felt their allegiance was not properly rewarded and they began to press for greater representation in local governments. A minority Uzbeki faction has also supported sporadic rebellions in an effort to oust the regime of President Rahkmonov. To date, the Tajiki

Uzbeks have not raised any demands for autonomy or unification with their kin in neighboring Uzbekistan.

Uzbekistan: Tajiks
1.2 million (5%)
Politically active since 1989
In the early 1990s, the Tajiks politically mobilized to press for the creation of an autonomous republic that would encompass the country's Tajik-dominant regions. The Tajiks were concerned that they would lose their separate identity in a newly independent Uzbekistan. The autonomy movement was short-lived due to low-level repression by federal authorities, divisions within the group, and a lack of external support. The Tajiks did achieve official recognition as a separate nationality group and Tajik was designated as an official language. The protection of their cultural rights remains a primary concern for group members.

Yugoslavia: Montenegrins
679,900 (6%)
Politically active since the 1990s
Although it is a constituent part of the Federal Republic of Yugoslavia, Montenegro has developed a democratic, multiparty, and multiethnic political system. President Djukanovic's government has adopted European standards for human rights and minority rights legislation and helped promote the development of civil society. While the region exercises broad autonomy in terms of the government and the economy, the Djukanovic regime has stopped short of a formal declaration of independence and called for a loose affiliation of Montenegro with Serbia. Montenegro's cooperation with the West during and after the Kosovo crisis has increased the threat of a direct takeover by Belgrade.

China: Christians
15–30 million (1.2–2.4%)
Not politically active
China recognizes only government-registered religious organizations and places of worship, on the basis of which it reports that there are 15 million Catholics and Protestants in the country. Other sources suggest there are some 30 million unofficial adherents, and expectations are that these numbers will continue to grow. Since the mid-1990s the government has cracked down on believers, including Christians, Buddhists, and Muslims. Thousands of house church groups have been destroyed, adherents are subject to harassment, and religious leaders have been arrested and detained for lengthy periods.

China: Mongols

6 million (0.48%)

Politically active since 1989

In 1949, China incorporated Inner Mongolia into the People's Republic of China after the region had experienced a brief period of independence. As in other minority regions, the PRC has pursued policies of assimilation and Sinification in the region. During the 1990s the Mongolians have engaged in violent protests and riots to press for independence or unification with Mongolia or, at the minimum, genuine autonomy. Due to large-scale government transfers of Han Chinese, Mongolians are now reported to be outnumbered by a 4 to 1 ratio. The Mongols contend that economic benefits accrue disproportionately to the Han and that the region has been subject to widespread environmental damage due to nuclear testing.

India: Reang (also referred to as the Bru)

200,000 (0.02%)

Politically active since 1997

The Reang are tribal peoples dispersed across three states in India's northeast: Mizoram, Tripura, and Assam. Asserting that they treated as aliens, the Bru National Union and its militant arm, the Bru National Liberation Front, are seeking the creation of an autonomous development council within Mizoram. Authorities contend that their ultimate objective is the formation of a separate Reangland state made up of portions of Mizoram, Tripura, and Assam. The death of a Mizo forest ranger in 1997, reportedly at the hands of Bru rebels, led Mizos to engage in violent anti-Reang riots. Some 40,000 Bru fled Mizoram, and many continue to reside in neighboring Tripura and Assam. The Reang rebels are reported to have links with major insurgent groups in Assam, Tripura, and Manipur.

India: Christians

18.9 million (1.9%)

Politically active since 1998

Since 1998, attacks by Hindu nationalists against church leaders and Christian properties have been reported in more than half of India's twenty-five states, mostly in the north and the west. Most attacks occurred after the February 1998 electoral victory of the Hindu nationalist Bharatiya Janata Party. Most of India's Christians are members of indigenous tribes or Scheduled Castes, formerly referred to as untouchables. Various Christian associations have organized peaceful demonstrations to protest the violence and urge the government to take action against right-wing Hindu groups.

Indonesia: Dayaks
3.6 million (1.7%)
Politically active since 1994

The Dayaks are indigenous peoples who reside primarily in Kalimantan on the island of Borneo, one of the poorest regions of Indonesia. The mostly Christian Dayaks are concerned with encroachments on their land by businesses and migrants and the protection of their lifeways. Many Muslim Madurese and Javanese migrants have been settled in the region through the government's transmigration program. Violent clashes between the Dayaks and migrants have occurred since 1996 along with Dayak protests against their treatment by governmental officials. There have been some calls for an independent Dayak republic. The Indonesian Dayaks are kindred to the politically active Dayaks of Malaysian North Borneo.

Burma: Karenni (also referred to as Kayah)
270,000 (0.6%)
Politically active since 1946

The Kayah are among numerous subgroups that constitute the mostly Christian Karenni indigenous peoples. As with their ethnic kin, the Karen, the Karenni unsuccessfully sought to preserve their autonomy prior to the country's independence. An armed struggle arose shortly after the 1948 independence declaration. Since then, successive governments have relied on military means to suppress the Karenni and other minority groups seeking autonomy or secession. During the mid-1990s the Myanmar junta was able to negotiate cease-fire agreements with several minorities, including the Karenni. However, by 1995 the main Kayah organization, the Karenni National Progressive Party, had resumed armed rebellion.

Burma: Wa
500,000 (1%)
Politically active since 1974

Prior to the late 1980s the Wa, indigenous peoples who are located in Shan state, primarily pursued their political objectives through umbrella organizations such as the former Burmese Communist Party (BCP). In 1989 they formed the United Wa State Army to press for autonomy. The UWSA signed a cease-fire agreement with the military regime in the same year, but by 1994 dissatisfaction over the lack of implementation, especially regarding the promotion of development projects, led the rebels to resume armed struggle. During the early and mid-1990s, the Wa were also involved in violent intercommunal conflicts with the Shan people.

Pakistan: Christians

2.6 million (2%)

Politically active since 1991

The Christians are among Pakistan's poorest people, and in the 1990s they have mobilized to protest against government policies and violent attacks against their community by the majority Muslims. Along with the requirement that each citizen carry an identity card that lists his or her religious affiliation, Christians and other religious minorities have been subject to harassment and discrimination as a result of a vague blasphemy law enacted in 1993. Christian organizations are seeking equal rights for their community, including compensation for victims of religious violence and state protection against future incidents.

Pakistan: Sarakis

19.4 million (14%)

Politically active since the 1990s

Since the 1990s the Sarakis have sought recognition as a separate nationality based on their language, Saraki. They straddle Punjab and Sindh provinces and are demanding the creation of a new province of Sarakistan. Thus far they have pursued their goals through conventional political means, including an alliance with Pakistan's other non-Punjabi ethnic groups, all of whom contend that Punjabis dominate the country's economic, military, and political structures.

Pakistan: Shi'is

19.5 million (14%)

Politically active since 1984

Intercommunal violence between the minority Shi'i and majority Sunni Muslim communities since the mid-1980s has claimed thousands of lives in Pakistan. Violent attacks have occurred in all four of Pakistan's provinces, although Shi'is are concentrated in Punjab province. They have engaged in numerous political protests demanding protection of their religious rights and opposing large-scale attacks against their community by Sunni extremist groups who contend that the Shi'is are not Muslims.

Sri Lanka: Muslims

1.34 million (7.1%)

Politically active since the 1980s

Over a third of the country's Muslims reside in the north and east of Sri Lanka, where the Tamil rebel group, the LTTE, has been waging a violent fifteen-year campaign for independence. Since the mid-1980s the Muslims, who primarily speak Tamil, have been drawn into the Tamil conflict as targets of violent attacks by the Tamil rebels. Hundreds of Muslims have been killed, and over one hundred thousand have fled northern areas. Politically the Muslims are seeking a separate regional council in the east to protect their interests and identity. Though the Sri Lankan government's 1995 devolution plan provides autonomy in Muslim-majority areas, the plan has been rejected by the LTTE.

Liberia: Gios, Krahns, Mandingoes
Gios: 175,000 (6.3%)
Krahns: 95,000 (3.4%)
Mandingoes: 45,500 (1.6%)
Politically active since the 1980s
Most of Liberia's population consists of indigenous tribes such as the Gios, Krahns, and Mandingoes. Although the Americo-Liberians, who are descendants of freed American slaves, constitute a very small minority, they have controlled the country's political and economic structures for over 130 years. In 1980, a military coup by a Krahn, Samuel Doe, broke the Americo-Liberians' dominance. During Doe's autocratic rule his Krahn tribe, along with the Mandingoes, who over the past few centuries had migrated to the country from neighboring states, received the bulk of the government's political and economic patronage. An abortive coup attempt in 1985 supported by the Gio and Mano groups resulted in violent reprisals by the Krahns. In 1989, an Americo-Liberian, Charles Taylor, launched what was to be an eight-year civil war in which up to two hundred thousand Liberians died. Supported by the Gio and Mano, Taylor's forces deposed Doe and sought violent retaliation against the Krahns and Mandingoes. A peace agreement between the various parties, including the Economic Community of West African States, led to elections in 1997, in which Taylor was elected president. Since then, Krahns and Mandingoes have been targeted in violent attacks by Taylor's supporters.

Namibia: Caprivi
100,000 (6.2%)
Politically active since the 1990s
The majority of the residents of the Caprivi Strip, a remote stretch in Namibia's northeast, are Lozi-speakers whose ethnic kin are located across the border in Zambia. The Caprivi encompass at least three tribal groups, and they have the country's lowest per capita income. In October 1998, the Namibian government began a security crackdown on the region to counter a fledgling separatist movement led by the Caprivi Liberation Army. The Caprivi claim that

they are seeking to protect their cultural identity. Over twenty-five hundred Caprivians who fled to Botswana in the ensuing months refuse to return to Namibia while residents in the Caprivi Strip report harassment by security forces.

Nigeria: Ijaw
8 million (7.2%)
Politically active since 1992
Most Ijaw reside in the Niger Delta, whose vast oil reserves produce 90 percent of the country's hard currency earnings. The Christian Ijaws, who are subdivided by dialect, are the largest and poorest community in the delta and the fourth largest ethnic group in Nigeria. Since 1998, various tribal organizations have engaged in numerous protests, including occupying the facilities of oil companies and taking hostages, in a campaign for more economic development and political participation in the region. Some elements within the group are now calling for autonomy and even independence. Governmental repression of the Ijaws was reported in 1998 and 1999.

Sudan: Copts
200,000 (0.6%)
Politically active since 1983
The Sudanese Copts are followers of the Egyptian Coptic Orthodox Church. Since the early 1980s, when *shari'a* law was imposed in the Sudan, the Copts have been subject to various forms of political, economic, and religious discrimination, including restrictions on obtaining citizenship and employment in the government and banking sectors. At least twenty-five thousand Copts have fled the country. Previously, the mainly northern-based Copts were a professional, educated class. Although the Copts have participated in Christian organizations that have used conventional means to oppose the Islamicization process, they have not joined the armed rebellion of the southerners, many of whom also are Christians.

Sudan: Nuba
850,000 (2.5%)
Politically active since 1985
Although they are black Africans like the people of southern Sudan, the Nuba consider themselves to be northerners (who are mainly Arab Muslims). Most live in the Nuba Mountains near the center of the country. Many have adopted Arab culture, but the community consists of both Muslims and Christians. The Nuba cooperated with the southern rebel movement in the

1980s in order to counter the north's efforts to Islamicize the country. Since then they have been subject to genocidal actions by government forces, especially after 1992, when a jihad was declared against the region. In the latter half of the 1990s, some one hundred thousand to two hundred thousand Nuba are thought to have been killed or to have died from starvation. Thousands of others have been forcibly relocated into government "peace camps," and some quarter of a million have fled to regions under the control of the southern rebels.

Tanzania: Zanzibaris
700,000 (2.3%)
Politically active since the 1990s
The twin islands of Unguja and Pemba, collectively referred to as Zanzibar, were ruled for centuries by the sultan of Oman. In 1964, newly independent Zanzibar joined mainland Tanzania. Zanzibaris are overwhelmingly Muslim but are divided between a majority who are of African or mixed descent (Shirazi) and the Arab minority, who prior to independence dominated the island's political and economic structures. Violent communal conflicts between the two groups first surfaced in the 1960s. These tensions reemerged in the 1990s, especially as the majority of Zanzibaris (most Arabs and many Shirazi) demanded greater autonomy. Controversial elections on the islands in 1995, in which the country's ruling party was declared the winner over the islands' pro-autonomy party, have exacerbated relations between Zanzibar and Tanzania. In 1997, a number of leaders of the pro-autonomy party were charged with conspiracy to overthrow the Zanzibar government.

Trinidad and Tobago: Africans and East Indians
Africans: 600,000 (43%)
East Indians: 520,000 (40%)
Politically active since the 1950s
Trinidad and Tobago's Africans are the descendants of slaves and West Indians who migrated to the region in the late 1800s. They are largely an urban, professional class, most of whom reside on the larger island of Trinidad. The East Indians, who live mainly in rural areas, trace their roots to South Asia, primarily India. The majority of Africans are Christians; Hinduism is the religion of most East Indians. For most of Trinidad and Tobago's thirty-seven years of independence, Africans have held political power, largely through the People's National Movement. However, since elections in 1995, the country has its first East Indian prime minister and a primarily East Indian cabinet. Africans now fear that they will be subject to discrimination, and the East Indians believe that their years of limited political participation have been corrected.

Although violent intercommunal conflict has not broken out, tensions are high as social organizations of each communal group intensify their rhetoric against the other. There is also a nonviolent separatist movement on the island of Tobago.

Appendix D
Background Characteristics of Ethnopolitical Groups and Risk of Rebellion

Anne Pitsch

Tables D.1 through D.6 each present information on a region, sorted alphabetically by country and group.

The following variables are listed in the tables.

Country: country in which the group resides.

Group: full name of the group. Where two similar groups are combined for the purposes of coding, both names are given, separated by a comma. Where a group has a common alternative name, it is given in parentheses.

GPOP98: estimated group population (in 000s) for 1998 based on the U.S. Census Bureau's estimate of country population for 1998. The bases of group population estimates are discussed in appendix E.

CPOP98: estimated country population (in 000s) for 1998 (U.S. Census Bureau).

PROP98: estimate of group size as a proportion of the country population.

Type: type of the group. See chapter 1, pp. 16–18.

Risk Indicator: risks of future rebellion, or escalating current rebellion, based on conditions measured in 1998. Scores of greater than 0.5 signify substantial risks. See chapter 7 for a discussion of how the index is derived.

Table D.1. Background Characteristics of Ethnopolitical Groups and Risk of Rebellion: Western Democracies and Japan

Country	Group	GPOP98	CPOP98	PROP98	Type	Risk Indicator
Australia	Aborigines	261	18613	0.0140	indigenous	-3.98
Canada	French Canadians	1166	30675	0.0380	ethnonational	-5.30
Canada	Indigenous peoples	951	30675	0.0310	indigenous	-3.98
Canada	Quebecois	5583	30675	0.1820	ethnonational	-3.34
France	Basques	259	58805	0.0044	ethnonational	0.77
France	Corsicans	365	58805	0.0062	ethnonational	-0.54
France	Muslims (noncitizens)	2235	58805	0.0380	ethnoclass	-0.18
France	Roma (Gypsies)	312	58805	0.0053	ethnoclass	-7.03
Germany	Turks	1970	82079	0.0240	ethnoclass	0.03
Greece	Muslims	128	10662	0.0120	religious sect	-3.87
Greece	Roma (Gypsies)	181	10662	0.0170	ethnoclass	-5.30
Italy	Roma (Gypsies)	99	56783	0.0018	ethnoclass	-7.03
Italy	Sardinians	1647	56783	0.0290	ethnonational	-3.34
Italy	South Tyrolians	290	56783	0.0051	national minority	-2.13

Country	Group					
Japan	Koreans	71	125932	0.0056	ethnoclass	-4.08
New Zealand	Maori	352	3625	0.0970	indigenous	-5.30
Nordic countries	Saami	65	18456	0.0035	indigenous	-5.30
Spain	Basques	2113	39134	0.0540	ethnonational	0.77
Spain	Catalans	6261	39134	0.1600	national minority	-3.34
Spain	Roma (Gypsies)	744	39134	0.0190	ethnoclass	-4.23
Switzerland	Foreign workers	1408	7260	0.1940	ethnoclass	-7.03
Switzerland	Jurassians	160	7260	0.0220	national minority	-5.08
United Kingdom	Afro-Caribbeans	1179	58970	0.0200	ethnoclass	-7.03
United Kingdom	Asians	1651	58970	0.0280	ethnoclass	-5.72
United Kingdom	Catholics in Northern Ireland	702	58970	0.0119	ethnonational	0.03
United Kingdom	Scots	5661	58970	0.0960	ethnonational	-5.30
United States of America	African Americans	33519	270312	0.1240	ethnoclass	-1.18
United States of America	Hispanics	27032	270312	0.1000	ethnoclass	-2.03
United States of America	Native Americans	2119	270312	0.0078	indigenous	-2.03
United States of America	Native Hawaiians	330	270312	0.0012	indigenous	-5.30

Table D.2. Background Characteristics of Ethnopolitical Groups and Risk of Rebellion: Eastern Europe and the NIS

Country	Group	GPOP98	CPOP98	PROP98	Type	Risk Indicator
Albania	Greeks	117	3331	0.0350	national minority	−2.43
Azerbaijan	Armenians	181	7856	0.0230	national minority	2.10
Azerbaijan	Lezgins	196	7856	0.0250	indigenous	−3.86
Azerbaijan	Russians	1964	7856	0.2500	national minority	−4.38
Belarus	Poles	427	10409	0.0410	national minority	−0.70
Belarus	Russians	1374	10409	0.1320	national minority	−2.65
Bosnia	Croats	740	3366	0.2200	national minority	−0.70
Bosnia	Muslims	1279	3366	0.3800	ethnonational	0.15
Bosnia	Serbs	1346	3366	0.4000	national minority	0.89
Bulgaria	Roma	733	8240	0.0890	ethnoclass	−7.03
Bulgaria	Turks	700	8240	0.0850	national minority	−2.13
Croatia	Roma	35	4872	0.0075	ethnoclass	−5.30
Croatia	Serbs	247	4872	0.0530	national minority	0.67
Czech Republic	Roma	267	10286	0.0260	ethnoclass	−2.50
Czech Republic	Slovaks	309	10286	0.0300	ethnonational	−2.13
Estonia	Russians	408	1421	0.2870	national minority	1.98
Georgia	Abkhazians	89	5109	0.0175	ethnonational	−0.82
Georgia	Adzhars	296	5109	0.0580	ethnonational	−2.13
Georgia	Ossetians (South)	163	5109	0.0320	ethnonational	−0.82
Georgia	Russians	245	5109	0.0480	national minority	−2.77
Hungary	Roma	572	10208	0.0560	ethnoclass	−5.30
Kazakhstan	Germans	522	16847	0.0310	national minority	−2.43
Kazakhstan	Russians	5846	16847	0.3470	national minority	−0.70

Kyrgyzstan	Russians	814	4522	0.1800	national minority	0.15
Kyrgyzstan	Uzbeks	583	4522	0.1290	national minority	-0.70
Latvia	Russians	821	2385	0.3440	national minority	-4.08
Lithuania	Poles	252	3600	0.0700	national minority	-2.13
Lithuania	Russians	313	3600	0.0870	national minority	-5.30
Macedonia	Albanians	460	2009	0.2290	national minority	-2.03
Macedonia	Roma	241	2009	0.1200	ethnoclass	-3.34
Macedonia	Serbs	48	2009	0.0240	national minority	-3.34
Moldova	Gagauz	156	4458	0.0350	national minority	-3.34
Moldova	Slavs	1195	4458	0.2680	national minority	0.67
Romania	Magyars (Hungarians)	1993	22396	0.0890	national minority	0.15
Romania	Roma (Gypsies)	2083	22396	0.0930	ethnoclass	-3.86
Russia	Avars	543	146881	0.0037	ethnonational	-0.54
Russia	Buryat	411	146881	0.0028	indigenous	-2.13
Russia	Chechens	896	146881	0.0061	indigenous	-0.82
Russia	Ingush	235	146881	0.0016	indigenous	0.77
Russia	Karachay	147	146881	0.0010	indigenous	-3.34
Russia	Kumyks	250	146881	0.0017	ethnonational	-3.34
Russia	Lezgins	2497	146881	0.0170	indigenous	-2.03
Russia	Roma	294	146881	0.0020	ethnoclass	-4.23
Russia	Tatars	5581	146881	0.0380	ethnonational	-5.08
Russia	Tuvinians	206	146881	0.0014	indigenous	-3.34
Russia	Yakut	382	146881	0.0026	indigenous	-2.13
Slovakia	Hungarians	582	5393	0.1080	national minority	-2.13
Slovakia	Roma	502	5393	0.0930	ethnoclass	-5.30
Tajikistan	Russians	210	6020	0.0350	national minority	-2.43

continued on next page

Table D.2. (cont.)

Country	Group	GPOP98	CPOP98	PROP98	Type	Risk Indicator
Turkmenistan	Russians	288	4298	0.0670	national minority	–5.82
Ukraine	Crimean Russians	1654	50125	0.0330	national minority	1.98
Ukraine	Crimean Tatars	251	50125	0.0050	ethnonational	1.98
Ukraine	Russians	11028	50125	0.2200	national minority	–3.87
Uzbekistan	Russians	1308	23784	0.0550	national minority	–5.82
Yugoslavia	Croats	134	10526	0.0120	national minority	–2.13
Yugoslavia	Hungarians	448	10526	0.0400	national minority	0.67
Yugoslavia	Kosovar Albanians	1569	10526	0.1400	national minority	1.98
Yugoslavia	Roma	421	10526	0.0400	ethnoclass	–7.03
Yugoslavia	Sandzak Muslims	206	10526	0.0184	religious sect	0.77

Table D.3. Background Characteristics of Ethnopolitical Groups and Risk of Rebellion: East, Southeast, and South Asia

Country	Group	GPOP98	CPOP98	PROP98	Type	Risk Indicator
Afghanistan	Hazaris	4711	24782	0.1900	communal contender	2.10
Afghanistan	Pashtuns	9421	24782	0.3800	communal contender	-0.70
Afghanistan	Tajiks	6198	24782	0.2500	communal contender	2.10
Afghanistan	Uzbeks	1488	24782	0.0600	communal contender	2.10
Bangladesh	Biharis	255	127567	0.0020	national minority	0.03
Bangladesh	Chittagong Hill tribes	765	127567	0.0060	indigenous	0.67
Bangladesh	Hindus	13395	127567	0.1050	religious sect	-7.03
Bhutan	Lhotshampas	668	1908	0.3500	national minority	0.67
Burma	Kachins	710	47305	0.0150	indigenous	-0.54
Burma	Karens	3311	47305	0.0700	ethnonational	0.67
Burma	Mons	946	47305	0.0200	indigenous	-1.07
Burma	Rohingya (Arakanese)	1314	47305	0.0320	indigenous	0.67
Burma	Shans	4257	47305	0.0900	ethnonational	0.67
Burma	Zomis (Chins)	993	47305	0.0210	indigenous	0.67
Cambodia	Vietnamese	340	11340	0.0300	national minority	-4.38
China	Hui Muslims	8658	1236915	0.0070	religious sect	-4.23
China	Tibetans	5442	1236915	0.0044	ethnonational	0.67
China	Turkmen	8658	1236915	0.0070	indigenous	1.98
Fiji	Fijians	401	803	0.5000	communal contender	-5.30
Fiji	Indians	345	803	0.4300	communal contender	-1.28
India	Assamese	12792	984004	0.0130	indigenous	0.67
India	Bodos	4920	984004	0.0050	indigenous	0.67

continued on next page

Table D.3. (cont.)

Country	Group	GPOP98	CPOP98	PROP98	Type	Risk Indicator
India	Kashmiris	6888	984004	0.0070	ethnonational	1.98
India	Mizos	590	984004	0.0006	indigenous	−3.34
India	Muslims	112176	984004	0.1140	religious sect	0.03
India	Nagas	3050	984004	0.0031	indigenous	−0.54
India	Scheduled tribes	76752	984004	0.0780	indigenous	0.77
India	Sikhs	13680	984004	0.0200	ethnonational	0.67
India	Tripuras	787	984004	0.0008	indigenous	1.98
Indonesia	Acehense	3620	212942	0.0170	ethnonational	0.67
Indonesia	Chinese	5749	212942	0.0270	ethnoclass	−1.28
Indonesia	East Timorese	852	212942	0.0040	ethnonational	1.98
Indonesia	Papuans	1065	212942	0.0050	indigenous	0.67
Laos	Hmong	210	5261	0.0400	indigenous	0.67
Malaysia	Chinese	5652	20933	0.2700	communal contender	−2.50
Malaysia	Dayaks	628	20933	0.0300	indigenous	−3.34
Malaysia	Indians	1675	20933	0.0800	communal contender	−2.50
Malaysia	Kadazans	607	20933	0.0290	indigenous	−3.34
Pakistan	Ahmadis	4730	135135	0.0350	religious sect	−1.28

Pakistan	Baluchis	5405	135135	0.0400	national minority	-0.54
Pakistan	Hindus	2703	135135	0.0200	religious sect	-1.07
Pakistan	Mohajirs	10811	135135	0.0800	communal contender	-1.18
Pakistan	Pashtuns (Pushtuns)	10811	135135	0.0800	communal contender	-0.54
Pakistan	Sindhis	16216	135135	0.1200	communal contender	-0.54
Papua New Guinea	Bouganvillians	138	4600	0.0300	ethnonational	-2.13
Philippines	Igorots	1088	77726	0.0140	indigenous	-3.34
Philippines	Moros	3886	77726	0.0500	ethnonational	0.67
Singapore	Malays	520	3490	0.1490	national minority	-5.30
South Korea	Honamese	6081	46417	0.1310	communal contender	-5.08
Sri Lanka	Indian Tamils	1136	18934	0.0600	ethnoclass	0.03
Sri Lanka	Sri Lankan Tamils	2272	18934	0.1200	ethnonational	0.67
Taiwan	Aboriginal Taiwanese	372	21908	0.0170	indigenous	0.77
Taiwan	Mainland Chinese	3067	-21908	0.1400	communal contender	-3.02
Taiwan	Taiwanese	18403	21908	0.8400	communal contender	-2.92
Thailand	Chinese	6604	60037	0.1100	ethnoclass	-7.03
Thailand	Malay-Muslims	1801	60037	0.0300	national minority	0.67
Thailand	Northern hill tribes	600	60037	0.0100	indigenous	-2.28
Vietnam	Chinese	1067	76236	0.0140	ethnoclass	-5.82
Vietnam	Montagnards	1296	76236	0.0170	indigenous	0.67

Table D.4. Background Characteristics of Ethnopolitical Groups and Risk of Rebellion: North Africa and the Middle East

Country	Group	GPOP98	CPOP98	PROP98	Type	Risk Indicator
Algeria	Berbers	7620	30481	0.2500	indigenous	0.62
Bahrain	Shi'a	539	618	0.8700	religious sect	-1.28
Cyprus	Turkish Cypriots	142	749	0.1900	ethnonational	-2.13
Egypt	Copts	5944	66050	0.0900	religious sect	-4.23
Iran	Arabs	2069	68960	0.0300	national minority	-5.08
Iran	Azerbaijanis	16550	68960	0.2400	national minority	-5.08
Iran	Baha'is	593	68960	0.0086	religious sect	-1.28
Iran	Bakhtiari	690	68960	0.0100	indigenous	-5.08
Iran	Baluchis	1379	68960	0.0200	indigenous	-5.08
Iran	Christians	310	68960	0.0045	religious sect	-4.23
Iran	Kurds	4827	68960	0.0700	ethnonational	-5.08
Iran	Turkmen	1379	68960	0.0200	national minority	-5.08
Iraq	Kurds	4244	21722	0.2000	ethnonational	0.77

Iraq	Shi'is	13033	21722	0.6000	religious sect	1.98
Iraq	Sunnis	4344	21722	0.2000	communal contender	-7.03
Israel	Arabs	1015	5644	0.1800	ethnoclass	0.77
Israel	Palestinians	2431	8255	0.2945	ethnonational	1.98
Jordan	Palestinians	2217	4435	0.5000	ethnonational	-2.77
Lebanon	Druze	210	3506	0.0600	communal contender	-3.34
Lebanon	Maronite Christians	876	3506	0.2500	communal contender	-3.34
Lebanon	Palestinians	350	3506	0.1000	ethnonational	-1.28
Lebanon	Shi'is	1122	3506	0.3200	communal contender	1.98
Lebanon	Sunnis	701	3506	0.2000	communal contender	-5.30
Morocco	Berbers	10859	29347	0.3700	communal contender	-3.34
Morocco	Saharawis	229	29347	0.0078	indigenous	0.67
Saudi Arabia	Shi'is	3118	20786	0.1500	ethnonational	-2.13
Syria	Alawi	1834	16673	0.1100	religious sect	-5.08
Turkey	Kurds	12913	54567	0.2000	communal contender	1.98

Table D.5. Background Characteristics of Ethnopolitical Groups and Risk of Rebellion: Africa South of the Sahara

Country	Group	GPOP98	CPOP98	PROP98	Type	Risk Indicator
Angola	Bakongo	1412	10865	0.1300	communal contender	0.89
Angola	Cabinda	196	10865	0.0180	communal contender	0.89
Angola	Ovimbundu	4020	10865	0.3700	communal contender	2.10
Botswana	San Bushmen	43	1448	0.0300	indigenous	−2.28
Burundi	Hutus	4707	5537	0.8500	communal contender	1.47
Burundi	Tutsis	775	5537	0.1400	communal contender	−2.65
Cameroon	Bamileke	4058	15029	0.2700	communal contender	−3.77
Cameroon	Kirdis	1653	15029	0.1100	indigenous	−5.08
Cameroon	Westerners	3006	15029	0.2000	communal contender	0.25
Chad	Southerners	2737	7360	0.3800	communal contender	0.77
Congo (former Zaire)	Hutus	1470	49001	0.0300	ethnoclass	−3.65
Congo (former Zaire)	Luba	1960	49001	0.0400	communal contender	−0.85
Congo (former Zaire)	Lunda, Yeke	980	49001	0.0200	communal contender	−3.65
Congo (former Zaire)	Ngbandi	980	49001	0.0200	communal contender	−3.65
Congo (former Zaire)	Tutsis	980	49001	0.0200	ethnoclass	2.10
Djibouti	Afars	154	441	0.3500	indigenous	−3.34
Eritrea	Afars	154	3842	0.0400	ethnonational	−2.13
Ethiopia	Afars	2336	58390	0.0400	indigenous	0.89
Ethiopia	Amhara	14598	58390	0.2500	communal contender	−1.91
Ethiopia	Oromo	23356	58390	0.4000	communal contender	−0.70
Ethiopia	Somalis	3503	58390	0.0600	indigenous	0.89
Ethiopia	Tigreans	5839	58390	0.1000	communal contender	−3.65
Ghana	Ashanti	5179	18497	0.2800	communal contender	−3.65

Country	Group					
Ghana	Ewe	2405	18497	0.1300	communal contender	-3.65
Ghana	Mossi–Dagomba	2960	18497	0.1600	communal contender	-3.65
Guinea	Fulani	2243	7477	0.3000	communal contender	-0.85
Guinea	Malinka	2243	7477	0.3000	communal contender	-3.65
Guinea	Susu	1495	7477	0.2000	communal contender	-3.65
Kenya	Kalenjin	3400	28337	0.1200	indigenous	-3.65
Kenya	Kikuyu	6234	28337	0.2200	communal contender	0.37
Kenya	Kisii	1700	28337	0.0600	communal contender	-2.43
Kenya	Luhya	3967	28337	0.1400	communal contender	0.37
Kenya	Luo	3684	28337	0.1300	communal contender	0.37
Kenya	Maasai	425	28337	0.0150	indigenous	-3.65
Madagascar	Merina	3616	14463	0.2500	communal contender	-3.34
Mali	Tuareg	607	10106	0.0600	communal contender	-3.87
Mauritania	Black Moors	817	2511	0.3500	ethnoclass	-4.23
Mauritania	Kewri	879	2511	0.3500	communal contender	-1.07
Namibia	Basters	41	1622	0.0250	ethnonational	-3.34
Namibia	Europeans	81	1622	0.0500	ethnoclass	-7.03
Namibia	San Bushmen	49	1622	0.0300	indigenous	-2.28
Niger	Tuareg	774	9672	0.0800	ethnonational	-3.34
Nigeria	Ibo	18790	110532	0.1700	communal contender	-1.91
Nigeria	Ogani	553	110532	0.0050	communal contender	2.10
Nigeria	Yoruba	22106	110532	0.2000	communal contender	1.68
Rwanda	Hutus	6365	7956	0.8000	communal contender	0.15
Rwanda	Tutsis	1512	7956	0.1900	communal contender	-2.65
Senegal	Diolas in Casamance	875	9723	0.0900	ethnonational	0.67
Sierra Leone	Creoles	102	5080	0.0200	ethnoclass	-5.60

continued on next page

Table D.5. *(cont.)*

Country	Group	GPOP98	CPOP98	PROP98	Type	Risk Indicator
Sierra Leone	Limba	406	5080	0.0800	communal contender	-3.65
Sierra Leone	Mende	1534	5080	0.3000	communal contender	-1.91
Sierra Leone	Temne	1524	5080	0.3000	communal contender	0.89
Somalia	Isaaq	821	6842	0.1200	communal contender	-0.70
South Africa	Asians	1114	42835	0.0260	communal contender	-7.03
South Africa	Coloreds	3684	42835	0.0860	communal contender	-3.77
South Africa	Europeans	5568	42835	0.1300	communal contender	-5.30
South Africa	Xhosa	7282	42835	0.1700	communal contender	-5.08
South Africa	Zulus	6125	42835	0.1430	communal contender	-3.34
Sudan	Southerners	8388	33551	0.2500	ethnonational	0.67
Togo	Ewe	2159	4906	0.4400	communal contender	-0.97
Togo	Kabre	1128	4906	0.2300	communal contender	-5.08
Uganda	Acholi	887	22167	0.0400	communal contender	-1.07
Uganda	Baganda	3547	22167	0.1600	ethnonational	-5.08
Zambia	Bemba	2554	9461	0.2700	communal contender	-1.91
Zambia	Lozi	473	9461	0.0500	communal contender	0.89
Zimbabwe	Europeans	99	11044	0.0090	ethnoclass	-5.30
Zimbabwe	Ndebele	1767	11044	0.1600	communal contender	-0.54

Table D.6. Background Characteristics of Ethnopolitical Groups and Risk of Rebellion: Latin America and the Caribbean

Country	Group	GPOP98	CPOP98	PROP98	Type	Risk Indicator
Argentina	Indigenous peoples	363	36285	0.0100	indigenous	−5.08
Bolivia	Highland indigenous peoples	4304	7828	0.5500	indigenous	0.67
Bolivia	Lowland indigenous peoples	157	7828	0.0200	indigenous	0.67
Brazil	Afro-Brazilians	82186	169806	0.4840	ethnoclass	−3.34
Brazil	Amazonian Indians	278	169806	0.0020	indigenous	−0.54
Chile	Indigenous peoples	621	14787	0.0420	indigenous	−5.30
Colombia	Blacks	1543	38581	0.0400	ethnoclass	−5.08
Colombia	Indigenous peoples	386	38581	0.0100	indigenous	−0.54
Costa Rica	Antillean Blacks	72	3605	0.0200	ethnoclass	−5.08
Dominican Republic	Haitian Blacks	800	7999	0.1000	ethnoclass	0.37
Ecuador	Blacks	1234	12337	0.1000	ethnoclass	−5.08
Ecuador	Indigenous highland peoples	3516	12337	0.2850	indigenous	0.77
Ecuador	Lowland indigenous peoples	123	12337	0.0100	indigenous	−0.82
El Salvador	Indigenous peoples	288	5752	0.0500	indigenous	−3.34
Guatemala	Indigenous peoples	5043	12008	0.4200	indigenous	0.62
Guyana	Africans	276	708	0.3900	communal contender	−2.50
Guyana	East Indians	345	708	0.5000	communal contender	−5.30
Honduras	Black Karibs	117	5862	0.0200	ethnoclass	−3.34
Honduras	Indigenous peoples	410	5862	0.0700	indigenous	−5.08
Mexico	Mayans	1084	98553	0.0110	indigenous	0.77
Mexico	Other indigenous peoples	6209	98553	0.0630	indigenous	−2.50
Mexico	Zapotecs	591	98553	0.0060	indigenous	−3.34

continued on next page

Table D.6. (cont.)

Country	Group	GPOP98	CPOP98	PROP98	Type	Risk Indicator
Nicaragua	Indigenous peoples	229	4583	0.0500	indigenous	1.98
Panama	Blacks	356	2736	0.1300	ethnoclass	−7.03
Panama	Chinese	109	2736	0.0400	ethnoclass	−7.03
Panama	Indigenous peoples	164	2736	0.0600	indigenous	−3.34
Paraguay	Indigenous peoples	106	5291	0.0200	indigenous	−4.08
Peru	Blacks (Afro-Peruvians)	261	26111	0.0100	ethnoclass	−3.34
Peru	Highland indigenous peoples	9922	26111	0.3800	indigenous	−0.54
Peru	Lowland indigenous peoples	313	26111	0.0120	indigenous	−0.54
Venezuela	Blacks	2280	22803	0.1000	ethnoclass	−5.08
Venezuela	Indigenous peoples	342	22803	0.0150	indigenous	−0.54

Appendix E
Estimating 1990s Populations of Groups in the Minorities at Risk Study

Ted Robert Gurr and Marion Recktenwald

Because communal groups are cultural entities rather than territorially bounded political communities, there are no standard sources or procedures for estimating their populations.[1] Rather, there are multiple sources and different bases for estimating group size. The 1999 update of the Minorities at Risk (MAR) data set includes new group population estimates for 1995 and 1998, expressed in two forms: as a proportion of country population and as an absolute number, rounded to the nearest thousand.

The 1995 and 1998 estimates were arrived at by the authors based on a systematic review of existing data and sources, using standardized procedures for resolving discrepancies. The procedures and guidelines are described in this appendix. It must be emphasized that all estimates of group size, in the MAR data set and elsewhere, are inherently arbitrary and imprecise. We have sought to reduce the appearance of precision by rounding to the nearest thousand, but for most groups we could easily have rounded to the nearest ten thousand or hundred thousand without any loss of relative accuracy. Similarly, proportions have been rounded to the nearest thousandth, sometimes hundredth, depending on the reliability of the source data. Further rounding is not appropriate, because these proportions will be used for future estimations of group population size. Note also that population estimates for years prior to 1995 in previous versions of the MAR data set have not been revised.

General Procedures

All estimates of group size in the MAR data set are derived from estimates of the group's proportion of country population in a target year. The general procedure is to identify the most reliable recent estimate of the group's size as a proportion of country population. The proportion then is applied to U.S. Census Bureau estimates of country population for 1995 and 1998.[2] Some sources report group size in percentages, in which case the task usually is simple. Other sources report estimates of absolute numbers. When using absolute numbers, we express the number as a proportion of total country population for the year of reference: for example, if the estimate is derived from a 1989 census, we express the estimate as a proportion of the country's 1989 population. The 1995 and 1998 estimates of group size then are determined by applying the proportion derived from the 1989 data to country population estimates for those years.

Sources of Data

Our first step was to list existing estimates of group population from Minority at Risk files for 1990 and 1995 and to cross-check them against general sources. The most comprehensive source of estimates is the Central Intelligence Agency's *World Factbook 1998,* which reports group size in percentages of country population but does not specify sources.[3] We also checked demographic estimates in reports from Minority Rights Group, some of which provided comparative information that we regarded as superior—because more internally consistent and detailed than others. For groups in the Soviet and Yugoslav successor states, we checked data from the USSR's 1989 census and Yugoslavia's 1981 census, respectively.[4] These had provided the basis for the MAR data set's 1990 and 1995 estimates and also, by inspection, proved to be the source of estimates in the CIA's *Factbook.* For African groups we checked the data reported in the second edition of *Black Africa: A Comparative Handbook.*[5] This source was used in previous MAR work and proved, again by inspection, to be the principal source of the CIA's African estimates. Some countries regularly report census and intercensal data on the populations of minority groups and regions—for example, most Western European countries; the British Commonwealth, including India and Canada; South Africa; and the United States. We took current data for these countries mainly from recent editions of *The Statesman's Year-Book,* a London-based publication that consistently reports census and other statistical data from country sources.[6]

These sources and others cited in the list that follows often provided discrepant estimates. Literally hundreds of decisions had to be made about which were most reliable. In general, we used the following order of precedence:

For groups enumerated in censuses, the census reports as summarized in the sources identified earlier. In the Soviet and Yugoslav successor states, for example, we used the republic-level data from their 1989 and 1981 censuses, respectively, with a few adjustments noted below.

For indigenous populations in Latin America, the census and expert estimates compiled by Mary Lisbeth Gonzalez, in "How Many Indigenous People?"[7]

For the Roma, a group that is notoriously undercounted (or not enumerated at all) in most European censuses, Jean-Pierre Liegeois and Nicolae Gheorghe, *Roma/Gypsies: A European Minority.*[8] This source's estimates (in absolute numbers) are attributed to the Gypsy Research Centre, René Descartes University, Paris, 1994.

For groups in Africa south of the Sahara, Donald George Morrison, Robert Cameron Mitchell, and John Naber Paden, *Black Africa: A Comparative Handbook.*[9]

For groups not covered above, the CIA's *World Factbook 1998* cross-checked against country- and group-specific estimates from various sources, including materials in the information files compiled by the Minorities at Risk project on the 275 groups in Phase III. When several estimates were available from equally good (or bad) sources, we looked for convergence and consistency with nonstatistical information and, in a few cases, opted to take a midpoint between two extreme values. Usually we resolved such discrepancies by relying on the multiple-sourced estimates developed in the MAR project's previous work.[10]

Sources of Indeterminacy and How We Dealt with Them

In addition to the inherent fuzziness of determining who belongs to an ethnocultural or religious group, there are limitations to the accuracy of all the sources of estimates described in the preceding section.

Census data, the optimum source of information, is based on individuals' self-reports of their group identifications. As noted, we used census data when available. But there are substantial intercensal variations in reported group size. In Peru, for example, the indigenous population declined from 32 percent of country population in 1972 to 27 percent in 1981. In Australia over roughly the same period, the number of self-identified Aborigines increased far more than might be explained by natural increases.[11] Some such changes may be due to differences in the comprehensiveness of census coverage or in the ways that census questions are asked and answers recorded. Others are due to changes in individual choices about self-identification. As a consequence census data may be regarded as best approximations of group size but approximations nonetheless. We use data from the most recent censuses, usually ones conducted in the 1990s.

Expert estimates are the only general alternative to census data, and indeed in much of Africa and the Middle East they are the only sources of estimates. Several problems arise when using such estimates, the most obvious being, first, the existence of multiple estimates, and, second, the lack of information about the ways in which or the sources from which estimates are derived. Another problem is that expert sources often report absolute numbers without giving a year of reference. For example, an otherwise useful global reference, *Ethnic Groups Worldwide,* reports numbers of group members without any years of reference *or* sources. Most of the more detailed studies prepared by the Minority Rights Group, many of them summarized in the *World Directory of Minorities,* provide more demographic details.[12] We gave precedence to sources that compiled estimates for a particular type of group or region, on the assumption that the authors imposed some quality control on estimates or at least were consistent in the types of information used. In a relatively small number of instances we relied on assessments by group or country experts.

State formation has a major impact on group population percentages. Croatia's secession from Yugoslavia, for example, drastically reduced the Croat population remaining under Belgrade's control. The new internationally recognized states of the 1990s are European postcommunist states, all of whose 1980s censuses reported on ethnic identification within each constituent republic. We used these republican census results to obtain percentages that we then applied to 1990s population estimates for the newly independent states, all of which inherited communist-era boundaries.

Population movements, especially refugee flows, lead to changes over time in group population percentages such that a proportion based on information from the 1980s sometimes cannot be reliably applied to country population in the 1990s. This factor especially affects estimates of minority populations in the Soviet and Yugoslav successor states as well as estimates of communal group size in the Greater Horn of Africa. Widely used sources of minority population estimates, such as the CIA's *World Factbook* and *Black Africa: A Comparative Handbook,* usually do not or cannot take account of such movements. We have used refugee data and expert estimates, where possible, to adjust data derived from these sources. In particular, we have adjusted estimates of the size of Russian and German minorities in the post-Soviet republics, Tatars in Ukraine, Serbs in Croatia and Bosnia, and Tutsis and Hutus in the states of the Great Lakes region to take account of recent population movements.

Differential population growth leads to changes over time in group percentages of country population. Disadvantaged minorities, for example, typically have higher birthrates than others. We did not attempt to correct for this factor, other than to rely on the most recent census and expert estimates available. In our judgment it is a relatively small source of error, or indeterminacy, by comparison with others described here.

Net Changes in MAR Population Estimates

Many MAR estimates of group population for 1995 were revised as a result of the process described here, and all 1998 estimates are derived from and consistent with the corrected 1995 proportions. Most changes are technical: we identified and corrected for past errors in projecting population estimates from 1990 to 1995, used a consistent source for 1995 and 1998 country population estimates, and corrected computational and data entry errors. More substantial changes are few, affecting less than a tenth of the groups. Some are due to decisions to redefine the group. For example, all Brazilians with some African ancestry, rather than those of purely African descent, are now counted as Afro-Brazilians. The Quebecois provide a second example: the group is now defined demographically as the Francophone population of Quebec rather than the total population of the province. Other substantive changes are due to identification of better sources, especially more reliable expert estimates and more recent census data. The aggregate impact of all changes is small, however. In 1990 the aggregate population of all minorities in the MAR survey was 17.3 percent of the global population; in 1998—using corrected data and an expanded set of groups—it is 17.5 percent.

Notes

Preface

1. See Richard Haas's *Conflicts Unending: The United States and Regional Disputes* (New Haven, Conn.: Yale University Press, 1990); Daniel Moynihan's *Pandemonium: Ethnicity in International Politics* (Oxford and New York: Oxford University Press, 1993); and Samuel P. Huntington's *The Clash of Civilizations and the Remaking of World Order* (New York: Simon & Schuster, 1996).

2. The term *short peace* was used to characterize the declining global trend in armed conflict by Jonathan Wilkenfeld and Ernest J. Wilson at a seminar at the University of Maryland's Center for International Development and Conflict Management in September 1998.

3. On the procedures, data, and 1980s findings of the Minorities at Risk project, see chaps. 1–4 in Ted Robert Gurr, *Minorities at Risk: A Global View of Ethnopolitical Conflicts* (Washington, D.C.: United States Institute of Peace Press, 1993).

1. The Ethnic Basis of Political Action in the 1980s and 1990s

1. For overviews of scholarly interpretations of the nature of ethnicity, see Nathan Glazer and Daniel P. Moynihan, eds., *Ethnicity: Theory and Experience* (Cambridge, Mass.: Harvard University Press, 1975); and Richard H. Thompson, *Theories of Ethnicity: A Critical Appraisal* (Westport, Conn.: Greenwood Press, 1989). The quotation is from Virginia Q. Tilley, "State Identity Politics and the Domestic Ethnic Arena" (paper presented at the annual meeting of the International Studies Association, Minneapolis, April 1998), 5. See her article "Terms of the Debate: Untangling Language on Ethnicity and Ethnic Movements," *Ethnic and Racial Studies* 20 (July 1997): 497–522. Similar constructivist conceptualizations are used by David A. Lake and Donald Rothchild, eds., in their introduction to *The International Spread of Ethnic Conflict: Fear, Diffusion, and Escalation* (Princeton, N.J.: Princeton University Press, 1998), 5–9; and by Valery Tishkov, *Ethnicity, Nationalism, and Conflict in and after the Soviet Union: The Mind Aflame* (London: Sage Publications for the International Peace Research Institute, Oslo, 1997), 12–22. A sociobiological or evolutionary alternative to the constructivist approach has been developed by Pierre L. van den Berghe, *The Ethnic Phenomenon* (Westport, Conn.: Praeger, 1981, 1987), and assessed empirically by Tatu Vanhanen, "Domestic Ethnic Conflict and Ethnic Nepotism: A Comparative Analysis," *Journal of Peace Research* 36, no. 1 (1999): 55–73.

2. J. M. Coetzee, "Against the South African Grain," *New York Review of Books,* September 23, 1999, 51.

3. Martin O. Heisler, "Ethnicity and Ethnic Relations in the West," in *Conflict and Peacemaking in Multiethnic Societies,* ed. Joseph V. Montville (Lexington, Mass.: Lexington Books, 1990), 21–54, quotation p. 45.

4. Ted Robert Gurr, *Minorities at Risk: A Global View of Ethnopolitical Conflicts* (Washington, D.C.: United States Institute of Peace Press, 1993), 3–4.

5. There is a vast theoretical and comparative literature on nationalism to which Gellner and Smith are among the most influential contributors. See Ernest Gellner, *Nations and Nationalism* (Oxford: Oxford University Press, 1983); and Anthony D. Smith, *The Ethnic Origins of Nations* (Oxford and New York: Basil Blackwell, 1986). A critical analysis of old and new manifestations of nationalism is Liah Greenfeld, *Nationalism: Five Roads to Modernity* (Cambridge, Mass.: Harvard University Press, 1992).

6. Rashid Khalidi, *Palestinian Identity: The Construction of a Modern National Consciousness* (New York: Columbia University Press, 1998).

7. See Vamik D. Volkan, "On Chosen Trauma," *Mind and Human Interaction* 4 (1991): 3–19; Volkan, *Bloodlines: From Ethnic Pride to Ethnic Terrorism* (New York: Farrar, Straus & Giroux, 1997); and Khalidi, *Palestinian Identity* (note 6).

8. James D. Fearon and David D. Laitin, "A Cross-Sectional Study of Large-Scale Ethnic Violence in the Postwar Period" (unpublished paper, Department of Political Science, University of Chicago, September 30, 1997). Heterogeneity in the MAR data set can be reduced, for some analytic purposes, by selecting out all advantaged minorities that dominate the state apparatus.

9. Some of the MAR coding categories provide information on the extent of segmentation and conflict within each ethnic group.

10. The criticism has been posed most generally by Fearon and Laitin in "A Cross-Sectional Study" (note 8). Other suggestions for inclusion have come from users of the project's data set and are actively sought from future users and readers of this study.

11. Fearon and Laitin, "A Cross-Sectional Study" (note 8) contend that "selection bias" affects current list groups because groups are most likely to come to our attention when they initiate collective action; others tend to be overlooked. Fearon and Laitin are engaged in a collaborative effort with the Minorities project to make the roster of groups more representative. Valery Tishkov observes that the project's 1990 roster of 233 ethnic groups is "selective" and says that "many more 'unnoticed' ones do not fight, choosing instead to live peaceful and cooperative lives" in *Ethnicity, Nationalism, and Conflict* (note 1), 296. Also see his critique of large-*n* studies of ethnic conflict like the Minorities study, "Ethnic Conflicts in the Former USSR: The Use and Misuse of Typologies and Data," *Journal of Peace Research* 36, no. 5 (1999): 571–591.

12. An account of historical patterns of ethnic and national conflict in Europe is Sandra Halpern, "The Spread of Ethnic Conflict in Europe: Some Comparative-Historical Reflections," in Lake and Rothchild, *International Spread of Ethnic Conflict* (note 1), 151–184. An overview of minority status and strategies in the 1980s is "Minorities in the Western Democracies and Japan," chap. 6 in Gurr, *Minorities at Risk* (note 4). Other recent comparative studies of the region are Guntram F. A. Werther, *Self-Determination in Western Democracies: Aboriginal Politics in a Comparative Perspective* (Westport, Conn.: Greenwood Press, 1992); Ian M. Cuthbertson and Jane Leibowitz, eds., *Minorities: The New Europe's Old Issue* (Boulder, Colo.: Westview Press for the Institute for East-West Studies, 1993); and John T. Ishiyama and Marijke Breuning, *Ethnopolitics in the New Europe* (Boulder, Colo.: Lynne Rienner, 1998).

13. All the non-Russian republican nationalities except Byelorussians met the "at risk" criteria in the 1980s. So did Croats, Slovenes, Serbs (a politically advantaged minority), and Kosovar Albanians in Yugoslavia, and Slovaks in the former Czechoslovakia. Yugoslavia's Bosnian Muslims and Macedonians were not included in the 1980s study because they did not then meet the general criteria for inclusion.

14. Case and regional studies make up most of the voluminous literature on ethnic and national politics and conflict in the postcommunist states. Broadly comparative studies include Barnett R. Rubin and Jack Snyder, eds., *Post-Soviet Political Order: Conflict and State-Building* (London and New York: Routledge, 1998); Tishkov, *Ethnicity, Nationalism, and Conflict* (note 1); and Kumar Rupesinghe, Peter King, and Olga Vorkunova, eds., *Ethnicity and Conflict in a Post-Communist World: The Soviet Union, Eastern Europe, and China* (New York: St. Martin's Press, 1992). A comparative survey of the status, interests, and political activities of the new Russian minorities is Vladimir Schlapentokh, Munir Sendich, and Emil Payin, eds., *The New Russian Diaspora: Russian Minorities in the Former Soviet Republics* (Armonk, N.Y., and London: M. E. Sharpe, 1994). For references on the Roma, see the sketch of the Roma in East Central Europe on pp. 143–150.

15. Most studies of national and minority status and conflicts in Asia deal with subregions. An important exception is Michael E. Brown and Sumit Ganguly, eds., *Government Policies and Ethnic Relations in Asia and the Pacific* (Cambridge, Mass.: MIT Press, 1997). Useful recent regional studies are Ishtiaq Ahmed, *State, Nation, and Ethnicity in Contemporary South Asia* (London and New York: Pinter, 1996), and William Safran, ed., "Nationalism and Ethnoregional Identities in China," special issue of *Nationalism and Ethnic Politics* 4 (spring/summer 1998): 83–99. The MAR data provide the basis for two studies that encompass the entire region: Gurr, "Democracy and the Rights of Ethnic and Regional Minorities in Asia," in *Democracy* *and Communism: Theory, Reality, and the Future,* ed. Sung Chul Yang (Seoul: Korean Association of International Studies, Conference Series No. 3), 105–140; and Gurr, "A Risk Assessment Model of Ethnopolitical Rebellion," in *Preventive Measures: Building Risk Assessment and Crisis Early Warning Systems,* ed. John L. Davies and Ted Robert Gurr (Lanham, Md.: Rowman and Littlefield, 1998), 15–26.

   16. Broadly comparative studies of communal conflict in the Middle East include Milton J. Esman and Itamar Rabonovich, eds., *Ethnicity, Pluralism, and the State in the Middle East* (Ithaca, N.Y.: Cornell University Press, 1988); Saad Eddin Ibrahim, "Ethnic Conflict and State-Building in the Arab World," *International Social Science Journal* 156 (1998): 229–242; and Ofra Bengio and Gabriel Ben-Dor, *Minorities and the State in the Arab World* (Boulder, Colo.: Lynne Rienner, 1999).

   17. For comparative studies of ethnic conflict in Africa, see note 21. For an empirical analysis of ethnic and other bases of conflict in Zaire, see Kisangani N. Emizet, "Political Cleavages in a Democratizing Society: The Case of the Congo (formerly Zaire)," *Comparative Political Studies* 32 (April 1999): 185–228. Tutsis in Rwanda and Burundi were included in the Minorities study in the 1980s; the Banyarwandans of Zaire were added in the 1990s because of new discriminatory policies imposed on them. For details about their background and changing status, updated through January 2000, see the Minorities project's Web site at *www.bsos.umd.edu/cidcm/mar.*

   18. For broadly comparative studies of indigenous groups, see Donna Lee Van Cott, ed., *Indigenous Peoples and Democracy in Latin America* (New York: St. Martin's Press, 1995); and George Psacharopoulos and Harry Anthony Patrinos, eds., *Indigenous People and Poverty in Latin America: An Empirical Analysis* (Washington, D.C.: World Bank, 1994). Recent comparative studies of Afro–Latin Americans are Peter Wade, *Race and Ethnicity in Latin America* (London: Pluto Press, 1997); and Norman Whitten and Arlene Torres, eds., *Blackness in Latin America and the Caribbean: Social Dynamics and Cultural Transformations,* 2 vols. (Bloomington: Indiana University Press, 1998).

   19. During the heyday of the civil rights movement in the United States almost all African Americans sought equal rights and status and, in the extreme case, a "revolution" that would empower all peoples of color. These are demands for "access." A much smaller group supported the Republic of New Africa, an organization whose objectives were avowedly separatist. The Nation of Islam also can be seen as a manifestation of the separatist objective, realized in this instance by creation of an alternative society-within-a-society.

   20. Some Chinese communities are categorized in the Minorities study as national minorities, some as communal contenders, depending on their relationships with the governments of their host countries. In Malaysia, for example, they are politically organized communal contenders. The term *diaspora* in the narrow sense refers to people who have been dispersed from a specific homeland and taken up permanent residence elsewhere but retain a strong sense of identification with their place of origin. The archetypical examples are Jews and, in this century, Armenians and Palestinians. Recently the term has been used more broadly, for example, for Africans in the Americas, labor migrants, refugees, and national minorities. For the narrow usage, see William Safran,

"Diasporas in Modern Societies: Myths of Homeland and Return," *Diaspora* 1 (1991). For more diverse conceptions see Gabriel Sheffer, ed., *Modern Diasporas in International Politics* (London: Croom Helm, 1986); and Yossi Shain and Martin Sherman, "Dynamics of Disintegration: Diaspora, Secession, and the Paradox of Nation-States," *Nations and Nationalism* 4, no. 3 (1998): 321–346. A comparative study of five transborder people in the post-Soviet states is Charles King and Neil J. Melvin, eds., *Nations Abroad: Diaspora Politics and International Relations in the Former Soviet Union* (Boulder, Colo.: Westview Press, 1998). The diaspora concept is not used analytically in the Minorities at Risk study.

21. Two general analyses of the sources of communal conflict in postcolonial African societies are James R. Scarritt, "Communal Conflict and Contention for Power in Africa South of the Sahara," chap. 9 in Gurr, *Minorities at Risk* (note 4); and "African State Management of Ethnic Conflict," chap. 1 in Donald Rothchild, *Managing Ethnic Conflict in Africa: Pressures and Incentives for Cooperation* (Washington, D.C.: Brookings, 1997). On the colonial origins of these patterns, see Crawford Young, *The African Colonial State in Comparative Perspective* (New Haven, Conn.: Yale University Press, 1994).

2. Long War, Short Peace

1. Only 268 groups are included in this analysis. Seven additional groups from countries in the 500,000–1 million population range were added in 1998 and are included in comparisons later in this chapter.

2. On the causes and sequences of political action by African Americans, see Doug McAdam, *Political Process and the Development of Black Insurgency, 1930–1970* (Chicago: University of Chicago Press, 1982); and Ted Robert Gurr, ed., *Violence in America*, vol. 2, *Protest, Rebellion, Reform* (Newbury Park, Calif.: Sage Publications, 1989), especially chaps. 3, 7, and 8. Armed attacks on urban police were carried out mainly by the Black Liberation Army, not—as was commonly supposed—by the Black Panthers.

3. Figures 2.1 and 2.2 are constructed by averaging coded data for the two different kinds of ethnopolitical conflict across all groups in the study in each period. Before 1990 the number of groups is 233; in the 1990s it is 275. *Active groups* are those that, in any given five-year period, used any of the forms of protest or rebellion shown in table 2.2. Each group's protest and rebellion score is the highest recorded in the Minorities data set in each five-year period. The scales used range from 0 to either 6 or 7, as shown in table 2.2. Two different means are calculated and shown in the figures. Mean protest and rebellion for *active groups* is a measure of the relative intensity of their political actions. Mean protest and rebellion for *all groups* is an indicator of the changing volume of ethnopolitical conflict in the world system. Note that the figures exclude conflict between rival communal groups. The Minorities at Risk project's coded information on intercommunal conflict needs to be analyzed and interpreted with caution because reporting on conflict between rival groups has not been as thorough as reporting on conflict between communal groups and states. With this caveat, we also observe a parallel long-term increase in the frequency and intensity of communal conflict, which escalated sharply in the 1980s and 1990s.

4. Figures 2.3 through 2.9 were constructed applying the same procedures used for figures 2.1 and 2.2 (see note 3) to annual data. The Minorities at Risk project did not code annual data on ethnopolitical conflict prior to 1985.

5. Peter Wallensteen and Margareta Sollenberg, "Armed Conflict, 1989–98," *Journal of Peace Research* 36, no. 5 (1999): 593–606. This survey includes wars between as well as within states, but three-quarters of the conflicts covered are wars between politically organized communal groups and governments. Of the five new armed conflicts that began in 1998, however, the Kosovo rebellion was the only one involving a communal group.

6. A. J. Jongman and A. P. Schmid, *World Conflict and Human Rights Map 1998* (Leiden: PIOOM [Interdisciplinary Research Programme on Causes of Human Rights Violations], Department of Political Sciences, Leiden University, 1998). In contrast to the Wallensteen surveys, which count only battle-related deaths, PIOOM includes estimates of all people who die directly or indirectly as a result of conflict, many or most of whom are usually unarmed civilians.

7. Daniel Byman and Steve Van Evera, "Hypotheses on the Causes of Contemporary Deadly Conflict," *Security Studies* 7, no. 3 (1998): 1–50. On the same general theme, see Yahya Sadowski, *The Myth of Global Chaos* (Washington, D.C.: Brookings Institution Press, 1998).

8. Data are compiled annually, mainly from UN sources, and reported in *World Refugee Survey 1998* (Washington, D.C.: U.S. Committee for Refugees, 1998). The totals include 3.7 million Palestinians, most of them survivors or descendants of those who fled the Israel-Arab war of 1949. The totals do not include internally displaced persons, who number at least 15 million.

9. The asterisks for 1995–98 in figures 2.4 through 2.9 signal that this period includes data for only four years. The numbers of active groups therefore may be slightly understated by comparison with previous five-year periods.

10. See Edmond J. Keller, "Transnational Ethnic Conflict in Africa," in *The International Spread of Ethnic Conflict: Fear, Diffusion, and Escalation*, ed. David A. Lake and Donald Rothchild (Princeton, N.J.: Princeton University Press, 1998); and Barry R. Posen, "The Security Dilemma and Ethnic Conflict," *Survival* 35, no. 1 (1993): 27–47.

11. A useful collection of essays on democratization and ethnopolitical groups' status and strategies is Larry Diamond and Marc F. Plattner, eds., *Nationalism, Ethnic Conflict, and Democracy* (Baltimore and London: Johns Hopkins University Press, 1994). The conditions for and extent of democratization in each postcommunist country are analyzed by contributors to Karen Dawisha and Bruce Parrott's four edited volumes on *Democratization and Authoritarianism in Postcommunist Societies* (Cambridge and New York: Cambridge University Press, 1997).

12. These are the operational rules for identifying new episodes: "New" episodes of protest are dated to the year in which ethnopolitical movements shifted from symbolic and organizational activities to collective action, i.e., strategies of demonstrations, strikes, rallies, or rioting aimed at the state (from 2 or less to 3 or more on the protest scale in table 2.2). "New" episodes of rebellion are dated to the year in which the group initiated organized campaigns of terrorism, local rebellion, guerrilla war, or civil war against the state (actions 2 or higher on the rebellion scale in table 2.2). Most of these episodes of organized violence were preceded by protest or isolated incidents of violence. Episodes of protest and rebellion were not counted if the initiating group used the same strategy during the previous decade. The analysis excludes intercommunal violence, i.e., violent conflict between communal contenders in which the state was not directly a party to conflict.

13. The nationalist movements that precipitated the breakup of the Soviet Union and Yugoslavia are included in the analysis reported in table 2.2 but are excluded from tables 2.3 and 2.4. The latter include only movements that fell short of internationally recognized independence, e.g., the Serbs in Croatia and Bosnia, and the Chechens and Tatars in Russia.

14. Short-lived protests also were organized by Greeks in Albania (1993) and Russians in Kazakhstan (1996). Neither had resurfaced through 1999.

15. The two Russian minorities in Ukraine are analyzed separately because they live in different regions and have distinct political histories, status, and grievances.

16. Russian nationalists in Russia and Ukraine have sought to undermine the Ukrainian state and constrain its policy choices in various ways. See Marion Recktenwald's sketch on pp. 57–63 and her dissertation, "The Russian Diaspora in Ukraine: Russian Influences on Its Political Behavior" (Ph.D. diss., University of Maryland, 1998).

17. William Easterly and Ross Levine, "Africa's Growth Tragedy: Policies and Ethnic Divisions," *Quarterly Journal of Economics* (November 1997): 1203–1250.

18. Ted Robert Gurr, *Minorities at Risk: A Global View of Ethnopolitical Conflicts* (Washington, D.C.: United States Institute of Peace Press, 1993), 145–146.

19. This analysis of prior political action is based on the Minorities at Risk codings of violent and nonviolent protest and rebellion in five-year increments from 1945–49 through 1980–84 and annual codings of protest and rebellion from 1985 onward. Contextual information also was taken into account. We lacked enough information to analyze antecedents of two of the fifty-two new rebellions.

20. See, e.g., Robert I. Rotberg, ed., *Vigilance and Vengeance: NGOs Preventing Ethnic Conflict in Divided Societies* (Washington, D.C.: Brookings Institution Press, 1996); and chapters by Steven L. Burg, "Nationalism and Civic Identity: Ethnic Models for Macedonia and Kosovo," and Michael S. Lund, Barnett R. Rubin, and Fabienne Hara, "Learning from Burundi's Failed Democratic Transition, 1993–1996: Did International Initiatives Match the Problem?" both in Barnett R. Rubin, ed., *Cases and Strategies for Preventive Action*, vol. 2 of *Preventive Action Reports* (New York: Century Foundation Press, 1998).

21. The Bodo and Tuareg meet the criteria of indigenous people used in the Minorities study: they are conquered descendants of earlier inhabitants of a region who live mainly in conformity with traditional social, economic, and cultural customs that are sharply distinct from those of dominant groups. The Bougainville islanders are kin to nearby Solomon Islanders and are culturally distinct from the people of mainland Papua New Guinea. Rather than being "conquered," however, the Bougainvillians were joined to Papua New Guinea for the convenience of Australian administration of international trust territories, not conquest. Their demands for control of their own land and resources are typical of indigenous peoples elsewhere.

22. Stephen M. Saideman, "Is Pandora's Box Half Empty or Half Full? The Limited Virulence of Secessionism and the Domestic Sources of Disintegration," in Lake and Rothchild, *International Spread of Ethnic Conflict* (note 10).

3. The Etiology of Ethnopolitical Conflict

1. This is a substantial revision and extension of theoretical arguments presented in "Minorities, Nationalists, and Ethnopolitical Conflict," in *Managing Global Chaos: Sources of and Responses to International Conflict,* ed. Chester A. Crocker and Fen Osler Hampson with Pamela Aall (Washington, D.C.: United States Institute of Peace Press, 1996), 53–77. Victor Assal and Robert Tomes suggested useful changes in the argument.

2. Rodolfo Stavenhagen, "Reflections on Some Theories of Ethnic Conflict," *Journal of Ethno-Development* 4, no. 1 (July 1994): 15.

3. Arguments about the salience of group identity can be found in many sources; my thinking about them has been especially influenced by Donald L. Horowitz, *Ethnic Groups in Conflict* (Berkeley and Los Angeles: University of California Press, 1985). The concept of incentives incorporates arguments about the motivating forces of relative deprivation, from my *Why Men Rebel* (Princeton, N.J.: Princeton University Press, 1970), and of rational goal-seeking. The notion of capacity is analogous to Charles Tilly's concept of mobilization as developed in *From Mobilization to Revolution* (Reading, Mass.: Addison-Wesley, 1978), 69–90. The significance of opportunities external to the group is central to theoretical models developed by Doug McAdam, *Political Process and the Development of Black Insurgency, 1930–1970* (Chicago: University of Chicago Press, 1982); and by Sidney Tarrow, *Power in Movement: Social Movements, Collective Action, and Politics* (New York: Cambridge University Press, 1994). Milton J. Esman gives political opportunity a prominent role in his comparative analysis of ethnic political movements, *Ethnic Politics* (Ithaca, N.Y.: Cornell University Press, 1994). The process by which groups organize for and sustain collective action is assumed to be fundamentally a rational one, as analyzed by Mark Irving Lichbach in *The Rebel's Dilemma* (Ann Arbor, Mich.: University of Michigan Press, 1995).

4. See Virginia Q. Tilley, "State Identity Politics and the Domestic Ethnic Arena" (paper presented at the annual meeting of the International Studies Association,

April 1998), and also contributions to Paul Brass, ed., *Ethnic Groups and the State* (London: Croom-Helm, 1985).

5. The relevance of racial differences for group identity has been analyzed by Pierre L. van den Berghe, most recently in "Does Race Matter?" *Nations and Nationalism* 1, no. 3 (November 1995): 357–368.

6. Jonathan Fox finds that 105 of 268 minorities in the Minorities at Risk study in the 1990s differ in religious belief from dominant groups. Religious issues are important for only 39 (37 percent) of the religiously distinct minorities. When religious issues *are* important, though, they are associated with higher levels of discrimination against the minority and more intense rebellions. See Fox, "The Salience of Religious Issues in Ethnic Conflicts: A Large-*n* Study," *Nationalism and Ethnic Politics* 3 (autumn 1997): 1–19.

7. Contention about language in heterogeneous societies is the topic of extensive comparative research. See, for example, Horowitz, *Ethnic Groups in Conflict* (note 3), *passim;* and the writings of David D. Laitin, most recently his *Identity in Formation* (Ithaca, N.Y.: Cornell University Press, 1998).

8. Horowitz, *Ethnic Groups in Conflict* (note 3), 141–185. Also see articles on Israelis, Afrikaners, and Hindus in "Chosen Peoples," special issue of *Nations and Nationalism* 5, no. 3 (1999): 331–430.

9. On patterns of relative deprivation and the conditions under which they lead to political violence, see Gurr, *Why Men Rebel* (note 3), chap. 2. On group interests and mobilization, see Tilly, *From Mobilization to Revolution* (note 3), 69–90.

10. Dennis Chong, *Collective Action and the Civil Rights Movement* (Chicago: University of Chicago Press, 1991), provides a sensitive analysis of minority group members' non-material incentives for taking part in collective action.

11. Ryan Dudley and Ross A. Miller, "Group Rebellion in the 1980s," *Journal of Conflict Resolution* 42 (February 1998): 77–96. Other global evidence on the close connections among discrimination, inequalities, grievances, and ethnopolitical action in the 1980s is reported in T. R. Gurr, "Why Minorities Rebel: A Cross-National Analysis of Communal Mobilization and Conflict since 1945," *International Political Science Review* 14, no. 2 (1993): 161–201; and in Gurr, *Minorities at Risk: A Global View of Ethnopolitical Conflicts* (Washington, D.C.: United States Institute of Peace Press, 1993), chaps. 2 and 3. In Africa, by contrast, mobilization has been demonstrated empirically to be more important than grievances as a cause of protest and rebellion; see James R. Scarritt and Susan McMillan, "Protest and Rebellion in Africa: Explaining Conflicts between Ethnic Minorities and the State in the 1980s," *Comparative Political Studies* 28 (October 1995): 323–349.

12. An index of historical loss of group autonomy is one of the strongest correlates of minorities' political grievances, protest, and rebellion in the 1980s; see Gurr, "Why Minorities Rebel" (note 11), 178–179.

13. Many empirical studies have explored the complex relations between government repression and dissent, and most are consistent with the general proposition given here, however much they may differ on the details. A recent empirical example is Christian A. Davenport, "The Weight of the Past: Exploring Lagged Determinants of Political Repression," *Political Research Quarterly* 49, no. 2 (1996): 377–403. A review of arguments and evidence is Mark Irving Lichbach, "Deterrence or Escalation? The Puzzle of Aggregate Studies of Repression and Dissent," *Journal of Conflict Resolution* 31 (1987): 266–297. The issue has just begun to be studied with reference to ethnopolitical groups. A reanalysis of Gurr, "Why Minorities Rebel" (note 11), compares different sources of minority grievances and finds that a recent history of repression against the group is a more important determinant of current grievances than either political discrimination or a history of lost autonomy; see T. R. Gurr and Will H. Moore, "Ethnopolitical Rebellion: A Cross-Sectional Analysis of the 1980s with Risk Assessments for the 1990s," *American Journal of Political Science* 41 (October 1997): 1093.

14. Robert Bates suggests that intergroup hostilities in Kenya are liable to come to a head during the next national election campaign (personal communication, January 1999).

15. Tarrow, *Power in Movement* (note 3), 123. The frame concept is derived from the work of Erving Goffman, *Frame Analysis: An Essay on the Organization of Experience* (Cambridge, Mass.: Harvard University Press, 1974).

16. See chap. 1, note 5, for general references on nationalism and national self-determination. Also see Walker Conner, *Ethnonationalism: The Quest for Understanding* (Princeton, N.J.: Princeton University Press, 1994); and a review essay by Thomas A. Koelble, "Towards a Theory of Nationalism: Culture, Structure, and Choice Analyses Revisited," *Nationalism and Ethnic Politics* 1 (winter 1995): 73–89.

17. On trends in political action by indigenous groups see Gurr, *Minorities at Risk* (note 11), chap. 4. The history of the indigenous rights movement is reviewed by Franke Wilmer, *The Indigenous Voice in World Politics: Since Time Immemorial* (Newbury Park, Calif.: Sage, 1993). On the emergence of transnational networks that link local and regional indigenous movements with environmental actors, see Pamela L. Burke, "The Globalization of Contentious Politics: The Amazonian Indigenous Rights Movement" (Ph.D. diss., University of Maryland, 1999), and her sketch on pp. 96–99 of this volume.

18. International efforts to guarantee minority rights have a centuries-long European history, as demonstrated by Stephen D. Krasner and Daniel T. Froats, "Minority Rights and the Westphalian Model," in *International Spread of Ethnic Conflict,* ed. David A. Lake and Donald Rothchild (Princeton, N.J.: Princeton University Press, 1998), 227–250. Recent developments are reviewed in Hugh Miall, ed., *Minority Rights in Europe: Prospects for a Transnational Regime* (New York: Council on Foreign Relations Press for Royal Institute of International Affairs, 1994).

19. Personal communication dated July 19, 1998.

20. Two recent comparative studies of the mobilization of separatist movements are Daniele Conversi, *The Basques, the Catalans, and Spain: Alternative Routes to Mobilization* (Reno, Nev.: University of Nevada Press, 1997); and R. Andersen, B. Bull, and K. Duvold, eds., *Separatism: Culture Counts, Resources Decide* (Bergen: Chr. Michelsen Institute, 1997).

21. Such appeals are rarely studied in a systematic way. Two exceptions are a microanalysis of the kinds of appeals used to mobilize support for African nationalist movements in Rhodesia by Will H. Moore, "Rebel Music: Appeals to Rebellion in Zimbabwe," *Political Communication and Persuasion* 8 (1991): 125–138; and Christian A. Davenport's "Rereading the Voice of the Vanguard Party: A Content and Rhetorical Analysis of the Black Panther Party Intercommunal Newsletter from 1969–1973," in *The Black Panther Party Reconsidered: Reflections and Scholarship*, ed. Charles Jones (Baltimore, Md.: Black Classic Press, 1998).

22. The general argument presupposes a loss of security that occurs when a state is no longer willing or able to protect a group against its rivals. In this circumstance the advantage lies, or is perceived to lie, with the group that takes preemptive action against its immediate rivals. The question is whether preemptive attacks are most likely against rivals who live in enclaves or next door. See Barry R. Posen, "The Security Dilemma and Ethnic Conflict," *Survival* 35, no. 1 (1993): 27–47; and Stephen Van Evera, "Hypotheses on Nationalism and War," *International Security* 15, no. 3 (1994): 5–39.

23. The cited studies use Minorities at Risk indicators, sometimes in combination with other data: Erik Melander, *Anarchy Within: The Security Dilemma between Ethnic Groups in Emerging Anarchy* (Uppsala, Sweden: Department of Peace and Conflict Research, Uppsala University, Research Report 52, 1999); Monica Duffy Toft, "Do Settlement Patterns Matter?" (unpublished paper, Center for Science and International Affairs, Harvard University, 1998); and James D. Fearon and David D. Laitin, "Weak States, Rough Terrain, and Large-Scale Ethnic Violence since 1945" (paper presented at the annual meeting of the American Political Science Association, Atlanta, September 1999).

24. Tarrow develops a general argument that social networks and preexisting institutions provide the basis for mobilization for social movements; see his *Power in Movement* (note 3), 21–22 and 54–61. The institutional origins of civil rights protest are documented by McAdam in *Political Process and the Development of Black Insurgency* (note 3). Jonathan Fox analyzes the role of religious institutions in facilitating political opposition by 105 religiously distinct minorities in "Do Religious Institutions Support Violence or the Status Quo?" *Studies in Conflict and Terrorism* 22, no. 2 (1999): 119–139, finding that they support opposition only in special circumstances, either when religious institutions are threatened or when the group has a nonreligious political agenda.

25. There is theoretical debate about the relative ease of pursuing sustained political action through new and flexible organizations in which spontaneity and solidarity are high and pursuing it through long-established organizations in which hierarchy and the imperatives of institutional survival trump enthusiasm. See Lichbach's discussion, "The Unintended Consequences of Dissident Organization," in *Rebel's Dilemma* (note 3), 263–275. The argument here is somewhat different: it is easier to build political movements among people who already interact frequently and routinely, whether they do so informally or through existing organizations.

26. Lichbach, *The Rebel's Dilemma* (note 3), 256. Evidence of the importance of coalition formation in ten recent revolutions is summarized in chap. 14 of Jack A. Goldstone, T. R. Gurr, and Farrokh Moshiri, eds., *Revolutions of the Late Twentieth Century* (Boulder, Colo.: Westview Press, 1991).

27. Pranab Bardhan, "Method in the Madness? A Political-Economy Analysis of Ethnic Conflicts in Less Developed Countries," *World Development* 25, no. 9 (1997): 1390.

28. The most enduring cleavages divide the rival clans, or "tribes," of rural Kurdistan. These differences are compounded by the more recent emergence of differences in interest between urban and rural Kurds, especially in Iraq and Turkey. In Iraq the PDK represents mainly traditional, rural Kurdish interests, and the PUK has more "modern" leadership and is more closely attuned to interests of urban Kurds. Governments in the region have been able to exploit such divisions for their own purposes. Since 1996, for example, the Turkish government has been able to get the Iraqi KDP to participate in its efforts to suppress rebellious Turkish Kurds who have taken sanctuary in Iraq. Divisions among the Kurds are discussed by most writers on the subject, but see especially Martin van Bruinessen, *Agha, Shaikh, and State: The Social and Political Structures of Kurdistan* (1978; reprint, London: Zed Press, 1991).

29. Discussions of the instrumental interpretation of ethnopolitical action are incorporated in William A. Douglass, "A Critique of Recent Trends in the Analysis of Ethnonationalism," *Ethnic and Racial Studies* 11, no. 2 (April 1988): 192–206; and George M. Scott, Jr., "A Resynthesis of the Primordial and Circumstantial Approaches to Ethnic Group Solidarity: Towards an Explanatory Model," *Ethnic and Racial Studies* 13 (April 1990): 147–171.

30. The concept of political opportunity is widely used in analyses of the origins and dynamics of social movements, for example, by Tilly, *From Mobilization to Revolution* (note 3), and McAdam, *Development of Black Insurgency* (note 3). The discussion here follows from Tarrow's definition of political opportunity structure as "the dimensions of the political environment that provide incentives for people to undertake collective action by affecting their expectation for success or failure" (*Power in Movement* [note 3], 85). The distinction between durable factors (Tarrow's structures) and transient factors is mine.

31. Deepa Khosla, "Third World States as Intervenors in Ethnic Conflict: Implications for Regional and International Security," *Third World Quarterly* 20, no. 6 (1999): 1143–1156. Her analysis uses coded data on international support from the Minorities at Risk project.

32. Studies that document the international dimensions of social movements in Latin America include Arturo Escobar and Sonia E. Alvarez, eds., *The Making of Social Movements in Latin America* (Boulder, Colo.: Westview Press, 1992); Alison Brysk, "Acting Globally: Indian Rights and International Politics in Latin America," in *Indigenous Peoples and Democracy in Latin America,* ed. Donna Lee Van Cott (New York: St. Martin's Press, 1995); and Pamela Burke, "The Globalization of Contentious Politics:

The Amazonian Indigenous Rights Movement" (Ph.D. diss., University of Maryland, 1999).

33. See the sketch on pp. 188–194 and Michael S. Lund, Barnett R. Rubin, and Fabienne Hara, "Learning from Burundi's Failed Democratic Transition, 1993–96: Did International Initiatives Match the Problem?" in *Cases and Strategies for Preventive Action*, vol. 2 of *Preventive Action Reports*, ed. Barnett R. Rubin (New York: Century Foundation Press, 1998), 47–92.

34. Barbara Harff developed the concept and operational measures of accelerators as a means to analyze and anticipate the onset of genocides and political mass murder. She and collaborators have extended the approach to ethnic wars and regime failures. Accelerator analysis begins with theoretical specification of the general causes of the conflict or crisis under consideration, such as incentives and political opportunities. Accelerators include events that change the parameters of these causal variables. See Barbara Harff, "Early Warning of Humanitarian Crises: Sequential Models and the Role of Accelerators," in *Preventive Measures: Building Risk Assessment and Crisis Early Warning Systems*, ed. John L. Davies and T. R. Gurr (Lanham, Md.: Rowman & Littlefield, 1998), 70–78; John L. Davies and Barbara Harff with Anne L. Speca, "Dynamic Data for Conflict Early Warning," pp. 79–94, in the same volume; and Barbara Harff and T. R. Gurr, "Systematic Early Warning of Humanitarian Emergencies," *Journal of Peace Research* 35 (September 1998): 551–579.

35. My first venture into the study of ethnopolitics outside the United States focused on Australian Aborigines, as reported in T. R. Gurr, "Outcomes of Public Protest among Australia's Aborigines," *American Behavioral Scientist* 26 (January–February 1983): 353–374.

36. See Gurr, *Minorities at Risk* (note 11), chaps. 2 and 6.

37. On strategies for accommodating ethnopolitical interests in Western democracies, see, for example, Martin O. Heisler, "Ethnicity and Ethnic Relations in the Modern West," in *Conflict and Peacemaking in Multiethnic Societies*, ed. Joseph V. Montville (Lexington, Mass.: Lexington Books, 1990), 21–52; chapters on Canada, Northern Ireland, Spain, and Belgium in *The Politics of Ethnic Conflict Regulation: Case Studies of Protracted Ethnic Conflicts*, ed. John McGarry and Brendon O'Leary (London and New York: Routledge, 1993); and Saul Newman, *Ethnoregional Conflict in Democracies: Mostly Ballots, Rarely Bullets* (Westport, Conn.: Greenwood Press, 1996).

38. On India's strategies for managing regional autonomy and separatist movements, see Gurharpal Singh, "Ethnic Conflict in India: A Case-Study of Punjab," in McGarry and O'Leary, *Politics of Ethnic Conflict Regulation* (note 37), 84–105; and Kanti Bajpai, "Diversity, Democracy, and Devolution in India," in *Government Policies and Ethnic Relations in Asia and the Pacific*, ed. Michael E. Brown and Sumit Ganguly (Cambridge, Mass.: MIT Press, 1997), 33–82. Steven M. Saideman suggests that India's low level of economic development may be at the heart of the government's inability to forestall secessionist rebellions, i.e., that the strategies that appear to encourage separatism are a function of limited resources (personal communication).

39. Protest is far more common than rebellion in contemporary democracies; for comparative evidence, see G. Bingham Powell, Jr., *Contemporary Democracies: Participation, Stability, and Violence* (Cambridge, Mass.: Harvard University Press, 1982); and T. R. Gurr, "Protest and Rebellion in the 1960s: The United States in World Perspective," in *Violence in America*, vol. 2, *Protest, Rebellion, Reform*, ed. T. R. Gurr (Newbury Park, Calif.: Sage Publications, 1989), 111–115.

40. On the problematic consequences of the recent wave of democratization, see Samuel P. Huntington, "Democracy's Third Wave," *Journal of Democracy* 2 (spring 1991): 12–34. On its implications for ethnopolitical conflict, see Larry Diamond and Marc F. Plattner, eds., *Nationalism, Ethnic Conflict, and Democracy* (Baltimore: Johns Hopkins University Press, 1994); and Amy L. Chua, "Markets, Democracy, and Ethnicity: Toward a New Paradigm for Law and Development," *Yale Law Journal* 108 (October 1998): 1–107.

41. James D. Fearon, "Commitment Problems and the Spread of Ethnic Conflict," in *International Spread of Conflict*, ed. Lake and Rothchild (note 18), 107–126. Also see Ian Bremmer, ed., *Understanding Nationalism: Nation-Building and Ethnic Minorities in the Post-Communist States* (Ithaca, N.Y.: Cornell University Press, 1996).

42. From Milovan Djilas, *Fall of the New Class: A History of Communism's Self-Destruction* (New York: Knopf, 1998), quoted by Michael Ignatieff, "Prophet in the Ruins," *New York Review*, March 4, 1999, 30.

43. Chua makes a strong theoretical argument that democratization and marketization both have conflict-enhancing effects, in "Markets, Democracy, and Ethnicity" (note 40), 106:

> marketization and democratization—to the extent that they are successful—may, in countries such as South Africa, Kazakhstan, and Vietnam, and throughout the developing world, catalyze ethnic tensions in a highly determinate and predictable fashion. The market will not lift the great majority of citizens out of poverty. Rather, it will aggravate, at least in appearance and probably in reality, the existing ethnic maldistribution of wealth. Democracy will not make all voters imagine themselves as coparticipants in a fraternal national community. Rather, the competition for votes will more likely foster the emergence of ethnic political entrepreneurs (particularly among the impoverished majority) and active ethnonationalist movements.

44. See Barnett R. Rubin, *The Fragmentation of Afghanistan* (New Haven, Conn.: Yale University Press, 1995). Information on the composition of the *shuras* is from his article "Afghanistan under the Taliban," *Current History* 98 (February 1999): 81.

45. Donald Rothchild interprets the breakdown of settlements in Angola as a commitment problem in chap. 5 of *Managing Ethnic Conflict in Africa: Pressures and Incentives for Cooperation* (Washington, D.C.: Brookings Institution, 1997). A useful comparative analysis of the interplay between warfare and political maneuvering in attempts to settle southern African conflicts, including Angola, is Thomas Ohlson and Stephen John Stedman with Robert Davies, *The New Is Not Yet Born: Conflict Resolution in Southern Africa* (Washington, D.C.: Bookings Institution, 1994).

46. A conceptual analysis of diffusion, contagion, and other international effects on internal conflicts is William Foltz, "External Causes," in *Revolution and Political Change in the Third World,* ed. Barry M. Schutz and Robert O. Slater (Boulder, Colo.: Lynne Rienner, 1990). Hill and Rothchild have done a series of empirical studies of transnational contagion of conflict, including Stuart Hill and Donald Rothchild, "The Contagion of Political Conflict in Africa and the World," *Journal of Conflict Resolution* 30 (December 1986): 716–735; and Stuart Hill, Donald Rothchild, and Colin Cameron, "Tactical Information and the Diffusion of Peaceful Protests," in *International Spread of Ethnic Conflict,* ed. Lake and Rothchild (note 18), 61–88.

47. Saideman, "Is Pandora's Box Half-Empty or Half-Full? The Limited Virulence of Secessionism and the Domestic Sources of Disintegration," in *International Spread of Ethnic Conflict,* ed. Lake and Rothchild (note 18), 127–150.

48. See Paula Garb, "Ethnicity, Alliance Building, and the Limited Spread of Ethnic Conflict in the Caucasus," in *International Spread of Ethnic Conflict,* ed. Lake and Rothchild (note 18), 185–199.

49. The Miskitos had strong incentives for opposing the Sandinista regime, first, because it tried to suppress Miskito indigenous rights organizations, second, because it forcibly relocated thousands of Miskitos from villages along the Coco River. Support from the CIA enhanced the capabilities of some Miskito exiles; others chose not to accept U.S. assistance but fought anyway. See chaps. 3 and 6 in T. R. Gurr and Barbara Harff, *Ethnic Conflict in World Politics* (Boulder, Colo.: Westview Press, 1994).

50. David R. Davis, Keith Jaggers, and Will H. Moore, "Ethnicity, Minorities, and International Conflict Patterns," in *Wars in the Midst of Peace: The International Politics of Ethnic Conflict,* ed. David W. Carment and Patrick James (Pittsburgh: University of Pittsburgh Press, 1997); and Will H. Moore and David R. Davis, "Transnational Ethnic Ties and Foreign Policy," in *International Spread of Ethnic Conflict,* ed. Lake and Rothchild (note 18), 89–104. Both studies use data from the Minorities at Risk study in combination with data on dyadic interactions between states.

51. Fred W. Riggs, "The Modernity of Ethnic Identity and Conflict," *International Political Science Review* 19 (July 1998): 269–288. There is an extensive literature on the connections between modernization and ethnic conflict, much of it reviewed by Saul Newman, "Does Modernization Breed Ethnic Political Conflict?" *World Politics* 43 (1991): 451–478.

52. See Charles Tilly, *Big Structures, Large Processes, Huge Comparisons* (New York: Russell Sage, 1984); and *The Contentious French* (Cambridge, Mass.: Belknap Press, 1986).

53. Susan Olzak, "Ethnic Protest in Core and Periphery States," *Ethnic and Racial Studies* 21 (March 1998): 187–217.

54. Susan Olzak and Kiyoteru Tsutsui, "Status in the World System and Ethnic Mobilization," *Journal of Conflict Resolution* 42 (December 1998): 691–720. This study uses the Minorities at Risk data set for indicators of ethnic protest and violence.

55. This, like other macro-theories sketched here, is a simplification of a more nuanced and complex argument. See Jonathan Friedman, "Transnationalization, Socio-political Disorder, and Ethnification," *International Political Science Review* 19 (July 1998): 233–250; and *Cultural Identity and Global Process* (London: Sage Publications, 1994).

4. Incentives for Ethnopolitical Conflict

1. Most analyses in this chapter are based on 1994–95 data. The MAR indicators of discrimination and restrictions have been updated through 1998 and are consistent with the general patterns described here, except for a gradual decline in restrictions. Chapter 5 reports on trends in discrimination and restrictions for the full decade.

2. Article 1(1), UN General Assembly Resolution 2016A (XX), December 21, 1965.

3. Both these amplifications are consistent with the intent and substance of international agreements on human rights: for example, the 1981 UN Declaration on the Elimination of All Forms of Intolerance and of Discrimination Based on Religion or Belief. See Vernon Van Dyke, *Human Rights, Ethnicity, and Discrimination* (Westport, Conn.: Greenwood Press, 1985).

4. Restrictions on the Kurds in Turkey have varied in severity, depending on the government in power. Cultural restrictions have eased somewhat since the 1970s; political restrictions remain high. An excellent recent analysis is Henri J. Barkey and Graham E. Fuller, *Turkey's Kurdish Question* (Lanham, Md.: Rowman & Littlefield for the Carnegie Commission on Preventing Deadly Conflict, 1998).

5. The electoral defeat of nationalist-dominated governments in Romania in 1996 and in Slovakia in 1998 have led to modification of some of these restrictive policies. See the sketch of Hungarians in Slovakia on pp. 183–187.

6. Of the 275 minorities in this survey 151 are categorized as "national peoples," all of whom were historically autonomous or are now detached segments of a transnational people. Another 68 are culturally distinct communal groups contending for power in heterogeneous postcolonial societies. Most of them also were autonomous before the onset of colonial rule. The main class of exceptions to the generalization consists of "ethnoclasses," ethnically or culturally distinct descendants of slaves or immigrants who occupy distinct social and economic niches in contemporary societies.

7. The coding refers to Ukrainian Russians outside Crimea; the status and political activities of Russians in Crimea are distinct, and as a consequence they are coded as a separate group.

8. Ramses Amer, "Vietnam's Politics and the Ethnic Chinese since 1975," *Sojourn* 11, no. 1 (1996): 76–104. Later in the 1980s economic and political restrictions on the Chinese were substantially eased.

9. Spearman's correlation coefficient between the five-category scale of economic discrimination in 1994–95 and the four-category scale of extent of groups' collective economic disadvantage in 1994–95; $n = 260$ groups with coded data on both variables.

10. For an extensive analysis of military and ethnic interconnections and conflicts in postcolonial states, see Donald L. Horowitz, *Ethnic Groups in Conflict* (Berkeley and Los Angeles: University of California Press, 1985), chaps. 11–13. Cynthia Enloe also has written extensively on the subject, for example, in *Ethnic Soldiers: State Security in Divided Societies* (Athens, Ga.: University of Georgia Press, 1980).

11. A joint project is under way with David D. Laitin and James Fearon to code language differences in the Minorities project more precisely.

12. David D. Laitin, "Language Conflict and Violence" (working paper, prepared for the Committee on International Conflict Resolution, National Academy of Sciences, Washington, D.C., September 13, 1998). Horowitz analyzes the importance of language as a symbol of group status in plural societies, citing a number of Asian examples, in *Ethnic Groups in Conflict* (note 10), 216–224.

13. Quoted by S. W. R. De A. Samarasinghe, "Sri Lanka: Affirmative Action and Equity in a Multi-Ethnic Society," *Development and Democracy* (Colombo) (1993): 46.

14. Many studies of conflict behavior provide evidence about the circumstances in which state repression provokes future resistance. See, for example, Mark Irving Lichbach's review of empirical studies, "Deterrence or Escalation? The Puzzle of Aggregate Studies of Repression and Dissent," *Journal of Conflict Resolution* 31 (June 1987): 266–297; T. David Mason, "Nonelite Response to State-Sanctioned Terror," *Western Political Quarterly* 42 (1989): 467–492; Dipak K. Gupta, Harinder Singh, and Tom Sprague, "Government Coercion of Dissidents: Deterrence or Provocation?" *Journal of Conflict Resolution* 37 (1993): 301–339; and Christian Davenport, "The Weight of the Past: Exploring Lagged Determinants of Political Repression," *Political Research Quarterly* 49 (June 1996): 377–403.

15. From documents captured in the 1991 Kurdish uprising; quoted by Aryeh Neier, "Putting Saddam Hussein on Trial," *New York Review,* September 23, 1993, 47.

16. The scale also included a 0 category used mainly to code situations of past or future ethnopolitical conflict in which no repression was used. In the most recent update of the Minorities data set, a set of twenty-two annually coded categories of repression is employed. This more precise information is used for the risk assessments reported in chapter 7.

17. Politicides are episodes of mass political murder. See Barbara Harff, "Recognizing Genocides and Politicides," in *Genocide Watch*, ed. Helen Fein (New Haven, Conn.: Yale University Press, 1992), 27–41, for a conceptual discussion and a comprehensive list of cases of genocide and politicide since 1945.

18. A recent study documents 34,363 killings and disappearances committed by agents of the Guatemalan state during this period: Patrick Ball, Paul Kobrak, and Herbert F. Spirer, *State Violence in Guatemala, 1960–1996: A Quantitative Reflection* (Washington, D.C.: American Association for the Advancement of Science, Science and Human Rights Program, 1999).

19. The analysis of repression was applied only to the 268 groups in the first stage of the Phase III data collection. The seven groups in countries with populations in the 500,000–1 million range, added in 1998, were not included.

20. In the Lhotsampas and Royhinga Muslim cases, governments sought to expel members of the groups on grounds that they were aliens, prompting the establishment of exile-based resistance movements that remained active at the end of the decade.

21. Harff, "Recognizing Genocides and Politicides" (note 17), identifies about forty communal groups that were intended victims of genocide or politicide between the 1950s and early 1990s. The scale of repression used in the Minorities study is based on strategies used by government rather than intent. Most of the victimized groups identified by Harff are coded in the Minorities analysis as targets of strategies of "dirty war" or preemptive control.

5. Democratic Governance and Strategies of Accommodation in Plural Societies

1. Mark Howard Ross develops a strong theoretical argument that, whereas adversarial democracy often exacerbates conflict in ethnically divided societies, democracy as a set of principles and practices for joint problem solving has more constructive effects. See his "Democracy as Joint Problem-Solving: Addressing Interests and Identities in Divided Societies," *Nationalism and Ethnic Politics* 4 (winter 1998): 19–46.

2. An overview of the Chittagong Hills conflict is Michael Maxwell, "Peace for the Chittagong Hill Tracts?" *Fourth World Bulletin* (summer 1998): 64–69.

3. In the conclusion to David A. Lake and Donald Rothchild, eds., *The International Spread of Ethnic Conflict: Fear, Diffusion, and Escalation* (Princeton, N.J.: Princeton University Press, 1988), 345. A useful analysis of how new democracies provide opportunities for abuse by nationalist myth makers is Jack Snyder and Karen Ballentine, "Nationalism and the Marketplace of Ideas," *International Security* 21, no. 2 (1996): 5–40.

4. Michael S. Lund, Barnett R. Rubin, and Fabienne Hara, "Learning from Burundi's Failed Democratic Transition, 1993–1996: Did International Initiatives Match the Problem?" in *Cases and Strategies for Preventive Action*, ed. Barnett R. Rubin (New York: Century Foundation Press for the Center for Preventive Action, 1998), 59, 80–81.

5. Christian Davenport, "Human Rights and the Democratic Proposition," *Journal of Conflict Resolution* 43 (February 1999): 92–116. Also see the theoretical arguments and evidence in Jacek Kugler, ed., "The Democratic Transition Process," special issue of *Journal of Conflict Resolution* 43 (April 1999): 139–258.

6. The relative advantages of majoritarian and power-sharing or consociational approaches to democracy in ethnically divided societies are widely debated, for example, by Donald L. Horowitz in "Democracy in Divided Societies," *Journal of Democracy* 4, no. 4 (1993): 18–38; and Arend Lijphart in his classic study, *Democracy in*

Plural Societies (New Haven, Conn.: Yale University Press, 1977); and, more recently, "Electoral Systems, Party Systems, and Conflict Management in Segmented Societies," in *Critical Choices for South Africa: An Agenda for the 1990s*, ed. Robert Schrire (Cape Town, South Africa: Oxford University Press, 1990). These and other models are reviewed by Ben Reilly and Andrew Reynolds, *Electoral Systems and Conflict in Divided Societies*, Papers on International Conflict Resolution No. 2 (Washington, D.C.: National Academy Press, 1999); and Timothy D. Sisk, *Power Sharing and International Mediation in Ethnic Conflicts* (Washington, D.C.: United States Institute of Peace Press, 1996), chaps. 3 and 4. A comparative analysis by Frank S. Cohen, "Proportional versus Majoritarian Ethnic Conflict Management in Democracies," *Comparative Political Studies* 30 (October 1997): 607–630, reports empirical evidence that proportional electoral systems are more effective than majoritarian systems in managing conflict in ethnically heterogeneous societies.

7. The types are defined using annually coded information on political institutions from the Polity III data set; see Keith Jaggers and Ted Robert Gurr, "Tracking Democracy's Third Wave with the Polity III Data," *Journal of Peace Research* 32 (November 1995): 483–488. Political and civil rights are not measured directly in the Polity study, but the democracy index constructed from information on political institutions correlates very closely (+.90) with Freedom House indices of political rights and civil liberties. Appendix A, pp. 289–294, lists countries in each of the four categories used here and details the basis of the classification.

8. On the problematic outcomes of democratic transitions in the post-Soviet states, see Airat R. Aklaev, *Democratization and Ethnic Peace: Patterns of Ethnopolitical Crisis Management in a Post-Soviet Setting* (U.K.: Ashgate, 1999); Karen Dawisha and Bruce Parrott, eds., *Democratic Changes and Authoritarian Reactions in Russia, Ukraine, Belarus, and Moldova* (Cambridge: Cambridge University Press, 1997); and, by the same authors, *Conflict, Cleavage, and Change in Central Asia and the Caucasus* (Cambridge: Cambridge University Press, 1997). On the postcommunist states of Eastern Europe, see Andreas Klinke, Ortwin Renn, and Jan Paul-Lehners, eds., *Ethnic Conflicts and Civil Society: Proposals for a New Era in Eastern Europe* (U.K.: Ashgate, 1998).

9. Marina Ottaway, *Africa's New Leaders: Democracy or State Reconstruction?* (Washington, D.C.: Carnegie Endowment for International Peace, 1999). A broadly comparative study of democratic transitions in Africa and how they interact with ethnopolitics is Earl Conteh-Morgan, *Democratization in Africa: The Theory and Dynamics of Political Transitions* (Westport, Conn.: Praeger, 1997). Also see Timothy D. Sisk and Andrew Reynolds, eds., *Elections and Conflict Management in Africa* (Washington, D.C.: United States Institute of Peace Press, 1998).

10. Some groups in nondemocratic states used both strategies during the period under study, typically in a sequence that began with protest and shifted within a year or two to rebellion.

11. Harff proposes that the most severe kinds of ethnic conflict, genocides and political mass murder of ethnic groups, are likely to follow from political upheaval, defined as "abrupt change in the political community caused . . . by the formation of

a state through violent conflict, when national boundaries are reformed, or after defeat in war," in Ted Robert Gurr and Barbara Harff, *Early Warning of Communal Conflicts and Genocide: Linking Empirical Research to International Responses*, Monograph Series on Governance and Conflict Resolution (Tokyo: United Nations University Press, 1996), 48. I reported that half of the serious ethnopolitical conflicts ongoing in the early 1990s began within five years after state formation or within three years after revolutionary seizures of power, in "Peoples against States: Ethnopolitical Conflict and the Changing World System," *International Studies Quarterly* 38, no. 3 (1994): 361–362.

12. *Third World* is used here in its usual omnibus way to encompass the countries of South, Southeast, and East Asia (except Japan), the Middle East, Africa, and Latin America and the Caribbean. Their great diversity and the lack of a suitable alternative label are both acknowledged. Some of the analyses that follow were done separately for Latin American, African, and Asian groups; regional effects were not great enough to qualify the generalizations reported here. Nonetheless, more fine-grained reanalysis of regional patterns and changes in democratization, group status, and ethnopolitical conflict are well worth doing.

13. In South Africa protest by most communal groups did not change appreciably after 1994 but declined to 0 among the Xhosa, the principal communal supporters of the African National Congress. In South Korea protest by the Honamese, the people of the long-neglected southwest region, declined sharply after 1988, when they gained effective political representation in Seoul.

14. In twenty-three of the twenty-five countries, autocratic regimes experimented with democracy; in Fiji and Thailand long-established democracies temporarily reverted to autocracy. Seven of the thirty-two transitional regimes and their minorities are not included in this analysis, because their partial democratic institutions predate 1980 or were instituted after 1995; hence reliable before-and-after comparisons of ethnopolitical conflict cannot be made for them. See general note and *a* in table 5.3 for details.

15. From unpublished analyses by Michael Haxton of the components of the democracy index used in the Polity III data set described in note 7.

16. For general and comparative discussions of policies of preference and "affirmative action" as means to manage ethnic conflict see, for example, Donald L. Horowitz, *Ethnic Groups in Conflict* (Berkeley and Los Angeles: University of California Press, 1985), chaps. 14 and 16; Michael Wynan, *The Political Economy of Ethnic Discrimination and Affirmative Action* (New York: Praeger, 1990); Devanason Nesiah, *Discrimination without Reason? Preferential Policies in the USA, India, and Malaysia* (Delhi: Oxford University Press, 1997); and Crawford Young, ed., *Ethnic Diversity and Public Policy* (New York: St. Martin's Press for the UN Research Institute for Social Development, 1998). A case study of remedial policies for disadvantaged minorities in an autocratic regime is Barry Sautman, "Preferential Policies for Ethnic Minorities in China: The Case of Xinjiang," *Nationalism and Ethnic Politics* 4 (spring/summer 1998): 86–118.

17. Observers of state socialism will be quick to point out that Soviet policies toward non-Russian peoples were not even-handed, that communist Bulgaria treated its Turkish Muslim minority abominably, that many Russians were and are openly prejudiced against visible minorities and Jews. The fact remains that, according to our coded data on intergroup differentials and discrimination, the socialist states had on average a significantly better record than the Western democracies. This issue is discussed at greater length in Ted Robert Gurr, *Minorities at Risk: A Global Survey of Ethnopolitical Conflicts* (Washington, D.C.: United States Institute of Peace Press, 1993), chaps. 2 and 7.

18. Discrimination and restrictions were coded biennially for 1990–91, 1992–93, and 1994–95; they were coded annually for 1996, 1997, and 1998. Because the codings for the bienniums refer to conditions at the end of each period, the effective span covered in the comparisons that follow is 1991 to 1998. The data cover too brief a span to support a country-by-country comparison of discrimination before and after democratic transitions. Changes in political restrictions are not analyzed here, because they parallel changes in political discrimination.

19. A few instances of this phenomena are evident in the Minorities project's case studies, but we have not tried to catalogue, compare, or generalize from them.

20. The OSCE's missions aimed at managing ethnic and regional conflicts are surveyed by P. Terrence Hopmann, *Building Security in Post–Cold War Eurasia: The OSCE and U.S. Foreign Policy*, Peaceworks no. 31 (Washington, D.C.: United States Institute of Peace Press, 1999). See chapter 8 for additional evidence.

6. The Challenge of Resolving Ethnonational Conflicts

1. The justifiability of autonomy as a solution to ethnic and regional conflicts is widely debated. The circumstances in which secession is justified, normatively and politically, are analyzed by Allen Buchanan, *Secession: The Morality of Political Divorce from Fort Sumter to Lithuania and Quebec* (Boulder, Colo.: Westview Press, 1991). Jan and Brigitta S. Tullberg develop a general model for ethnic separation and migration as a solution to ethnic conflicts that has prompted extensive discussion and criticism; see their "Separation or Unity? A Model for Solving Ethnic Conflicts," *Politics and Life Sciences* 16 (September 1997): 237–248, and the commentaries that follow.

2. Ruth Lapidoth, *Autonomy: Flexible Solutions to Ethnic Conflicts* (Washington, D.C.: United States Institute of Peace Press, 1997). Of the eleven autonomies she examines, two were established after protracted conflict—Eritrea and the Palestinian National Authority. In addition to a survey of cases, she provides a useful overview of different concepts of and institutional arrangements for autonomy. An excellent general analysis of the doctrine of self-determination and a comparative assessment of nine autonomy arrangements is Hurst Hannum, *Autonomy, Sovereignty, and Self-Determination: The Accommodation of Conflicting Rights* (Philadelphia: University of Pennsylvania Press, 1990). Recent comparative analyses of separatist movements and autonomy arrangements include Galina Starovoitova, *National Self-Determination: Approaches and Case Studies* (Providence, R.I.: Thomas J. Watson Jr. Institute for International Studies, 1997); and Metta Spencer, ed., *Separatism: Democracy and Disintegration* (Lanham, Md.: Rowman & Littlefield, 1998).

3. "Canada's Natives Reclaim 'Our Land,'" *Washington Post*, April 2, 1999.

4. Barbara F. Walter, "The Critical Barrier to Civil War Settlement," *International Organization* 51, no. 3 (1997): 335.

5. The difficulties of settling civil and ethnic wars have been widely and intensively analyzed. Walter (note 4) contends, based on a large-n comparative analysis, that security guarantees are a necessary condition for successful settlement. Comparative case studies identify a more diverse set of relevant factors; see, for example, Roy Licklider, ed., *Stopping the Killing: How Civil Wars End* (New York: New York University Press, 1993); I. William Zartman, *Elusive Peace: Negotiating an End to Civil Wars* (Washington, D.C.: Brookings Institution Press, 1995); and Fen Osler Hampson, *Nurturing Peace: Why Peace Settlements Succeed or Fail* (Washington, D.C.: United States Institute of Peace Press, 1996). Lloyd Jensen emphasizes the need to create power structures that address the problems of power asymmetry between rebels and governments in "Negotiations and Power Asymmetries: The Cases of Bosnia, Northern Ireland, and Sri Lanka," *International Negotiations* 2 (1997): 21–41.

6. Patrick M. Regan, "Conditions of Successful Third-Party Intervention in Intrastate Conflicts," *Journal of Conflict Resolution* 40 (June 1996): 349. The role of mediation and intervention by outside powers has been widely and thoroughly analyzed, for example, by I. William Zartman, *Ripe for Resolution: Conflict and Intervention in Africa* (New York: Oxford University Press, 1989); and Patrick M. Regan, *Civil Wars and Foreign Powers: Outside Interventions in Intrastate Conflicts* (Ann Arbor, Mich.: University of Michigan Press, 2000).

7. All 275 groups in the Minorities study were screened for inclusion in this analysis. There may have been other armed separatist conflicts since 1960 by groups not covered in the study. It also is possible that we have misjudged the relative importance of political autonomy as a group objective in a few instances. In several cases, including the secessionist movement by the Gagauz in Moldova, armed conflict was minimal. None of these potential sources of error in exclusion or inclusion is likely to alter the general pattern of results reported here.

8. For details of the settlement process and agreement, see Mara Stankovitch, ed., "Compromising on Autonomy: Mindanao in Transition," *Accord: An International Review of Peace Initiatives*, no. 6 (London: Conciliation Resources, 1999).

9. The eighteen ongoing wars include twelve listed in table 6.1 as persisting or escalating in 1998–99 plus the six conflicts in which large-scale rebellion continues despite negotiated settlements or concessions.

10. See Peter Wallensteen and Margareta Sollenberg, "Armed Conflicts, Conflict Termination and Peace Agreements, 1989–1996," *Journal of Peace Research* 34, no. 1 (1997): 339–358. The authors and I have compared our interpretations of specific

cases; the two studies differ in criteria used but show the same general trend. Wallensteen and Sollenberg are concerned with formal agreements that bring an end to armed internal conflicts; this study focuses on settlements that provide gains to the contenders even if they do not lead to a complete cessation of fighting. Similar conclusions about the shift toward negotiated settlements are reached in Roy Licklider's comparative assessment of the results of these and other studies, "Early Returns: Results of the First Wave of Statistical Studies of Civil War Termination," *Civil Wars* 1 (autumn 1998): 121–132.

11. See Stephen John Stedman, "Negotiation and Mediation in Internal Conflicts," in *The International Dimensions of Internal Conflict*, ed. Michael E. Brown (Cambridge, Mass.: MIT Press, 1996); and "Spoiler Problems in Peace Processes" (paper prepared for the Committee on International Conflict Resolution, National Academy of Sciences, Washington, D.C., July 1, 1998).

12. See Francis Mading Deng, "The Identity Factor in the Sudanese Conflict," and Nelson Kasfir, "Peacemaking and Social Cleavages in Sudan," in *Conflict and Peacemaking in Multiethnic Societies,* ed. Joseph V. Montville (Lexington, Mass.: Lexington Books, 1990), 343–389. Millard Burr's detailed quantitative study, *Quantifying Genocide in the Southern Sudan, 1983–1993* (Washington, D.C.: U.S. Committee for Refugees Issue Paper, October 1993), estimates that 1.3 million southern Sudanese died of war-related causes between May 1983 and May 1993. An update of this report says that renewed war, including fighting among contending southern factions, brought the death toll by early 1999 to 2 million.

13. Some governments may have tried but failed to reach accommodation during the early stages; we have not tried to catalog such efforts. Also, the time horizon was much shorter in the postcommunist states. Their new and weakly institutionalized governments typically had only a year or two in which to anticipate and devise effective responses to ethnonational movements. Of course, in some instances, including Croatia and Georgia, the nationalist leaders of new governments chose policies that provoked rebellions.

14. For comparative studies of autonomy agreement, see the sources in note 2, especially Hannum, *Autonomy, Sovereignty, and Self-Determination*, and Lapidoth, *Autonomy: Flexible Solutions to Ethnic Conflict*. Hannum focuses on the legal basis of autonomy agreements, Lapidoth on the political and institutional factors that determine their effectiveness in mitigating conflict.

15. It is ironic that these peaceful accommodations have received little attention from scholars or journalists by comparison with the attention given to the Russian military assaults on Chechnya. For example Valery Tishkov, in *Ethnicity, Nationalism, and Conflict in and after the Soviet Union* (London: Sage Publications, 1997), devotes two chapters to the Chechen war (pp. 183–227) and two pages to successful negotiation and compromise in Tatarstan (pp. 242–243). For a more detailed account of the Tatarstan negotiations, see Cynthia S. Kaplan, "Ethnicity and Sovereignty: Insights from Russian Negotiations with Estonia and Tatarstan," in *The International Spread of Ethnic Conflict: Fear, Diffusion, and Escalation,* ed. David A. Lake and Donald

Rothchild (Princeton, N.J.: Princeton University Press, 1998), 251–274. The estimate of more than forty agreements is given in the *Washington Post*, February 26, 1999. Only some of these regions represent minority peoples and none gained powers as extensive as Tatarstan (Philip Roeder, personal communication).

16. A systematic discussion of how state interests mesh with minority objectives is Marvin W. Mikesell and Alexander B. Murphy, "A Framework for Comparative Study of Minority-Group Aspirations," *Annals of the Association of American Geographers* 81, no. 4 (1991): 588–590.

17. The majority-Russian population of Crimea does have regional autonomy; and the Crimean Tatar minority has its own assembly that is accepted by the government in Kiev essentially because it has been a counterweight to Russian Crimeans. On the status of non-Crimean Russians in Ukraine, see the sketch by Marion Recktenwald on pp. 57–63.

18. For more detailed discussions, see Lapidoth, *Autonomy: Flexible Solutions to Ethnic Conflicts* (note 2), 179–201, who identifies issues that need to be considered in negotiating autonomy agreements and a list of factors that contribute to their success; and Kjell-Åke Nordquist, "Autonomy as a Conflict-Solving Mechanism—An Overview" in *Autonomy: Applications and Implications,* ed. Markku Suksi (Netherlands: Kluwer Law International, 1998), 59–77, which analyzes the joint effects of international and internal conditions that determined the success of eleven autonomies established between 1920 and 1987.

19. On variants of federalism, see the contributions to Guénther Bächler, ed., *Federalism against Ethnicity? Institutional, Legal, and Democratic Instruments to Prevent Violent Minority Conflicts* (Zurich: Verlag Rügger for the Swiss Academy of Human and Social Sciences, 1997). A historically grounded discussion of nonterritorial autonomy is John Coakley, "Approaches to the Resolution of Ethnic Conflict: The Strategy of Non-Territorial Autonomy," *International Political Science Review* 15, no. 3 (1994): 297–314.

20. The Sri Lankan government has made many unsuccessful attempts to resolve the conflict, of which this was only one. The principal reason for failure is that Tamil militants reject any compromise with their objective of independence. See Ketheshwaran Loganathan, *Sri Lanka: Lost Opportunities; Past Attempts at Resolving Ethnic Conflict* (Colombo: Centre for Policy Research and Analysis, University of Colombo, 1997).

7. Assessing Risks of Future Ethnic Wars

1. This includes twenty-one ethnopolitical groups involved in low-level rebellions, scores of 2–4 on the 1998 rebellion indicator used in the Minorities project, and twenty groups involved in major armed conflicts, scores of 5–7 on the same indicator. Groups whose armed actions largely ended in 1998 are not counted.

2. Jan Eliasson, "Responding to Crises," *Security Dialogue* 26, no. 4 (1991): 405 ff. The same idea is incorporated in UN Secretary-General Boutros Boutros-Ghali's widely cited 1992 *Agenda for Peace* (New York: United Nations, June 17, 1992), which calls for proactive responses to impending conflicts and identifies fact-finding and early warning as means to that end. The expansion of the UN Security Council's role in preventive action since 1992 is reviewed by Juergen Dedring, "The Security Council in Preventive Action," in *Preventing Violent Conflicts: Past Record and Future Challenges,* ed. Peter Wallensteen, Report No. 48 (Uppsala, Sweden: Department of Peace and Conflict Research, Uppsala University, 1998), 45–65.

3. Agneta Pallinder, *Establishing an Early Warning Network in the Former Soviet Union,* report prepared for International Alert, London, March 1995; Aldo A. Benini, Anthony V. Minnaar, and Sam Pretorius, "Persistent Collective Violence and Early Warning Systems: The Case of KwaZulu-Natal, South Africa," *Armed Forces and Society* 24 (summer 1998): 501–518.

4. These analyses can be highly structured. A conceptually sophisticated framework designed for use by intelligence analysts is Ashley J. Tellis, Thomas S. Szayna, and James A. Winnefeld, *Anticipating Ethnic Conflict* (Santa Monica, Calif.: RAND Corporation, 1997).

5. Michael S. Lund, *Preventing Violent Conflicts: A Strategy for Preventive Diplomacy* (Washington, D.C.: United States Institute of Peace Press, 1996), is one of the first sustained and systematic treatments of the subject. The Center for Preventive Action, established by the Council on Foreign Relations, has issued several regional reports and a volume of comparative studies: Barnett R. Rubin, ed., *Cases and Strategies for Preventive Action,* vol. 2 of *Preventive Action Reports* (New York: Century Foundation Press, 1998). Other recent comparative and prescriptive studies of preventive action include Wallensteen, *Preventing Violent Conflicts* (note 2); Janie Leatherman, William DeMars, Patrick Gaffney, and Raimo Väyrynen, *Breaking Cycles of Violence: Conflict Prevention in Intrastate Crises* (West Hartford, Conn.: Kumarian Press, 1999); and Hugh Miall, Oliver Ramsbotham, and Tom Woodhouse, *Contemporary Conflict Resolution: The Prevention, Management, and Transformation of Deadly Conflicts* (Cambridge: Polity Press, 1999).

6. "The Cost-Effectiveness of Conflict Prevention: Report to Carnegie Commission on Preventing Deadly Conflict" (New York: Carnegie Commission, July 25, 1997), chap. 5.

7. Donald Krumm, "Early Warning: An Action Agenda," in *Preventive Measures: Building Risk Assessment and Crisis Early Warning Systems,* ed. John L. Davies and Ted Robert Gurr (Lanham, Md.: Rowman & Littlefield, 1998), 248. A recent essay advocating early warning of humanitarian crises is James F. Miskel and Richard J. Norton, "Humanitarian Early-Warning Systems," *Global Governance* 4 (July–September 1998): 317–330. A good discussion of early warning failures and how to overcome them is Philip A. Schrodt and Deborah J. Gerner, "The Impact of Early Warning on Institutional Responses to Complex Humanitarian Crises" (paper presented at the Third Pan-European International Relations Conference, Vienna, September 1998).

8. See contributions to Davies and Gurr, *Preventive Measures* (note 7); and Susanne Schmeidl and Howard Adelman, eds., *Early Warning and Early Response*

(New York: Columbia University Press International Affairs Online, 1998). Other examples are to be found in reports of the State Failure Task Force, a project initiated at the request of Vice President Albert Gore's office in 1994. The Task Force is an ongoing government-funded effort that uses a variety of empirical techniques to assess the risks of major political crises and internal wars two years in advance of their onset. Its techniques and results have gained some credibility among U.S. intelligence and foreign policy specialists. A public report of the study's principal findings is Daniel C. Esty, Jack A. Goldstone, Ted Robert Gurr, Barbara Harff, Marc Levy, Geoffrey D. Dabelko, Pamela T. Surko, and Alan N. Unger, "State Failure Task Force Report: Phase II Findings," *Environmental Change and Security Project Report* (Washington, D.C.: Woodrow Wilson Center), no. 5 (summer 1999): 49–72.

9. Barbara Harff has developed and is testing this kind of approach to early warning. The first step is assessments of risks, based on theoretical models of the conflicts about which early warnings are needed. The second step is to monitor and analyze theoretically specified accelerators and de-accelerators of conflict. Applications of this approach to genocides and politicides (political mass murder) are reported in Barbara Harff, "Early Warning of Potential Genocide: The Cases of Rwanda, Burundi, Bosnia, and Abkhazia," in *Early Warning of Communal Conflicts and Genocide: Linking Empirical Research to International Responses,* Ted Robert Gurr and Barbara Harff (Tokyo: United Nations University Press, 1996), chap. 3; Harff, "Early Warning of Humanitarian Crises: Sequential Models and the Role of Accelerators," in *Crisis Early Warning Systems,* ed. Davies and Gurr (note 7), 70–78; and Harff, "Could Humanitarian Crises Have Been Anticipated in Burundi, Rwanda, and Zaire? A Comparative Study of Anticipatory Indicators," in *Journeys through Conflict: Narratives and Lessons,* ed. Hayward Alker, Ted Robert Gurr, and Kumar Rupesinghe (Lanham, Md.: Rowman & Littlefield, forthcoming). She also is applying the approach to ethnic wars, regime crises, and a larger sample of genocides and politicides as part of the State Failure project (note 8).

10. In one such study, Will H. Moore and Ted Robert Gurr used the residuals from a regression model to derive forecasts. The assumption was that groups with lower-than-predicted magnitudes of rebellion in the last half of the 1980s (negative residuals) had the highest potential for ethnopolitical rebellion in the first half of the 1990s. The study is reported in Ted Robert Gurr and Will H. Moore, "Ethnopolitical Rebellion: A Cross-sectional Analysis of the 1980s with Risk Assessments for the 1990s," *American Journal of Political Science* 41, no. 4 (1997): 1079–1103. A second study compared the high-risk groups identified in statistical analysis with high-risk groups identified in a parallel study that specified a priori risk factors for the first half of the 1990s and profiled groups on the risk factors using then-current Minorities at Risk data. The latter method is applied to data on Asian minorities in Gurr, "A Risk Assessment Model of Ethnopolitical Rebellion Applied to Asian Minorities in the Late 1990s," in *Crisis Early Warning Systems,* ed. Davies and Gurr (note 7), 15–26. The two approaches gave somewhat different results, as reported in Will H. Moore and Ted Robert Gurr, "Assessing Risks of Ethnorebellion in the Year 2000: Three Empirical

Approaches," in *Early Warning and Early Response,* ed. Schmeidl and Adelman (note 8). The cases listed in the text are those in which both methods forecasted an increase in rebellion after 1995.

11. We also experimented with an indicator that set the threshold between rebellion and nonrebellion at 3 on the rebellion scale but were unable to estimate a model that permitted accurate differentiation using this indicator. In other words, it is easier to identify the risk factors that determine whether a group is likely to engage in *any* kind of rebellion than it is to identify the factors associated with risks of the most serious rebellions. We think this is due to the volatility and unpredictability associated with violent political interactions. The escalation, or de-escalation, of conflicts once force has been used is complex, interactive, and highly dependent on circumstances and therefore is not easy to anticipate using a deterministic model.

12. A three-year period to score protest was used rather than the two years used for rebellion because we could estimate a better model using the longer period. The likely reason is that protest has greater short-term variability than rebellion. Protests are more likely to focus on immediate, often single, issues rather than the broad nature of groups' relations with authority. A three-year span provides a more accurate assessment of a group's propensity to protest.

13. These findings are reported in Ted Robert Gurr, "Why Minorities Rebel: A Global Analysis of Communal Mobilization and Conflict since 1945," *International Political Science Review* 14 (April 1993): 161–202; and in articles by Gurr and Moore (note 10).

14. The indicators used do not assess the degree of mobilization per se (Tilly defines it as the extent to which group resources are under collective control) but two preconditions for mobilization: the extent to which group members live in proximity to one another and the existence of organizations that give expression to their aspirations and objectives. Charles Tilly, *From Mobilization to Revolution* (Reading, Mass.: Addison-Wesley, 1978), chap. 3.

15. Detailed evidence on spillover and insecurity effects in six zones of regional conflict during the Cold War is summarized in Monty G. Marshall, *Third World War* (Boulder, Colo.: Rowman & Littlefield, 1999).

16. The shift in strategies by indigenous peoples toward greater reliance on nonviolent forms of political action in the 1990s was greatly facilitated by broad programs of political support from regional and international organizations, as discussed in chapter 3.

17. For more thorough empirical studies of the linkages between religious differences and communal conflict, see Ted Robert Gurr, "Peoples against States: Ethnopolitical Conflict and the Changing World System," *International Studies Quarterly* 38 (September 1994): 347–377; and Jonathan Fox, "The Salience of Religious Issues in Ethnic Conflicts: A Large-*n* Study," *Nationalism and Ethnic Politics* 3 (autumn 1997): 1–19. Two empirical studies that focus specifically on Islam are Manus I. Midlarsky, "Democracy and Islam: Implications for Civilizational Conflict and the Democratic

Peace," *International Studies Quarterly* 42 (December 1998): 485–511; and Daniel E. Price, *Islamic Political Culture, Democracy, and Human Rights: A Comparative Study* (Westport, Conn.: Praeger, 1999). None of these studies provides strong support, direct or indirect, for a connection between religion in general or Islam in particular and the occurrence of severe conflict. Bruce B. Lawrence argues on historical and doctrinal grounds that Islam is not inherently violent; see his "Rethinking Islam as an Ideology of Violence," in Paul Salem, ed., *Conflict Resolution in the Arab World: Selected Essays* (Beirut: American University of Beirut, 1997).

18. These conflicts usually terminate only after a hurting stalemate has been reached and after protracted negotiations; see chapter 6.

19. The Tibetans and Uighurs are among the half-dozen highest-risk Asian groups identified in Gurr and Harff, *Early Warning of Communal Conflicts and Genocide* (note 9), 19–20; and Gurr, "A Risk Assessment Model of Ethnopolitical Rebellion," in *Preventive Measures*, ed. Davies and Gurr (note 7), 21–23. These studies used early 1990s data and a different methodology to diagnose risks.

20. For a comprehensive recent survey of African conflicts, see "Africa's Wars," *Current History* 98 (May 1999).

8. Conclusions

1. This important point also is made by David A. Lake and Donald Rothchild in their introduction to *The International Spread of Ethnic Conflict: Fear, Diffusion, and Escalation* (Princeton, N.J.: Princeton University Press, 1998), 27–28.

2. See Thomas Ohlson and Stephen John Stedman with Robert Davies, *The New Is Not Yet Born: Conflict Resolution in Southern Africa* (Washington, D.C.: Brookings Institution, 1994).

3. The other was a localized rebellion by Muslims in southern Thailand that was largely over by late 1999. A few other ethnic wars that observers thought were settled in the mid-1990s flared up again in the late 1990s—for example, the Russian war with Chechnya and the separatist rebellions of the Shan, Karen, and Wa in Burma.

4. Only some of these forty regions were potentially secessionist. A recent analysis of Russia's successful management of regional conflicts is Daniel S. Treisman, *After the Deluge: Regional Crises and Political Consolidation in Russia* (Ann Arbor, Mich.: University of Michigan Press, 1999). However, Graeme P. Herd contends that after August 1998 the centrifugal tendencies accelerated and that Russia's federal system of governance "is disintegrating not by design but by default" in "Russia: Systemic Transformation or Federal Collapse?" *Journal of Peace Research* 36 (May 1999): 259–269, quotation from p. 259.

5. See Steven L. Burg, "Nationalism and Civic Identity: Ethnic Models for Macedonia and Kosovo," in *Cases and Strategies for Preventive Action*, vol. 2, *Preventive Action Reports*, ed. Barnett R. Rubin (New York: Century Foundation Press, 1998), chap. 2, for a study of preventive strategies for Kosovo written before the conflict intensified. Studies that document the descent into war and repression after the fact include Mohamed Sahnoun's firsthand account, *Somalia: The Missed Opportunities* (Washington, D.C.: United States Institute of Peace Press, 1994); Valery Tishkov's analysis of the origins of the Chechen war, "Ambition and the Arrogance of Power," in *Ethnicity, Nationalism, and Conflict in and after the Soviet Union: The Mind Aflame,* (London: Sage Publications for the International Peace Research Institute, Oslo, 1997), chaps. 9, 10; and Howard Adelman and Astri Suhrke, eds., *The Path of a Genocide: The Rwanda Crisis from Uganda to Zaire* (New Brunswick, N.J.: Transaction, 1999).

6. Robert O. Keohane, "The Demand for International Regimes," in *International Regimes*, ed. Stephen D. Krasner (Ithaca, N.Y.: Cornell University Press, 1983), 153.

7. See, for example, Hugh Miall, ed. *Minority Rights in Europe: Prospects for a Transnational Regime* (New York: Council on Foreign Relations Press, 1994); and Jennifer Jackson Preece, "National Minority Rights vs. State Sovereignty in Europe: Changing Norms in International Relations?" *Nations and Nationalism* 3, no. 3 (1997): 345–364.

8. Preece, "National Minority Rights vs. State Sovereignty," 357–360, quotations from pp. 345–346, 359. The parallel evolution of international norms about ethnic conflict and secessionist movements is surveyed by Rajat Ganguly and Raymond C. Taras, *Understanding Ethnic Conflict: The International Dimension* (New York: Longman, 1998), chap. 2.

9. For a detailed assessment of alternative institutional designs for managing communal conflicts, see "Democratic Levers for Conflict Management," in *Democracy and Deep-Rooted Conflict: Options for Negotiators* (Stockholm: IDEA, 1998), 133–259.

10. Connie Peck, *The United Nations as a Dispute Settlement System: Improving Mechanisms for the Prevention and Resolution of Conflict* (The Hague: Kluwer Law International, 1996).

11. Recent works that emphasize international responsibilities for preventing internal conflict include, in addition to Peck, *United Nations as a Dispute System* (note 10), Hugh Miall, Oliver Ramsbotham, and Tom Woodhouse, *Contemporary Conflict Resolution: The Prevention, Management, and Transformation of Deadly Conflicts* (Cambridge: Polity Press, 1999); and Peter Wallensteen, ed., *Preventing Violent Conflicts: Past Record and Future Challenges* (Uppsala, Sweden: Department of Peace and Conflict Research, Uppsala University, 1998). The evolution of the United Nations' policies of coercive intervention is traced in James Mayall, ed., *The New Interventionism, 1991–1994: United Nations Experience in Cambodia, Former Yugoslavia, and Somalia* (Cambridge: Cambridge University Press, 1996). A useful overview is provided in chap. 4 of Ganguly and Taras, *Understanding Ethnic Conflict* (note 8).

12. We did not attempt to determine what specific kinds of international support for ethnopolitical groups have had conflict-dampening effects. This question is best answered through more fine-grained comparative and case studies.

13. John Pomfret, "Kosovo Hits Close to Home," *Washington Post*, May 7, 1999.

14. See Burg, "Nationalism and Civic Identity" (note 5). An agreement to normal-ize the Kosovo educational system, negotiated in 1996 with mediation by a U.S. non-governmental organization, the Center for Preventive Action, was never implemented.

15. The Ogoni's rebellious neighbors, the Ijaw, were profiled for the Minorities project after the chapter 7 risk assessment was completed. The Ijaw have high risks of escalating ethnorebellion.

Appendix B

1. Discriminant indicators of transnational kindred group support were also con-structed for military support (KMILSUP5) and material support (KMATSUP5).

2. Discriminant indicators of transnational state support were also constructed for military support (SMILSUP5), material support (SMATSUP5), and political sup-port (SPOLSUP5).

3. In addition, a discriminant indicator of regional and international organization support was also constructed for military support (IMILSUP5). A composite indica-tor was also created (ISUP5).

4. Transnational support from kindred groups does not vary much from year to year (unlike support from political organizations: SSUP and IPOLSUP); nearly all groups who received kindred support enjoyed that support in each of the years coded, so only the 1998 value is used.

5. The indicator is coded for 1990–95 and again for 1998. The following are the categories in the scale from which the risk assessment indicator is constructed:

- No political movements or organizations representing group interests are reported.
- Group interests are promoted by umbrella organizations that also represent other collective interests.
- Group interests are promoted by one or more conventional political movements or parties that draw their support mainly or entirely from the group.
- Group interests are promoted mainly by conventional political movements or par-ties but also by militant organizations that have limited support within the group.
- Group interests are promoted mainly by militant organizations but also by some conventional organizations.
- Group interests are promoted only by militant organizations.

6. The Minorities project codes detailed information on types of support received by each minority from kindred groups, foreign states, and international actors. These data are being used in much more discriminating analyses of these and other issues, for example, Deepa Khosla, "Third World States as Intervenors in Ethnic Conflict: Implications for Regional and International Security," *Third World Quarterly* 20, no. 6 (1999): 1143–1156; and R. William Ayres and Stephen M. Saideman, "Is Sep-aratism as Contagious as the Common Cold or as Cancer? Testing the International and Domestic Determinants of Secessionism," *Nationalism and Ethnic Politics* 6 (forthcoming).

7. The long-term increase in indigenous political action up to 1990 is documented in Ted Robert Gurr, *Minorities at Risk: A Global View of Ethnopolitical Conflicts* (Washington, D.C.: United States Institute of Peace Press, 1993), chap. 4. Also see chapter 2 in this volume.

Appendix E

1. For a detailed discussion and examples of problematic demographic information on communal groups, see T. R. Gurr, *Minorities at Risk: A Global View of Ethnopolitical Conflicts* (Washington, D.C.: United States Institute of Peace Press, 1993), 10–15.

2. There is one principal advantage of the population estimates produced by the International Programs Center of the U.S. Census Bureau over those produced by the United Nations. Both organizations base their estimates on the most recent data from censuses, vital registration, and demographic surveys and evaluate/adjust these data with well-established demographic techniques. However, the software used by the U.S. Census Bureau allows for much more detailed specification of the components of population change than does the program used by the United Nations. As a result, while the general trends in the estimates of both sources parallel one another, the Census Bureau's estimates more closely reflect the specific contours in the underlying data. For example, the impact of major refugee movements and other significant demographic events are able to be fixed in the year in which they actually occur, rather than being, in effect, distributed over a five-year period. The Census Bureau International Data Base is available at *http://www.census./gov.ipc/www.idbnew.html* (personal communication from Matthew Christenson and Peter Way of the International Programs Center, August 1999).

3. *The World Factbook 1998* (Washington, D.C.: Office of Public Affairs, Central Intelligence Agency, 1998). Another general source was identified after the MAR demographic data were updated: Philip M. Parker, *Ethnic Cultures of the World, A Statistical Reference,* vol. 3, *Cross-Cultural Statistical Encyclopedia of the World* (Westport, Conn.: Greenwood Press, 1997). Parker gives estimates of group size for circa 1994, combining related groups across countries; for example, he lists a single total for Kurds in seven countries. In the thirty or so instances where direct comparisons can be made, most of Parker's estimates are close to ours but some are as little as half or as much as twice the MAR estimates for 1998. Parker does not identify specific sources. Nonetheless, the MAR project will cross-check its estimates against his when the next population update is done.

4. See the summary tables compiled by Monty G. Marshall in *Minorities at Risk* (note 1), 210–216.

5. Donald George Morrison, Robert Cameron Mitchell, and John Naber Paden, *Black Africa: A Comparative Handbook,* 2d ed. (New York: Irvington Publishers and Paragon House, 1989).

6. Brian Hunter, ed., *The Statesman's Year-Book: Statistical and Historical Annual of the States of the World for the Year 1994–95* (New York: St. Martin's Press, 1994 and other annual editions).

7. Mary Lisbeth Gonzalez, "How Many Indigenous People?" in *Indigenous People and Poverty in Latin America: An Empirical Analysis,* ed. George Psacharopoulos and Henry Anthony Patrious (Washington, D.C.: World Bank Regional and Sectoral Studies, 1994), 21–40.

8. Jean-Pierre Liegeois and Nicolae Gheorghe, *Roma/Gypsies: A European Minority* (London: Minority Rights Group International, 1995), 7.

9. Morrison, et al., *Black Africa: A Comparative Handbook* (note 5).

10. The MAR files include worksheets, one for each group, that list estimates of group size in 1990, 1995, and 1998 and record the sources and computations used to develop the estimates used in the corrected Phase III data.

11. The Peru data are from Gonzalez, "How Many Indigenous People?" (note 7), 30. On Australia, see L. R. Smith, *The Aboriginal Population of Australia* (Canberra: Australian National University Press, 1980).

12. David Levinson, *Ethnic Groups Worldwide: A Ready Reference Handbook* (Phoenix: Oryx Press, 1998); Minority Rights Group, *World Directory of Minorities* (Chicago and London: St. James Press, n.d. [1994]).

Index

Ted Robert Gurr is distinguished university professor at the University of Maryland and is founder and director of the Minorities at Risk project, based at the university's Center for International Development and Conflict Management. He has written or edited twenty books and monographs, including the award-winning *Why Men Rebel, Violence in America, Ethnic Conflict in World Politics,* and *Minorities at Risk.*

Professor Gurr has taught at Princeton University, Northwestern University, and the University of Colorado. He has held a Ford Foundation faculty fellowship, a Guggenheim fellowship, a German Marshall Fund senior fellowship, and a Fulbright senior fellowship. In 1988–89 he was a peace fellow at the United States Institute of Peace. He was president of the International Studies Association in 1993–94, and in 1996–97 he held the Swedish government's Olaf Palme Visiting Professorship at the University of Uppsala. Since 1994 he has been senior consultant to the White House–initiated State Failure Task Force.

United States Institute of Peace

The United States Institute of Peace is an independent, nonpartisan federal institution created by Congress to promote research, education, and training on the peaceful management and resolution of international conflicts. Established in 1984, the Institute meets its congressional mandate through an array of programs, including research grants, fellowships, professional training, education programs from high school through graduate school, conferences and workshops, library services, and publications. The Institute's Board of Directors is appointed by the President of the United States and confirmed by the Senate.

Peoples versus States

This book is set in Adobe Caslon; the display type is Helvetica. The Creative Shop designed the book's cover, and Mike Chase designed the interior. Pages were made up by Helene Y. Redmond. Virginia Rich copyedited the text, which was proofread by Karen Stough. The index was prepared by Sonsie Conroy. The book's editor was Nigel Quinney.